CHICAGO

CROSSROADS OF AMERICA

Olivia Mahoney

CHICAGO HISTORY MUSEUM

Dedicated to the Trustees and Staff of the Chicago Historical Society, 1856 to the present

For my parents, Olivia Reid and John Saris Mahoney, who loved Chicago–O. M.

Chicago**History**Museum

The long-term exhibition *Chicago: Crossroads of America* opened to the public at the Chicago History Museum on September 30, 2006.

Published in the United States of America in 2006 by the Chicago Historical Society.
Copyright © 2006 by the Chicago Historical Society.

Chicago History Museum
1601 North Clark Street
Chicago, Illinois 60614
www.chicagohistory.org

Edited by Rosemary K. Adams
Designed and typeset by Joan Sommers Design
Printed in Singapore through Imago

Pages ii–iii: From left to right, details of: Ruins of the Chicago Fire, October 1871 (p. 46); Millennium Park, 2005 (p. 184)

Pages iv–v: From left to right, details of: The Ferris Wheel at the 1893 World's Columbian Exposition (p. 175); Valley Mould and Iron Company blast furnace, 1956 (p. 29).

Pages xiv–xv: From left to right, details of: Terminal at O'Hare International Airport, 1978 (p. 35); Livestock pens and workers herding sheep at the Union Stock Yard, c. 1910 (p. 18).

Page xvi: Traffic jam on Dearborn Street, 1909. Photograph by Frank M. Hallenbeck.

Pages 38–39: From left to right, details of: New buildings under construction after the Great Chicago Fire, October 1871 (p. 49); Demonstrators near Grant Park, August 28, 1968. Photograph by Declan Haun.

Page 40: Fire raging during Chicago's West Side riots, April 1968 (p. 77).

Pages 84–85: From left to right, details of: Maxwell Street Market, c. 1905 (p. 94); South Chicago neighborhood residents, c. 1910. Photograph by John Becker.

Page 86: The Dan Ryan Expressway and Robert Taylor Homes, 1964.

Pages 112–113: From left to right: Copper-plated cast medallion from the Carson Pirie Scott Building, 1898–99 (p. 128); *The Carson Pirie Scott Building*, 1903 (detail) (p. 128).

Page 114: Art class at Hull-House, 1924.

Pages 168–169: From left to right, details of: Swimming and wading at Clarendon Beach at Sunnyside Avenue, 1921 (p. 183); Entrance to the Blue Note Café, Chicago, c. 1955 (p. 188).

Page 170: Cover of *The Super Bowl Shuffle* by the Chicago Bears Shufflin' Crew, 1985 (p. 208).

Contents

The following members of The Guild of the Chicago Historical Society generously provided funding for this publication.

Mrs. T. Stanton Armour
Mrs. Charles A. Ault III
Mrs. J. Stephen Baine
Mrs. Peyton J. Barkley
Mrs. James N. Bay
Mrs. Thomas M. Begel
Mrs. Edward F. Blettner
Mrs. Philip D. Block III
Mrs. Joseph D. Boggs
Mrs. William A. Boone
Mrs. James J. Brennan
Mrs. Arnold F. Brookstone
Mrs. Murray C. Brown
Mrs. Vincent Buonanno
Mrs. Robert Adams Carr
Mrs. Henry T. Chandler
Mrs. Jonathan D. Clair
Mrs. Charles F. Clarke Jr.
Marcia S. Cohn
Mrs. William A. Crane
Miss Diane Curtis
Mrs. William W. Darrow
Mrs. Donald B. Davidson
Mrs. Stewart S. Dixon
Mrs. Raymond H. Drymalski
Mrs. Roger P. Eklund
Mrs. Samuel Ellis
Mrs. Stephen B. Friedman
Mrs. Isak V. Gerson
Trudene L. Giesel
Mrs. Paul C. Gignilliat
Mrs. John S. Graettinger
Mrs. Harry E. Green
Mrs. Evelyn Greene
Miss Harriet Gülis
Mrs. Donald H. Haider
Mrs. George E. Hale
Mrs. Chalkley J. Hambleton

Miriam Ewing Hamill
Ms. Sally M. Hands
Mrs. L.H. Healy Jr.
Mrs. Quentin G. Heisler Jr.
Mrs. Harlow N. Higinbotham
Mrs. David C. Hilliard
Mrs. Edward Hines
Mrs. R. Thomas Howell Jr.
Mrs. Thomas D. Hoyt
Mrs. William B. Hummer
Mrs. Willard K. Jaques
Mrs. Gary T. Johnson
Paula Werlein Jürisson
Mrs. Philip E. Kelley
Mrs. S. Warner Kenly
Mrs. Joseph A. Konen Sr.
Mrs. Harold W. Lavender Jr.
Mrs. Jay A. Lipe
Mrs. Glen A. Lloyd
Mrs. David E. Mason
Mrs. Frank D. Mayer
Mrs. James M. McMullan
Ms. Ann S. Merritt
Ms. Erica C. Meyer
Mrs. B. John Mix Jr.
Courtney M. Morris
Mrs. John K. Notz Jr.
Mrs. William F. O'Connor
Mrs. Thomas P. O'Mara
Mrs. Elliott N. Otis
Mrs. Beverly W. Pattishall
Mrs. Edward S. Petersen
Mrs. Marlene Welsh Phillips
Mrs. Philippe O. Piette
Mrs. Charles A. Pollock
Mrs. Charles S. Potter
Mrs. Charles S. Potter Jr.
Mrs. Jay D. Proops

Mrs. John Shedd Reed
Mrs. Tobin M. Richter
Mrs. John W. Robinson
Mrs. Thomas I. Rodhouse
Miss Harriet Cary Ross
Holly B. Rothschild
Mrs. John S. Runnells II
Mrs. Robert E. Sargent
Mrs. Charles E. Schroeder
Mrs. Gordon I. Segal
Mrs. Richard J.L. Senior
Mrs. Thomas C. Sheffield Jr.
Mrs. Richard D. Simonds
Ms. Margaret Snorf
Mrs. Sarah D. Sprowl
Ms. Lisbeth Cherniack Stiffel
Mrs. John Stoetzel
Mrs. Harvey J. Struthers Jr.
Mrs. Raynor F. Sturgis
Mrs. Steven Z. Szczepanski
Mrs. John W. Taylor III
Mrs. S.F. Thompson
Mrs. Howard J. Trienens
Mrs. Edgar J. Uihlein
Mrs. Peter E. Van Nice
Mrs. Jonathan A. Veeder
Mrs. Thatcher Waller
Mrs. Gordon K. Ware
Mrs. Morris S. Weeden
Mrs. William C. Weinsheimer
Mrs. John R. Weiss
Mrs. John A. Werhane
Ms. Nanette K. Wollack
Mrs. Freeman J. Wood Jr.
Mrs. George B. Young

Preface and Acknowledgments

By 1856, a critical mass of people, innovative ideas, money, and transportation networks converged along Lake Michigan and launched Chicago as the fastest-growing city in the world. Business dominated Chicago, driving the physical transformation of the city and its rapid population growth from about 30,000 citizens in 1850 to just under 100,000 in 1856. Almost half of the city's population was foreign born. Irish immigrants had flooded into Chicago to work on the Illinois & Michigan Canal since the 1830s, and thousands of Germans began their steady immigration in 1850, joined by English, Scots, Welsh, Norwegians, Swedes, and Danes. The city's railroads made it a central exchange point between the eastern and western rail lines, and the combination of rail and water networks allowed Chicago to thrive as a national processing and distribution center for grain, lumber, and meat enterprises that in turn fostered business innovations such as the McCormick Reaper Works and the Union Stock Yard.

Chicago struggled to become a city in the midst of this commercial juggernaut. Muddy streets and outbreaks of cholera and typhoid plagued efforts to make order and civility commonplace, but a new sewer system in 1852, raised street grades in 1856, and street railways by 1859 contributed to an urban infrastructure that made the city more livable. By 1856, the city's position as the crossroads of America was firmly established, and a sense of unlimited opportunity and potential focused all eyes on the future and creating the ideal city.

But the future has no meaning without a past. The twelve men who met on April 24, 1856, in the Marine Bank Building at Lake and LaSalle streets to form the Chicago Historical Society–William Barry, Mason Brayman, William Brown, John Harris Kinzie, Ezra McCagg, George Manierre, Mahlon Ogden, William Ogden, Charles Ray, J. Young Scammon, Mark Skinner, and Samuel Ward–embodied this belief. These prominent citizens actively participated in the commercial life of the city and were unabashed boosters of Chicago and its potential; many had witnessed firsthand Chicago's growth from a frontier outpost to a town to a nascent city. Yet the vision of a city consumed solely by commerce with business running amuck troubled them, and Chicago's reputation in the East as a place capable of making money but nothing else hurt their pride. While the ideal city would have commerce at its core, business needed the counterbalance of cultural institutions that promoted literature, art, and music. To be the great city everyone envisioned, wrote Isaac Arnold, one of the Historical Society's leading early members, Chicago must have "culture, taste, beauty, art, literature or there is danger that our city will become a town of mere traders and money getters; crude, unlettered, sharp, and grasping." Among the many cultural endeavors available, the study of history, which helped instill the values of patriotism, Republican virtues, and religious faith, was regarded as essential to a healthy nation and to growing cities like Chicago, whose patrons equated local advancement with national progress.

It was not unusual then for a group of business and civic leaders to institutional-
ize the pursuit of historical knowledge and tie it to the city's fortunes. Each founding
member was acutely aware of how quickly vestiges and memories of the past could be
obliterated and forgotten and how fleeting the present was. The origins of the Chicago
Historical Society reflect the collision of two powerful ideals: some of the members saw
the Society as part and parcel of Chicago's expanding economy and thus regarded it as
an essential component of the future ideal city in the making; other members stressed
its role as cultural custodian, seeing its chief role as preserving the past and present worlds
that rapid urbanization and industrialization—both hallmarks of Chicago—were destroying. Both of these ideals helped to nurture the fledgling Chicago Historical Society, and
the founding members hoped fervently that in focusing on the past the Society would
not only have value in the present, but also always have a place in the future city.

One hundred and fifty years later that hope has held fast. The completion of the
150th Anniversary Museum Building Project and the opening of the Chicago History
Museum reaffirm the value that history and the Chicago Historical Society hold for the
city today and into the future. Ever mindful of its own legacy as the cultural custodian of
Chicago's history and as a key element in making a vibrant city, the Museum has re-com-
mitted itself to presenting history to the public through exhibitions, publications, web-
sites, and educational programs that reach out not only to its members, but also to all of
the families, adults, children, students, and schoolchildren and teachers in the Chicago
region. Creating a meaningful past that encompasses the sweep of more than 400 years of
Chicago's history and presents a compelling story of the city's evolution to these many
audiences is a daunting challenge. The long-term exhibition *Chicago: Crossroads of America*
and this accompanying catalogue, curated and authored by Olivia Mahoney, chief curator of the Chicago History Museum, achieves this in spectacular fashion.

Designed as the lynchpin of the new Museum and the culmination of a century
and a half of collecting, preserving, and interpreting the city's history, *Chicago: Crossroads
of America* replaces the Chicago History Galleries, a visitor favorite since 1978. The exhibition explores the city's history using crossroads as a literal point of reference for chart-
ing its physical evolution and chronicling the vast movement of people, ideas, and products through the city by way of regional, national, and international social and
transportation networks. Crossroads also serves as a powerful metaphor for the dynamic
urban life that developed in this Midwestern metropolis and which has significantly
shaped American culture and society over the past 150 years. Featuring more than 1,200
artifacts and documents drawn from the Museum's vast collection of more than 22 million items, the exhibition explores place and identity; the interconnections among local,
regional, national, and international events, movements, and people; globalization; and
urbanization as powerful lenses to illuminate the continuities and discontinuities
between Chicago's past, present, and future.

Under the leadership of President Douglas Greenberg, and with the enthusiastic
support of the Board of Trustees, chaired By R. Eden Martin, the Historical Society ini-

To be the great city everyone envisioned, Chicago must have "culture, taste, beauty, art, literature or there is danger that our city will become a town of mere traders and money getters; crude, unlettered, sharp, and grasping."

tiated a major fundraising effort in the late 1990s to enhance its capacity to serve the people of metropolitan Chicago. Creating a new long-term exhibition on the history of Chicago was embraced as essential to realizing this goal. Making History: Campaign 2000, cochaired by trustees Potter Palmer IV and Mrs. John J. Louis Jr., raised more than $12 million to support the new exhibition. In 2001, Board Chair M. Hill Hammock and President Lonnie Bunch proposed that the new Chicago history exhibition become part of a larger museum project, which included a children's gallery, a costume and textile gallery, an exhibition of treasures from the Museum's collection, and extensive remodeling of the lobby and corporate rental spaces. A second fundraising effort, spearheaded by trustees John Rowe and Paul Snyder, provided critical additional support that enabled the expanded project to be completed. Throughout every aspect of the 150th Anniversary Museum Building Project, the Board of Trustees has shouldered an important leadership role, establishing an engaging vision for the Chicago History Museum, ensuring that the project goals were met, providing generous encouragement to the staff, and generating citywide enthusiasm for the new Museum. We are especially grateful to the board for its ongoing commitment to the project and for the collective and individual efforts of the trustees on behalf of this exhibition, catalogue, and building project. Our special thanks go to the board chairs whose tenures spanned this project—R. Eden Martin, M. Hill Hammock, and John W. Rowe—who rallied the support to begin the project and to launch a new chapter that builds on the institution's 150-year legacy.

The Guild of the Chicago History Museum made the publication of this catalogue possible, and we are deeply grateful to every member for supporting this initiative. Nancy Rogers, president of the Guild, boldly embraced this idea, and carried out a fundraising effort with enthusiasm and determination. The individual donors who supported this catalogue are listed on page viii.

A long-term exhibition and catalogue of this magnitude is not possible without the expertise and efforts of many. Every staff member at the Chicago History Museum has contributed in myriad ways to this project, and we cannot thank them enough for their creativity, stamina, and Herculean efforts. Nathaniel Arata, Michael Cleavenger, Jill Darrah, Gena Johnson, Paula Werlein Jurisson, and Monika Otting were amazing fundraisers. Special thanks go to Usama Alshaibi, Peter Alter, Patrick Ashley, Tamara Biggs, Joy Bivins, AnneMarie Chase, Olivia Chen, Luciana Crovato, Alison Eisendrath, Ginny Fitzgerald, Yasmin Dalal, Linda Evans, Lori Hall-Araujo, Rob Kent, Timothy Long, Sam Mangen, Lesley Martin, Lynn McRainey, Rob Medina, Heidi Moisan, Leigh Moran, Dan Oliver, Ralph Pugh, Nancy Ross, John Russick, Marie Scatena, Helga Spence, Michael Spock, Laura Stephens, Carrie Van Horn, Debbie Vaughan, and Kathleen Wadell for their contribution to the exhibition and the catalogue.

Work on developing a new core exhibition on Chicago's history began in 1998 under the direction of Phyllis Rabineau, vice president for interpretation and education, who hired Gerald Hilferty Associates to conduct an exhibition master plan for a new Chicago history exhibition in association with architectural master planning by Nicholai

xii   PREFACE AND ACKNOWLEDGMENTS

Studios; Selinda Research Associates conducted front-end evaluation for the exhibition to help the staff identify and better understand visitor expectations. Ms. Rabineau gave the project legs, and her efforts to encourage staff to embrace the challenges and opportunities of the project with imaginative solutions imbued it with a spirit of innovation that carried through to the end.

Olivia Mahoney brought her extensive experience as a curator and her seasoned historian's perspective to every aspect of this exhibition and catalogue, and both bear the stamp of her high standards for excellence and her commitment to making historical scholarship accessible to the broader public. Her stature as one of the nation's leading history museum curators, her familiarity with the Museum's collection, and her impressive record of successfully initiating and completing large, compelling exhibitions and publications made her an ideal choice to lead the curatorial effort. Thanks to years of hard work and her dedication to fulfilling the mission of this institution, the Chicago History Museum is proud to present a compelling new Chicago history gallery. We deeply appreciate Ms. Mahoney's remarkable contribution to the Museum and the city.

An exhibition team worked closely with Ms. Mahoney to plan and implement the exhibition and the catalogue. Melinda Spitzer and Courtney Collie, assistant curators, played an indispensable role in developing the exhibition and writing interpretive labels; they also provided invaluable assistance with content research, compiling the exhibition checklist, and reading early drafts of the manuscript for this catalogue. Without their hard work, dedication, and collegial support, the exhibition and catalogue would not have been possible. Jill Grannan developed flip books for the exhibition and was a critical creative force in developing the Second City audio tour. Jennifer Bridge conducted research and provided imaginative concepts for interactive and media components of the exhibition. Volunteer Ellen Bouleanu was extremely helpful as a researcher, proofreader, and fact-checker for the exhibition and the catalogue; we are also grateful to Shera Miller and Tim McCarthy for volunteering their time to this project. Kathleen Sam Plourd, director for collections and curatorial affairs, oversaw the deinstallation of the former Chicago History galleries and the installation of the new *Crossroads* exhibition. She led a group of staff who worked diligently and creatively to ensure that the exhibition design and fabrication reflected the highest curatorial standards and were completed according to schedule. Julie Katz, registrar, brought her expertise to every phase of the exhibition. She also oversaw all aspects of the loan, move, and installation of 'L' Car No. 1, the largest artifact every brought into the Museum. Her careful attention to every detail of this very complex loan ensured that one of Chicago great treasures has a pivotal place in the exhibition. We are especially grateful to the Chicago Transit Authority for facilitating this loan and its spirit of cooperation. Emily Benedict, project registrar, expertly managed and tracked the hundreds of artifacts and documents in the exhibition, worked on case layouts, cheerfully and efficiently coordinated the photography of exhibition artifacts, and completed the exhibition checklist. Museum conservators Carol Turchan,

Holly Lundberg, and Kimberly Smith skillfully treated artifacts and documents, which were expertly photographed for this publication by the Museum's outstanding photographers, John Alderson and Jay Crawford. Larry Schmitt, director of properties, and Sarah Delezen, project director, Alter Construction Company, deftly coordinated construction, design, and fabrication work. Rosemary Adams, director of print and multimedia publications, eagerly took on the monumental task of editing the exhibition labels and coordinating their production; the prose is clearer and the salient ideas more accessible because of her astute wordsmithing. She edited this catalogue and managed it through the many stages of production with efficiency and dispatch to ensure it met publication standards and deadlines. She was ably assisted by editors Gwen Ihnat and Emily Nordstrom and interns Bridget Campbell and Jacqueline Bransky. Joan Sommers of Sommers Design brought Chicago style to the design of the catalogue.

The Museum turned to its many partners and friends to gauge the accuracy and value of the exhibition. Groups made up of community partners, museum peers, scholars, and educators reviewed the exhibition plans and offered valuable guidance and suggestions for ensuring that the city's diverse communities are reflected in the exhibition, for creating a compelling visitors experience, for incorporating new scholarship to present better the city's history, and for strengthening the exhibition as a learning experience for schoolchildren. We are extremely grateful to the following individuals for participating in these discussions and reviews: Harold Arai, Henry Binford, Timuel Black, Bob Boone, Greg Borzo, Kathy Catrambone, Spencer Crew, Michael Conzen, Michael Ebner, Claire Elderkin, Maria Finitzo, Ann Fortescue, Thomas Frye, Lisa Grengg, Barbara Griffin, Elaine Heumann Gurian, Barbara Henry, Suellen Hoy, Janet Kamien, Jenny Karposov, Ann Keating, Bill Lavicka, Nhi T. Lieu, Jim Lemonides, Jan Lorys, Deborah L. Mack, David Maenza, Dominic Pacyga, Hamang Patel, C. Niobe Ngozi, Christopher Reed, Jon Rice, Lisa Roberts, Carl Smith, Michael Spock, A. T. Stephens, Martin Sullivan, Selma Thomas, Bernard Turner, James Volkert, Donna Ward, and Elliot Zashin. In addition, Professors Keating and Ebner read the manuscript for the catalogue and offered many helpful suggestions and invaluable advice.

IQ Magic provided initial design concepts in conjunction with architectural design services by Hodgetts & Fung. Patrick Gallagher & Associates, Design & Production, Inc., and Hammond, Bebbe, Ruppert, and Ainge were hired to complete exhibition design, fabrication, and architectural design services. We are especially grateful to Craig Brandt for his elegant architectural designs. Selma Thomas of Watertown Productions served as executive producer of all multimedia components; we are grateful to The History Channel for its many contributions to the *Crossroads* exhibition and it longstanding support of the Museum.

Gary T. Johnson, *President*
Russell Lewis, *Executive Vice President and Chief Historian*

Introduction

WNBQ Studios, c. 1949, including from left to right; *Kukla, Fran, and Ollie* with Burr Tillstrom and *Studs' Place* with Studs Terkel.

An ancient crossroads of travel and trade, Chicago played a key role in the making of modern America. In terms of location, Chicago enjoyed a critical advantage, situated at the midpoint of North America, straddling its inland water routes that provided access to the continent's vast, and resource rich, interior. As a result, Chicago served as a watery crossroads of travel and trade for Native Americans for thousands of years, and later, for European explorers and fur trappers. But Chicago did not develop into a major urban crossroads until the mid-nineteenth century when powerful forces of national expansion and industrialization transformed America from an agrarian republic into a powerful nation.

Established at the dawn of America's industrial age, Chicago grew with the nation, attracting people, extracting resources, adopting ideas and absorbing cultural forms from near and far in a complex process that often yielded new results. At its most basic level, the process involved shipping raw materials (lumber, grain, livestock, iron ore) from outlying rural areas to the city, where they were turned into manufactured goods (furniture, canned meat, steel rails) and shipped back out again to markets across the country and around the world. On another level, the process involved the adoption of ideas, including radical anarchist views from Europe that led to the Haymarket Affair and progressive theories of social reform from England

Chicago Union Station rail yard, c. 1910.

Workers at Allied Structural Steel Companies, c. 1950.

that inspired the establishment of Hull-House and nurtured a local Arts and Crafts Movement. On yet another level, the process involved absorbing cultural forms from elsewhere, including jazz and blues from the American South, transforming them into modern, urban sounds and dispersing them to mainstream America via studio recordings and live radio broadcasts.

As a national economic, social and cultural crossroads, Chicago exerted considerable influence on the rest of the country. While it did not act alone in shaping a modern nation, Chicago often led the way. Chicago railroads created a national market while its industries developed new production methods and a myriad of innovative products that changed daily life. As one of the nation's largest hubs of overseas immigration and black migration, Chicago helped diversify American society. Chicago's labor and racial strife exacerbated deep fissures in American society, but its unions and minorities gained fundamental rights for all citizens. Meanwhile, slums, vice, violent crime and political corruption gave Chicago an unsavory reputation that contributed to a general sense that American cities were unfit, dangerous places to live. Chicago's revolutionary architecture transformed the urban landscape and its retail practices fostered the rise of consumer society. Chicago reformers changed American social service, public education and the use of public space, while its lively cultural scene helped create American pop culture. In these and many other ways, Chicago shaped the American experience and the world we inhabit.

Traders at the Chicago Board of Trade, c. 2004.

Windows of The Reliance Building, c. 1970.

This publication, and the exhibition upon which it is based, were developed for the 150th anniversary of the Chicago Historical Society in 2006. They both include five thematic areas that explore various aspects of the city's dynamic nature:

1. *City on the Make*, which examines Chicago as a crossroads of economic and cultural exchange from prehistoric time to the present;
2. *City in Crisis*, which shows how conflicting social, economic, and political forces converging at the crossroads can explode in violent disorder, disrupting and changing the city;
3. *Sweet Home Chicago*, an overview of how Chicago's communities unite and divide along the lines of race, ethnicity and class;
4. *Second to None*, a presentation of Chicago's many innovations and their far-reaching impact; and
5. *My Kind of Town*, a discussion of Chicago as a cultural crossroads where generations of people have gathered to play and celebrate.

By no means a complete history, the exhibition and book focus on a selection of stories that best illustrate Chicago's crossroads nature and its national influence. Within the overall thematic approach, individual stories are arranged chronologically to illustrate how the city changed over time. Moreover, key themes overlap. Economic exchange and innovation run throughout, for example, reflecting Chicago's entrepreneurial nature, while additional stories of crisis and play appear outside their particular areas. In addition, themes of race, class, and gender illuminate the complex and often contested nature of Chicago's past. The overriding goal has been to provide an informative, provocative, and engaging view of Chicago, one that will encourage museum visitors and readers to explore the city on their own with new-found insight, understanding and appreciation.

"This will be the gate of commerce. Everything

Robert Cavalier de LaSalle, 1682

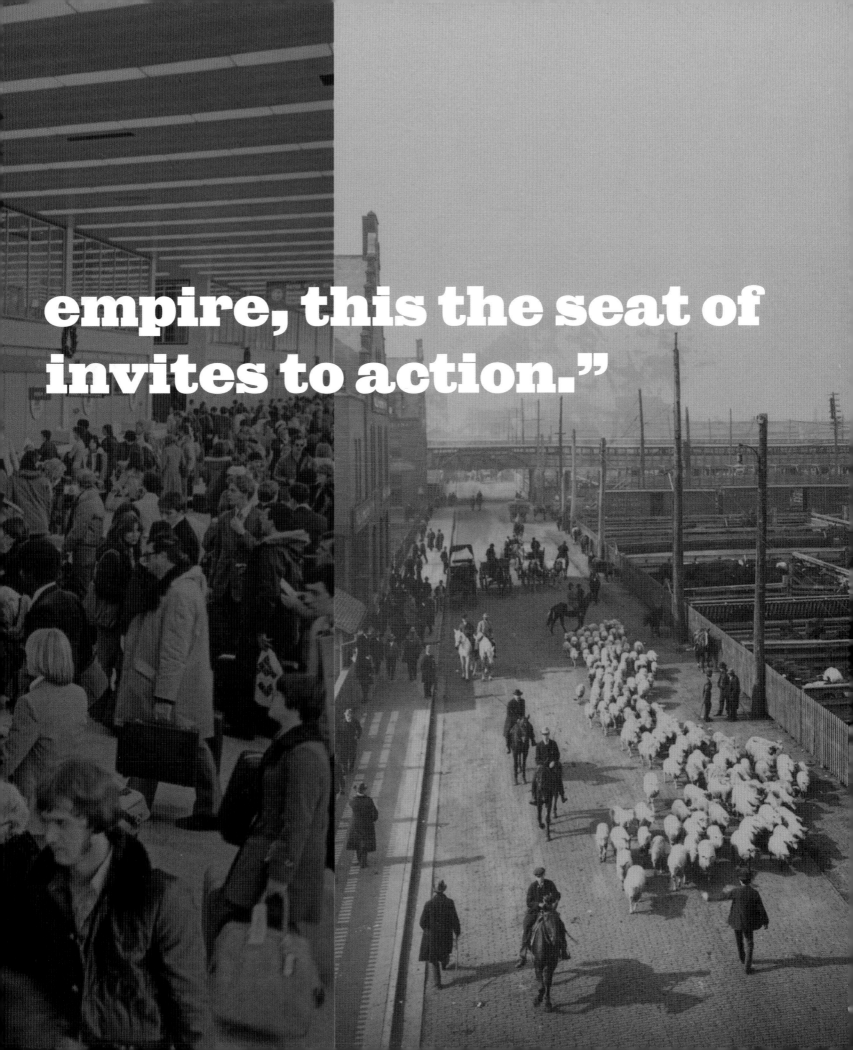

empire, this the seat of
invites to action."

Chapter One CITY ON THE MAKE

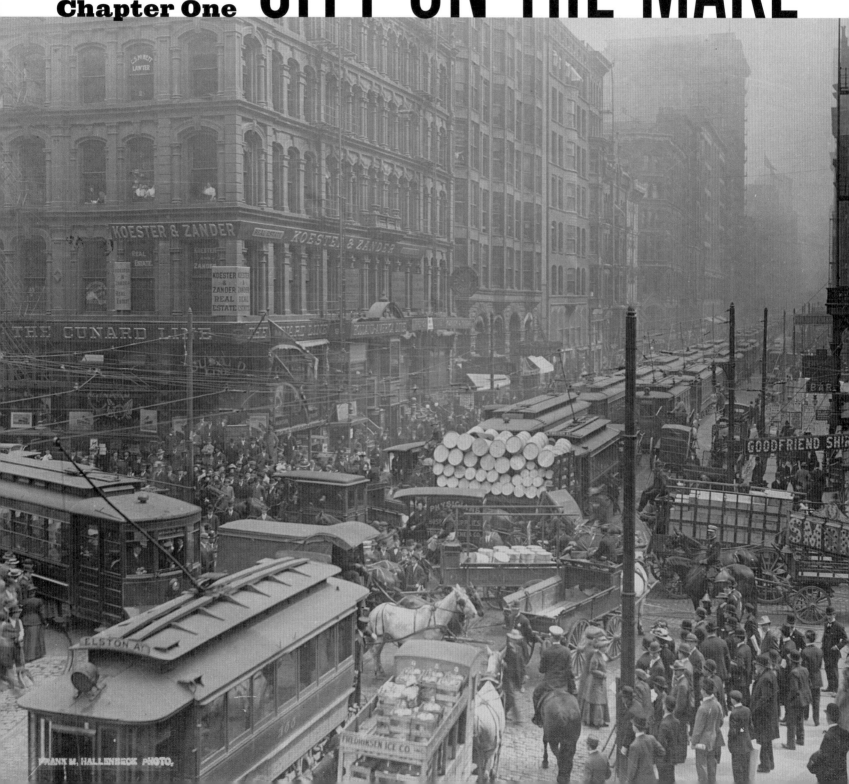

Blessed with a superb location, Chicago is a natural crossroads of economic exchange. Generations of Native Americans, European explorers, and early fur traders utilized the site's waterways to reach distant markets, but Chicago's economic potential remained largely untapped until the early nineteenth century. Beginning in the 1820s, a rapid expansion of industry and commerce swept across the United States, transformed an agrarian republic into an industrialized, and increasingly urbanized, nation. Revolutionary in nature, the process transformed Chicago from a frontier outpost with 100 people in 1830 into a bustling city of 300,000 by 1870.

Chicago's explosive growth astonished the world, but its driving ambition and preoccupation with money offended many contemporary observers who considered the city brash and vulgar. Yet the city paid little heed to its critics, preferring instead to concentrate on the business at hand. By 1890, less than sixty years after its inception, Chicago had emerged as a major industrial metropolis, second only to New York City in size and economic output.

Over the ensuing decades, Chicago continued to flourish. Still, many critics continued to complain that the city had a greedy, ruthless heart, a view fully articulated by author Nelson Algren in *Chicago: City on the Make*. Published in 1951, the book is a satirical portrait of Chicago as a city of hustlers out to make a profit at anyone's expense. According to Algren, the hustling began with city founders, who swindled American Indians out of their land, and it hasn't stopped since. While Algren's view may be harsh, the phrase — "city on the make" — struck a chord, for Chicago is essentially an economic crossroads, rather than a political or cultural capital. Accordingly, Chicago is primarily concerned with economic matters. While some may deride the city's ambitions, others applaud its entrepreneurial spirit, penchant for business, and driving determination.[1]

Historically, Chicago has experienced three major overlapping economic periods: Checagou, the pre-industrial era from about 2000 BCE through the 1830s; Big Shoulders, the age of heavy industry from the 1840s through the 1970s; and The New Economy, from the 1980s to the present.

CHECAGOU

Archeological evidence reveals that long-distance trading first developed in Illinois about 4,000 years ago during the Late Archaic Period. Native people traded as far north as Canada and south to the lower Mississippi River Valley.

Although people first arrived in Chicago between ten and twelve thousand years ago, archaeological evidence indicates that formal trading did not appear until about 2000 BCE, during the Late Archaic Period. By that time, the region's indigenous people were living in semi-permanent villages and growing crops in addition to hunting wild game. They used local waterways as regional trading networks that extended as far north as Lake Superior, where they acquired copper, and south to the Illinois, Mississippi, and Ohio river valleys, where they traded for chipping stones and small shells. During the subsequent Mississippian and Late Prehistoric periods, Native Americans continued to use these well-established routes of travel and trade.[2]

Beginning in the late seventeenth century, the entire Great Lakes region experienced a series of profound changes set into motion by European conquest of the New World. At the time, several competing Old World powers claimed various parts of North America. While France controlled a large part of Canada, Great Britain had a string of colonies along the Atlantic seaboard. Spain held Florida and lands west of the Mississippi River. Although the vast Great Lakes–Mississippi River region remained unclaimed, France sought to expand its empire in that direction. In 1673, French authorities sent Jacques Marquette, a Jesuit priest, and Louis Joliet, a Canadian fur trader, to explore the Mississippi River as a possible trade route to the Orient and to investigate the entire region for future economic development. Accompanied by several Native American guides, the voyageurs departed in several canoes from St. Ignace at the northern tip of Lake Michigan. They crossed into Green Bay and the Fox River, then carried their trappings across a land bridge to the Wisconsin River, and continued to the Mississippi River, which, as they discovered, flowed south, not west. Pushing onward, they reached what is now Arkansas, but turned back when they learned of a hostile Spanish presence further south.

Paddling upstream, they reached the Illinois River, a major water route that took them to the Des Plaines River. Informed by their own guides or perhaps by

The grooved ax, one of the most common tools of the Archaic Period, originally had a wooden handle lashed to the groove for better leverage. The tapered end was used to chop or split wood, while the blunt end served as a hammer.

Arrival of Marquette at the Chicago River by Herman A. MacNeil. Plaster bas-relief panel for the Marquette Building, 1894.

The panel commemorates Father Jacques Marquette's arrival in Chicago on December 4, 1674. The previous year, Marquette and Louis Joliet had passed through Chicago on their return journey from the lower Mississippi River. This time, poor health and harsh weather forced Marquette to remain in a temporary shelter on the Chicago River's South Branch for several months before traveling to Kaskaskia to preach to the Illinois Indians. Marquette died of an intestinal infection on May 16, 1675, near the present site of Ludington, Michigan.

Native Americans they encountered along the way, Marquette and Joliet were following an ancient trade route that brought them to the Chicago Portage, a marshy land bridge that led to the Chicago River, which flowed into Lake Michigan. Joliet wrote to French officials, "an all water transit between Lake Erie and the Mississippi was possible," and he enthusiastically called for the digging of a "ditch," or canal, between the Chicago and Illinois rivers to stimulate trade and commerce throughout the region.[3]

Several years later, in 1682, France sent Robert Cavalier de LaSalle to further explore the Mississippi River. Passing through Chicago, LaSalle also recognized the site's commercial potential and made a bold prediction. Although he disdained Joliet's notion of a canal, LaSalle declared that a great city would arise here, one that would command a New World empire. Reaching the Gulf of Mexico, LaSalle claimed the entire valley and all its tributaries, including the Missouri River, for France. Named in honor of King Louis XIV, the territory held great promise. For decades, French trappers had been hunting beaver, otter, muskrat, and other small, fur-bearing mammals in Canada and shipping their luxurious pelts to Europe, where they were made into gentlemen's hats, ladies' muffs, and other fashionable apparel. As trappers depleted the supply of animals, they moved steadily southward toward Chicago, arriving around 1670, several years before the French explorers.[4]

Neither the fur trappers nor explorers entered an empty world. Indeed, several tribes of Native Americans lived throughout the region, principally the Miami and Illinois Indians. These tribes had migrated to Illinois from Ohio and Michigan, respectively, during the mid-1600s, forced out by hostile Iroquois Indians. Members of the Central Algonquin cultural group of the Eastern Woodland Indians, the Miami

Passing through Chicago, LaSalle boldly predicted that a great city would arise here, one that would command a New World empire.

and Illinois spoke a similar language and lived in small, scattered villages, built dome-shaped homes known as wigwams, and survived by hunting, fishing, and growing small plots of corn, beans, and squash. As noted by Marquette and Joliet, they called their home *checagou* after the wild leek (or onion) plant that grew in abundance along the marshy riverbanks and traded with other tribes throughout the area. The European fur trade, however, changed their way of life forever.[5]

A complex enterprise, the fur trade involved Native Americans working alongside European trappers. Whereas native people had once bartered for food, tools, and decorative items amongst themselves, they now exchanged small animal pelts for manufactured European goods, primarily guns, liquor, trade beads, and jewelry. In the process, they formed complex alliances with rival European powers that eventually embroiled them in bloody tribal conflicts and protracted colonial wars over who would control the New World.

As the French fur trade moved into Chicago, it drew Potawatomi, Sacs, and Ottawa Indians from Michigan and Wisconsin to the area. Longtime trading partners with the French, these tribes hunted throughout the area for decades, but the Fox Wars prevented them from establishing permanent villages until the 1740s and 1750s. A long and bloody conflict, the Fox Wars pitted the Mesquakie Indians, otherwise known as the Fox, against France and their Indian allies. Starting in 1712, the conflict continued on an intermittent basis for twenty years, closing the Chicago Portage and forcing French trappers to use alternative routes, primarily the Wabash River, to reach rich hunting grounds further south.[6]

After France achieved victory in 1733, Chicago emerged as a key crossroads of the international fur trade as French and Indian trappers used its waterways to access regional hunting grounds and the Great Lakes–St. Lawrence River–Atlantic Ocean trade route. France's reign, however, came to an end after Great Britain won the French and Indian War in 1763. As a result, France relinquished all of its territorial claims around the Great Lakes, but French trappers remained in the region for years, even as British merchants in Montreal sent trappers into the region to hunt and create new alliances with local tribes. Great Britain's reign, however, only lasted until 1783, when the United States acquired the territory after winning the American Revolution.

Around 1785, Jean Baptiste Point DuSable (c. 1754–1818) arrived in Chicago. Of African and French descent, DuSable previously had worked as a fur trader near present-day Michigan City, Indiana. Like many other traders of the time, DuSable married a Native American woman. Known as Catherine, she undoubtedly helped DuSable establish good trading relationships with local tribes. The couple established a homestead on the north bank of the Chicago River, an ideal location for a frontier outpost. A resourceful entrepreneur, DuSable developed an extensive farm and trading post that eventually included a large frame house built in the

Brass holy water font, 1752. In addition to explorers and trappers, French authorities sent Catholic missionaries to Illinois to convert Native Americans. Construction workers found this font in 1894 near the Chicago River's South Branch, a regular route of travel and trade during the French colonial era.

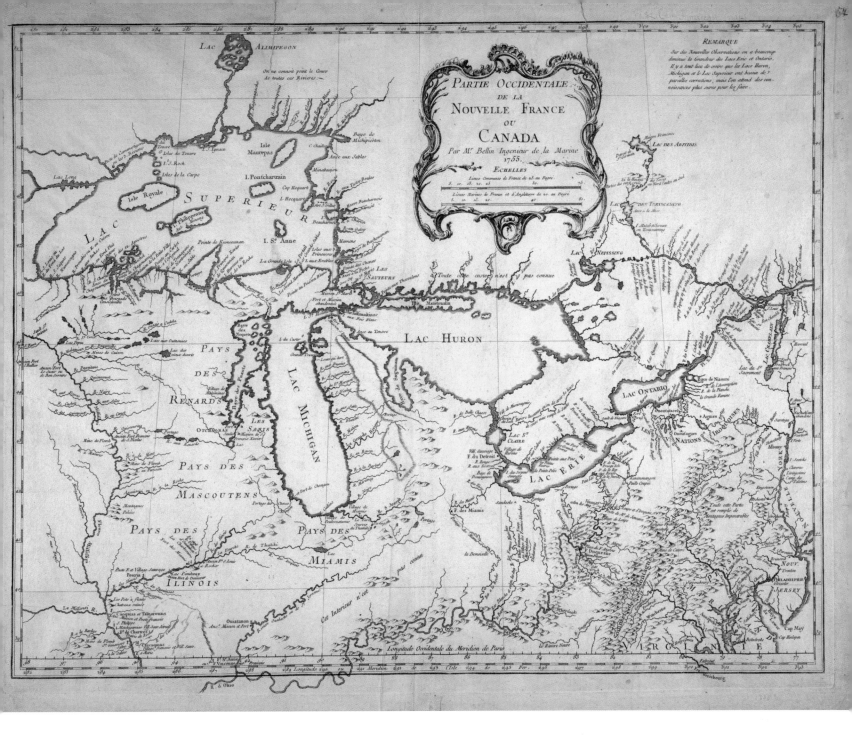

By 1755, France claimed a vast empire in the New World, including Chicago. As shown on this map, the Chicago Portage, or land bridge between the Chicago and Des Plaines rivers, served as an important link in the international fur trade that flourished for decades.

French colonial style with a long front porch, several barns, a flour mill, bake house, milk house, smokehouse, chicken house, workshop, thirty "big horned beasts" or cattle, thirty-eight pigs, and two horses for plowing.[7]

Although no written records survive, it is safe to assume that DuSable traded with Native Americans and fur traders passing through the area. The fact that he and his wife remained in Chicago for fifteen years attests not only to their personal stamina, but also suggests that they were making a good living. In 1800, DuSable sold his property to Jean Lalime, a French Canadian trader, and moved to St. Charles County in what is now Missouri. Unfortunately, DuSable lost his property claims when France sold the Louisiana Territory to the United States in 1803 and died impoverished.[8]

DuSable's departure signaled the beginning of a new era in Chicago history, one shaped by the powerful forces of American expansion. By 1800, thousands of

An imaginary portrayal of Jean Baptiste Point DuSable depicts him in the prime of life when he lived in Chicago. Born c. 1754, DuSable arrived in Chicago around 1785 and remained here until 1800. No real portraits of DuSable are known to exist.

The Kinzie Home and Fort Dearborn by an artist unknown. Oil on canvas, c. 1900.

Standing on opposite banks of the Chicago River, Fort Dearborn (left) and the home of fur trader John Kinzie (right) anchored the frontier community. The cabin was originally built by Chicago's first permanent settler, Jean Baptiste Point DuSable, around 1785. He lived there for fifteen years before selling the property to Jean Lalime, a French Canadian fur trapper who in turn sold it to Kinzie in 1803.

ME.TE.A,
A POTTAWATOMIE CHIEF.

PUBLISHED BY F. W. GREENOUGH, PHILAD.ª

Like other Native Americans, Chief Me-Te-A resisted the encroachment of white settlers into tribal territory. Together with Ottawa Chief Blackbird, Me-Te-A led the attack on Fort Dearborn on August 15, 1812.

Great Britain presented Ottawa Chief Blackbird with this silver loyalty medal for leading the attack on Fort Dearborn. The front of the medal bears a portrait of King George III while the reverse carries the royal coat of arms.

settlers from the eastern United States were pouring into the Northwest Territory, established by Congress in 1787 (eventually, this area became the five states of Ohio, Michigan, Indiana, Wisconsin, and Illinois). Yet, the region remained contested and dangerous. While Native Americans resisted the encroachment of settlers and frequently clashed with them, Great Britain exerted pressure from its base in Canada. In response, the United States government ordered the construction of several forts, including those at Fort Wayne, Indiana, and Chicago. In April 1803, Captain John Whistler and six soldiers arrived from Fort Detroit to survey a site at the mouth of the Chicago River. The following August, Whistler returned with nearly seventy soldiers and commenced building Fort Dearborn, named after General Henry Dearborn, President Thomas Jefferson's secretary of war. Designed by Whistler, Fort Dearborn stood on a sandy, eight-foot-high hill on the river's south bank, facing the DuSable–Lalime homestead. In addition to protecting settlers, the rough-hewn garrison served as a fur-trading post, governed by a set of regulations enacted by Congress to regulate trade with Native Americans.[9]

Fort Dearborn remained a quiet outpost of the western frontier until the War of 1812, waged between the United States and Great Britain over trans-Atlantic trade and control of the Great Lakes territory. The war involved a complex alliance between the British and some local Native Americans who hoped to regain control of their homelands and the fur trade from the United States. Amidst growing tensions, conflict erupted in Chicago on the morning of August 15, 1812, when a group of soldiers and their families, led by Captain William Wells and a contingent of Miami Indians, evacuated Fort Dearborn, heading for the safety of Fort Wayne. As they neared the present site of Prairie Avenue and Eighteenth Street, approximately five hundred Potawatomi and Ottawa Indians, led by Chiefs Blackbird and Me-Te-A, staged an attack, killing sixty-seven people and capturing forty-one prisoners. The next day, tribal warriors burned Fort Dearborn to the ground, leaving Chicago with several prisoners who remained in captivity for months.[10]

Two years after the United States defeated Great Britain in 1814, the army erected a new fort at Chicago. While the second Fort Dearborn stood ready to protect white settlers from further attack, it primarily operated as a fur-trading post, even as Chicago's first industry declined. Brief sketches of three frontiersmen from this era illustrate how the forces of economic change affected Chicago and its early residents.

The first is Gurdon Saltonstall Hubbard (1802–86), who was born in Vermont but moved with his parents to Montreal in 1815. Three years later, in April 1818, the sixteen-year-old Hubbard started working for the American Fur Company and passed through Chicago for the first time on his way to a network of trading posts on the Illinois River. An ambitious entrepreneur, Hubbard gradually gained control of all trade throughout the region of the Iroquois and Kankakee rivers, one of Illinois's richest hunting grounds. In addition, his brief marriage to Watseka, the niece of a

A miniature portrait of Gurdon S. Hubbard captures him at age 26. By then, his youthful days as a frontier fur trader had passed, and he was pursuing other business interests that eventually made him one of Chicago's wealthiest citizens.

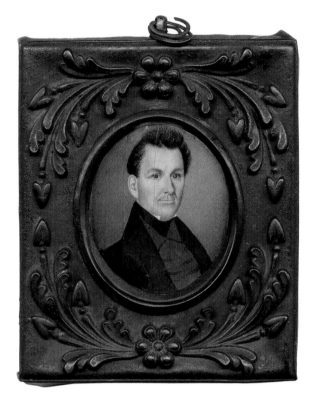

Originally from Detroit, Jean-Baptiste Beaubien moved to Chicago in 1817 and worked for the American Fur Company. He formed close trading alliances with native people by virtue of his marriage to an Ottawa woman.

The Ottawa chief Shabbona lived near the Kankakee River south of Chicago, an area that teemed with beaver and other wildlife. Shabbona formed close trading alliances with many white traders, including Jean-Baptiste Beaubien.

Potawatomi chief, helped him establish vital trading relationships among Native Americans. During the 1820s, Hubbard continued to work as a fur trader, gaining the Native American name Pa-pa-ma-ta-be, or Swift Walker, for his ability to cover great distances by foot in a short amount of time. In turn, he gave his name to Hubbard's Trace, a vital trade route between Danville and Chicago. But Hubbard faced uncertainty as the fur trade declined. Over-trapping and the massive influx of settlers who turned Illinois's lush wilderness into farmland greatly diminished the supply of fur-bearing animals. As the trade died out, Hubbard developed other ventures and eventually moved to Chicago, arriving in 1833, the same year Chicago incorporated as a town. Hubbard invested in several operations, including meat-packing, shipping, real estate, banking, and insurance.[11]

Jean-Baptiste Beaubien (1787–1863), one of Hubbard's contemporaries, was born to a large, well-established French Creole family in Detroit. Like Hubbard, Beaubien started working for the American Fur Company as a young man. Originally assigned to a trading post in Milwaukee, Beaubien moved to Chicago in 1819 to assist John Kinzie, the company's chief agent. Eventually, Beaubien assumed control of the operation and, by virtue of his marriage to Maw-naw-bun-no-quah, an Ottawa woman, he formed a close trading alliance with Shabbona, an Ottawa chief who lived near the Kankakee River. Although Beaubien continued to work for the American Fur Company until 1835, he developed other means of support. Like Hubbard, Beaubien invested in real estate, including valuable acreage around Fort Dearborn, and became involved in local politics, eventually serving as a Cook County administrator.[12]

Mark Beaubien (1800–81), Jean-Baptiste's younger brother, also moved to Chicago from Detroit in search of opportunity. The younger Beaubien, however,

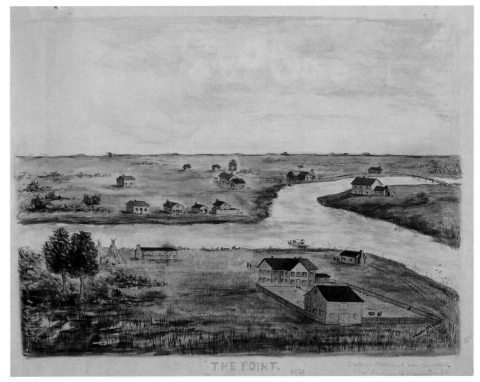

Wolf's Point 1833, by Justin Herriott, c. 1902.

Located where the North, South, and Main branches of the Chicago River meet, Wolf's Point attracted early settlers and business establishments, including the Sauganash Tavern, the large, two-story building in the foreground.

A beloved figure from Chicago's frontier era, Mark Beaubien owned and operated the Sauganash Tavern, one of the city's earliest hotels and gathering places where he reportedly played fiddle "like hell."

Beaubien played this fiddle later in life, perhaps for the 1880 reunion of the Old Settlers at Chicago's Calumet Club.

did not arrive until 1825, by which time the fur-trade era had nearly ended. A new economy, however, was beginning to emerge as Yankee settlers, entrepreneurs, and merchants moved into the area. In 1829, Beaubien established the Sauganash Tavern at Wolf's Point, near the fork of the Chicago River, naming it after a mixed-race British/Indian fur trader also known as Billy Caldwell. The Sauganash served as a hotel, restaurant, and social gathering place for the growing community of traders and settlers. Strong drink, hearty food, and the merry sounds of Beaubien's fiddle entertained customers and friends until he closed the establishment in 1834. Afterward, Beaubien ran a ferryboat service on the Chicago River and worked as a lighthouse keeper before moving, first to Naperville/Lisle, then to Kankakee after the Civil War. Returning to Chicago in 1880 for a reunion of Old Settlers, Beaubien hopped on a table with his fiddle and, much to everyone's delight, played a spirited version of "Fisher's Hornpipe," a familiar dance tune. When asked about Chicago's astonishing growth, Beaubien uttered, "There was no town; didn't expect no town."[13]

Indeed, Chicago remained a frontier backwater through the 1820s, even as settlers poured into southern and central Illinois. But Chicago's fortunes changed in the decade's final year when the Illinois state legislature appointed the Illinois &

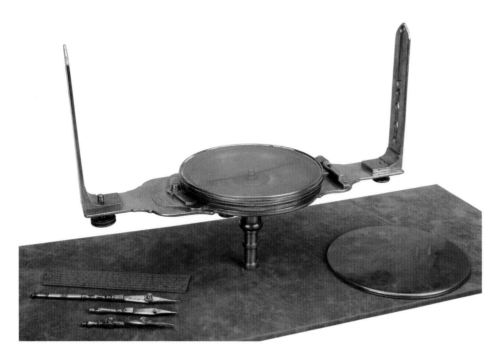

Surveyor's compass and drafting instruments used by James Thompson to plot Chicago as the northern terminus of the Illinois & Michigan Canal in 1830.

Chicago's first mayor, William Butler Ogden, served one term (1837), then turned his attention to business matters, particularly the development of Chicago's railroads. Ogden's visionary efforts helped make Chicago the nation's rail capital.

Michigan Canal Commission to construct a canal linking the Chicago and Illinois rivers. Like Louis Joliet, they believed a canal would stimulate trade and commerce throughout the area by providing a vital connection from Lake Michigan to the Mississippi River, then the country's most important commercial water route. The commission employed James Thompson, a civil engineer from downstate Illinois, to survey Chicago as the canal's northern terminus. On August 4, 1830, Thompson filed a survey and plat for Section 9, Township 39, Range 14; it consisted of a simple grid applied over a three-eighths mile square, bound on the north and south by Kinzie and Madison streets, and by State and Des Plaines streets on the east and west. The area included a good portion of the Chicago River, but not its mouth, as the federal government still controlled the area surrounding Fort Dearborn.[14]

Supporters hoped the canal would stimulate regional growth similar to that of upstate New York after the Erie Canal opened in 1825. Indeed, plans for a new canal attracted a flood of new settlers and sparked wild land speculation. In 1833, Chicago had 350 residents; within four years, its population had exploded to 4,170. Chicago land values grew even faster with property values increasing a thousand-fold to more than two million dollars by 1836. The boom, however, quickly crashed with the Panic of 1837, one of the worst economic depressions in U.S. history. Directly tied to western land speculation, including Chicago's, the panic closed every bank in the country and brought the economy to a screeching halt. But, on March 4 of that same year, Chicago incorporated as a city and subsequently held its first mayoral election, selecting William Butler Ogden, a young entrepreneur from upstate New York, over former fur trader John H. Kinzie.[15]

As mayor, Ogden presided over an elected council of fellow citizens with this gavel. They met in an upper room of the Saloon Building at Lake and Clark streets.

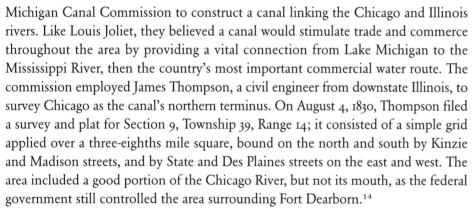

In 1833, Chicago had 350 residents; within four years, its population had exploded to 4,170. Chicago land values grew even faster with property values increasing a thousand-fold to more than two million dollars by 1836.

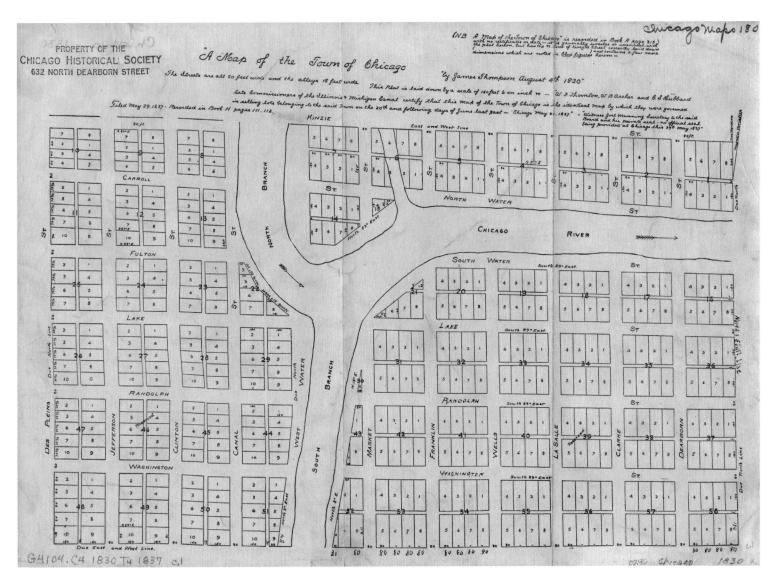

A Map of the Town of Chicago, by James Thompson, August 4, 1830.

Thompson's original map burned in the Great Fire of 1871, but the Chicago History Museum retains a copy created in 1840.

Clearly, Chicago had entered a new era, a change accelerated by national events. Three years prior to Chicago's incorporation, Congress passed the Indian Removal Act of 1830. According to its terms, Native Americans living in the eastern United States had to relinquish their homelands and move to reservations west of the Mississippi River, supposedly away from the path of white settlement. As one of many tribes forced to leave the Midwest, the Sauk Indians of western Illinois were expelled to eastern Iowa in 1831, but the following April, Chief Black Hawk and

WA-BAUN-SEE,
A POTTAWATOMIE CHIEF.

Left: The Treaty of Chicago forced Native Americans to relinquish their land claims and move west to reservations in Iowa and Kansas. As a parting gesture, Potawatomi Chief Aptakisic, or Half Day, presented this ceremonial war club to Stephen F. Gale, an early settler.

Right: Wabaunsee, a prominent Potawatomi chief fought with Great Britain against the United States during the War of 1812 and participated in the attack on Fort Dearborn. In 1833, he signed the Treaty of Chicago, relinquishing tribal claims in the area, but traveled to Washington, D.C., the following year to protest its terms. During Wabaunsee's visit, the artist Charles Bird King painted his portrait, the source of this lithograph.

approximately one thousand followers re-entered the state to plant spring crops. Their actions alarmed white settlers and stirred the U.S. military into action. Even troops at Fort Dearborn were put on alert, although no fighting took place anywhere near Chicago. Further west, however, conflict erupted as American soldiers pursued Black Hawk's band into Wisconsin, where he eventually surrendered in July 1832.[16]

The last armed Native American resistance east of the Mississippi River, the Black Hawk War triggered the final removal of Native Americans from Chicago. In 1833, the United Bands of Chippewas, Ottawas, and Potawatomies signed a treaty relinquishing the last of their Illinois and Wisconsin land claims to the U.S. government. Treaty signatories included several early fur traders, among them Potawatomi Chief Waubansee, Ottawa Chief Shabonna, Gurdon Hubbard, and Jean-Baptiste Beaubien. Over the next few years, several thousand Native Americans left the Chicago area for western reservations where they established new homes. Unknown numbers slipped across the border into Wisconsin or moved further north to Canada, blending in with other tribes and remaining in the area.[17]

The forced departure of Native Americans opened the door for white settlers who arrived in Chicago by foot, horse, wagon, and boat. Many hailed from New England, giving Chicago a decidedly Yankee tone, while others came from central Indiana and Illinois. Numerous merchants, Protestant churches, and residential homes sprang up near the river, which retained its central importance to the community. City directories from the 1840s list numerous grain merchants and meatpacking plants, reflecting Chicago's connections to rural Midwest farming communities. Firmly established by 1840, Chicago's economic foundation would continue to expand over the next several decades, creating a dynamic crossroads of commerce and industry.

THE ILLINOIS AND MICHIGAN CANAL, CONNECTING CHICAGO AND THE WEST WITH THE HEAD WATERS OF THE MISSISSIPPI.

The Illinois & Michigan Canal opened in 1848 and connected Chicago to the Illinois River Valley, a rich farming region. Canal traffic stimulated the growth of the city as a central marketplace of agricultural products.

BIG SHOULDERS

Hog Butcher for the World,
Tool Maker, Stacker of Wheat,
Player with Railroads and the Nation's Freight Handler;
Stormy, husky, brawling,
City of the Big Shoulders.
— from the poem *Chicago* by Carl Sandburg, 1916

When Carl Sandburg penned his famous poem, Chicago stood at the peak of its industrial power. Many of its major industries, including railroad, meatpacking, furniture, iron and steel, farm machinery, and mail order were the world's largest, while hundreds of smaller manufacturing companies produced an astonishing array of goods for regional, national, and international markets. As a result, Chicago dominated the Midwest economy and helped fuel the nation's spectacular growth between the Civil War and World War I.

Chicago's Big Shoulders era began in the 1840s, and while a great location and ambitious entrepreneurs certainly fueled its meteoric rise, government also played a role. Indeed, the Illinois state government launched Chicago with the chartering of the Illinois & Michigan Canal in 1829 and subsequent plotting of the town one year later. Delayed by the Panic of 1837 and an economic depression that lasted seven years, the canal finally opened for business in 1848. Stretching more than one hundred miles through some of the best farmland in the world, the canal performed a critical function. While farmers used the canal to ship grain, produce, and livestock to Chicago, city factories and merchants shipped manufactured goods, including agricultural tools and equipment, household furniture, dishware, clothing, shoes, and books to rural and small town customers.[18]

Simultaneous to its growth as a canal town, Chicago became a major inland port with hundreds of ships docking at its wharves each day. Beginning in the mid-1830s, after the federal government funded harbor improvements, steamships from eastern cities arrived, carrying much-needed supplies and manufactured products eagerly sought by early residents. The ships returned to the East Coast loaded with grain, some of which made its way to overseas markets in Great Britain and Europe. In addition, lake schooners brought lumber, iron ore, and farm products, primarily fruits and vegetables, from Wisconsin and Michigan, establishing an important circuit of regional trade.[19]

Chicago's growing importance as an inland port led to the 1847 River and Harbor Convention, the first such event in city history. Organized by western interests, the convention attracted representatives from several states who wanted to send a strong message to President James K. Polk after he vetoed previous measures aimed at internal improvements. Convention attendees included Illinois congressmen Abraham Lincoln and "Long John" Wentworth, as well as William Butler Ogden, Chicago's former mayor and one of the city's leading entrepreneurs. Held from July 5 through 7, the convention addressed the need to improve Chicago's shallow harbor and river, which could not accommodate large vessels.[20]

As important as waterways were to Chicago's growth, they could not compare to the railroads. Railroads justly are credited with building Chicago, primarily because they allowed the city to extend its reach throughout the region and across the country, creating a national network of trade, manufacturing, and distribution with Chicago at the center. The city's first railroad company, the Galena & Chicago Union Railway, owned by Ogden, began operations in 1848 with the Pioneer locomotive, a small, secondhand engine purchased from upstate New York and shipped by frigate to Chicago. Initially used to construct the company's first line of track, the Pioneer took its maiden passenger run on November 20, 1848, carrying nearly one hundred people about ten miles west to the Des Plaines River. Returning with a load

Built by John Gregory on Goose Island, the two-masted *Mary A. Gregory* hauled cargo across the Great Lakes to Chicago for nearly fifty years. In 1924, Captain John Harry Woltman towed the schooner into Lake Michigan and set her ablaze, a customary burial for retired ships, but saved the bowsprit (left), megaphone, and lanterns.

Founded by William Butler Ogden in 1859, the Chicago & North Western Railway eventually became one of the nation's largest systems with 10,000 miles of track spanning nine states. The company remained in operation until purchased by the Union Pacific Corporation in 1995.

Originally used by a railroad company in upstate New York, the Pioneer locomotive arrived in Chicago in 1848. At the time, Chicago did not have a single operating railroad, but the Pioneer sparked a boom that made the city a national hub of transportation.

of farmer's wheat, the Pioneer created tremendous excitement among Chicago businessmen who saw a golden opportunity.[21]

Two years later in 1850, Senator Stephen A. Douglas, with Congressman Wentworth's help, passed the Illinois Central Railroad Bill calling for a line from Dubuque, Iowa, to Mobile, Alabama, with a branch line to Chicago. The bill also provided generous land grants to the states of Illinois, Mississippi, and Alabama — valuable acreage that they sold to pay off government construction loans — thereby making the Illinois Central the first land-grant railroad in American history. Douglas's national triumph brought personal fortune as well, as he sold lakefront property in Chicago for the railroad's right-of-way into the city. The creation of the Illinois Central sparked a rail boom that transformed Chicago. During the 1850s, as several East Coast railroads built lines to Chicago, the city developed its own operations with the founding of the Chicago, Rock Island & Pacific; the Chicago, Burlington & Quincy; the Chicago & North Western; and the Chicago, Alton & St. Louis. These companies used large gangs of immigrant laborers, primarily Irish, to lay thousands of miles of track outward from Chicago to farms, towns, and cities throughout the region. Moreover, all Chicago lines, except the Chicago, Alton & St. Louis, made vital connections to the transcontinental railroad that stretched nearly two thousand miles from Omaha, Nebraska, to Sacramento, California. Thus, Chicago railroads linked the country's eastern and western halves together in a national network of trade and transportation.[22]

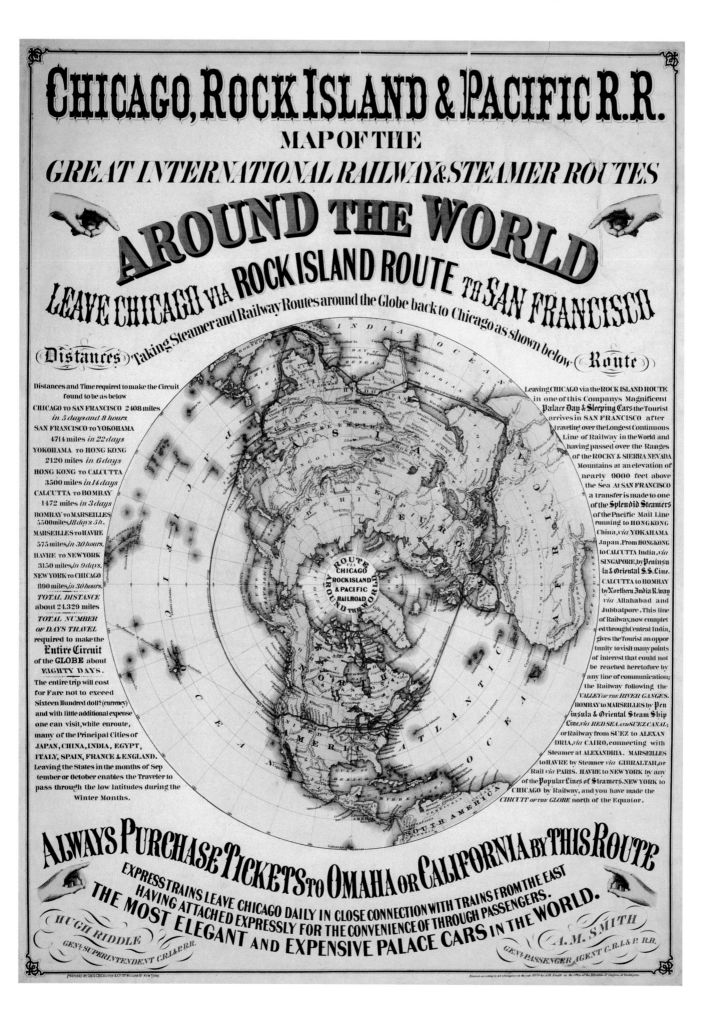

Opposite: Travel broadside from the Chicago, Rock Island & Pacific Railroad Company, 1870.

Using railway and steamer routes, passengers could leave Chicago and travel around the world. Few people, however, could afford the trip, and railroad companies primarily relied upon domestic traffic to generate income.

Right: The Great Age of American Railroads lasted from the 1870s through the 1940s. During that time, Chicago served as the nation's rail capital with thousands of passengers passing through the city on a daily basis. To serve their needs, railroad companies used Pullman sleeping, dining, and observation cars and employed scores of porters, cooks, waiters, and maids.

A working model of a Pullman sleeping car berth, c. 1930, illustrates its basic functions: the lower passenger seats folded down to form a bed while an upper bed lay behind a pull-down panel. Outer drapes and interior window shades provided privacy for sleeping passengers.

As America's rail capital, Chicago experienced tremendous growth. Hundreds of trains arrived daily, shipping raw materials, products, and people in and out of the city at a phenomenal rate. Shipping freight took priority and realized tremendous profits. In 1884, for example, the Chicago, Rock Island & Pacific Railway transported 3.6 million tons of freight, earning more than eight million dollars in revenue, while the Chicago, Burlington & Quincy Railroad shipped more than seven million tons of freight, taking in eighteen and a half million dollars. Freight on these lines and others operating in Chicago included raw products shipped into the city from distant markets and manufactured goods going back out again. Many of these products were made in Chicago for western settlers, including mechanical reapers, windmills, barbed wire, prefabricated wooden housing, household goods, and clothing.[23]

In addition to a voluminous amount of freight, Chicago railroads transported a heavy load of passengers. Each day, thousands of people passed through the city's mammoth passenger stations. Indeed, Chicago served as a national "jumping off" place for routine travel as well as a mass migration of people moving west. In 1884, for example, the Chicago, Rock Island & Pacific Railway carried 2.8 million passengers, earning 3.3 million dollars, while the Chicago & North Western Railway carried 8.5 million passengers with revenues of 6 million dollars.[24]

Chicago's rail traffic created thousands of local jobs and fostered the growth of a new American industry: tourism. To attract passengers, railroads purchased luxurious cars made by the Pullman Palace Car Company of Chicago. Established in 1867 by George M. Pullman, the company transformed travel with the innovative and comfortable sleeping cars, lavish dining cars equipped with their own kitchens, observation cars for viewing the scenery, and luxurious parlor cars furnished with velvet upholstery, mahogany paneling, crystal chandeliers, and brass fixtures. Staffed exclusively by African American porters and waiters, Pullman cars provided first- and

The Union Stock Yard, c. 1910, supplied dozens of Chicago meatpacking plants with a fresh supply of pork, beef, and lamb on a daily basis. Note the sign for Clay, Robinson & Company on the building at left; they were one of the leading livestock dealers in the country.

second-class passengers with added comfort on long-distance journeys. By 1900, Pullman employed more blacks than any other employer in the nation. Although wages remained low, working for Pullman allowed many African Americans to advance economically over the next several decades. In 1925, a group of porters and A. Philip Randolph organized the International Brotherhood of Sleeping Car Porters and Maids, the first African American union chartered by the American Federation of Labor. The union helped workers secure better wages and working conditions, despite stiff resistance from company officials. Pullman porters remained a familiar presence on trains through the 1960s, but their numbers dwindled as rail passenger service declined.[25]

Directly related to its growth as a rail center, Chicago's meatpacking industry assumed gigantic proportions. As early as the 1830s, Chicago received livestock and processed meat with several small operations, such as Myrick's Yards located a few miles south of the city. During the 1850s, the industry grew rapidly as Chicago railroads expanded, bringing an increasing number of animals into the city each day. As a result, numerous stockyards sprang up across the city, and while the resultant traffic, dirt, and noise annoyed many Chicagoans, livestock trader John B. Sherman saw opportunity. With one million dollars in financial backing from nine railroad companies, Sherman consolidated smaller yards into one large operation, known as the Union Stock Yard, outside the city limits on the Southwest Side. Construction began on June 1, 1865; about six months later, on December 25, the yards opened for busi-

Silver loving cup presented to William H. Thompson Jr., president of the Chicago Live Stock Exchange. Thompson served as president of the exchange from 1888 until 1902 and worked diligently to make Chicago the national headquarters of the beef industry.

The "Billionth Animal" arrived at the Union Stock Yard in 1954, a time when trucking and decentralization were beginning to threaten Chicago's industry. Officials staged the ceremony to drum up more business with typical Chicago fanfare.

A badge from the Chicago Live Stock Exchange, c. 1900, bears its motto: "Success Comes to Those Who Hustle Wisely."

ness. With 320 acres and 500 pens that could hold 20,000 cattle, 75,000 hogs, and 20,000 sheep, the facility was the world's largest stockyard. Designed by the engineer Octave Chanute, the stockyards were also a marvel of modern technology with 30 miles of sewers and hundreds of modern pumps that delivered 500,000 gallons of water from the west branch of the Chicago River each day to the animals.[26]

Farmers and ranchers throughout the Midwest and Great Plains shipped pigs, cattle, sheep, and horses to the stockyards via the railroads, which had fifteen miles of track in and around the facility. In 1871, the stockyards received more than 500,000 cattle and 2,000,000 hogs; over the ensuing years, they received millions more, reaching the "Billionth Animal" in 1954, a remarkable achievement. The yards were a unique and colorful crossroads of the urban and rural worlds. They looked and smelled like a gigantic feedlot, but they featured a gracious six-story hotel, a modern bank, and commodious office building where hundreds of traders, clerks, and general office hands worked. Each day—rain or shine, in blazing heat or freezing cold—cowboys, traders, farmers, ranchers, buyers, and bankers met on the yards' common ground to conduct business. A brawling and oftentimes brutal world, the Union Stock Yard also provided comradeship, adventure, and a tangible connection to rural life for urban employees.[27]

The Chicago Live Stock Exchange increased the city's ties to rural America. Established in 1884, the Exchange was a group of cattle dealers based at the Union Stock Yard. Their motto, "Success Comes to Those Who Hustle Wisely," succinctly captured the essence of Chicago entrepreneurship and routinely appeared on association badges and letterhead. The association's first president, William H.

Invented in Chicago, the mechanical pig-hoist revolutionized the ancient art of butchering. It sped up the process and made mass-production possible by lifting the animal onto a disassembly line.

An 1891 map of the Union Stock Yard provides a glimpse into Chicago's largest industry. The 160-acre facility housed 100,000 animals, more than any other stockyard in the world. Its pungent odors filled the Southwest Side and often wafted over the Loop.

A bronze bull's head is one of a pair from the main gate of the Union Stock Yard.

The gate, designed in 1865 by Chicago architects Daniel H. Burnham and John W. Root, still stands on Exchange Avenue, a lonely vestige of the city's meatpacking heyday.

Bidding on champion feeder cattle at the Union Stock Yard, 1947.

Daily life at the Union Stock Yard involved fiercely competitive bidding for the best "live meat on the hoof." Note the auctioneer stand at left.

Like his father before him, Fred Hatch Jr. worked as a livestock commission man at the Union Stock Yard. Commission men served as the link between rural farmers and urban packers, negotiating the best selling price while trying to keep the buyer happy. Hatch's son Eldon also worked as a commission man until the yards closed in 1971.

Winners of the Angus Steer competition at the International Live Stock Exposition, 1954. Chicago's exposition showcased top quality animals in high-stakes competition. Proud winners took home cash prizes and enhanced reputations.

Thompson, worked as head buyer for the G. H. Hammond Company and later became president of the National Live Stock Association, which often held its annual convention in Chicago. Other members, like John Clay, headed their own firms. Clay, a native of Scotland, arrived in Chicago in 1872, and launched his career as a cattleman buying and selling cattle for British interests. He later managed the Swan Ranch in Wyoming, one of the largest spreads in the country, and eventually established his own trading company. A forward-thinking businessman, Clay helped modernize cattle ranching by introducing better land management, scientific breeding methods, and up-to-date business practices.[28]

Clay also helped organize the International Livestock Exposition, an annual event that drew thousands of people to Chicago. Financed by the Union Stock Yard & Transit Company, the first exposition opened on December 1, 1900, in the Dexter Park Ampitheater, a large, domed structure located next to the yards. Livestock experts from across the country judged various classes of cattle, sheep, swine, and horses. In the cattle division, monetary prizes ranged from ten dollars for a fourth-place finish to one hundred dollars for the Grand Champion steer or heifer. Wealthy dealers held special competitions; for example, Clay sponsored a stock-judging contest for agricultural departments at Midwestern and western colleges. The winner took home a cast "Bronze Bull" trophy that became the exposition's official symbol. According to Clay, the exposition brought the West to Chicago, giving the city a "genuine outburst of agrarian loyalty" while providing ranchers with valuable information on breeds and animal husbandry. Aimed at big breeders, rather than small ranchers or farmers, the exposition later moved to the International Ampitheater and remained on Chicago's calendar until 1975.[29]

Ultimately, Chicago's livestock operations were part of a giant food industry with regional, national, and international connections. Central to its existence were

A boldly-designed poster from 1949 commemorates the 50th anniversary of the International Live Stock Exposition. Note the exposition's "Bronze Bull" symbol on the farmer's flag and the image of the International Ampitheater below the horse's hooves.

A trade card from Swift and Company's display at Chicago's 1893 World's Columbian Exposition features a refrigerator rail car packed with freshly butchered meat. Invented by Gustavus F. Swift, the refrigerator car made long-distance shipments possible, a crucial step in the industrial food chain.

Packinghouse workers, c. 1945, helped Chicago live up to its reputation as "hog butcher for the world," a phrase coined by Carl Sandburg in his poem *Chicago*. Though dirty and often dangerous, meatpacking jobs provided steady employment for generations of Chicagoans.

dozens of meatpacking plants that ringed the yards. They included the familiar names of Swift, Armour, Morris, Hammond, and Cudahy, along with several smaller plants. To increase production, and therefore profits, Chicago packers improved or developed new ways of working that revolutionized production into a highly mechanized process. The pig-hoist, for example, consisted of a steam-powered wheel that raised the live hog by its hind leg and attached it to an elevated steel rail, allowing workers to kill, scald, scrape, and gut the suspended animal in a matter of minutes. Additional innovations included ice-cooled refrigerator units that made year-round butchering possible, and the refrigerated railroad car, developed in 1882 by Gustavus F. Swift, that made the shipment of dressed meat to distant markets, such as New York City, not only possible but highly profitable.[30]

By 1900, Chicago meatpacking companies employed nearly twenty-five thousand workers, more than any other local industry. Most workers were immigrants, primarily Irish, Italian, Eastern European, and beginning in the early twentieth century, African American migrants from the South. By the early 1900s, Chicago packers produced 82 percent of all meat consumed in the United States, an astonishing figure that reveals the effects of mechanization on the nation's eating habits. In addition, Chicago meatpackers shipped their products overseas, selling various products such as tinned meat and beef boullion in Great Britain and Europe. Meatpacking companies also produced a wide variety of by-products shipped across the country and overseas, including beef extract, gelatin, glue, fertilizer, soap, horsehair, wool, leather, and celluloid, the first form of plastic. Additionally, the industry spawned dozens of smaller industries, including the manufacturing of shoes, gloves, luggage, and sporting goods that diversified Chicago's economy and employed thousands of people.[31]

The industry, however, had a dark side. Workers endured long hours, dangerous conditions, filthy environments, and notoriously low wages. Worker unrest came to

During the 1904 stockyard strike, approximately 30,000 unionists and their children staged a parade along Ashland Avenue on August 6. According to the *Chicago Daily News*, "two hundred little children dressed in white and waving tiny flags . . . marched at the head of the women workers."

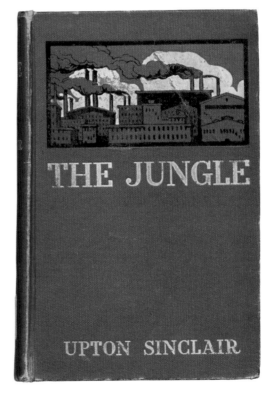

More than a century after its publication in 1906, Upton Sinclair's *The Jungle* remains a powerful indictment of unfair labor practices and harsh working conditions in Chicago's meatpacking industry.

a head in 1904 when the Amalgamated Meat Cutters Union struck several large plants for better wages. The companies shot back by hiring unemployed men, primarily African Americans, as strikebreakers. As the strike dragged on through the summer, tensions ran high and the situation grew increasingly violent as workers and strikebreakers clashed. Finally, in September, the two sides settled: workers agreed to end the strike, and management agreed to take workers back as needed. Wages, however, remained at pre-strike levels, a devastating defeat for the union.[32]

The strike attracted national attention, prompting novelist Upton Sinclair to secretly investigate working conditions in Chicago's meatpacking plants. Sinclair published his findings in *The Jungle*, a fictionalized account of the meatpacking industry told through the story of a Lithuanian immigrant family and their struggles to survive in America. Published in 1906, *The Jungle* sold more than 100,000 copies within the first year and raised a storm of controversy. Although Sinclair intended to raise public awareness of unfair labor practices in the meatpacking industry, the book's graphic descriptions of unsanitary conditions and practices in Chicago's packing plants shocked the public, who pressured Congress to pass the Pure Food and Drug Act on June 30, 1906. A landmark bill of the Progressive Era, the act forbade foreign and interstate commerce in adulterated or fraudulently labeled food and drugs; under its provisions, contaminated products could be seized and condemned, and offenders could be fined and jailed.[33]

Chicago's packing plants also created a host of environmental and social concerns. Pungent odors and smokestack pollution permeated the air and frequently wafted northward across the city. Animal and factory waste lay everywhere and the run-off gave "Bubbly Creek" its infamous nickname. In general, life in the Back of the Yards neighborhood proved difficult for most residents who struggled with harsh

Pungent odors and smokestack pollution from the stockyards permeated the air and frequently wafted northward across the city.

A popular item of the late nineteenth century, horn chairs utilized discarded cattle horns from meatpacking plants. Meatpackers also supplied animal glue and leather hides to the furniture industry.

conditions on a daily basis. Yet the industry provided employment for thousands of people and remained Chicago's largest employer for decades. As early as the 1920s, however, the industry began to decline, the result of new stockyards and modernized meatpacking plants opening in western states. The trend eventually forced Chicago's major packing plants to close, along with the Union Stock Yard itself in 1971. The few small packinghouses that remained in Chicago packed pre-butchered meat shipped in from other locations.[34]

Chicago Furniture

A similar story of growth and decline can be told about Chicago furniture. A small shop industry prior to the Civil War, furniture manufacturing flourished afterward as Chicago grew into a major crossroads of trade and industry. Key ingredients included an ample supply of lumber from the north woods of Michigan and Wisconsin; glue, horsehair, feathers, leather, and animal horns from the Union Stock Yard; steam-powered machinery; a large pool of immigrant labor; willing investors; an increased demand for fashionable, yet affordable, home furnishings for the middle class; large mail-order houses; and a national network of railroad lines for mass distribution. By 1895, Chicago was the nation's largest furniture producer with 276 firms employing some 28,000 workers, outranking New York, Philadelphia, and

Employees of the Tonk Manufacturing Company, 1893. Furniture manufacturing, Chicago's second largest industry, employed tens of thousands of workers, including many young children.

An elaborately carved walnut headboard made by the W. W. Strong Company in 1873 illustrates the quality of craftsmanship found in Chicago during the late nineteenth century. The headboard belongs to a bedroom set installed in the Palmer House's bridal suite.

Grand Rapids, Michigan. Only Chicago's meatpacking and railroad companies employed more people.[35]

Several large companies dominated the industry: A. H. Andrews and Co., W. W. Strong, Tonk Manufacturing, Johnson Chair Company, and S. Karpen & Brothers. Together with smaller firms scattered across the city and outlying communities, they employed thousands of workers to mass produce chairs, desks, bedsteads, piano stools, upholstered parlor suites, and other furniture for the home, school, and office. Additionally, several companies such as Cudell & Lehmann, the Tobey Furniture Company, and John A. Colby & Company employed sophisticated designers and highly skilled craftsmen to produce fine furniture for wealthier clientele.[36]

Like other manufacturers in Chicago, the furniture industry employed a large number of immigrants, particularly highly skilled craftsmen from Germany. In addition to knowledge, they brought strong beliefs about workers' rights with them when they moved to America. Beginning in 1855 with the Cabinet Makers Society of Chicago, they organized some of Chicago's most important unions, most notably Furniture Workers Union No. 1 in 1872. During the 1870s and 1880s, many furniture workers became involved in radical socialist and anarchist movements that called for labor to overthrow management and take control of production. More specifically, they participated in the Great Railway Strike of 1877—a nationwide sympathy strike for railroad workers that spread to Chicago—the eight-hour-day movement, and the 1886 Haymarket Affair.[37]

Despite labor unrest, Chicago continued to produce more furniture than any other city in the nation. Companies large and small used local retail stores and mail-order companies, primarily Montgomery Ward's and Sears, Roebuck & Co., to

Established in 1918, the Great Northern Chair Company of Chicago specialized in making inexpensive but sturdy bentwood chairs for restaurant use. This chair, made in 1939, was modeled after the type first made by the Thonet factory in Vienna, Austria.

S. Karpen & Bros. *26th Annual Catalog*, published in 1906, featured a wide array of chairs and settees upholstered in various fabrics and leather. Established by German immigrant brothers in 1880, the company remained in business until 1952.

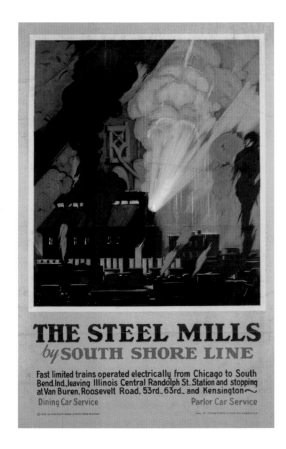

The South Shore Line, a privately owned transit company, encouraged people to visit Chicago's steel district with colorful posters that conveyed the industry's power and might.

market new lines and relied upon Chicago's superior position as a transportation crossroads to ship orders by water, rail, and eventually, by truck, to customers across the country. Chicago retained its position as the nation's largest center of furniture manufacturing until the Great Depression of the 1930s, when many companies suffered serious losses and had to close. Afterward, the industry relocated to North Carolina and other southern states where lumber and labor were more readily available and less expensive.[38]

Iron and Steel

Like the meatpacking and furniture industries, Chicago's iron and steel industry tapped the rural hinterland for raw materials: in this case, iron ore from northern Michigan, coal from Pennsylvania and southern Illinois, and limestone from Indiana. At dozens of plants scattered across the city, workers converted these materials into rails and car wheels for the burgeoning railroad industry, shaped steel for agricultural machinery, as well as steam engines, boilers, stoves, barbed wire, printing presses, iron pipes, pumps, bolts, screws, saws, cutlery, horseshoe nails, and dozens of other types of industrial products sold to local, regional, and national markets. From its inception in the 1850s, Chicago's iron and steel industry flourished, growing with the city and its ever-expanding rail network to become the nation's fourth largest producer, behind Pennsylvania, Ohio, and New York, by 1880. Statistics from 1885 reveal the Chicago industry's massive scale: 246 establishments with a combined capital of nearly $22 million employed 19,180 workers who produced more than $38 million worth of iron and steel.[39]

The North Chicago Rolling-Mill Company, the city's first and largest such facility, began operations in 1857 on the North Branch of the Chicago River.

A steelworker processes molten iron into steel in an open hearth furnace at U.S. Steel's South Works mill, c. 1950.

Steel-toed boots, c. 1970, worn by engineer Herb Post at U.S. Steel South Works.

Originally, the mill re-rolled iron rails, but started producing the nation's first steel rails in 1865. Stronger and more durable than iron, steel rails greatly aided the development of a national rail network. Additional rolling mills included the Chicago Iron Company in Bridgeport, the American Iron and Steel Works on Canal and West Lake streets, and the Chicago Steel Works on Noble Street, a firm that specialized in making attachments for agricultural equipment produced by the McCormick Reaper Works and other manufacturers. The city's rolling mills also played a crucial role in developing the modern skyscraper, a revolutionary accomplishment achieved in Chicago by William Le Barron Jenney in 1885 with the Home Insurance Building. Unlike previous structures that used heavy exterior walls for support, Jenney's skyscraper and those that followed used an interior iron or steel frame that provided strong, yet lightweight support, allowing buildings to soar higher than ever before.[40]

A red-enameled iron alloy letter, c. 1970, is one of three remaining letters from the Wisconsin Steel Works, a mammoth mill in South Deering. The plant's abrupt closing in 1980 threw nearly 3,500 employees out of work, devastating the local economy.

Valley Mould and Iron Company blast furnace, 108th Street and the Calumet River, 1956. During its heyday, Chicago's steel industry shaped the landscape and character of the Southeast Side.

As demand continued to increase during the late nineteenth century, Chicago's iron and steel manufacturers moved away from the crowded central city in order to expand their facilities. While North Chicago Rolling-Mill Company moved to Calumet, twelve miles south of the Loop, Inland Steel opened a plant in Chicago Heights, twenty miles south of the city limits. On a much larger scale, the United States Steel Corporation, the country's first billion-dollar organization founded in 1901 by Chicago lawyer Elbert H. Gary, broke ground for a massive new plant across the state line in Lake County, Indiana, in 1906. Located on a former marsh and sand dunes, the site lay about halfway between eastern coal fields and northern iron ore mines—far-flung sites linked by ship and rail lines. The company established a town for its workers, naming it after the company's founder, and hired private contractors to construct miles of affordable tract housing for workers and their families. By December 1906, six months after its incorporation, Gary had ten thousand residents; by 1920, its population had mushroomed to fifty-five thousand. Like Chicago, Gary attracted European immigrants and their descendants who dominated the ranks of the steel industry for decades.[41]

Concentrated outside city limits, Chicago's steel industry flourished during the 1910s and 1920s when the emerging American automobile industry and World War I increased demand. Although the industry nearly bottomed out during the Great Depression, business rebounded during World War II with orders from the U.S. military. Afterward, as German and Japanese industries lay in shambles, American steel manufacturing, led by Chicago-area companies, dominated the world market. By 1948, local firms and their allied industries employed over 500,000 people, more than half the total number of people working in Chicago. Five years later, Chicago surpassed Pittsburgh as the nation's largest steel producer with an output exceeding twenty million tons. For the next twenty years, Chicago's steel industry flourished with the construction of steel-frame skyscrapers, super-highways, and the military build-up associated with the Cold War, and the Korean and Vietnam wars.[42]

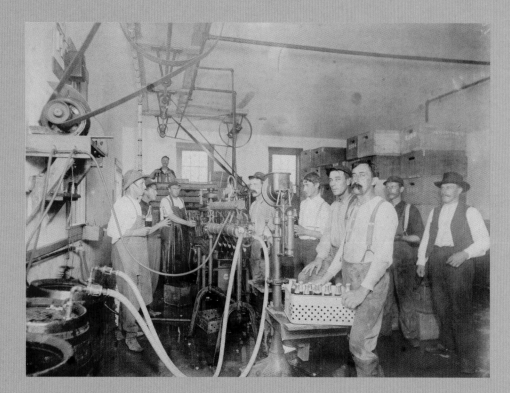

Bottling beer at Siebel's Brewing Academy, 1422–24 Montana Street, Chicago, 1909.

Chicago Breweries

At one time, Chicago made more beer than Milwaukee. During the nineteenth century, European immigrants from Germany, Ireland, Poland, and other countries tapped Old World skills, Midwestern grains, and modern technology to establish Chicago's brewing industry as one of the nation's finest. Companies such as Keeley, Wacker, Seipp, and Schoenhofen employed scientific methods, modern refrigeration, and high-speed bottling machines to create one of the country's most mechanized industries. By 1900, Chicago's sixty breweries were producing more than 100 million gallons of beer per year, primarily for local consumption. Horse-drawn beer wagons became a familiar sight in Chicago neighborhoods, supplying local taverns with tasty brew. Many breweries established their own taverns and supplied them with products for thirsty customers. Chicago remained a beer-making capital until Prohibition and the Great Depression put most breweries out of business.

Issued at the time of the 1893 World's Columbian Exposition, a colorful advertisement for Wacker and Birk Brewing Company features the figure of Columbia unveiling her "favorite brands" of beer, symbolized by a shield bearing the Chicago flag and company logo. The upside-down "Y" symbolized the three branches of the Chicago River.

Birk Brothers Brewing Company delivery wagon on Belmont Avenue, c. 1895.

Concentrated outside city limits, Chicago's steel industry flourished during the 1910s and 1920s when the emerging American automobile industry and World War I increased demand.

The boom collapsed however, as Chicago and the Midwest experienced the effects of deindustrialization during the 1970s and 1980s. More foreign competition, the increased use of plastics, and the end of the Cold War lessened demand for American steel. Some companies, including Wisconsin Steel and South Works, closed down completely, while others such as Inland and Republic Steel cut scores of employees. This turn of events left thousands of people without jobs and had a devastating impact on steel district communities. Yet Chicago's steel industry survived into the twenty-first century as a much smaller enterprise while still producing a considerable amount of steel for domestic and foreign use. As of 2006, a few large mills continue to operate, including Mittal Steel USA in East Chicago and U.S. Steel/Gary Works. In addition, many small mills that recycle scrap metal, as well as steel service centers that store and ship steel, operate throughout the area.[43]

THE NEW ECONOMY

The rise and decline of Chicago's Big Shoulder industries reflects global economic change and illustrates how the city has to adapt and respond or risk losing its position as a national crossroads. After World War II, the United States emerged as the world's most powerful nation with a strong economy based on manufacturing. That economy, however, soon began to change to one that relied more upon the exchange of information and services, rather than industrial production. The process, known as deindustrialization, not only affected the United States, but also Great Britain and Western Europe. Like the nineteenth century's shift from hand-labor to mechanization, deindustrialization had a transforming effect. While some Chicago industries, including furniture manufacturing and publishing moved to southern states, to Mexico, or overseas for cheaper labor and lower production costs, many others including meatpacking and mail order virtually disappeared from the city. In addition, several major companies, including Bell & Howell and Motorola, lured by lower taxes and more room for expansion and employee parking, moved to suburban areas. As companies moved, many employees followed, leaving city neighborhoods for new homes in communities in the suburbs that grew at astonishing rates. Between 1967 and 1987, Chicago lost 360,000 manufacturing jobs due to plant closings or major layoffs.[44]

Together, the twin forces of deindustrialization and suburbanization threatened the city's economic survival. Chicago was not alone, however, as most American cities struggled at this time. Fortunately, Chicago had an advantage. Unlike other cities, such as Detroit, which relied upon a single industry—automobile manufacturing—for economic survival, Chicago had a mixed economy with well-established

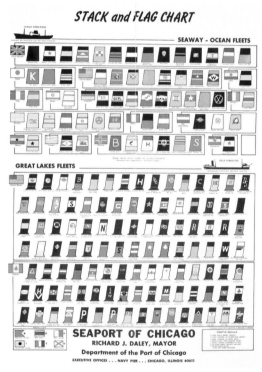

Continental Grain Silos photograph by Jay Wolke, 1984. The shipping of grain is one of Chicago's oldest industries.

A stack and flag chart from the mid-1960s illustrates how the opening of the St. Lawrence Seaway in 1958 stimulated Great Lakes shipping and made Chicago more of an international port.

commercial, financial, and service sectors dating to the city's inception. Government, finance, banking, insurance, retail, health care, education, and other white-collar industries had helped Chicago flourish during the previous century. Now they would become its major employers.

Moreover, Chicago had strong leadership in Mayor Richard J. Daley, who held office from 1955 to 1976. Armed with considerable political clout and backed by private investors as well as the federal government, Daley carried out an ambitious — and controversial — urban renewal program during the 1950s and 1960s. Primarily aimed at saving the Loop as a financial center, the program cleared away hundreds of acres of slums that ringed the downtown perimeter, replacing thousands of dilapidated housing units with high-rise public housing projects such as Stateway Gardens, Robert Taylor, Henry Horner, and Cabrini Green. Daley also convinced authorities at Rush and Mercy Hospitals and the Illinois Institute of Technology to remain in the city rather than move to the suburbs and brought a new branch of the University

Modern highways keep Chicago's economy humming despite frequent back-ups. As intended, they route traffic around the city's central business district to keep that area less congested.

Sign for Interstate 94, c. 1980. I-94 is one of several highways that make Chicago a modern crossroads of transportation and commerce.

of Illinois to the West Side. For the Loop itself, Daley authorized the construction of new government buildings and enthusiastically encouraged the building of Marina Towers and Lake Point Tower. These new high-rise structures helped recast Chicago's image as a forward-looking city.[45]

Daley directed a massive effort to expand and modernize Chicago's transportation network in order to maintain the city's position as a national crossroads of travel and trade. Projects included a new Port of Chicago in Calumet, the region's primary port. Actually a series of several harbors from Waukegan to Burns Harbor, the port chiefly handles local barge traffic, but also includes an enlarged Calumet–Sag Channel and Lake Calumet near the Indiana border that can handle ocean-going vessels. Connected to the Atlantic Ocean via the St. Lawrence Seaway, the complex became an international port and the largest terminal on the Great Lakes.

Chicago also remained the nation's rail capital. Although the increased use of automobiles and airplanes caused a steep decline in passenger traffic after World War

At O'Hare Airport's official dedication on March 23, 1963, President John F. Kennedy declared: "This is an outstanding airport . . . it can be classified as one of the wonders of the world."

II, Daley supported the expansion of Chicago's freight yards on the city's Southwest Side. The use of "piggyback" service, a system that places freight trucks on top of flatbed cars, allowed for more tonnage and greater flexibility in the shipment of goods across the country. As the price of gasoline increased steadily during the 1970s and 1980s, rail traffic continued to grow with tens of thousands of freight cars passing through the city each day.[46]

In addition, Daley directed a complete overhaul of Chicago's antiquated highway system. During the 1920s and 1930s, the city's automobile and truck traffic increased steadily, but after World War II, its roads could no longer handle the exponential boom of traffic. Many streets throughout the city doubled as highways, including U.S. Routes 12, 30, 41, 45, and 66. Each day, they carried thousands of cars and trucks through congested city neighborhoods, bisecting local streets and snarling traffic for hours. To remedy the situation, Chicago, like other major cities, used massive amounts of federal aid to build a new highway system that provided better access to the city while bypassing its neighborhoods. The resultant Edens, Kennedy, Eisenhower, Stevenson, Dan Ryan, Calumet, and Kingery expressways relieved local congestion, but at a cost. Construction disrupted and destroyed several Chicago neighborhoods, a hotly contested political issue and a painful loss for many residents. In turn, the new highways connected Chicago to an interstate highway system that includes the Tri-State Tollway, U.S. Route 55, 57, 90/94, and 80. Chicago's massive, interlocking system of highways plays a crucial role in the economic life and health of the city.[47]

Perhaps most importantly, Chicago expanded O'Hare International Airport on the city's far Northwest Side. The original site, selected in 1945 by a committee appointed by Mayor Edward Kelly, included farms, country clubs, an assembly plant used by Douglas Aircraft during World War II, and a small airport with four runways known as Orchard Field. In 1949, the Chicago City Council renamed the field after Lt. Commander Edward H. "Butch" O'Hare, a Congressional Medal of Honor recipient from Chicago who died in World War II (today, the initials "ORD" used on tickets and baggage tags remind travelers of the airport's early years). O'Hare officially opened in 1955 with a single terminal for commercial traffic, attracting seventeen carriers and serving more than 176,000 passengers in its first year. The following year, the city of Chicago annexed the airfield, thereby acquiring a critical new source of tax revenue. Over the next three years, Kelly's successor, Richard J. Daley, promoted airport expansion to include 7,200 acres, additional terminals (international and domestic), cargo buildings, airplane hangers, parking, and rental car facilities.[48]

At the airport's formal dedication on March 23, 1963, President John F. Kennedy declared: "There is no other airport in the world which serves so many people and so many airplanes. This is an outstanding airport . . . and it can be classified as one of the wonders of the world." By 1965, O'Hare served more than twenty million

The building of O'Hare International Airport assured that Chicago would remain a central crossroads of the new economy. At the airport's formal dedication, President John F. Kennedy placed a wreath on the monument to Edward H. "Butch" O'Hare while Mayor Richard J. Daley and a large crowd of Chicagoans observed.

The United Airlines terminal during the holiday rush, 1978. Based in Chicago, United Airlines operates the largest terminal at O'Hare International Airport.

passengers, a feat aided by transferring all operations from Midway Airport, an outdated facility on the Southwest Side that had served Chicago since the 1930s. Over the next decade, O'Hare continued to add new facilities (such as a hotel and a parking garage) and attract more passengers (forty million by 1976). In 1988, United Airlines, based in Elk Grove Village, opened a new terminal designed by world-renowned Chicago architect Helmet Jahn. A stunning achievement, the modern terminal recalls Chicago's cathedral-like railway stations of the late nineteenth century with an exposed steel frame structure, vaulted ceiling, and spacious waiting areas.[49]

A booming economy drew seventy million passengers to O'Hare in 1997, but the tremendous increase in traffic resulted in many delays that annoyed passengers while eroding company profits. In response, Mayor Richard M. Daley, the first Mayor Daley's son, announced the O'Hare Modernization Plan. Originally estimated at $6.6 billion, the plans, recalculated in 2006 at $20 billion, will reconfigure existing runways into a parallel layout, add several new runways, and construct a new terminal on the West Side. Although supporters claim that the plans will keep O'Hare vital, create hundreds of thousands of new jobs, and add billions of dollars in revenue each year, critics claim that costs far exceed benefits, and they question

Anchoring the south end of the LaSalle Street canyon, the Chicago Board of Trade building opened in 1930. The architectural firm of Holabird and Root designed the stepped-back skyscraper, which remains one of the city's most familiar landmarks.

plans to acquire 433 acres in Chicago, Des Plaines, Elk Grove Village, and Bensenville—which will destroy some residential areas.[50]

Although controversial, revitalizing O'Hare promises to maintain Chicago's vital connections to regional, national, and international markets. While these markets provide opportunity, they also compete with Chicago, as did other Midwest cities during the Big Shoulders era. In today's economy, however, competition is intensely global, with distant cities vying with Chicago for a share of the market. Motorola, Inc., inventor of the cell phone, for example, faces stiff competition from Asian companies. Similarly, European trading companies compete with the Chicago Board of Trade (CBOT) and Chicago Mercantile Exchange (CME), two of the city's most venerable institutions that have adopted new strategies to remain competitive.

A gleaming figure of Ceres, the Greek goddess of grain, soars high above the Chicago Board of Trade Building. A much smaller plaster model reveals a faceless figure clutching a shaft of wheat in one hand and a bag of money in the other, appropriate symbols of the company and city.

Modern computers have revolutionized trading at the Chicago Mercantile Exchange and Chicago Board of Trade, but many traders still trade face-to-face on the floor.

Colorful jackets and platform shoes help traders stand out in the busy pits of the Chicago Board of Trade where competition is fierce.

Buttons from the Chicago Mercantile Exchange announce the company's technological advance in trading and advertise new products.

Founded in 1848, the CBOT originally dealt in farm commodities, primarily Midwest grain (oats, wheat, corn, and beans). During the Civil War, CBOT introduced futures trading, a revolutionary practice that obligates the seller to deliver specific goods at stipulated prices sometime in the future. While futures trading involved risk, it actually helped control wild fluctuations in the marketplace and helped foster trade. By 2006, CBOT traders were exchanging fifty different types of futures and option products through open auction in trading room pits, or increasingly, via high-speed computers. Likewise, the CME, founded in 1898 as the Chicago Butter and Egg Board, has revolutionized trading. In 1972, the company introduced futures trading on seven foreign currencies, including the British pound, Deutsche mark, and Japanese yen. Since then, the CME has become the world's largest regulated marketplace for foreign exchange trading. In 1992, the CME adopted Globex, a computerized trading platform that increased efficiency and profits. In 2004, the CME and CBOT formed a common computerized link to expedite transactions, an alliance that has paid off for both companies.[51]

Although Chicago survived the effects of deindustrialization better than many American cities, its economic future remains uncertain. While companies such as the CBOT and CME have changed with the times, their success is not easily duplicated, and some economists wonder if other Chicago-based companies will be able to survive. Competition from other regions and other parts of the world is steep, and Chicago has discovered that a central location, while still important, is not as critical in the postindustrial, decentralized world of the New Economy.[52] Will Chicago relearn how to "hustle wisely" and remake itself as a vital economic crossroads of the twenty-first century? Only time will tell.

"Chicago Shall Rise Again"

Chicago Tribune, October 11, 1871

Chapter Two CITY IN CRISIS

Life at the crossroads is not always peaceful. In a complex urban milieu such as Chicago, competing social, economic, and political forces are ever-present, creating tensions that periodically explode in crisis. Like other major cities in the United States and around the world, Chicago has experienced several great crises in its past. They include the Great Fire of 1871, the 1886 Haymarket Affair, the 1919 Race Riot, the Gangland Era of the 1920s, and events in the year 1968, when the West Side and the Democratic National Convention both erupted in violence. Although their causes differ, each crisis severely disrupted Chicago, tearing the city's social fabric and testing its ability to respond and recover.

As watershed moments in Chicago history, the crises also shaped the city's identity in complex and often contradictory ways. The Great Chicago Fire, for example, gave rise to the city's most enduring and reassuring legend of survival, resilience, and recovery. In contrast, the 1886 Haymarket Affair and the 1919 Race Riot raised troubling questions of racial and economic justice in American society, leaving contested, often bitter legacies. The Gangland Era gave Chicago a sordid reputation for violent crime while fostering the American myth of urban gangsters as modern-day Robin Hoods. Finally, the events of 1968 left Chicago's West Side in ruins and hampered the city's efforts to attract another political convention for decades. Overall, Chicago's crises, coupled with those experienced by other cities, contributed to a growing sense that American cities were dangerous places to live or visit. This notion arose during the late nineteenth century when cities such as Chicago were emerging and experiencing new types of urban crisis unprecedented in what had been a predominately rural nation. Anti-urban feelings would remain part of the American landscape well into the twentieth century, and it is no surprise that Chicago had a hand in their continuance.

THE GREAT CHICAGO FIRE

One of the worst urban disasters in American history, the Great Fire of 1871 left Chicago in ruins, but ultimately transformed the city into a modern crossroads. By 1871, Chicago had come a long way from its days as a frontier outpost. A burgeoning transportation network and flourishing industries made Chicago a rising star among American cities. The city also boasted a lively retail district, several cultural institutions (including the Chicago Historical Society, founded in 1856), a well-established public school system, a university, and numerous hospitals, parks, and churches. With a population of 300,000, Chicago was one of the nation's largest and most promising cities.[1]

At the time of the fire, most Chicagoans lived within a two-mile radius of the central city. Whites made up the vast majority (nearly 99 percent), but nearly half of them were immigrants, primarily from Germany and Ireland. While they lived in relatively mixed neighborhoods, the poor Irish and a small community of African Americans (about three hundred people) lived in segregated communities, reflecting widespread racial and ethnic prejudice.

Regardless of their status, most Chicagoans lived in wooden structures, usually made of highly flammable pine boards harvested from the north woods of Michigan and Wisconsin. Shoddy construction methods used on brick buildings, including the lack of protective firewalls, and miles of wooden streets and sidewalks added to the volatile mix.[2]

Furthermore, Chicago industries typically burned coal and fires broke out on a regular basis. One such fire on the evening of Saturday, October 7, provided the city with an ominous warning. The blaze started in the boiler room at Lull & Holme's Planing Mill, one of several large lumberyards along the river. Despite firefighters' best efforts, the roaring flames burned four city blocks. Chicagoans inadvertently added to the risk of living in a wooden city by using kerosene lanterns, their only reliable source of light. In addition, many city dwellers kept livestock—pigs, chicken, horses, milk cows—for their own consumption or trade, and wooden barns filled with hay often caught fire at the drop of a match or lantern. Weather also played a role; during the summer and fall of 1871, Chicago experienced a long, hot, dry spell that turned the city into a virtual tinderbox.[3]

A lithograph view of pre-fire Chicago captures the early city's hustle and bustle.

Although the blaze destroyed entire buildings, many small objects made of fireproof materials survived, including a multitude of ceramic doll heads.

Memories of the Chicago Fire in 1871 by Julia Lemos.
Oil on canvas, 1912.

Long after the fire, Julia Lemos, who escaped the
burning city with her five small children, painted this
naïve but compelling view of Chicago's most
destructive event.

These factors made Chicago extremely vulnerable to fire. Around 9:00 P.M. on
the evening of Sunday, October 8, disaster struck. A fire from an unknown source
started on the city's Southwest Side, in or near a barn behind the home of Catherine
and Patrick O'Leary on DeKoven and Jefferson streets. Exactly who or what started
the fire remains a mystery, but strong winds from the southwest quickly fanned the
blaze into a roaring wall of flames that the city's small fire department, exhausted
from the night before, could not handle. Before midnight the fire jumped the south
branch of the Chicago River and headed toward the city's commercial district. A
newly installed bronze bell at the Cook County Court House pealed in alarm as the
fire destroyed everything in its path. Jumping the main branch of the river, it roared
into the city's North Division, burning the Water Works (but not its Water Tower)
and elegant mansions together with hundreds of smaller, more modest homes.[4]

As the fire raged, thousands of Chicagoans fled for their lives. From the central
district they streamed northward across numerous bridges that spanned the river creating a crush of people and widespread panic; one young boy wrote, "It was all we
could do to breathe." Many sought refuge along the lakefront, and some people
jumped into the water for safety. Burning all day and through the night of Monday,
October 9, the fire finally died out early the next morning, after reaching the city's
northern limits near Fullerton Avenue. At last, as a cooling rain began to fall,

Although no one knows who or what started the Great Fire, Catherine O'Leary and her cow became the scapegoats. Popular accounts and imagery made the story a national legend.

Chicagoans faced a scene of complete and utter destruction. The fire had burned over two thousand acres in a path more than four miles long and nearly a mile wide. It killed nearly 300 people, left 100,000 homeless (one-third of the city's entire population), and destroyed more than 18,000 buildings worth $200 million. What had once been a vibrant, up-and-coming city lay in ruins.[5]

On Tuesday, shortly after noon, Chicago Mayor Roswell B. Mason and several members of the Common Council, the city's governing body, assembled at the First Congregational Church, located at Washington and Ann streets. They quickly converted the church into an official headquarters, passed an ordinance prohibiting the sale of liquor "in any saloons until further orders," and established a temporary Relief Committee. Additional measures included swearing in ordinary citizens for special police service, fixing the price of bread, and asking the public to exercise great caution in the use of fire and to completely refrain from using kerosene lanterns for several days. In addition, Mason asked the Illinois Governor, John M. Palmer, to send state militia troops to help local police maintain order. Mason placed them under Lieutenant-General Philip H. Sheridan of the U.S. Army, a Civil War hero and commander of the Division of the Missouri, a vast military region with headquarters in Chicago. Under Sheridan's command for two weeks, the highly visible force of local, state, and federal troops provided a sense of security, calming Chicagoans' fears of looters and other criminal elements thought to be descending upon the city. In the end, very little actually happened along these lines, but a precedent had been set, and martial law would be imposed again during subsequent Chicago crises.

On another front, the Relief Committee tended to the real and immediate needs of the victims. Under the direction of 10th Ward Alderman Orren E. Moore, the committee immediately set to work, sending citizen-scouts to unburnt portions of the city to watch for new fires, and ordering intact churches and schools to open their doors and provide food and shelter for the homeless. Several local physicians

Roswell B. Mason, mayor of Chicago at the time of the Great Fire.

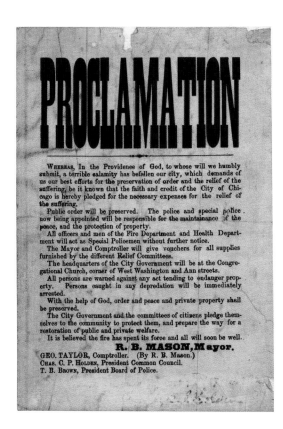

Issued on the morning of October 10, 1871, Mayor Roswell B. Mason's proclamation to the people of Chicago decreed that "public order will be preserved" and ended on a note of optimism.

Fire Marshall William H. Musham wore this leather helmet during the fire. His initials are on the front, above the visor.

Trying to Save a Wagonload of Goods from the Fire by Alfred R.Waud captures the frenzied rush of Chicagoans escaping the burning city. Waud, a noted Civil War artist, made several sketches of the fire, an invaluable record of events as no photographs are known to exist.

volunteered to provide medical assistance, and a special task force, using water wagons voluntarily supplied by a city street contractor, carried fresh water from city parks and wells to the burnt district.[6]

The committee also distributed food, clothing, blankets, and other supplies shipped to Chicago from other cities in response to Mayor Mason's urgent telegrams sent during and immediately after the fire. Organized by James Fisk and Jay Gould of the Erie Railroad, who had a vested interest in the fortunes of Chicago, the first supply train arrived from New York City on the evening of October 11 with seven cars loaded with provisions. According to a report from Relief Headquarters, the shipment included coats, trousers, and vests (one hundred each), four hundred bar-

A panoramic view of the ruins between Wabash (left) and Michigan (right) avenues, looking north from Congress Street, reveals a scene of utter devastation. Reaching 2,000 degrees Fahrenheit, the fire destroyed nearly everything in its path.

A fused clump of carriage bolts testifies to the fire's intense heat.

rels of sugar and coffee, and another hundred barrels of flour. The following day, four additional express trains brought more supplies, and the cash value of New York's largesse totaled approximately $250,000. Boston sent $100,000 while St. Louis sent six carloads of food, one carload of clothing, $50,000 from the City Council, and $70,000 from concerned citizens. Smaller but no less welcome assistance came from Springfield, Fort Wayne, Milwaukee, and many other cities across the country; in addition to basic supplies and $100,000, Cincinnati established a train "kitchen-car" on the West Side that had the capacity for feeding 10,000 people a day and remained open through late winter. Altogether, Chicago received nearly five million dollars worth of contributions in cash and goods, including nearly three million from the state of Illinois.[7] The aid came at a critical time, right before the onset of winter. Without it, Chicagoans would have struggled to meet basic needs, illustrating just how dependent they—and all urban Americans—had become on manufactured goods and a national network of distribution.

Although the Relief Committee performed nobly, the city's official Relief and Aid Society assumed its duties on Friday, October 13. Originally founded as a charitable organization to care for the poor, the society established various committees to address different aspects of the crisis. The Committee on Sick, Sanitary, and

An engraving published in *Frank Leslie's Illustrated Newspaper* on November 4, 1871, records a scene at Grace Church where the pastor and his assistants were "serving out rations for the destitute." Such coverage made the Great Chicago Fire a national, and international, event.

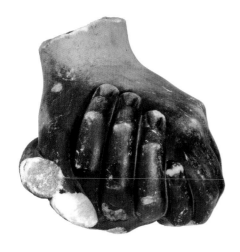

Charred and fused silver watches found in the vault of Wendell-Hyman Jewelry Company attest to the fire's heat and penetrating force.

Like many relics of the fire, a pair of marble statuary hands are from an unknown source.

Hospital Measures cared for those in physical distress and vaccinated more than 60,000 people against a feared outbreak of smallpox, while the Committee on Housing erected thousands of temporary shelters for the homeless, restoring a sense of physical order to the devastated city. To retain skilled laborers for rebuilding efforts, the committee housed them in single-family units, but placed tenement dwellers in multi-family barracks. While the separation reinforced class distinctions, those directing the effort believed that the skilled might leave if they had to live among the lower classes.[8]

Despite its devastating impact, the fire had only affected one-fourth of the city, leaving many residential and manufacturing areas intact, including the mammoth Union Stock Yard and numerous meatpacking plants on the city's Southwest Side. Chicago's transportation network also survived. The Illinois & Michigan Canal lay outside the path of the fire, and while railroad companies lost depots, equipment, and rolling stock within the central city—all covered by insurance—the extensive web of lines radiating out from Chicago maintained crucial connections of trade and transportation throughout the region and across the country. These connections maintained the city's position as a national crossroads even as it lay in ruins.[9]

With so much of the city left, it is not surprising that Chicago started to rebuild immediately. On the morning of October 10, real estate agent William D. Kerfoot erected a small, wooden structure at 89 Washington Street, between Clark and Dearborn streets, a few feet in front of his original location. On top, he placed a sign that read "W. D. Kerfoot's Block: First in the Burned District," a tongue-in-cheek reference to the fact that several businesses occupied the same structure, including surveyors, a lawyer, a plumber, and another real estate agent. On the front, Kerfoot attached another sign: "All gone but Wife, Children, and Energy." Kerfoot's infectious humor made his building an informal headquarters of news and commerce in the immediate aftermath of the fire.[10]

W. D. Kerfoot's Block by W. J. Burton.
Oil on canvas, 1872.

Within days of the fire, William D. Kerfoot, an enterprising real estate agent, erected the first building in the burnt district at 89 Washington Street.

Other Chicagoans turned to God for comfort and inspiration. On the afternoon of October 10, Mayor Mason issued a formal proclamation that began, "Whereas, In the Providence of God, to whose will we humbly submit" and added, "With the help of God, order and peace and private property shall be preserved." Several Christian ministers described the fire as a sign from God, sent to cleanse the city of sinful elements: the saloons, theaters, brothels, and gambling houses that filled the streets of Chicago and corrupted its people. Accordingly, the fire had provided Chicagoans with a second chance to start over and make a better, more virtuous city. Secular commentators held similar views. "Cheer Up," proclaimed the *Chicago Tribune* in a famous editorial dated October 11, "The Christian world is coming to our relief. The worst is over . . . and we can resume the battle of life with Christian faith and Western grit. Let us all cheer up!" The editorial went on to state that "CHICAGO SHALL RISE AGAIN" and even more emphatically that "CHICAGO MUST RISE AGAIN!"[11]

Chicago, however, needed more than good cheer to clear the mounds of charred rubble that choked the streets. Wagon-teams hauled debris to the lakefront, filling in the basin between the outlying track and breakwater of the Illinois Central Railroad. As the clean up progressed, hundreds of temporary structures sprang up throughout the burnt district. More permanent structures followed despite the difficulties of establishing real estate titles burned in the Court House. By December, Chicago had issued 250 building permits; new restrictions banned the use of wood for any building in the downtown area, making brick the preferred material, followed by lime- and sandstone. Using state money, Chicago rebuilt bridges and viaducts destroyed in the fire, re-establishing important commercial, as well as psychological, connections. The Water Works, civic buildings, hotels, railroad depots, churches, schools, and residential districts were rebuilt, which expanded the city's central core and outer reach, particularly on the South Side where many middle- and upper-income people moved after the fire to escape the city's dirt, noise, overcrowded conditions, and low-income residents. Its large homes, spacious lots, and tree-lined streets gave the South Side a gracious air that seemed far removed from the city's hustle and bustle.[12]

Chicago's rapid recovery from the fire astonished contemporary observers and subsequent generations. A view looking north from the corner of Randolph and Market streets shows new buildings under construction a few weeks after the catastrophe.

To showcase the city's recovery and rebounding potential, civic leaders led by Potter Palmer and Cyrus McCormick sponsored the first annual Inter-State Industrial Exposition in September 1873, less than two years after the disaster. Held in a sprawling glass and iron building on the lakefront, the exposition ran for eighteen days. An important regional event, the show drew thousands of people who not only marveled at the extensive displays of industrial products, fine arts, and natural history, but also at the resurrected city itself, which continued to rebuild at a rapid rate.[13]

Chicago's recovery, however, did not exist in a vacuum, and soon outside forces slowed the process. The Panic of 1873, one of the worst economic depressions in United States history, began that September when several important Eastern banks failed, chief among them Jay Cooke & Company of New York City. Hardest hit were bankers, manufacturers, and farmers of the South and West—in other words, Chicago's bread and butter. The depression lasted four years, and like the earlier Panic of 1837, burst the bubble of Chicago's booming economy. According to the historian A. T. Andreas, the depression's damaging effect rivaled or surpassed that of the fire, although rebuilding efforts kept the city's economy from going completely under. Between 1873 and 1877, trade and manufacturing slowed and twenty-one banks failed. Unemployment and labor unrest both grew, culminating in the participation

A boy sitting in remains of the courthouse bell provides a sense of its massive size. When the fire started, the bell rung out in alarm until flames engulfed the building, causing the bell tower to collapse. The bell crashed to the floor, shattering in pieces. Afterward, clever entrepreneurs created miniature souvenir bells that became treasured family heirlooms.

of many Chicago workers in the Great Railway Strike of 1877, the first nationwide strike in American history.[14]

Yet Chicago, like the nation, rebounded. With the passage of time, the Great Chicago Fire became the city's most important legend with both heroes and scapegoats, the latter being Catherine O'Leary, whose status as an immigrant Irish woman made her an easy target for those looking for someone to blame. Not surprisingly, the Chicago Historical Society, whose supposedly fireproof building at Dearborn and Ontario streets lay in ruins after the blaze, amassed a large collection of fire materials in the aftermath. The collection, primarily built by fire survivors and their descendants, includes first-person accounts, artists' sketches, photographs, paintings, and hundreds of "relics" burned or melted, some beyond recognition, by the intense heat. Dozens of charred toys, dishes, coins, keys and watches, molten screws, washers and nails, and blackened marble statuary bear witness to the fire's destructive nature. By comparison, cherished dolls, buried silver, and a fire marshal's helmet remind subsequent generations that all was not lost.

Over the years, the Museum has commemorated the event in numerous exhibitions, publications, and public events. In 1996, the Chicago Historical Society launched a new Web feature, *The Great Chicago Fire and the Web of Memory*, which reaches audiences, both near and far, through cyberspace. Likewise, the city of Chicago has commemorated the anniversary of the fire as a means to celebrate the city's survival and rebirth. Yet not everyone has been honored. Indeed, most people continued to blame Catherine O'Leary, or at least her cow, for starting the fire even though the City Council absolved her of all guilt in 1997.[15] Truly a momentous event, the Great Chicago Fire has become a common touchstone for all Chicagoans, a useful civic reminder that we can survive a crisis and begin anew.

The Great Chicago Fire has become a common touchstone for all Chicagoans, a useful civic reminder that we can survive a crisis and begin anew.

The Great Chicago Fire left behind tons of rubble containing small, recognizable treasures from everyday life, including a wide array of children's toys.

Doll carried by Elizabeth Richardson as she and her family fled the Great Chicago Fire from their home at 136 Schiller Street. Fifty-nine years later, Elizabeth donated her beloved doll to the Chicago Historical Society.

THE HAYMARKET AFFAIR

In the decades following the Great Fire, Chicago expanded at an astonishing rate and its burgeoning industries required a large work force to keep them running. While laborers welcomed the opportunity to work, they often toiled in brutally harsh conditions. Most men earned one dollar a day, while women and children averaged five cents per hour. They put in ten, twelve, and even fourteen hours a day in dirty, poorly lit facilities. Hazardous working conditions, seasonal slowdowns, sudden layoffs, and the increasing use of machines that replaced human labor created a great deal of uncertainty and unpredictability for workers with few financial resources.[16]

To gain some control over their lives, Chicago workers joined the growing American labor movement. During the 1870s and 1880s, the movement focused on making the eight-hour day standard across the country. Although the Illinois State Legislature had passed a law in March 1867 declaring eight hours to be the legal limit, most employers did not comply. On May 1 of that year, more than ten thousand Chicago trade union workers left their jobs and marched through the streets, demanding their rights. While some employers agreed to the worker's terms, others refused, and more strikes ensued. In response, owners hired unemployed workers from other cities and the movement failed. Several years later, Samuel Gompers and other labor leaders revived the effort. In 1884, the Federation of Organized Trades and Labor Unions of the United States and Canada convened in Chicago and declared that the eight-hour day would go into effect across the country on May 1, 1886. On that day, tens of thousands of Chicago laborers walked off their jobs, joining a national strike that involved more than 300,000 workers.[17] Eighty thousand workers marched up Michigan Avenue led by Albert and Lucy Parsons, two of the main players in the drama of Haymarket.

Born in Alabama and raised in Texas, Albert Parsons served in the Confederate Army during the Civil War. Afterward, Parsons worked as a journalist, launching his own weekly newspaper, the *Spectator*, in which he advocated reunification with the North and full civil rights for former slaves. In addition, Parsons held a series of political posts in the Texas government and served as an officer in the state militia, protecting blacks from harassment and violence. Around 1872, Parsons and Lucy married. She was a former slave of mixed ancestry, possibly American Indian and Mexican, as well as white. Unwelcome in Southern society, the couple left Texas in 1873 and moved to Chicago, a magnet for people searching for work. At the time, however, the Panic of 1873 had plunged the entire nation into a deep depression. Although Albert found work as a typesetter, thousands of other people remained unemployed. Moved by the workers' plight, Parsons adopted socialist views that the wage labor system denied political liberty by creating social classes, class servitude, and class conflict.[18]

Workers at the Horn Brothers Furniture Company
assembled on April 30, 1886, the day before a national
strike in support of the eight-hour day. Tens of thousands
of Chicago workers participated in the strike.

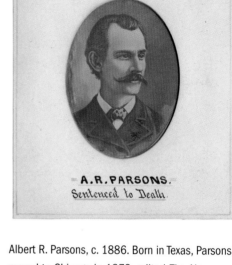

A. R. PARSONS.
Sentenced to Death.

Albert R. Parsons, c. 1886. Born in Texas, Parsons
moved to Chicago in 1873, edited *The Alarm*, a radical
newspaper, and spoke at the Haymarket rally.

AUGUST SPIES.
Sentenced to Death.

August Spies, c. 1886. Originally from Germany, Spies
edited the *Arbeiter-Zeitung*, Chicago's leading foreign
language socialist newspaper. Spies spoke first at the
Haymarket rally.

In Chicago, Parsons became increasingly involved in radical politics. During the Railway Strike of 1877, America's first nationwide labor protest, he chastised railroad executives, urged workers to join unions, and demanded the adoption of the eight-hour day. Although Parsons spoke against violence, he believed that anarchism, or the lack of formal regulation or government, provided the only solution to problems created by industrial capitalism. When asked to explain his beliefs, Parsons stated: "I am an Anarchist. . . . What is Socialism, or Anarchism? Briefly stated, it is the right of the toilers to the free and equal use of the tools of production and the right of the producers to their product." These activists believed in the destruction of capitalism and in the union as its replacement—the nucleus of a new social order.[19]

Known as the "Chicago idea," the combination of anarchism and revolutionary unionism was articulated in 1883 by Parsons, as well as August Spies, a German socialist from Chicago and other radicals attending a socialist congress in Pittsburgh. In addition, they formed the International Working People's Association (IWPA), a loose-knit federation of revolutionary groups across North America. They published their views in *The Alarm*, edited by Parsons, and the *Arbeiter-Zeitung*, a German newspaper edited by Spies that enjoyed a wide circulation in Chicago. Both newspapers advocated the use of violence to overthrow capitalist "oppressors." Dynamite became the weapon of choice. Easy-to-conceal dynamite, in the words of Gerhard Lizius, who wrote for both papers, "can be used against persons or things; it is better to use it against the former than against bricks and mortar. It is a genuine boon for the disinherited" against "rich loafers, who live by the sweat of other people's brows."[20]

Initially, anarchists did not support the eight-hour-day movement, believing it conceded the justness of a wage-system. By 1886, however, the eight-hour movement had picked up steam, and Parsons and Spies joined the effort. While sensing an opportunity to expand their base of support, they considered the eight-hour day a small, but necessary step toward the ultimate goal of revolution. Thus, the IWPA,

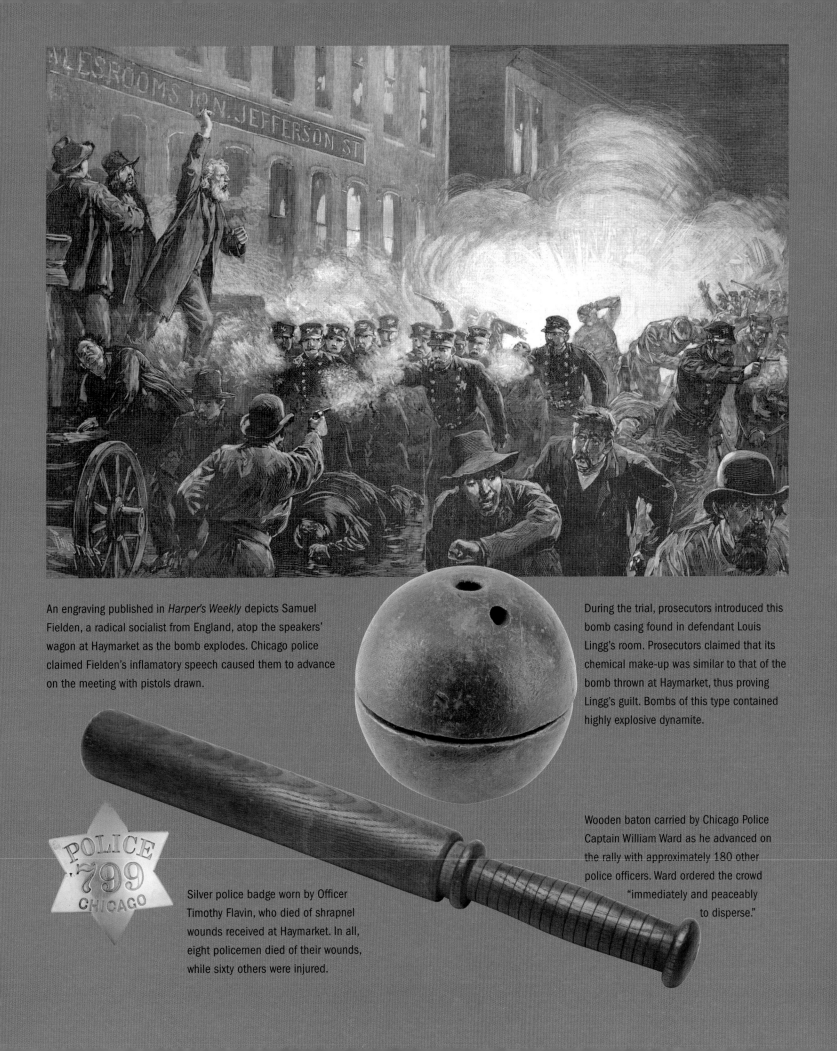

An engraving published in *Harper's Weekly* depicts Samuel Fielden, a radical socialist from England, atop the speakers' wagon at Haymarket as the bomb explodes. Chicago police claimed Fielden's inflamatory speech caused them to advance on the meeting with pistols drawn.

During the trial, prosecutors introduced this bomb casing found in defendant Louis Lingg's room. Prosecutors claimed that its chemical make-up was similar to that of the bomb thrown at Haymarket, thus proving Lingg's guilt. Bombs of this type contained highly explosive dynamite.

Silver police badge worn by Officer Timothy Flavin, who died of shrapnel wounds received at Haymarket. In all, eight policemen died of their wounds, while sixty others were injured.

Wooden baton carried by Chicago Police Captain William Ward as he advanced on the rally with approximately 180 other police officers. Ward ordered the crowd "immediately and peaceably to disperse."

SAMUEL FIELDEN.
Sentenced to Death.

LOUIS LINGG
Sentenced to Death.

acting with the Central Labor Union, organized the massive parade led by Parsons on May 1. Although tense, with police, private detectives, and militia troops standing guard throughout the city, the demonstration remained peaceful.[21]

Two days later, however, trouble erupted at the McCormick Reaper Works, the scene of many bitter clashes between labor and management over the years. On the afternoon of May 3, Spies addressed an open-air meeting of the Lumber Shovers' Union on strike for shorter hours. At the conclusion of his remarks, a group of two hundred men rushed toward the nearby McCormick plant, where picketing workers, locked out since February, were heckling nonunion laborers leaving work. The ensuing clash brought in Chicago police, wielding clubs and revolvers. Shooting into the crowd, they wounded many people, at least two fatally. After witnessing the violence, Spies rushed back to his office and wrote what came to be known as the "revenge" circular, printed in English and German, which exhorted, "Workingmen to Arms!!!" against the "hideous monster that seeks to destroy you."[22]

The next day, May 4, a second circular called for a mass meeting at Haymarket Square, on Desplaines Street, just north of Randolph. That evening, approximately two to three thousand people attended the rally, far less than organizers anticipated. Spies, Parsons, and their fellow anarchist Samuel Fielden spoke at length to the peaceful crowd, decrying capitalism and the existing social order. Around 10:20 P.M., 176 policemen arrived and ordered the crowd to disperse; by this time, only a few hundred people remained. As Fielden stopped speaking, someone threw a bomb that exploded with a terrible blast between police lines. Many officers fell, but after a moment of stunned silence, those left standing opened fire on the crowd, killing an unknown number of civilians and wounding between thirty and forty others in about five minutes. In all, eight policemen died of their wounds, while sixty others suffered injuries, many from police fire shot in the midst of mass confusion. Of those killed, only one policeman, Officer Mathias Degan, died directly as a result of the bomb—a fragment struck his left thigh, severing an artery.[23]

The Haymarket bomb threw Chicago into a panic. Gripped by fear and hysteria whipped up by the press, Chicagoans demanded revenge. Local police quickly rounded up anarchists and labor activists, most of them immigrants, and shut down

Left: Adolf Fischer, c. 1886. Originally from Germany, Fischer arrived in Chicago in 1881. An avowed anarchist, Fischer worked for the *Arbeiter-Zeitung* before being arrested as a conspirator in the Haymarket incident.

Center: Samuel Fielden, c. 1886. Arrested, tried, and sentenced to hang for the Haymarket incident, Fielden appealed to Governor Richard Oglesby and had his sentence commuted to life in prison. In 1893, Governor John Peter Altgeld pardoned Fielden.

Right: Louis Lingg, c. 1886. A German socialist and anarchist, Lingg arrived in Chicago ten months before the Haymarket bombing. Arrested, tried, and convicted, Lingg evidently committed suicide in his jail cell the day before his scheduled execution.

Michael Schwab, c. 1886. The associate editor of the *Arbeiter-Zeitung*, Schwab had his death sentence commuted to life in prison. In 1893, Illinois Governor John Peter Altgeld pardoned Schwab.

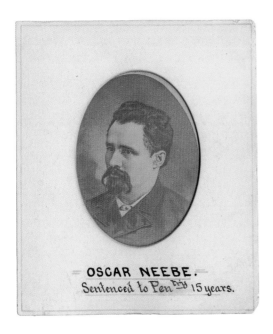

Oscar Neebe, c. 1886. Sentenced to fifteen years in prison for his role in the Haymarket Affair, Neebe also was pardoned by Governor John Peter Altgeld in 1893.

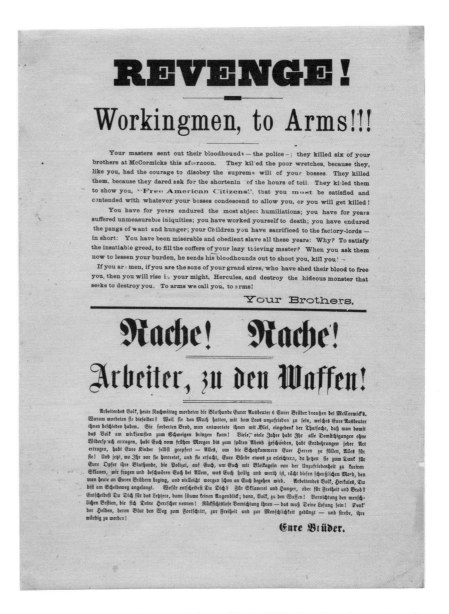

The "Revenge Circular," written by August Spies on May 3, 1886, after witnessing events at the McCormick Reaper Works. During the Haymarket trial, prosecutors introduced the broadside as evidence that Spies incited workers to use violence against authorities.

anarchist newspapers. Among those arrested were eight men who eventually stood trial for the murder of Officer Degan: August Spies, Samuel Fielden, Adolf Fischer, Michael Schwab, George Engle, Louis Lingg, and Oscar Neebe. Albert Parsons, who disappeared from Chicago on the night of the explosion, remained in hiding in Waukesha, Wisconsin, but, convinced of his innocence, turned himself into police on the day of trial. William Selinger and Rudolf Schnaubelt were indicted but not tried; Selinger turned state's evidence while Schnaubelt, accused of being the actual bomb thrower, fled the city, never to be seen again. The identity of the person who threw the bomb at Haymarket remains a mystery.[24]

Now considered to be one of the grossest miscarriages of justice in American history, the Haymarket trial began on June 21, 1886, in the Cook County Court House at the northwest corner of Dearborn and Hubbard streets. The presiding

The public hanging of August Spies, Albert Parsons, George Engel, and Adolf Fischer on November 11, 1887, attracted international attention. Before he died, Spies declared from the gallows: "The day will come when our silence will be more powerful that the voices you are throttling today."

judge, Joseph E. Gary, had a strong bias against the defendants; moreover, the jury had been stacked with people who shared Gary's views. Lacking any hard evidence, the prosecuting state's attorney, Julius S. Grinnell, built a case against the defendants on the grounds that their inflammatory speeches and writings had incited an unknown sympathizer to throw the bomb that fateful night. The anarchists essentially stood trial not for their deeds, but for their political beliefs, which Grinnell probed throughout the trial. Conversely, Judge Gary allowed the defense attorney, William P. Black, to cross-examine witnesses only on specific points brought out by the state, thus limiting the effectiveness of the defense.[25]

In the climate of fear that gripped Chicago that summer, the jury reached a swift verdict. On August 20, they found the defendants "guilty of murder in manner and form as charged in the indictment and fix the penalty at death" for all eight men except for Neebe, who received a fifteen-year prison term at the state penitentiary. Despite subsequent appeals by Black to the Illinois and United States Supreme Courts, four of the Haymarket defendants, Parsons, Spies, Engle, and Fischer, were hung on November 11, 1887 — known as Black Friday — in the courtyard between the courthouse and jail in front of 170 witnesses (reporters, members of the jury, doctors, and other officials). The day before, Louis Lingg, the only defendant linked to manufacturing dynamite, had allegedly committed suicide in his cell, two hours before Illinois Governor Richard J. Oglesby commuted the sentences of Fielden and Schwab to life imprisonment. Six years later, in 1893, Illinois Governor John Peter Altgeld pardoned the three survivors while denouncing the trial, in particular Judge Gary, for his biased handling of the case.[26]

While the Haymarket executions angered radicals and other labor activists across the United States and Europe, most Americans felt relief. For them, anarchy and its call for violent revolution posed a real and very frightening threat to the prevailing social order. Anarchy's European roots also disturbed many Americans who held a

Above: Dedicated in 1889, a monument to the police who marched on Haymarket Square depicts an officer with his right arm raised, signifying their efforts to disperse the crowd peacefully before the bomb exploded.

Below: Its counterpart, an 1893 monument dedicated to the Haymarket anarchists, features a defiant figure of Justice striding above the last words of August Spies inscribed on the base.

deep mistrust of foreigners who brought different ideas and customs with them when they immigrated to the United States. Ultimately, the Haymarket trial and executions were a way to restore civic order and control in an increasingly uncertain urban environment. Additional measures of control included a general clampdown on union activities across the country and, in Chicago, the construction of a new U.S. Army base twenty-seven miles north of the Loop in Highwood, Illinois. Occupying more than six hundred acres and named after commanding officer Philip H. Sheridan, the fort gave Chicago authorities new means to deal with any future labor unrest in the city.[27]

Like the event itself, the Haymarket Affair created a contentious legacy. On Memorial Day in 1889, the Chicago police erected a commemorative statue to their fallen comrades in Haymarket Square. Depicting a policeman raising his right arm in a protective gesture, the statue remained in place until a streetcar damaged it in 1925. Restored and moved to Union Park, it was returned to an area near Haymarket, but Vietnam War protestors defaced the statue on May 4, 1968. The following year, the Weathermen faction of the Students for a Democratic Society, who revered Chicago's anarchists, claimed responsibility for blowing up the statue twice. In 1972, the statue found a more secure home in the lobby of the Central Police Headquarters, but it was moved again in 1976 to the Timothy J. O'Connor Police Training Academy.[28]

Similarly, anarchist supporters dedicated a monument in Forest Park's Waldheim Cemetery in 1893 near the graves of Spies, Parsons, Engel, Fischer, and Lingg. An imposing figure of Justice, ready to draw the sword, places a laurel wreath on the head of a fallen worker. Inscribed on the base are the final words of August Spies: "The day will come when our silence will be more powerful than the voices you are throttling today." The remains of twenty-five supporters lie nearby, including those of Lucy Parsons; Emma Goldman, noted anarchist and feminist deported by the U.S. government in 1919; and the ashes of William "Big Bill" Haywood, founder of the International Workers of the World.[29]

More than a century later, the Haymarket Affair remains highly controversial, capable of stirring heated debate over its meaning and place in public memory. While many view the incident as a hallowed moment in the long struggle for workers' rights, others consider the anarchists' extreme views and violent methods dangerous to a democratic society. Nonetheless, in 2004, Chicago erected a monument to free speech and the labor movement at Desplaines and Halsted streets, near Haymarket Square. That same year, the city named a neighborhood park after Lucy Parsons, creating anger among many members of the Chicago Police Department. A watershed event, the Haymarket Affair will undoubtedly remain a lightning rod of controversy. Unlike the Great Chicago Fire, which inspired stories about the city's survival and recovery, the Haymarket Affair surfaced troubling questions about class, economic justice, workers' rights, and the limits of free speech in America.

The Eastland Disaster

S. S. "Eastland" of South Haven Mich.

Photo by D. J. Lewis

My Dear Mother: On Monday F.W. hope and arrived all after a very pleasant lake trip. Your Son, Gilbert

Launched in 1903, the poorly designed, top-heavy *Eastland* experienced many problems before capsizing in the Chicago River twelve years later.

Early on the morning of Saturday, July 24, 1915, approximately five thousand people gathered along the Chicago River between Clark and LaSalle streets for the Western Electric Company's annual employee picnic. Despite a light rain, the mood remained festive as hundreds of people began boarding the *S. S. Eastland*, one of five excursion boats hired by the company. As the boarding of 2,500 passengers continued, the *Eastland* began listing, first to the starboard (right) side, then to the port (left) side, and took on water. Although the crew tried to stabilize the ship by asking passengers to move from side to side, the *Eastland* continued to list and eventually reached a forty-five-degree angle on the port side.

At that point, water poured into the gangway and portholes on the main deck, creating panic everywhere. While some passengers and crew members jumped off the boat, landing on the nearby wharf or in the murky water, most remained on board, trapped below deck in a chaotic crush of people and furniture. At 7:28 A.M., the *Eastland* rolled over into the shallow waters and soft mud of the Chicago River, less than twenty feet from shore. Although trained rescue personnel and passers-by heroically saved 280 people, 844 people perished in the accident.

Why did the *Eastland* tip over? Although debated, the probable cause relates to the ship's faulty design. A tall, narrow ship built for speed, the *Eastland* was a top-heavy, unstable vessel with a history of problems and near accidents. Furthermore, the ship's owners made

Steering wheel from the stern deck of the *Eastland*, 1903. It was salvaged from the vessel in 1947 and donated to the Chicago Historical Society in 1969.

The capsized *Eastland* in the Chicago River, July 24, 1915. Note the rescue team on the left carrying a victim on a stretcher away from the ship.

several modifications to the ship that increased its instability, including the addition of several tons of concrete between the main deck and floor below a few months prior to the accident. Ironically, the sinking of the *Titanic* in 1912 also contributed to the disaster. In the wake of that tragedy, Congress passed an act requiring that the number of lifeboats and rafts be based on the number of passengers, rather than a ship's gross tonnage. As a result, when the *Eastland*'s owners increased the ship's capacity, they added three lifeboats and six rafts, totaling ten to fourteen tons, to the top deck, further destabilizing the ship.

While not as physically destructive as the Great Fire or as socially disruptive as the Haymarket Affair, the Eastland disaster devastated Chicago on an emotional level. Twenty-two families were completely wiped out, and more than 650 families lost someone, including many

Rescue worker leaping into the Chicago River at the site of the *Eastland* disaster, July 24, 1915. Although the tragedy claimed 844 lives, heroic efforts saved 280 people.

young children. Immediately after the accident, survivors and victims were taken to the Reid, Murdoch & Company warehouse across the river. Later in the day, the dead were taken to a temporary morgue set up in the Second Regiment Armory at Washington and Curtis streets, but the identification of bodies took weeks. Churches on the West Side, where most victims lived, held funeral services daily, often for several victims at a time. Meanwhile, the Eastland lay in the river until salvage crews righted the vessel nearly four weeks later on August 14, a grim reminder to all Chicagoans of the terrible tragedy. Public outrage resulted in several investigations and new laws requiring stiffer inspections, but a Chicago jury eventually found the ship's owners innocent of criminal neglect. Afterward, the Eastland, repaired and rechristened the U.S.S. Wilmette, served as a United States Navy training ship until scrapped in 1947.

FOR
VALUED SERVICES RENDERED
TO THE CORONER
EASTLAND DISASTER
1915

Four years after the event, Chicagoan August Holdorf received this badge from coroner Peter M. Hoffman for rendering "valued services" during the *Eastland* disaster.

The Great Migration of African Americans from the South to northern cities transformed the nation, creating social tensions that precipiated the Chicago Race Riot of 1919.

1919 RACE RIOT

Similar to the Haymarket Affair, the 1919 Race Riot illustrates how conflicting forces converging at the crossroads create tensions that explode into crisis. Its roots lay in the complex swirl of events and social upheaval associated with World War I. At the time, a booming economy and tight labor market caused by the draft created new opportunities for African Americans living in the South, where Jim Crow practices severely restricted their freedom. Drawn by employment opportunities and hoping for a better life, scores of blacks journeyed to northern cities such as Chicago in a mass movement known as the Great Migration.

One of the turning points in American history, the Great Migration had a profound impact on the North. In Chicago alone, more than fifty thousand African Americans arrived between 1916 and 1920, more than doubling the size of the city's black population. They came to work in various industries, primarily meatpacking and steel plants. For the most part, they settled on the South Side below Twelfth Street in an area known as the Black Belt, where a small community of African Americans had been living amidst a larger white community since the 1890s. Not surprisingly, the large and rapid influx of blacks created racial and social tensions in a city long dominated by whites, most of whom had never lived near blacks before. Similar tensions had erupted in Illinois race riots in Springfield (1908) and East St. Louis (1917), creating racial tension throughout the state. In addition, when the war ended in November 1918, thousands of white soldiers returned, expecting to find jobs; instead, they found blacks had taken their place, a situation that greatly exacerbated tensions that soon exploded into violence and mayhem.[30]

On July 27, 1919, Eugene Williams and four other black teenagers from the South Side decided to go swimming. Like other blacks excluded from "white" beaches

in the city, they patronized the Twenty-fifth Street Beach. Inexperienced swimmers, they used a large, homemade fourteen-foot log raft as a safety platform for swimming and diving, propelling it forward by kicking their legs. That day, they aimed for a post near the Twenty-ninth Street Beach, an area controlled by whites where a nasty fight between blacks and whites had just erupted. As Williams and his friends floated by a breakwater at Twenty-sixth Street, they noticed a white man throwing rocks at them. A projectile struck Williams in the forehead, knocking him back into the water. His panic-stricken friends tried to help, but to no avail. One of them, John Harris, swam to shore and notified a lifeguard at the Twenty-fifth Street Beach who called for a rescue boat, but by the time it arrived, Williams had drowned.[31]

A black policeman went with Williams's friends to the Twenty-ninth Street Beach, where they identified the rock-thrower standing in the crowd. The white officer on duty, Daniel Callahan, refused to arrest the man, or to allow the black policeman to arrest him. At that point, Harris and his friends ran back to the Twenty-fifth Street Beach, where they told the crowd what was happening a few blocks away. A crowd of African Americans ran to the scene, and soon, hundreds of blacks and whites gathered at the beach. After Officer Callahan arrested a black man, the crowd began to throw rocks and bricks at each other. A black man, James Crawford, fired a gun at several white policemen, injuring one of them. In return, a black policeman fired at Crawford, fatally injuring him. Many others in the crowd were also armed and they began shooting, starting a full-blown race riot that lasted the better part of five days.[32] That first evening, Sunday, July 27, white gangs, known euphemistically

The Chicago Race Riot began at the Twenty-ninth Street Beach on July 27, 1919, after the drowning death of Eugene Williams, a black teenager who had crossed an imaginary boundary in the water separating blacks from whites. Photographer Jun Fujita documented the events as they unfolded in a series of dramatic photographs.

For the better part of five days, rioting raged across the South Side and spread to other parts of the city. In all, the disturbance claimed 38 lives, injured 537 people, and damaged millions of dollars worth of property.

From the beach, rioting quickly spread across the South Side. Photographer Fujita followed a mob carrying bricks and stones as they chased a black man through the streets and alleyways.

as athletic clubs, including Ragen's Colts, Hamburgers, and Dirty Dozen, led the charge. Armed with bricks, stones, baseball bats, iron bars, and hammers, they crossed Wentworth Avenue and entered the black community. African Americans responded with sniper fire and knife attacks, but few ventured into white neighborhoods that evening. To regain control of the situation, Mayor William Hale "Big Bill" Thompson ordered nearly three thousand police, or 80 percent of the city's entire force, to surround the Black Belt, which left other parts of the city thinly protected; Thompson

also imposed a curfew and barred the sale of all alcoholic beverages. Preferring to handle the situation—and the city—himself, Thompson rejected suggestions from other city officials to ask Illinois Governor Frank O. Lowden to send in the state militia, which many thought would have immediately squelched the disturbance.[33]

By late evening, Thompson's measures were working, but violence erupted again Monday afternoon as blacks and whites continued to clash. At a special meeting of the City Council, all but five of the twenty-five aldermen present strongly urged Thompson to call for the state militia. Only once before in the city's history had the militia been summoned—after the Great Fire—and Thompson did not want to relinquish control to outside authorities. Under enormous pressure, however, he finally agreed and 3,500 troops arrived. They remained stationed in city armories, however, awaiting orders as rioting raged across the South Side. In all, 17 people died that night, while 172 blacks and 71 whites sustained injuries.[34]

On Tuesday, a citywide transit strike inadvertently helped calm matters down by reducing the number of workers going to the stockyards, but violence soon spread to the Loop as angry mobs roamed the streets. Rioting erupted on the city's West and North Sides and continued all Wednesday, with numerous attacks and more than thirty fires that threatened to engulf the South Side. Finally, at 1:00 P.M., Mayor Thompson—bowing to pressure from across the spectrum, including stockyard

Fujita recorded whites stoning a black man, who died of his injuries. Thirty-eight people died in the rioting (23 blacks, 15 whites) and more than five hundred were injured.

During the riot, roving bands of white youth entered black neighborhoods to intimidate residents and create mayhem. Fujita captured one such group raiding a home and throwing its contents onto the street.

After three days of rioting, Chicago Mayor William "Big Bill" Thompson finally called for the Illinois National Guard to restore order to the riot-torn city.

employers, black leaders, and white aldermen—called out the state militia to restore order. Moving into the South Side, the well-trained and disciplined soldiers quickly regained control of the streets.[35]

Tensions, however, remained high. The next day, white stockyard workers attacked returning black laborers, inflicting one fatality and setting off another pitched battle. On Saturday morning, the immigrant Polish-Lithuanian neighborhood behind the stockyards burned down, damaging nearly $250,000 in property and leaving more than nine hundred people homeless. As each side blamed the other, Mayor Thompson accused members of the International Workers of the World of setting the fire, posing as blacks to stir up more trouble. In the end, however, a grand jury charged white athletic clubs with starting the fires to arouse more hatred toward blacks. For the next several days, the stockyards remained tense, but on Thursday, August 7, twelve thousand blacks reported for work under the armed

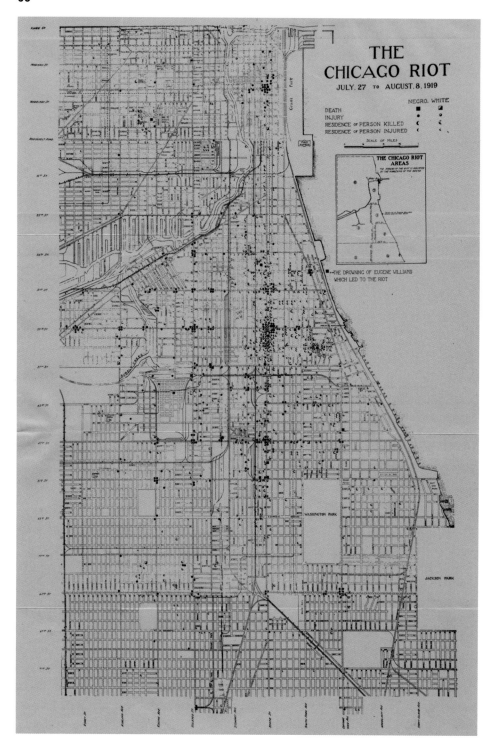

A map of the riot documents that most fighting took place in the Black Belt, east of the dividing line between whites and blacks on the South Side. Note the cluster of deaths and injuries at Thirty-fifth and State streets, the heart of the black community.

In the riot's aftermath, a wall of racial fear, mistrust, and hatred went up across the city, forming distinct residential zones where blacks and whites led separate lives.

Following the 1919 Race Riot, Olivet Baptist Church helped to anchor the black community by offering educational and social programs in addition to regular Sunday services. At one time, the church had more than ten thousand members.

and watchful guard of fifteen hundred policemen, a militia regiment, and hundreds of special deputies and detectives. As they entered the yards, ten thousand white union workers walked out, and later that day union officials called members to strike for a closed shop, which would exclude blacks who were barred from union membership. Ultimately neither happened, but tensions between union whites and nonunion blacks would plague the stockyards for years to come.[36]

Finally on August 8, twelve days after the rioting began, the state militia left the city. Their departure signaled the official end of the riot, which claimed 38 lives (23 blacks, 15 whites), injured 537 people (342 blacks, 195 whites), and damaged millions of dollars worth of property. Moreover, the riot deepened Chicago's racial divide, heightening suspicion, anger, and hatred between whites and blacks, feelings that had been bubbling beneath the surface for years. In racially changing neighborhoods, such as Hyde Park and Kenwood, where white property owners had organized formal associations to keep blacks out, the number of bombs thrown into black homes and businesses increased dramatically. This style of racial intimidation would continue for decades. In addition, beginning in the mid-1920s, whites on the South Side and throughout Chicago began using restrictive covenants that forbade the sale of property to blacks, Jews, and other minorities. Many other whites simply decided to leave, moving further south or west into South Shore, Beverly, and other newly developed areas where blacks did not live. Although this pattern of "white flight" emerged before 1919, the race riot greatly accelerated its pace and by 1925, the area between Twenty-sixth and Fifty-first streets had become 90 percent black.[37]

Surrounded by a sea of white neighborhoods, the Black Belt became a more self-sufficient community after the riot. Despite the harmful effects of segregation, the community flourished during the 1920s with hundreds of African American–owned and operated businesses, churches, political and social organizations, sports teams, and cultural institutions. The area became a national model of African American achievement, second only to Harlem. Yet, blacks did not enjoy equal access to jobs and housing and remained second-class citizens to whites. In its report to Governor Lowden on the riot, entitled *The Negro in Chicago*, the Chicago Commission on Race Relations identified issues of social and economic inequality as critical factors fueling the riot. If not addressed, the commission warned, there could be another riot.[38] Unfortunately, Mayor Thompson and his successors did little to help the black community or address Chicago's racial divisions.

Ultimately, the 1919 Race Riot proved to be a major turning point in Chicago history. It not only exposed the city's racial problems, but exacerbated them. In the riot's aftermath, a wall of racial fear, mistrust, and hatred went up across the city, forming distinct residential zones where blacks and whites led separate lives. Eventually, that wall made Chicago one of the most racially segregated urban crossroads in America, a city ripe for another round of racial disturbance in 1968.

GANGLAND CHICAGO

Closely following the 1919 Race Riot, Chicago's Gangland Era made urban crime an American tradition. The sordid history of Gangland Chicago begins in 1919 with the ratification of the Eighteenth Amendment, which forbade the export, import, manufacture, sale, or transportation of alcoholic beverages in the United States and its territories. The accompanying Volstead Act, passed by Congress the same year over President Woodrow Wilson's veto, provided for the enforcement of prohibition, specifically for the means to investigate and punish violators of the amendment. Originally advanced in the early 1800s as a movement for temperance, prohibition remained a hotly debated issue in American politics for decades, but by 1855, thirteen states had abolished liquor. Although support for prohibition waned during the Civil War, several reform groups led by the Woman's Christian Temperance Union (WCTU) revived the effort afterward. Founded in 1874, the WCTU campaigned for prohibition under the direction of its president, Frances E. Willard of Evanston, a northern suburb of Chicago. Like other temperance supporters, Willard believed that liquor caused most ills in American society and rallied public support to abolish its consumption. After Willard's death in 1898, the WCTU continued to campaign for a constitutional amendment to abolish liquor nationwide. During World War I, prohibitionists argued that making alcohol from

After moving from New York City to Chicago, Johnny Torrio established a bootlegger's empire eventually controlled by Al Capone.

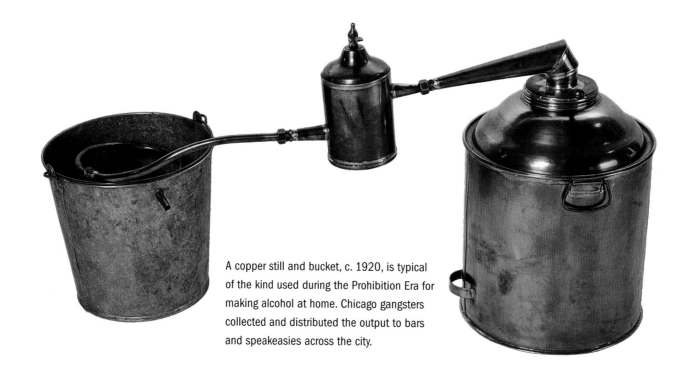

A copper still and bucket, c. 1920, is typical of the kind used during the Prohibition Era for making alcohol at home. Chicago gangsters collected and distributed the output to bars and speakeasies across the city.

Summoned from New York City by Johnny Torrio to help him run the show in Chicago, Al Capone waged an all-out war against rival gangsters to gain control of the city's illegal liquor traffic. Capone's brutal style made him the most notorious gangster in America.

grain deprived the armed forces of food and convinced the American public and Congress to pass laws that limited or prohibited the manufacture and sale of alcoholic beverages during the war. In 1917, Congress approved the Eighteenth Amendment abolishing liquor, and by 1919, three-fourths of the states had ratified the measure.[39]

Prohibition proved to be an instant failure. Scores of otherwise law-abiding citizens broke the law by making alcohol at home or by visiting thousands of private clubs known as speakeasies that sprang up across the country when legal bars closed. Prohibition also ushered in a new era of organized crime as criminal elements stepped into the picture and took control of a new and potentially lucrative business. In Chicago, they built upon a well-established underworld controlled by Big Jim Colosimo, otherwise known as "Diamond Jim," an Italian immigrant who arrived in Chicago as a youth and worked selling newspapers and shining shoes before turning to a more profitable life of crime. After Colosimo operated as a pickpocket and pimp, he married a brothel madam who helped him develop an extensive network of bordellos, gambling houses, and nightclubs in the Levee, Chicago's notorious vice district located on the South Side between Eighteenth and Twenty-second streets and Wabash and Clark streets.[40]

Established shortly after the Great Fire of 1871, the Levee teemed with hundreds of establishments, including the notorious Everleigh Club at 2131–33 South Dearborn Street, a luxurious bordello operated by two sisters, Ada and Minna Everleigh, who made a fortune. They, like Colosimo and other proprietors of the Levee, learned to appease city politicians, in particular First Ward Aldermen Mike "Hinky Dink" Kenna and "Bath House" John Coughlin, with votes and pay-offs that allowed vice to flourish despite public outcries for reform.

With the passage of Prohibition, Colosimo's right-hand man, Johnny Torrio, originally from New York City, saw a golden opportunity to expand into boot-legging, the illegal transportation and distribution of wine, beer, and distilled spirits. By now a rich man, Colosimo lacked the drive to take on the challenge, but Torrio would not be stopped, and it is widely believed that he paid Frankie Yale, a New York mobster, ten thousand dollars to take out Big Jim on May 11, 1920.[41]

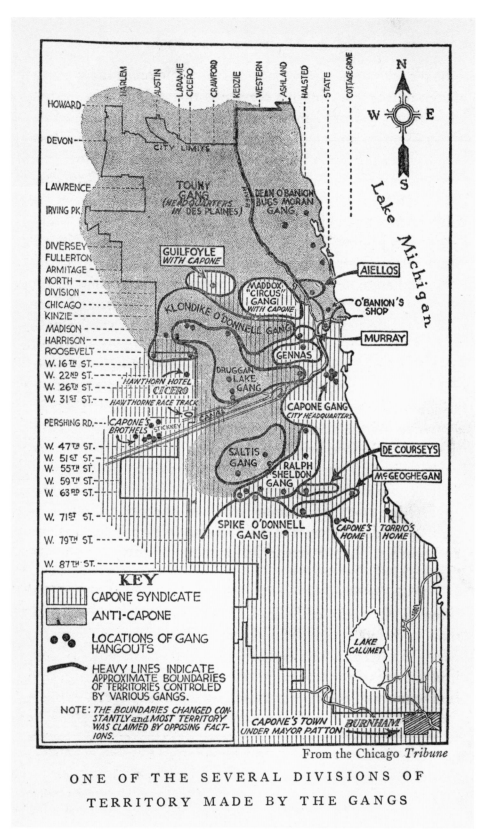

ONE OF THE SEVERAL DIVISIONS OF
TERRITORY MADE BY THE GANGS

From the Chicago *Tribune*

Charles Dion O'Banion, one of many gangsters to die in Chicago's Beer War, was shot in his North Side flower shop, probably at the direction of Al Capone.

George "Bugs" Moran, Capone's chief rival, controlled the North Side with O'Banion.

A map from c. 1925 charts Al Capone's control of the South Side and Roger Touhy's of the Northwest Side. In between lay a contested and bloody ground where rival gangs vied for territory and dominance during Chicago's Beer War.

The sordid history of Gangland Chicago begins in 1919 with the ratification of the Eighteenth Amendment, which forbade the export, import, manufacture, sale, or transportation of alcoholic beverages.

Early "Hymie" Weiss, O'Banion's successor, died on the steps of Holy Name Cathedral in one of Chicago's most shocking gangland slayings.

With Colosimo gone, Torrio moved to take over the liquor trade, consolidating several rival gangs into one efficient operation that ran more like a modern corporation than a crime outfit. While Torrio maintained overall control, a small group of select henchmen directed hundreds of gangsters to run daily operations. In December 1919, a young gangster from New York named Al Capone arrived to help Torrio run the show. Born in 1899, Capone grew up in an Italian neighborhood in Brooklyn; at age eleven, he joined a kids' gang, headed by the young Johnny Torrio. Reunited in Chicago, Torrio and Capone, who used the alias name of Al Brown, built a bootlegger's empire as the booze and money flowed — not only into their pockets but also into those of police, judges, and elected officials, most notably Mayor William Hale "Big Bill" Thompson, who oversaw one of the most corrupt political regimes in American history.

To keep the peace and maximize profits, Torrio persuaded rival gang leaders to divide the city and suburbs into territories that each would control while rival gangs stayed out. The plan gave Torrio–Capone a vast area on the city's South and Southwest Sides, including Calumet City, Burnham, and Cicero, along with a portion of the Near North Side and a small pocket between Division Street and North Avenue. Meanwhile, Charles Dion "Deany" O'Banion and George "Bugs" Moran controlled the North Side, while Roger "The Terrible" Touhy, son of a Chicago policeman, controlled a large territory on the Northwest Side with headquarters in Des Plaines. Smaller gangs, including the Genna brothers, Klondike–O'Donnell, Druggan, and Saltis, controlled smaller zones between the larger gang territories.[42]

As long as Mayor Thompson remained in office, the "peace plan" worked, but in 1923, Chicagoans elected William E. Dever, a reform candidate who promised to clean up City Hall and go after the gangsters. Dever's victory upset the delicate balance of power in Chicago's underworld and forced Torrio–Capone to the southwest suburb of Cicero, where they established a new headquarters after taking control of local politicians. The Torrio–Capone organization, however, faced a new challenge the following year when Deany O'Banion began feuding with the "Terrible Gennas" of the West Side over liquor distribution. Although Torrio and Capone stepped in to settle the dispute, O'Banion continued to challenge the Gennas over a gambling debt, in effect challenging the authority of Torrio–Capone. Furthermore, O'Banion set up Torrio in a police raid that took place May 19, 1924, at the Sieben Brewery, a large plant jointly owned by O'Banion, Torrio, and Capone. Fed up with O'Banion and facing a stiff penalty for bootlegging, Torrio made O'Banion pay for his actions. On November 10, three gunmen, probably hired by Capone, entered O'Banion's flower shop at 738 North State Street, opposite Holy Name Cathedral, and shot him in cold blood.[43]

O'Banion's murder launched an all-out war between rival gangs that became known as the Beer War. Despite Mayor Dever's best efforts, the violence continued

Chicago's Beer War reached a gruesome climax on February 14, 1929, when seven members of the Bugs Moran gang were shot to death in a North Side garage. Known as the St. Valentine's Day Massacre, the incident remains the bloodiest gangland slaying in American history.

In response to the St. Valentine's Day Massacre, the federal agent appointed Eliot Ness to clean up Chicago. Ness and his gang of "Untouchables" raided Capone's operations across the city, dismantling stills and arresting many bootleggers.

to escalate with sixteen gangland killings in 1924, forty-six in 1925, and seventy-six in 1926, an all-time high. Scores more were injured, including Torrio, who survived a vicious attack when emissaries of Hymie Weiss, O'Banion's successor, shot him in front of his Hyde Park home in January 1925. After spending sixteen days in Jackson Park Hospital and nine months in jail for the Sieben affair, Torrio relinquished his empire to Capone and left Chicago for Italy, where he lived for several years before returning to a life of organized crime in New York City.[44]

After Torrio's departure, Chicago's gang war continued unabated. On September 20, 1926, Hymie Weiss led an entourage of eleven cars to Cicero, Capone territory. They pulled up in front of the Hawthorne Restaurant, one of many Cicero establishments controlled by Capone and where he had just finished eating lunch with Frank Rio, his bodyguard. Armed with powerful machine guns, Weiss's men took aim and fired nearly one thousand bullets through the plate-glass window, smashing up the interior, but somehow missing all the patrons, including Capone, who lay flat against the floor. Three weeks later, on October 11, 1926, Weiss died in a hail of bullets across the street from Holy Name Cathedral, near the O'Banion flower shop headquarters. Although police connected Capone to the shooting, he denied complicity and remained a free man. But even Capone realized that matters had gotten out-of-hand. To regain control, he staged a conference at the Hotel Sherman in downtown Chicago to pressure rival gangs to stop fighting. While the conference solidified Capone's position as the city's most powerful gangster, he could not maintain control for long, and fighting soon erupted again.[45]

City Hall did little to stop the violence. In 1927, Big Bill Thompson, aided by a $500,000 campaign contribution from Capone, regained the mayoral seat, and once again he allowed gangsters to run amok. Capone's influence extended to the rank and file as well. He used neighborhood athletic clubs, such as Ragen's Colts,

With the help of newspapers, Hollywood movies, and popular television shows, the name "Chicago" became synonymous with "gangsters."

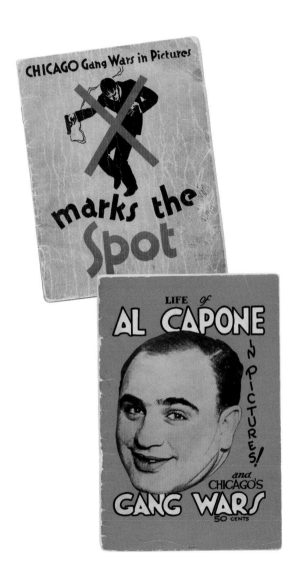

Pulp magazines filled with graphic images of gangland violence turned Chicago hoodlums into well-known celebrities and gave the city an international reputation for crime. The notorious Al Capone became one of the most famous figures in American history.

which had more than one thousand members, to run liquor and kill on demand. He also employed thousands of ordinary Chicagoans to make liquor at home, and for those struggling to make ends meet, Capone's regular payments helped them survive. Many came to regard Capone as a Robin Hood figure, someone who not only thumbed his nose at authority, but also shared the "take" with those in need. Furthermore, Capone made good newspaper copy, attracting readers who thrilled to his exploits and glamorous lifestyle. Ultimately, Capone became a national celebrity—an urban pirate who broke the law but made a fortune.[46]

Chicago's Beer War reached a bloody climax on February 14, 1929. That morning, a black touring car pulled up in front of a small brick garage at 2122 North Clark Street. According to eyewitness accounts, several policemen left the car and entered the building through the front door. Within minutes, neighbors heard a loud clattering noise followed by two muffled blasts; then they saw two men with hands in the air and three "policemen" exit the building, board the car, and drive away with the gong sounding. But what appeared to be a routine police raid turned out to be mass-murder, for inside the garage, seven men lay dead or dying, their bodies riddled with at least one hundred machine-gun bullets. The men belonged to the Bugs Moran gang, which used the Clark Street garage as a central liquor cache, and their murderers undoubtedly worked for Capone, although Big Al never faced any formal charges for ordering the worst gangland slaying in American history.[47]

With the St. Valentine's Day Massacre, Chicago gangsters, as described by the *Herald Examiner*, graduated "from murder to massacre." The shocking news finally stirred federal authorities to take action. The U.S. Justice Department created a special unit to go after Capone and chose as its head Eliot Ness, who developed a plan to destroy Capone. Taking a page from the gangsters' unwritten manual, Ness selected nine young men to work closely with him. Together, they became known as the "Untouchables" for refusing to accept customary bribes from gangsters, just as gangsters refused to talk to police or identify rivals who had attacked them. Over the next several months, Ness and his men carried out a series of raids against Capone's operations that destroyed more than two dozen breweries and distilleries, making headline news and reassuring the public that, at last, someone had taken charge.[48]

In addition, the Chicago Crime Commission (CCC), an independent agency established in 1919 to root out crime, launched its famous "Public Enemy" campaign on April 23, 1930. For the first time, it provided the American public with the names and photographic images of twenty-eight gangsters, including "Alphonse Capone, most notorious of gangsters" and George "Bugs" Moran, who "has made his peace with the Capone gang since . . . the St. Valentine's Day massacre." Aimed at driving twenty-eight criminals out of Chicago, the campaign struck a chord with the American public, many of whom were struggling in the early years of the Great Depression and no longer in the mood for sensational stories that glorified gangsters.[49]

Law enforcement finally cornered Capone on June 5, 1931, when the Internal Revenue Service indicted him for income tax evasion. Although Capone kept no written records of his transactions, federal agents had discovered account books from the Hawthorne Smoke Shop—actually a gambling front—that showed Capone had received more than one million dollars as his share of the profits, meaning he had failed to pay approximately $215,000 in taxes—small change for Capone, but enough to convict and sentence him to eleven years in jail.[50]

Capone's demise signaled the end of an era that formally closed two years later with the repeal of Prohibition, but a peculiar legacy developed in its wake. With the help of newspapers, Hollywood movies, and popular television shows, the name "Chicago" became synonymous with "gangsters." The city's violent reputation, however, had a romanticized quality. Although gangsters were dangerous criminals, they were also succeeding financially in ways that most Americans could only dream about. Today, nearly eighty years later, the appeal of Gangland Chicago continues. Although movies such as *The Road to Perdition* strip away some of the mythology with unmitigated violence, "Chicago Gangster" bus tours are more popular than ever. It is hard to imagine any future account of the city that will not include some kind of tribute, no matter how small, to Gangland Chicago and its denizens.

1968

Chicago's reputation for violence dramatically increased in 1968 when the West Side and Democratic National Convention both exploded in bloody chaos. These events revealed deep divisions in American society along the lines of race, class, and political ideology—divisions that converged at the crossroads of America and threatened to tear the nation apart. While the uproar at the Democratic National Convention has consistently received more attention from the media, historians, and the general public, the West Side riot had a far greater impact on the city.

Its root cause lay in the miserable conditions of the West Side itself, a sprawling ghetto where approximately 250,000 African Americans resided. During the early 1960s, the area became a focal point of the Civil Rights Movement led by Dr. Martin Luther King Jr. and the Southern Christian Leadership Council (SCLC). After years of protesting conditions in the South, King and his followers had achieved major victories with the passage of the Civil Rights Act in 1964 and Voting Rights Act of 1965. Flush with victory, King turned his attention to the North, selecting Chicago primarily because its slums were "the prototype of those chiefly responsible for the Northern urban race problem."

Before bringing the Civil Rights Movement to Chicago in 1966, Dr. Martin Luther King Jr. made several visits to the city. On June 21, 1964 he addressed a major rally in Soldier Field.

By 1960, Chicago's West Side had become one of the poorest urban neighborhoods in America. High levels of unemployment, residential overcrowding, and escalating crime rates plagued the area, creating conditions ripe for social unrest.

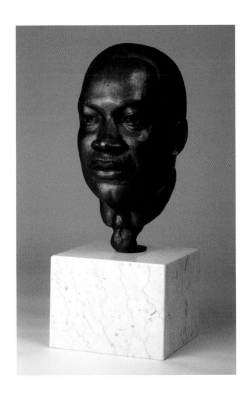

Bronze bust of Dr. Martin Luther King Jr. by Sara S. Miller, 1994.

King's Chicago campaign focused on eradicating slums and ending discriminatory housing practices.

Indeed, in 1959, the United States Commission on Civil Rights had labeled Chicago "the most residentially segregated large city in the nation," the result of de facto segregation practices that restricted black movement into white neighborhoods and the tendency of whites to move away from neighborhoods undergoing racial change. Furthermore, Chicago had a well-established local civil rights movement led by the Coordinating Council of Community Organizations (CCCO), a coalition of community-based organizations headed by Al Raby. Finally, King thought he had an ally in the city's mayor, Richard J. Daley, a life-long Democrat who publicly supported the goals of the Civil Rights Movement, but privately feared the effects on Chicago, which he ruled with an iron hand.[51]

King turned his attention to the North, selecting Chicago primarily because its slums were "the prototype of those chiefly responsible for the Northern urban race problem."

Armed with a message of hope and peaceful change, King arrived on Chicago's West Side in February 1966. At the time, 25 percent of the area's adult men were unemployed, the result of a steady decline in jobs across the city, as well as long-standing racial prejudice and exclusionary practices against blacks. The situation eroded the social and physical fabric of the neighborhood, creating one of the worst slums in America and a new kind of challenge for King. Whereas in the South they had focused on voting rights, King and the SCLC now struggled to find a focus for their campaign. They eventually settled on two main objectives: the eradication of slums and open housing.[52]

On both accounts, they faced enormous challenges exacerbated by Mayor Daley and his powerful political machine that kept most black politicians and ministers in line by doling out political appointments and patronage jobs to their constituencies. With such a big stake in the status quo, Chicago's black establishment not only failed to support King's efforts, but some members, such as Congressman William H. Dawson and the Rev. Joseph H. Jackson of Olivet Baptist Church, actually spoke out against King at Daley's urging. Despite such obstacles, King launched a campaign that included calls for civil disobedience, numerous demonstrations and prayer vigils, and a rally on July 10 at Soldier Field followed by a peaceful march of five thousand people to City Hall. There King, imitating his namesake, taped a full list of demands including open housing, better schools, and various political reforms on the door. In response, Daley met with King, Raby, and their aides the following day, but the meeting ended without any agreement.[53]

Although their campaign began to raise local and national awareness of racial discrimination in Chicago, King and his circle became increasingly frustrated and discouraged by the lack of an outright victory. Moreover, they experienced firsthand the heat of ghetto anger just two days after the Soldier Field rally where King had reiterated his familiar call for nonviolence. The clash, set off by a minor altercation between police and West Side residents over the use of a fire hydrant to cool off, quickly escalated into a full-blown riot that involved thousands of people over a span of four days. To restore order, Daley called in the National Guard but blamed King's staff for instigating the violence, despite the fact that King and Young had met with angry residents to soothe tensions. The riot left two people dead, over eighty injured, more than four hundred arrested, and upward of two million dollars in property damage.[54]

Afterward, King and other civil rights leaders met with Daley and convinced him to attach sprinklers to fire hydrants, open more swimming pools, and establish a civilian committee to review police-community relations. Although King could claim a small victory, he and others began to express doubt about the movement's effectiveness in Chicago, a city beset by many complex problems, including inner-city gangs whose youthful members had little use for King's efforts. Despite these

The assassination of Dr. Martin Luther King Jr. sparked nationwide rioting. In Chicago, the *West Side Torch,* a community newspaper, documented local events within a national context. The photograph of King's funeral procession is at the top of the page.

frustrations, King and his followers adopted a more aggressive approach later that summer by staging a series of open-housing marches through white, working-class neighborhoods on the city's Southwest and Northwest Sides. Between mid-July and early August, several hundred protestors marched on several different occasions through Gage Park, Chicago Lawn, Marquette Park, and Belmont-Cragin. Angry whites, prodded by members of the Ku Klux Klan and American Nazi Party who had flocked to Chicago in response to King's campaign, hurled racial insults and projectiles at King, including a rock that felled him to the ground. Although the marches stirred up racial hatred in Chicago, King pressed on, announcing plans to march on Cicero, a bastion of white ethnic pride and racial exclusion on the city's Southwest Side, where King claimed blacks would not only march but also "work and live."[55]

The march, which many feared would instigate a full-blown riot, never materialized. Instead, King announced its suspension after an intense three-day summit meeting with the Chicago Real Estate Board produced a set of suggestions and goals that would foster open housing in the city. The summit, however, did not produce an actual open-housing agreement and left many black Chicagoans deeply disillusioned. Indeed, some local civil rights workers criticized King afterward for settling for so little, while others questioned the emphasis on open housing, a middle-class issue that did little to assist impoverished, inner-city blacks. Claiming victory but describing the accord "a beginning" rather than an end, King departed for Atlanta, as did many members of his staff. Although some members of the SCLC remained behind, the Chicago campaign essentially had come to an end. King made this clear the following May when he announced that he saw "no need for further demonstrations" in Chicago after a newly established city agency announced a massive fair-housing educational campaign to address the issue of open housing in the city and suburbs.[56]

Although King had faltered in the North, he remained an important national figure and his assassination on April 4, 1968, sent the country into shock. That evening, President Lyndon B. Johnson addressed the nation on television; he praised King and pleaded for calm, as did Mayor Daley. Despite their efforts, the next day rioting erupted in hundreds of cities and towns across the country, including Chicago, as blacks expressed both sorrow and rage over their loss. Although city officials on Thursday night had canceled all days off for city police and alerted the National Guard, nothing prepared them for what happened in the wake of King's death. By 9:00 A.M. Friday morning, scores of black youth had walked out of school and taken to the streets. While some staged impromptu memorial services for King, others began smashing windows and looting businesses along Sixty-third Street on the South Side, Madison Street on the West Side, and Division Street on the North Side. Rioters threw stones at passing white motorists, forcing police to close Division and several West Side streets to all traffic, including city bus service.[57]

Responding with sorrow and anger over King's death, rioters burned more than twenty blocks on Chicago's West Side. The disturbance left deep scars on the city that have yet to heal.

As the rioting verged out of control, roving bands of looters trashed dozens of small businesses on the West Side, leaving the area decimated.

Outnumbered and overwhelmed, police did little to stop the rioting. According to eyewitness accounts, policemen kept their distance, sitting in squad cars as rioters took control of the streets. At 2:00 P.M., police superintendent James B. Conlisk telephoned Mayor Daley and recommended he call out the National Guard. Daley did not hesitate, and within minutes, Acting Governor Samuel Shapiro ordered 6,900 troops to Chicago. Meanwhile, the rioting escalated, particularly on the West Side. At 4:00 P.M., the first fire broke out at a looted furniture store at 2235 West Madison Street. Soon, dozens of other shops and buildings along Kedzie Avenue, Pulaski Road, and West Roosevelt Road succumbed, overwhelming firefighters who struggled to contain the maelstrom. Fires broke out on the North and South Sides as well, but nothing compared to the West Side where entire blocks burned to the ground. At 11:00 P.M., the National Guard finally arrived, but the young, inexperienced troops had difficulty restoring order until 3:00 A.M. when rioters finally retreated. Four hours later, rioting broke out again and police reported "serious sniping" at the Cabrini

In a scene reminiscent of the Great Fire, twenty-eight blocks of Madison Street lay in ruins. Property damage totaled nine million dollars.

Green high-rise public housing complex on the North Side. As the city reeled out of control, Conlisk cancelled all police furloughs and asked Daley to request U.S. troops to help restore order. The mayor agreed, and within hours, five thousand soldiers from bases in Texas and Colorado had arrived. Daley also imposed a 7:00 P.M. to 6:00 A.M. curfew on persons less than twenty-one years of age and banned the sale of firearms and ammunition in city and county stores. In certain hard-hit areas, he ordered police to close taverns and halt the sale of liquor and gas in cans.[58]

By Sunday morning, calm had descended, but the shocking damage totaled nine persons dead (all black), hundreds injured including ninety policemen, about two hundred families left homeless, and more than two thousand people arrested for looting and curfew violations. Fire had destroyed 162 buildings and damaged 22 others; 268 other apartments or stores were broken into and looted. In a scene reminiscent of the Great Fire, twenty-eight consecutive blocks of West Madison Street lay in ruins. Property damage totaled nine million dollars.[59]

Although Washington, D.C., and other cities experienced worse rioting than Chicago, Mayor Daley expressed disbelief that such an event could occur in his city, a comment that reflected his general attitude toward the plight of inner-city residents. Several days later on April 15, Daley tried to shift some of the blame for the riot to Chicago police who, he said, had shown too much restraint. As Daley explained, on the night of April 5, he had issued Police Superintendent Conlisk an order to "shoot to kill" arsonists or anyone with a Molotov cocktail and to "maim and detain" any looters. According to Daley, police had failed to follow these orders, which he reissued the morning of April 15. Daley's words created a firestorm of controversy, causing him to backpedal and retract the statement by accusing the media for misreporting what he had said. Although Daley alarmed many observers, including U.S. Attorney Ramsey Clark, who described his statement a "dangerous escalation," an overwhelming number of Chicagoans expressed support for Daley's firm stance against those who would disrupt the city.[60]

Indeed, the West Side riots, as the open-housing marches before them, contributed to a mounting backlash against the Civil Rights Movement that helped usher in a more politically conservative era during the 1970s. Moreover, the West Side riots left the community more impoverished than before as many businesses were destroyed in the mayhem and many residents who fled never returned. The West Side continued to decline for decades until the 1990s when some redevelopment began with the construction of the United Center and preparations for the 1996 Democratic National Convention. Today, nearly forty years later, parts of the West Side are experiencing a rebirth, but large sections of the area still bear scars left by the riot and its root cause: poverty.

1968 DEMOCRATIC NATIONAL CONVENTION

More immediately, the events of April 1968 had a direct impact on the Democratic National Convention staged in Chicago four months later. Although Chicago had hosted numerous political conventions (Democratic and Republican) in previous years, primarily because of its central location and position as the nation's rail hub, that year's convention would be dramatically different. Held during the height of the Vietnam War, the convention became a lightning rod for antiwar activists from all over the country. Indeed, they had been planning for months, as had Mayor Daley and the Chicago police.

Unlike today's conventions, those of an earlier era actually decided upon the nominee. As such, they became hotly contested battlegrounds where opposing candidates vied for delegates' votes. In 1968, the stakes could not have been any higher. On March 31, just a few days before the assassination of Martin Luther King Jr., incumbent President Lyndon B. Johnson, who faced a growing antiwar movement and low approval ratings, announced on national television that he would not seek reelection. His decision opened the door to other hopefuls, including Vice President Hubert Humphrey and senators Robert F. Kennedy of New York and Eugene McCarthy of Minnesota, both of whom had called for an end to the war. On June 5, an assassin's bullet felled Kennedy in San Francisco, dashing the hopes of many supporters across the country. Over the summer months, Humphrey and McCarthy continued to campaign with an eye toward the Chicago convention where they hoped to sway enough delegates to gain the nomination.[61]

Meanwhile, antiwar activists led by Rennie Davis and David Dellinger of the National Mobilization Committee to End the War (MOBE) and Abbie Hoffman and Jerry Rubin of the radical Youth International Party (or Yippies) made plans to disrupt the convention. While Davis called for a "massive confrontation" between antiwar demonstrators and delegates, Hoffman and Rubin taunted Daley and the establishment with threats, including the abduction or drugging of convention delegates. Anticipating thousands of demonstrators—and recalling the disruptive riots in April—Daley prepared for the worst-case scenario. Displaying a siege mentality, he had a seven-foot-high chain-link fence, topped by more than two thousand feet of barbed wire, built around the International Ampitheater, site of the convention, and ordered all manhole covers in the area sealed with tar. He put Chicago's nearly twelve thousand police officers on twelve-hour shifts, gave them specific battle plans, and equipped them with "Daley dozers," jeeps with barbed wire attached to the front to clear the streets of demonstrators. In addition, Daley brought in seventy five hundred army troops from Texas, Oklahoma, and Colorado and requested one thousand FBI and Secret Service agents. Secretly, the Chicago police's "Red Squad" had been

As Chicago Mayor Richard J. Daley welcomed delegates to the 1968 Democratic convention, others planned to disrupt the event by staging anti–Vietnam War protests.

By 1968, a growing number of Americans opposed the Vietnam War and expressed their views by wearing buttons that left no doubt of where they stood on the issue.

Daley addressed the delegates that evening, reassuring them that "as long as I am mayor of this city, there is going to be law and order."

In the weeks leading up to the 1968 Democratic National Convention, buttons worn by anti-Vietnam War protestors made their destination clear.

A broadside distributed by the Students for a Democratic Society (SDS) critiques Mayor Daley.

infiltrating peace groups for years to collect information, as had Daley's personal investigative body, the Chicago Department of Investigation. The black ghettoes were of particular concern to Daley, but he appeased residents with a $27-million public housing improvement program, new social centers, and a special touch football program for inner-city youth. Daley also introduced a resolution to City Council renaming a major thoroughfare on the South Side after Dr. Martin Luther King Jr.[62]

On the eve of the convention, several labor strikes (transit, electrical, taxi) added to the tension, but Daley maintained tight control over the city as antiwar protestors began to arrive on August 17, a week before the convention, to celebrate a hippie-like "Festival of Life" in Lincoln Park. Although police made a few arrests, including Rubin and Hoffman, the city remained calm until Sunday, August 25, when eight hundred antiwar demonstrators greeted convention delegates as they checked into the Conrad Hilton Hotel located at Michigan and Balbo avenues. Later that night, Chicago police attacked and beat several hundred protestors camping in Lincoln Park, clearing them out for violating an 11:00 P.M. curfew. Among those injured were several journalists whose reports helped turn public opinion against the police and Mayor Daley.[63]

On Monday, August 26, the convention began. Daley addressed the delegates that evening, reassuring them that "as long as I am mayor of this city, there is going to be law and order." A few miles away, however, police and protestors clashed in Grant Park, opposite the Hilton Hotel, and further north in Lincoln Park, where police once again beat protestors and journalists. The violence continued Tuesday night when police fought antiwar demonstrators in Lincoln Park as convention delegates argued late into the night about the war in Vietnam. As delegates debated about adding a peace plank to the party's platform, an angry Daley repeatedly drew a finger across his neck to signal the convention chairman that he should end the proceedings. Aired on national television, Daley's action belied the notion of an open convention. On Wednesday afternoon, the long-awaited peace rally organized by MOBE took place in Grant Park, the only place for which city officials had issued protestors a permit. Ten thousand people gathered peacefully, but there were several skirmishes between protestors, police, and National Guardsmen.

Later that night, shortly before 8:00 P.M., the worst fighting of the week erupted in front of the Hilton Hotel, where police and guardsmen attacked protestors with clubs, tear gas, mace, and their own fists. Known as the Battle of Michigan Avenue, the melee lasted about twenty minutes. Captured by television cameras and broadcast nationwide, the brutal scene stunned viewers at home and convention delegates who watched the same footage on television monitors installed around the convention hall. As the convention spun out of control, Daley reacted with red-faced anger at opponents who described Chicago police action as "state terror" and "Gestapo tactics." Later that night, convention delegates nominated Hubert Humphrey for president, but Daley missed the voting for he had walked out in anger.[64]

While convention delegates at the International Ampitheater fiercely debated their party's nomination, antiwar protestors and Chicago police waged a bloody battle several blocks north on Michigan Avenue (opposite).

The radical Youth International Party, or Yippies, billed their gathering in Chicago as a "Festival of Life" to counter the Democrats' "Convention of Death."

On Thursday, police and guardsmen continued to clash with demonstrators, arresting eighty people and turning back two marches heading toward the convention hall. In addition, they dispersed a crowd of three thousand demonstrators at Eighteenth Street and Michigan Avenue with tear gas. On Friday, police responded to reports of objects being thrown from windows by raiding the headquarters of Eugene McCarthy on the fifteenth floor of the Hilton Hotel and beating many staff members. By Friday afternoon, order returned, but in the coming weeks, nationally-renowned journalists such as Tom Wicker of the *New York Times* decried the mean streets of Chicago. Local newspapers, however, including the *Chicago Tribune*, supported Daley, along with the police and National Guard, for trying to protect the city, a sentiment widely shared by most Chicagoans who felt deeply threatened by the disturbance.[65]

Several months later, a national commission headed by Daniel Walker, president of the Chicago Crime Commission and future governor of Illinois, concluded that the disturbance at the Democratic National Convention had been a "police riot" and attributed their behavior to Mayor Daley's "shoot to kill" comments after the earlier unrest in April following King's assassination. On another level, the convention riots had an impact on national politics as a growing number of Americans, tired of the Vietnam War, and sickened by the violence in Chicago, brought more pressure to bear on the U.S. government to end the conflict. At the same time, a large portion of the electorate became more conservative, and in the November election, Richard Nixon, the Republican candidate, defeated Humphrey. On the local level, Daley won reelection in 1971, but the DNC debacle severely damaged his

Opposite: Chicago police officer's riot helmet worn by Max O. Ziegler while on duty during the 1968 Democratic National Convention. Most Chicagoans supported police action against demonstrators despite widespread condemnation across the country.

reputation outside the city, and Chicago would not host another presidential convention for thirty years.[66]

For many Chicagoans, the events of 1968 proved extremely disturbing. Unlike the Great Chicago Fire, these crises did not end well. Rather, like the Haymarket Affair and the 1919 Race Riot, they revealed and exacerbated deep fissures in American society, ones that proved difficult to heal, even with the passage of time. In this regard, Chicago has been a national crucible as well as a crossroads.

"This is Chicago, this is America."

Mayor Richard J. Daley, 1968

Chapter Three SWEET HOME CHICAGO

Known as the City of Neighborhoods, Chicago is a complex, contested cross-roads of the American dream. Indeed, the city is something of a paradox. Historically, Chicagoans have been sharply divided by issues of race, ethnicity, and class, but politically, they have been united under the banner of the Democratic Party for the better part of a century. While this may seem contradictory, there is an explanation deeply rooted in the same patterns of migration and immigration that shaped Chicago.

Paralleling national trends, Chicago has experienced several waves of migration and immigration. The first occurred during the 1830s, when Yankee settlers arrived. Primarily from New England and New York, they were part of a great wave of migration that populated the upper Midwest during the early nineteenth century. In Chicago, their numbers grew quickly, from a few hundred people in 1833 to nearly forty-five hundred by 1840. They established numerous businesses and assumed positions of civic and political leadership. Most lived in the central city near the main branch of the Chicago River, establishing homes, schools, and churches in a Yankee-like manner.[1]

During the 1840s and 1850s, immigrants from Ireland and Germany diversified—and divided—the growing city. The Irish, many of whom came to work on the Illinois & Michigan Canal, were predominately poor and Catholic. They settled outside the city's inner core, west of the Chicago River's South Branch near the canal and south of the city near the Illinois Central rail yards, another place of employment. Meanwhile, the German immigrants, who had more financial means than the Irish, but different customs and language, settled north of the river's Main Branch. In addition, a small community of

Chicago has been shaped by a succession of people from other regions of the United States and distant lands.

African Americans comprising free northern blacks and fugitive slaves moved to Chicago and lived south of the Loop.[2]

By 1870, Chicago had 300,000 residents. While the vast majority (nearly 99 percent) were white, almost half of them were immigrants and their numbers were growing. Millions of immigrants poured into the city during the late nineteenth and early twentieth centuries as the largest wave of immigration in American history reached Chicago. Between 1870 and 1920, more than twenty million immigrants streamed into the country from all parts of Europe. A large portion of them settled in cities like Chicago where they could find work. In a pattern repeated across America, the new immigrants settled according to ethnic background and economic means. While those who came to Chicago from western European countries tended to settle on the city's North Side, poorer immigrants from Eastern Europe congregated on the South and West Sides.[3]

Beginning around the time of World War I and continuing through the 1960s, Chicago experienced another great wave of settlement. Known as the Great Migration, this influx involved hundreds of thousands of southern blacks, seeking employment and more freedom. Restricted by racial prejudice, they settled in isolated enclaves on the city's South and West Sides. In a pattern typical of American cities, the inward migration of blacks prompted a "white flight" to suburban areas. By 1970, the vast majority of people living on the South and West Sides were African American, while the outer ring of neighborhoods and suburbs remained predominately white.[4]

Simultaneously, whites and other ethnic minorities from outlying areas continued to arrive in Chicago. This wave included many working- and middle-class whites from farming communities, small towns, and mid-size cities, as well as increasing numbers of Mexicans, who came to Chicago seeking better economic opportunities. After World War II, Native Americans from regional reservations and Japanese Americans interred during the war were relocated to the city. Additionally, poor whites from Appalachia settled in the Uptown area, making it one of the city's most impoverished communities.[5]

Finally, beginning in the late 1960s and continuing into the twenty-first century, Chicago experienced its latest wave of immigration from multiple countries, including Southeast Asia, Africa, India, Eastern Europe, and the Philippines, along with a massive influx of people from Mexico. While many of the new immigrants settled on Chicago's North Side and surrounding suburbs, Mexicans congregated on the city's West Side. Overall, the most recent wave of newcomers has made Chicago one of the most diverse cities in the world.[6]

During each successive wave, the powerful forces of race, ethnicity, and class determined Chicago's settlement patterns. Brief sketches of several Chicago neighborhoods will illustrate how this worked. Each area—Douglas/Grand Boulevard, the Near West Side, Pilsen, Lincoln Park, and Rogers Park and West Ridge—is a microcosm of Chicago history, a local crossroads that illustrates national and international issues.

Lithuanian American children, c. 1910.

Lithuanians were part of the great flood of European immigrants who made Chicago a multiethnic crossroads during the late nineteenth and early twentieth centuries. As shown by the map (opposite), Lithuanians settled on the city's Southwest Side, near the Union Stock Yard and meatpacking plants where many of them worked.

Asian Indians celebrating Indian Independence Day on Devon Avenue in 1999 represent the latest wave of immigration to affect Chicago. Most Asian Indians have settled on Chicago's North Side and in several suburban areas.

A community settlement map for 1900 reveals Chicago as a multiethnic and biracial crossroads.

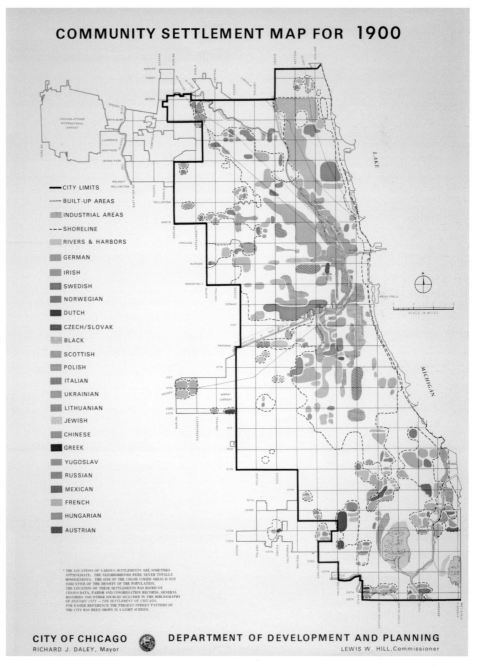

COMMUNITY SETTLEMENT MAP FOR 1900

- CITY LIMITS
- BUILT-UP AREAS
- INDUSTRIAL AREAS
- SHORELINE
- RIVERS & HARBORS
- GERMAN
- IRISH
- SWEDISH
- NORWEGIAN
- DUTCH
- CZECH/SLOVAK
- BLACK
- SCOTTISH
- POLISH
- ITALIAN
- UKRAINIAN
- LITHUANIAN
- JEWISH
- CHINESE
- GREEK
- YUGOSLAV
- RUSSIAN
- MEXICAN
- FRENCH
- HUNGARIAN
- AUSTRIAN

CITY OF CHICAGO
RICHARD J. DALEY, Mayor

DEPARTMENT OF DEVELOPMENT AND PLANNING
LEWIS W. HILL, Commissioner

The Morris Family moved to Chicago during the Great Migration of African Americans from the South to northern cities around the time of World War I. They lived on the South Side of Chicago where African Americans had been living since the late nineteenth century (see map).

Left: The Mandel Family, c. 1900, resided at 3400 South Michigan Avenue. They belonged to a small community of German Jews who moved from the city's central core to the Douglas area after the Great Chicago Fire.

Right: One of Chicago's leading citizens, Harlow N. Higinbotham, lived with his family at 2838 South Michigan Avenue. Higinbotham, a partner in Marshall Field & Company, served as president of the 1893 World's Columbian Exposition and supported many charitable organizations in the city.

DOUGLAS/GRAND BOULEVARD

Douglas is one of Chicago's oldest residential areas. It is bounded by Twenty-sixth Street on the north; Thirty-fifth Street, Vincennes Avenue and Thirty-ninth Street on the south; Lake Michigan on the east; and a set of railroad tracks adjacent to the Dan Ryan Expressway on the west. The area is named after Stephen A. Douglas, Illinois's powerful Democratic Senator during the 1850s. Douglas, who lived in Chicago before the Civil War, purchased a large portion of the area (seventy acres) as a residential development for wealthy Chicagoans. He established Groveland Park and Woodland Park as residential enclaves, but died before the area was fully developed. Spared by the Great Fire of 1871, the area came into its own afterward. Blessed with a convenient location and excellent transportation provided by the Illinois Central Railroad and horse-drawn omnibuses, the area attracted a large number of Chicagoans looking for more spacious homes and quieter surroundings than those found in the increasingly crowded and dirty inner city. In many ways, Douglas was Chicago's first suburb, with a mix of working-, middle- and upper-income families of Yankee, Irish, and German descent. By 1890, Douglas also included a small community of African Americans who primarily worked as servants for the wealthy.

The area remained predominately white until World War I, when large numbers of African Americans began moving into the area. Part of the Great Migration of southern blacks who moved North for economic opportunity and greater social freedom, the new arrivals were drawn to the area by a small, established community of blacks and the area's close proximity to the meatpacking plants, where many found employment.[7]

By 1900, a small community of African Americans lived in Douglas, including Reverend and Mrs. Reverdy Ransom. Originally from Ohio, Ransom served as minister of Bethel African American Methodist Episcopal Church. Together with Jane Addams, he also established Chicago's first settlement house for African American migrants who were moving to the city in ever-increasing numbers.

The Illinois Central Railroad tracks formed the eastern
boundary of Douglas/Grand Boulevard and gave residents
easy access to the Loop or points further south. This view
looks north from Thirty-fifth Street, c. 1895.

As whites moved away from the South Side during the 1920s, middle- and upper-income African Americans occupied the large brown- and greystone homes along South Park Avenue, now Dr. Martin Luther King Jr. Drive.

Establishing a pattern that would repeat itself across Chicago—and America—South Side whites moved out of the area as more blacks arrived. Most whites moved further south and west, establishing a ring of white neighborhoods around what became known as the Black Belt, which by 1900, extended southward into Grand Boulevard. Although the 1919 Race Riot further isolated Chicago's black community, a vibrant neighborhood formed during the aftermath with dozens of African American businesses, churches, and civic institutions. Despite many accomplishments, Chicago's African Americans remained geographically isolated and socially confined by racial discrimination, threats of violence, and the use of restrictive covenants preventing white homeowners from selling to people of color. The Great Depression hit the area, then known as Bronzeville, particularly hard, causing many black-owned businesses to fail. Decades-old residential housing deteriorated, as did the infrastructure. The situation prompted blacks to desert the Republican Party (the party of Abraham Lincoln) for the New Deal of the Democrats under Franklin D. Roosevelt, a political shift with enormous consequences for local and national politics. When the World War II economy attracted more blacks to the area, overcrowding made matters worse.[8]

After World War II, Chicago launched an ambitious program of urban renewal that dramatically reshaped the area. Mayor Richard J. Daley, who provided overall direction for the project, believed that the Loop had to be protected from encroaching slums and used massive amounts of federal money to clear acres of dilapidated low-rise housing and replace them with massive high-rise buildings to house the urban poor. Initially hailed as modern marvels, projects such as Stateway Gardens and the Robert Taylor Homes proved disastrous. The large concentration of poor residents, limited access to the outdoors, lack of proper policing, and inadequate community support systems created "high-rise ghettos" of poverty, crime, and despair.[9]

The Great Depression hit Bronzeville particularly hard, causing many black-owned businesses to fail. Decades-old housing deteriorated, as did the infrastructure.

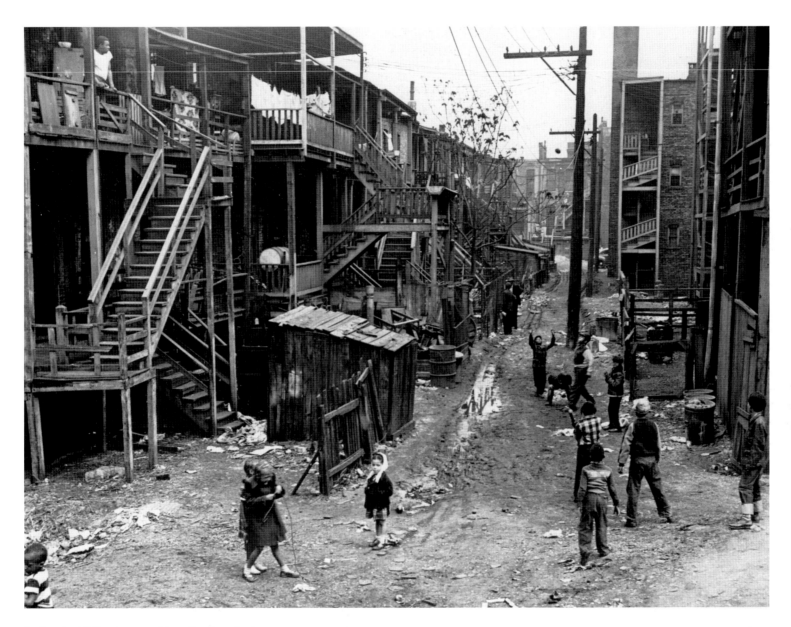

During the 1950s, slum conditions like those in the 500 block of Thirty-seventh Street prompted the push for affordable public housing on the South Side.

As the projects went up, many middle-class blacks left Douglas/Grand Boulevard for other neighborhoods in search of better housing and public schools. Their exodus began after the Supreme Court's 1948 ruling against the use of restrictive covenants and accelerated after Congress passed the Civil Rights Act of 1968 prohibiting discriminatory housing practices. Moving predominantly southward, they took up residence in many formerly all-white neighborhoods, such as South Shore and Chatham, which eventually turned into black communities as whites moved away.

An aerial view of the Southwest Side of Chicago from Damen Avenue and West Eighteenth Street, c. 1955.

The Maxwell Street market, c. 1905, remained a fixture of the West Side until the 1990s, when the University of Illinois at Chicago razed it for campus expansion.

The departure of middle-class blacks from Douglas/Grand Boulevard left a greatly impoverished district with most residents living below the poverty line and lacking opportunities for employment in the wake of Chicago's deindustrialization. During the 1990s, however, the return of middle-class blacks to the neighborhood sparked a revitalization effort that continues. Meanwhile, in accordance with the Supreme Court ruling in *Gautreaux v. Chicago Housing Authority* (1969), most of the South Side's high-rise public housing projects have been demolished, with residents rehoused in low-rise units scattered across the city and suburbs.[10]

THE NEAR WEST SIDE

Like Douglas, the Near West Side developed as a residential district during the 1850s. It is defined by Kinzie Street on the north; the Chicago River on the east; Sixteenth Street on the south; and Ogden Avenue on the west. The area originally attracted many upper-class whites who wanted to live away from the congested inner core of the city, as well as members of the working and middle class. During the late nineteenth century, the area attracted thousands of European immigrants, including Russian and Polish Jews, Italian Catholics, and Greek Orthodox, who formed ethnic communities bound by language, religious beliefs, and cultural traditions. While Jews settled southward to Sixteenth Street, Italians lived between Polk and Taylor streets, and Greeks settled between Harrison, Halsted, and Polk streets, and Blue Island. Predominately poor and uneducated, they faced enormous challenges in their new home, but found work in Chicago's burgeoning industries,

Three of the many thousand Chicago youth served by Hull-House, c. 1920.

primarily meatpacking. Many established small businesses that catered to local clientele, creating lively centers of commerce and employment in their own communities. Maxwell Street, Chicago's most famous open-air market, located at the intersection of Halsted and Maxwell streets, remained at the heart of the city's Jewish community for decades. Numerous synagogues and churches were established to meet the spiritual needs of their communities, and organizations like the Hebrew Institute and local parishes helped members locate jobs and housing, providing childcare and offering educational classes. In this regard, they rivaled Hull-House on Halsted Street. Established by Jane Addams and Ellen Gates Starr in 1889, Hull-House provided a wide range of social services to accommodate and Americanize recent immigrants, gaining worldwide recognition in the process.[11]

The Near West Side remained a predominately white ethnic enclave until the 1930s and 1940s, when large numbers of African Americans and Mexicans moved

The Near West Side remained a predominately white ethnic enclave until the 1930s and 1940s, when large numbers of African Americans and Mexicans moved into the area.

Left: Confirmation class at Saints Peter and Paul Slovak Church on the West Side, 1921. An important rite of passage for Catholic youth, the sacrament of confirmation involved elaborate ritual and community-wide celebration.

Right: Baptismal certificate for Christina Kozik from Saints Peter and Paul Slovak Church on the West Side, 1910. The Catholic Church anchored Chicago's immigrant communities, providing them with services from cradle to grave.

into the area. Drawn by economic opportunity, they found work in the city's meat-packing and manufacturing plants that flourished during World War II. Afterward, when Chicago's industrial base declined, many residents lost jobs, leaving them in a state of chronic unemployment. At the same time, large numbers of middle-class whites moved to neighborhoods further north or left Chicago for the suburbs, in part to flee blacks, but also to find better housing, schools, and basic services. The departure of the middle class, otherwise known as "white flight," furthered the area's decline, prompting the city to launch a massive program of urban renewal on the Near West Side. During the 1950s and 1960s, blighted areas were cleared, public housing erected, new highways built, and the University of Illinois at Chicago (UIC) established in what had been Little Italy. Destroying neighborhood businesses, including the eastern half of Maxwell Street for the Dan Ryan Expressway, and displacing thousands of residents, these projects stirred considerable controversy and alienated many supporters of Mayor Richard J. Daley, who directed the effort. The process continued in the 1980s and 1990s when UIC destroyed the last remnants of Maxwell Street for new athletic fields, relocating merchants to a new facility several blocks away.[12]

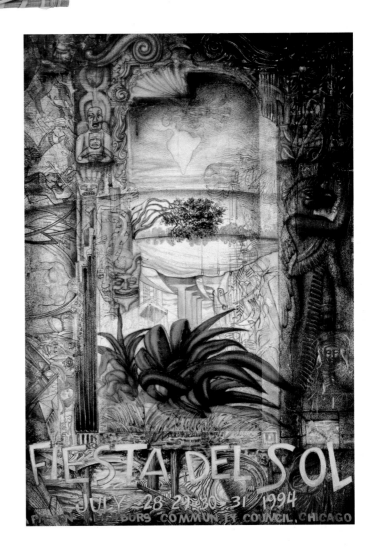

Left: Straw Crucifix, Pilsen, 1999, collected during the annual Way of the Cross ceremony that commemorates Christ's walk to Cavalry and subsequent crucifixion.

Right: Fiesta de Sol poster, 1994, announces the annual summer festival, one of many traditions retained by Chicago's Mexican community.

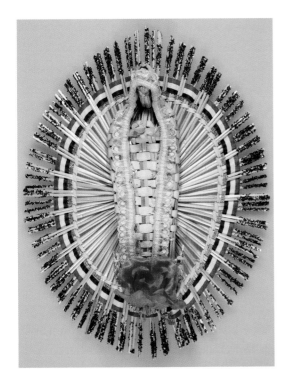

Our Lady of Guadalupe straw figure, Pilsen, 1999. Chicago's Mexican community retains a special devotion to Mary, the mother of Jesus and patron saint of Mexico, honoring her with small icons for the home.

PILSEN

Below the Near West Side, in an area known as the Lower West Side, lies the neighborhood of Pilsen. Its boundaries are Sixteenth Street to the north; Cermak Avenue to the south; the curving Chicago River to the east and south; and Western Avenue to the west. The area first drew German and Irish immigrants who were attracted by employment opportunities with the Illinois & Michigan Canal and the Burlington Railroad. After the Great Fire of 1871, displaced industries, including the McCormick Reaper Works, numerous lumber mills, and garment sweatshops relocated to the area, attracting thousands of Eastern European immigrants looking for work. A large percentage of the population came from Bohemia, and residents began to refer to the area as Pilsen, after the city of Plzen, the second largest city in West Bohemia (now the Czech Republic). Predominately Roman Catholic, the community established several churches, including Saint Procopius, the largest Bohemian congregation in the country, and the Polish congre-

Chicago's well-established pattern of ethnic succession transformed Pilsen into a Mexican community, one of many that emerged across America in the twentieth century.

gations of Saint Adalbert's and Saint Pius. These institutions not only provided residents with religious services, but also schools and social services that helped them adjust to life in America.[13]

A working-class neighborhood, Pilsen emerged as a stronghold of labor activism during the late nineteenth century. In 1877, Pilsen workers joined a nationwide railroad strike for better wages. Their actions culminated in the Battle of the Viaduct on Halsted Street near Sixteenth Street between U.S. Army troops and striking workers that killed thirty residents and injured hundreds more. On May 3, 1886, when laborers at the McCormick plant struck for the eight-hour day, Chicago police shot and killed two workers, prompting a protest meeting on May 4 at Haymarket Square that ended in tragedy when a bomb blast sparked a police riot. In 1910, workers at Hart, Schaffner, and Marx clothing manufacturers launched a strike that eventually involved thirty-five thousand workers and shut down Chicago's garment industry.[14]

Pilsen remained a predominately white, working-class enclave until the 1950s, when large numbers of Mexicans arrived. Many came from the Near West Side, displaced by urban renewal, while others came from Mexico to take jobs in Chicago's industries. At the same time, ethnic whites began moving away from Pilsen's urban congestion to the suburbs, where new homes and schools promised a better life. Chicago's well-established pattern of ethnic succession soon transformed Pilsen into a Mexican community, one of thousands that emerged across America during the late twentieth century as waves of immigrants from south of the border poured into the country. Despite the change in ethnicity, Pilsen remained a bastion of Roman Catholicism and labor activism. Churches that once served an Eastern European population now hold Spanish services, and community festivals such as the Via Cruces, or Way of the Cross, a procession that re-enacts Christ's journey to Calvary on Good Friday with people from the community cast as biblical figures, are annual events. Each August, Pilsen stages Fiesta del Sol (Feast of the Sun), a secular holiday brought from Mexico. Relatively isolated from the rest of Chicago by its location, physical barriers, and cultural traditions, Pilsen nonetheless is being transformed by the continual change of urban life, most notably the incursion of young artists and urban professionals seeking affordable housing.[15]

LINCOLN PARK

Lincoln Park, one of the North Side's oldest neighborhoods, originally lay outside Chicago's boundaries. It joined the city in 1853, when the state legislature annexed the northern portion adjacent to the city; the rest remained part of Lake View Township until Chicago annexed that area in 1889. Before the Great Fire of 1871, Lincoln Park included a mix of white people. While those of affluence,

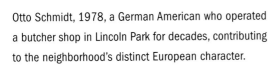

Otto Schmidt, 1978, a German American who operated a butcher shop in Lincoln Park for decades, contributing to the neighborhood's distinct European character.

most notably the merchant prince and hotelier Potter Palmer and his socialite wife, Bertha Honoré, resided in large homes near the lakefront, middle-class residents lived near the park, originally a cemetery located on the outskirts of town. Working-class families lived on the neighborhood's west side, near factories along the river's North Branch, and German immigrant merchants and farmers lived around North Avenue, near St. Michael's Roman Catholic Church, which they established in 1852.[16]

Although the fire destroyed most of the area, residents quickly rebuilt their homes and businesses, while the park developed into one of Chicago's crown jewels with lush gardens, winding walkways, ponds, fountains, and bicycle paths. Further west, more factories were established, including several furniture manufacturers and the Deering Harvester Works. These industries attracted immigrants from Italy and Eastern Europe, including Poles, Romanians, and Hungarians, who established working-class communities. Public transportation in the form of cable cars, later converted to electric trolleys, created commercial districts along Clark Street, Wells Street, and Lincoln Avenue that employed local residents and provided them with basic necessities. In 1900, the Northwestern Elevated Railroad opened a line from downtown to Wilson Avenue with stops in Lincoln Park, but the advent of the automobile clogged the area's narrow streets with traffic and noise, a problem that still plagues the area.[17]

Like much of Chicago, Lincoln Park thrived during the 1920s but deteriorated during the Great Depression as many neighborhood businesses failed and the city lacked the necessary funds to maintain infrastructure. After World War II, more low-income residents moved into the area, occupying buildings often operated by absentee landlords. When conditions deteriorated, concerned citizens formed the Old Town Triangle Association and later, the Lincoln Park Conservation Association,

Passport and wooden carrying case used by Nanni Helena Korolainen when she immgrated to Chicago from Finland in 1921. Nanni settled on the North Side and remained in Chicago for the rest of her life.

to stimulate neighborhood renewal through private rehabilitation of property. As renewal took hold, low-income Puerto Ricans and African Americans were displaced, a process accelerated by real-estate developers who constructed high-rise apartment buildings near Lincoln Park. One of Chicago's first neighborhoods to undergo gentrification, Lincoln Park attracted affluent whites back to the city during the 1980s and 1990s, a process that sent real estate values soaring. Today, Lincoln Park remains one of Chicago's most desirable neighborhoods, despite congestion and rising property taxes.[18]

ROGERS PARK AND WEST RIDGE

Located several miles north of Lincoln Park, Rogers Park is one of Chicago's most diverse neighborhoods. Its history begins in the late 1830s when Phillip Rogers, an Irish immigrant, began purchasing government land formerly occupied by Native American tribes after they were forced to leave the area according to the terms of the 1833 Treaty of Chicago. Rogers eventually owned approximately 1,600 acres of land, which his son-in-law, Patrick Touhy, subdivided in 1872, intending to attract people relocating after the Great Chicago Fire, as well as new arrivals. By 1878, enough people lived in Rogers Park to incorporate as a village, which it remained until Chicago annexed the area in 1893, along with West Ridge.

Then as now, Rogers Park had good connections to the city with the Chicago & North Western Railway, the Chicago, Milwaukee, & St. Paul Railroad, and by 1908, the Northwestern Elevated Railroad. With good transportation came more people and eventually, Rogers Park lost its suburban-like qualities with the construction of large apartment buildings instead of single-family homes. In addition, Loyola University, formerly Saint Ignatius College on Roosevelt Road, began to move its

During the 1950s and 1960s, Jewish merchants operated dozens of stores along Devon Avenue, attracting shoppers from the neighborhood and nearby suburbs.

facilities to a larger campus in Rogers Park. Commercial districts sprang up near several 'L' stops and along Clark Street and Devon Avenue. Thus, by World War I, Rogers Park had become a densely populated urban neighborhood. Most of its residents were native-born whites of mixed ancestry with few, if any, recent African American migrants from the South. Racial discrimination, along with higher housing costs, prevented blacks from moving into the area. During the Great Depression, Rogers Park, like most Chicago neighborhoods, deteriorated, and conditions worsened during World War II when a housing shortage resulted in overcrowding and subdivided apartments.[19]

Meanwhile, Rogers Park's neighbor, West Ridge, experienced a surge of growth. Unlike most areas of the city, West Ridge, also called West Rogers Park, still had room to grow. As its name implies, West Ridge lies west of Ridge Avenue and extends to the North Shore Channel that runs east of McCormick Road. The area remained predominately rural until the early 1900s when several brick manufacturers moved into the area, attracting immigrant workers from Germany and Scandinavia. After World War I, block after block of brick bungalows and two-flat apartment buildings sprang up to keep pace with an increasing population.

Between 1920 and 1930, West Ridge's population grew from 7,500 to nearly 40,000 people, and a lively commercial district developed along Devon Avenue. During the Great Depression, West Ridge continued to grow as more Chicagoans

During the Great Depression, Rogers Park, like most Chicago neighborhoods, deteriorated. Conditions worsened during World War II when a housing shortage resulted in overcrowding and subdivided apartments.

moved away from older sections of the city. After World War II, a large number of Russian and Polish Jews moved into the area, establishing a strong community with synagogues, schools, businesses, shops, and restaurants. West Ridge remained a Jewish enclave until the 1970s, when a new wave of immigrants moved into the area.[20]

As a result of the Immigration and Nationality Services Act of 1965 (also known as the INS or Hart-Celler Act), many people from developing countries moved to the United States. A large percentage came from India and Pakistan, and together these two groups settled in West Ridge and opened businesses on Devon Avenue. Despite their cultural and political differences, the two communities established a relatively harmonious community and transformed the area with distinctive shops, restaurants, and cultural institutions. In addition to serving the local population, Devon Avenue attracts residents from other parts of the city, as well as tourists, who want to experience one of Chicago's more colorful neighborhoods.

Rogers Park and West Ridge continue to evolve. By 2000, Rogers Park had become one of the most diverse neighborhoods in the city with a large number of eastern European, Asian, African American, and Hispanic people. Its 63,000 residents spoke more than 80 languages and the racial mix stood at 46 percent Caucasian, 30 percent African American, 28 percent Hispanic, and 6 percent Asian/Pacific Islander. Approximately 75 percent of Rogers Park residents lived in rental units, giving the area a fluid, transitory character. Similarly, West Ridge, with 73,000 people by 2000, had a very large non-native population (approximately 46 percent) but remained a neighborhood where most people owned their own homes.[21]

Once an enclave of Jewish merchants, Devon Avenue is now the commercial center of Chicago's Indian and Pakistani communities.

The 'L'

'L' Car No. 1

Built in 1892, 'L' Car No. 1 is the last remaining car from Chicago's first fleet of elevated cars owned and operated by the South Side Rapid Transit Company. It originally transported passengers from the Loop to the 1893 World's Columbian Exposition. At the time, a one-way fare cost five cents. The car was converted to electricity in the early 1900s and remained in operation until the early 1930s.

Chicago's elevated train system began operating in 1892 and played a key role in making the city an urban crossroads. The first line, built by the South Side Rapid Transit Company, began at Twelfth Street (now Roosevelt Road) and extended southward along State Street, reaching Jackson Park on May 1, 1893, just in time for the World's Columbian Exposition. It provided Chicagoans with an alternative to the cable car line that ran down Cottage Grove Avenue and promised quicker service with tracks running above the South Side's increasingly busy streets. At the time, elevated trains used steam locomotives to pull wooden passenger cars at fifteen miles per hour, three miles faster than the cable car.

Built by Jackson & Sharp Company of Wilmington, Delaware, the first set of 180 wooden cars arrived in Chicago on June 6, 1892. They resembled Chicago's Pullman railroad cars with mahogany paneling, etched glass windows, plush seating, and gas jet lighting fixtures; the cars were converted to electric operation in 1897. The new system, developed by Frank J. Sprague of Chicago, featured a multiple unit control system that supplied each car with its own power, the first such system in the world.

Encouraged by the success of the South Side line, new elevated lines sprung up across the city: a West Side line in 1893, the Loop in 1897, a North Side system in 1900, and a Ravenswood line in 1907. While providing much-needed urban transportation to residents, the 'L' also stimulated the growth of new housing and commercial developments away from the central city, significantly contributing to the expansion of Chicago neighborhoods. The 'L' also brought people, primarily daily commuters, back into the city, and returned them to the surrounding neighborhoods each evening. While many Chicagoans preferred other means of transportation, particularly the streetcar, the 'L' provided a vital service for generations of people. Cursed by some for its dirt and noise, and feared by others for its height and speed, the 'L' nonetheless serves people from all social classes and walks of life. In this regard, the 'L' unites Chicago and remains an integral part of the city's identity and character.[22]

Chicago aldermen in session, c. 1900. During the late nineteenth and early twentieth centuries, the Democratic Party exerted more control over the city council, laying the groundwork for the rise of the political machine during the 1930s.

CHICAGO POLITICS

Like the city's social fabric, Chicago politics are often contentious, but overall, the Democratic Party has been a dominant force since the late 1870s. Based on its original charter, Chicago has a city council type government with an elected mayor and aldermen representing various wards across the city. William B. Ogden, Chicago's first mayor and a Yankee from upstate New York, served a one-year term from 1837 to 1838, focusing his energies on building Chicago's infrastructure to make the city economically viable. His early successors, all from New England save one from Kentucky, followed a similar path.[23] During the mid-1850s, Chicago politics began to change. The arrival of Irish and German immigrants in the mid-nineteenth century not only diversified Chicago but introduced ethnic rivalry into its politics. During the 1850s, Chicago voters reacted against the large number of immigrants occupying "their" city. In the 1854 election, they selected Isaac L. Milliken of the Temperance Party, which opposed drinking, a well-established custom among the Irish and Germans. Although he only served one term, Milliken set the stage for the 1855 election of Levi D. Boone of the anti-Catholic, anti-immigration Know-Nothing Party. Once in office, Boone and the City Council immediately set out to hike the city's liquor license fees and enforce an old ordinance closing taverns and saloons on Sundays. Boone further incensed immigrants by refusing to hire them as police even as he beefed up the forces. On April 21, 1855, tensions erupted when a large anti-temperance crowd gathered at the courthouse in support of several tavern owners arrested for noncompliance. Acting on Boone's orders, police cleared the area, arresting nine protestors in the process. Afterward, a group of armed Germans from the North Side assembled at the Clark Street drawbridge, which Boone ordered raised until he had enough police assembled. When the bridge came down, Germans

Chicago ballot box, in use from c. 1890 to 1932.

The arrival of Irish and German immigrants in the mid-nineteenth century not only diversified Chicago but introduced ethnic rivalry into its politics.

Mayor Carter H. Harrison I (lower center of photograph) making a speech at the World's Columbian Exposition, October 28, 1893. That evening, a disgruntled office-seeker shot and killed Harrison in front of his home.

Carter H. Harrison I, Chicago's first five-term mayor, c. 1886. His son, Carter Harrison II, also served five terms.

stormed across, only to be met by more than two hundred policemen and state militia who quickly quelled what is known as the Lager Beer Riot. The action mobilized Chicago immigrants, who helped elect Thomas Dyer, a Democrat, as Chicago's mayor the following year.[24]

The elections of 1857 and 1861, however, were won by Republican candidates, an auspicious debut for the local wing of a new national party and a reflection of Chicago's patriotic fervor at the outbreak of the Civil War. Racial issues inserted themselves into Chicago politics for the first time in 1862 when voters, reacting negatively to Abraham Lincoln's Emancipation Proclamation, elected Francis Cornwall Sherman, a Copperhead Democrat, as mayor for three consecutive terms.[25]

For the next decade, Chicago remained a two-party town with some third-party action, but that changed in 1879 with the election of Carter H. Harrison I. Known as the Mayor of the Common Man, Harrison hailed from a wealthy Kentucky family. After graduating from Yale, he attended law school at Transylvania College in Lexington, then moved to Chicago and commenced practicing law in 1855. Harrison also worked in real estate before winning his first election in 1874 to the Cook County Board of Commissioners. Between 1875 and 1879, Harrison served

Campaign trucks for Anton J. Cermak in the Twenty-second Ward. Crossing ethnic and neighborhood boundaries, Cermak appealed to a broad constituency of voters who swept him to office in 1931.

in the U.S. Congress as a Democrat, and, in 1879, was elected mayor, the first of four consecutive two-year terms.[26]

Harrison, who sported a black slouch hat and rode around town on a white horse, developed a paternalistic rapport with the city's immigrant working class, frequenting their wards, learning their languages, and adopting a laissez-faire attitude toward their recreational habits of drinking and gambling. More important, Harrison supported the labor movement and the eight-hour cause. In spring 1886, when agitation peaked, Harrison did not intervene with striking workers or stop the planned rally at Haymarket Square on May 4. Instead Harrison attended the meeting, but left before the bomb exploded. In the aftermath Harrison, bowing to public pressure, clamped down on public gatherings and marches. During the anarchists' trial, the mayor noted that none of the Haymarket speakers suggested using force or violence, but if they had, he would have dispersed them at once. Harrison withdrew from the 1887 mayoral race, but he won a fifth term in 1893, taking office shortly before the World's Columbian Exposition opened. On the evening of October 28, 1893, shortly after delivering the fair's closing address, Harrison was assassinated at his home by Eugene Patrick Prendergast, a disgruntled office-seeker. Thousands of devoted supporters turned out for Harrison's funeral and burial in Graceland Cemetery.[27]

Campaign broadside for Anton J. Cermak, 1931. During his campaign for mayor, Cermak sought ethnic votes, including Greeks who lived on the city's North Side.

Cermak also reached out to Chicago's African American voters during the 1931 mayoral campaign. At the time, an increasing number of blacks were switching from the Republican to the Democratic Party for economic relief during the Great Depression.

Anton J. Cermak campaign button, 1931. Cermak's ties to Chicago labor unions helped him win the mayoral race.

Four years after Harrison's death, Chicago voters elected his son, Carter Harrison II, as their mayor. Like his father, Harrison served four consecutive terms, between 1897 and 1905, and a final fifth term, between 1911 and 1915. Although Harrison developed a solid base of aldermanic support, Chicago politics had not yet reached a "machine" level. In fact, a Republican candidate, William "Big Bill" Thompson successfully ran for mayor in 1915 and reigned throughout the Roaring Twenties. Widely considered one of the most corrupt mayors in American history, Thompson allowed bootleggers to work freely during two consecutive terms in office that coincided with the early years of Prohibition. Rampant corruption and Thompson's political courtship of African American voters, however, angered other Chicagoans, and they failed to reelect him in 1923, voting instead for a "reform" Democrat, William E. Dever. Although reelected in 1927, Thompson thus far remains Chicago's last Republican mayor.[28] Thompson's successor, Anton J. Cermak, developed the Chicago Machine. Cermak, born in 1873 in Austria-Hungary, now the Czech Republic, immigrated the following year with his parents to the United States. They settled in Braidwood, Illinois, where Cermak, after three years of schooling, joined his father working as a coal miner. In 1890, Cermak moved to Chicago and started his own hauling company, earning him the nickname "Pushcart Tony." Cermak entered the world of Democratic politics on the precinct level and won election to the state legislature in 1902. Seven years later, Cermak became alderman of the 12th Ward (Bridgeport), and in 1922 assumed the presidency of the Board of Cook County Commissioners. Both positions allowed Cermak to dole out patronage, gaining widespread support and power in return.[29]

In 1931, Cermak ran against "Big Bill" Thompson, Republican mayor during the 1920s Gangland Era and long associated with crime and corruption. Cermak's campaign of reform and, more important, his ability to form alliances across ethnic lines, swept him into office by more than 200,000 votes. As mayor, Cermak appointed people of different ethnic backgrounds to government positions and required them to work together. Cermak's political network helped Franklin Delano Roosevelt capture Chicago's vote in the 1932 presidential election, which involved the courtship of local African American voters who began leaving the Republican Party in droves during the Great Depression. Pushcart Tony's mayoral term, however, was cut short in 1933 when an assassin's bullet, intended for Roosevelt, struck him during a political rally in Miami, Florida. As they had for Carter Harrison I, Chicagoans mourned deeply their fallen leader, who was laid to rest in the Bohemian National Cemetery on the Northwest Side.[30]

Although Cermak's term ended abruptly, his political machine flourished under his successor, Mayor Edward J. Kelly. Like Cermak, Kelly cultivated ethnic support and also sought African American votes. Taking patronage to a new level, Kelly doled out thousands of jobs and political favors to party loyalists across the

Backed by party leaders, Daley successfully ran for mayor in 1955 and remained in office for twenty-one years. He ruled with an iron fist and maintained a well-oiled political machine.

city, ensuring him three more terms in office until 1947. Kelly's successor, civic leader Martin H. Kennelley, served two terms until he was pushed aside for Richard J. Daley.

An Irish American Catholic from the blue-collar neighborhood of Bridgeport, Daley rose through party ranks by working as an alderman's secretary and serving as a state legislator between 1936 and 1946.[31] Backed by party leaders, Daley successfully ran for mayor in 1955 and remained in office for twenty-one years. He ruled with an iron fist and maintained a well-oiled political machine by controlling City Council and the power of patronage. Daley also played politics at the national level, helping John F. Kennedy achieve victory in the closely contested 1960 presidential election and delivering the vote for Lyndon B. Johnson four years later. During the Johnson administration, Daley supported the president's efforts to build a "Great Society of the highest order" with programs such as Medicare and the War on Poverty, despite his personal misgivings about government welfare. Daley believed people should pick themselves up by their own bootstraps, as he had done, but willingly accepted the flow of millions of dollars in federal funds to support these programs in Chicago.[32]

Daley also took advantage of federal funds for urban renewal, launching an ambitious program of new highway construction and public housing projects that dramatically reshaped the city and living patterns of its residents. New highways displaced thousands of Chicagoans, leaving many angry and bitter toward the mayor, but they also relieved congestion within the city by routing automobile and commercial truck traffic around its perimeter. Included in Daley's program was the construction of a tollfree expressway to O'Hare Airport, then a small facility. Completed in 1960 at a cost of $300 million, the Northwest Expressway, later renamed the Kennedy, provided a critical connection to the Loop and allowed Daley to move forward with ambitious plans to expand O'Hare into an international facility that would sustain and enhance Chicago's role as a global crossroads of travel and trade. Perhaps Daley's most important single accomplishment, the construction of O'Hare International Airport nonetheless involved the awarding of lucrative contracts to close associates of the mayor without competitive bidding.[33]

Mayor Daley's public housing program stirred even more controversy. Early into his tenure, the City Council authorized the construction of several new public housing projects in black neighborhoods where public housing already existed. This kept poor blacks out of middle-class white neighborhoods, reinforcing segregation patterns in Chicago and appeasing white voters. Ultimately, the Supreme Court ruled against the practice in *Gautreaux v. Chicago Housing Authority* (1969), launching a new era of scattered-site housing that placed low-income residents in better neighborhoods across the metropolitan area. In the process, notorious projects such as the Robert Taylor Homes have been demolished, but they continue to tarnish Daley's

Campaign poster for Richard J. Daley, 1955. In his first campaign for mayor, Daley promised to "get things done" and rewarded his constituency with a flood of patronage jobs.

Mayor Richard J. Daley delivering a speech at City Hall, December 18, 1959. At the peak of his political powers, Mayor Daley controlled Chicago aldermen with a firm hand.

An anti-Daley broadside, c. 1970, mocks Chicago politics by portraying the mayor as a candidate for every major office.

Women of Chicago's 11th Ward carrying banners for Richard J. Daley during his second mayoral campaign, 1959.

Mayor Harold Washington's vision for reform was dashed as twenty-nine white aldermen formed a solid block of opposition in the City Council.

record, as do his handling of the riots on the West Side and Democratic National Convention in 1968.[34]

The haunting specter of racial politics continued to play out in Chicago during the administration of Harold Washington. In the years between Daley's death in 1976 and Washington's election in 1983, Michael Bilandic and Jane Byrne governed a city in economic decline and increasingly torn by issues of race, housing, education, employment, and crime. When the city failed to respond effectively after a crippling blizzard in January 1978, voters rejected Bilandic in favor of Byrne. Although she promised reform, a fractious political climate prevented much progress. Increasingly impatient with empty promises, Chicago blacks rallied around the candidacy of Harold Washington. Born in Cook County Hospital and raised on the South Side, Washington worked in the meatpacking industry and served in the U.S. Army before attending Roosevelt College and Northwestern University Law School. A loyal member of the Democratic Party, Washington entered the world of Chicago politics in 1954 as corporation counsel for the 3rd Ward. Working his way up party ranks, Washington won election to the Illinois House of Representatives in 1965 and retained his seat until 1976. Between 1977 and 1980, Washington served in the Illinois Senate, then as U.S. Congressman from January 1981 until his resignation in April 1983 after being elected the first black mayor of Chicago.[35]

Washington's election portended great change for politics as usual in Chicago, but the city's racial divisions proved too deep for him to govern effectively. After narrowly defeating Republican candidate Bernard Epton with more than 51 percent of the vote, Washington took office, declaring in his inaugural address: "We have a clear vision of what our people can become, and that vision goes beyond economic wealth, although that is a part of our hopes and expectations. . . . In our ethnic and racial diversity, we are all brothers and sisters in a quest for greatness." Washington's vision for reform, however, was soon dashed as twenty-nine white aldermen, previously allied with Mayor Daley, formed a solid block of opposition in the City Council. Thwarting the mayor's every initiative, they pitted themselves against twenty-one other aldermen, most of them African American, who supported Washington. Their raging debates, reported nationwide and dubbed "Council Wars," were, at times, humorous, but they resulted in political stalemate and frustration across the city. At the same time, Chicago struggled with a continuing loss of jobs (more than 100,000 since 1973) and growing budget deficits. Although Washington remained a popular figure, many Chicagoans, particularly business leaders, grew increasingly concerned over the city's economic decline. After winning a second term, however, Washington seemed to be gaining political momentum when he unexpectedly died of a heart attack on November 25, 1987. The fourth mayor to die in office, Washington left a void, temporarily filled by Eugene Sawyer, until the next election in 1989.[36]

SALE EL SOL PARA EL LATINO CON
Washington
VOTA DEMOCRATA
Perfora NO. **8**

A Spanish-language poster for Harold Washington, 1983, attests to his effort to reach new immigrant voters living in Chicago.

Harold Washington greets Chicagoans in 1983. The city's first African-American mayor, Washington served one full term in office but died eight months after his re-election.

In 1989, Richard M. Daley, son of the legendary Richard J. Daley, won his first term as Chicago mayor.

Tapping into his own heritage and that of many Chicago voters, a pin from Richard M. Daley's 1989 campaign features an Irish shamrock and the saying "Erin Go Braugh" ("Ireland Forever").

Once again, Chicagoans elected the son of a former mayor as their new leader. Richard M. Daley, fourth child and eldest son of the late Richard J. Daley, had previously served in the Illinois State Senate during the 1970s and as State's Attorney for Cook County from 1980 to 1989. In 1983, Daley tossed his hat into the mayoral ring, but lost in a three-way primary election involving Harold Washington and Jane Byrne. Daley's attempt, however, paved the way for his successful bid in 1989 when he defeated Eugene Sawyer in the primary and Timothy Evans and Edward Vrdolyak in the general election. Taking office at the end of this challenging decade in the city's history, Daley enjoyed a more prosperous time during the 1990s when Chicago regained both jobs and population, including a large number of young professionals in addition to new immigrants. Moreover, Daley united City Council's aldermen, staged the Democratic National Convention in 1996, took control of the public schools in an attempt to improve them, and championed Chicago as a tourist destination with citywide beautification efforts, most notably Millennium Park east of the Loop, but also in many neighborhoods. As a result, Daley has developed a wide base of political support across the city, winning five consecutive terms of office between 1989 and 2003.[37]

"The source of growth and change is innovation."

Paul O'Connor, 2002

When it comes to innovation, Chicago is second to none. The modern department store, mail order, and skyscrapers top a notable list of Chicago innovations that also includes progressive theories of education and social reform, the first nuclear chain reaction, and the birth control pill. In addition, Chicagoans developed many well-known consumer products, including the cell phone, Lincoln Logs, Tinkertoys, Wrigley Gum, Morton Salt, and the Weber Grill. Although the list of local innovations seems endless, it is also important to note why Chicago is such fertile ground for new ideas and products.

Innovation is a hallmark of urban society. Unlike rural societies that adhere to traditional ways, urban centers value change and attract people with new ideas. In Chicago, these innovators find especially fertile ground created by a combination of factors. As a major crossroads of travel and trade, the city has facilitated the introduction and exchange of new ideas. And as a city that sprang up without a set of well-established traditions, Chicago has typically been more open to new ideas than some older cities, such as Boston or Philadelphia. Furthermore, Chicago's financial resources and mixed economy have fostered creativity in many different fields, not just one or two (such as Detroit's automotive industry). Additional factors include a Midwestern penchant for practicality that makes complex ideas work and an extensive network of transportation and communication that rapidly distributes new ideas and products far and wide. The familiarity of Chicago innovations makes them seem ordinary. What was once revolutionary is now taken for granted, but the overall impact remains significant.[1]

Not surprisingly, many Chicago innovations addressed urban problems and, while they may have resolved immediate concerns, they often created new challenges. Skyscrapers, for example, provide vertical space in congested cities, but they tend to create social anonymity; modern retail practices supply a wide range of goods but help foster rampant consumerism. The birth control pill gives women control over reproduction but created bitter controversy within the Catholic Church. The first nuclear chain reaction led to the atomic bomb, man's most destructive weapon.

GIVE THE LADY WHAT SHE WANTS!

Today, Americans live in a consumer society unprecedented in world history. In contrast to previous eras, consumption, not production, keeps the national economy afloat, and when consumer spending dips, so does the stock market. Permeating every level of society, shopping is the American pastime, central to our way of life and personal identity. Now more than a century old, the current form of consumerism dates to the mid-nineteenth century when forward-thinking merchants in Chicago, Philadelphia, and New York pioneered new practices that transformed the routine chore of shopping into something far more pleasant. Although Chicago cannot claim every retail innovation, fixed prices, the money-back guarantee, department-store window displays, home delivery, and mail order all originated here.

The history of modern retail in Chicago begins with Potter Palmer. A reserved, twenty-six-year-old Quaker with a keen mind for business, Palmer moved to Chicago from upstate New York in 1852 and opened a small store at 137 Lake Street, the city's first commercial strip on the south side of the Chicago River. Palmer's arrival coincided with Chicago's emergence as a bustling port and rail center with numerous connections to eastern cities. Inspired by the Marble Palace, a dry goods store in New York City catering exclusively to women, Palmer kept the ladies in mind when he set up shop. For starters, he refused to install the customary whiskey barrel for men (thereby creating a more comfortable atmosphere for women), filled the shelves with quality goods, and installed an attractive display of merchandise in the storefront window, which he lit at night.

More importantly, Palmer routinely undersold the competition and introduced fixed pricing, a revolutionary concept that allowed customers to see how much an item cost before they decided to purchase. Customers and merchants typically dickered over every transaction, with each side trying to outwit the other for the best price possible. The practice resulted in erratic pricing—even for the same item—and a general lack of trust between merchant and shopper. On the other

Potter Palmer, 1868, established many of the customary practices of modern retail, including fixed prices and the money-back guarantee.

On October 10, 1868, Field & Leiter's staged a gala opening for their new store on State Street described as "the grandest affair of its kind which ever transpired even in Chicago, the city of grand affairs."

Marshall Field, c. 1900, succeeded Palmer as the crown prince of American retail, emphasizing quality merchandise and customer service.

hand, set prices eliminated haggling, reduced the element of risk, and created a more relaxing environment in which to shop.[2] As Palmer's store flourished, he stocked European imports that attracted a more affluent clientele. Even during the Panic of 1857, which destroyed many businesses in Chicago, Palmer turned a profit, allowing him to move to larger quarters at 139 Lake Street. But the street had problems. Located near the Chicago River and its pervasive stench, the low-lying street turned into a muddy quagmire after each rain. Within a year Palmer moved to a five-story marble-front building on State Street.

In addition to retail, Palmer excelled as a wholesaler, stocking huge quantities of yard goods, sheets, blankets, gloves, soaps, and other dry goods that small-town merchants purchased in large quantity to sell in their own shops. Palmer mastered the art of promotion by advertising in local newspapers on a daily basis, and on November 26, 1861, he posted a revolutionary announcement: "Notice. Purchases made at my establishment that prove unsatisfactory either in price, quality, or style, can be returned . . . for which the purchase money will be with pleasure returned. P. Palmer." No American merchant had ever made such a promise, but Palmer's practice eventually became standard for all retailers.[3]

Palmer remained in business until 1865, when he sold the business to rival merchants Marshall Field and Levi Z. Leiter, remaining a silent partner by investing $330,000 in the firm. Palmer then turned his attention to State Street, which he envisioned as Chicago's new commercial district to replace the aging and overcrowded Lake Street. Spending some two million dollars of his own fortune, Palmer purchased property along the narrow street and demolished its old wooden structures. To spur development, Palmer constructed two new buildings; on the south end, he erected the Palmer House Hotel, an eight-story marble structure with 225 rooms, while at the north end—where State and Washington streets intersect—he built a six-story limestone and marble building that he rented to Field and Leiter for fifty thousand dollars a year.[4]

Field & Leiter's move to State Street ushered in a new era in Chicago retail. On Saturday, October 10, 1868, they staged a gala opening described by the *Chicago Tribune* as "the grandest affair of its kind which ever transpired even in Chicago, the city of grand affairs." The upper floors belonged to wholesale; here, large quantities of goods were displayed and sold to other merchants who in turn sold them to their customers. While many Chicago merchants frequented Field's, storekeepers from cities and towns throughout the Midwest also shopped here, making the store a crossroads of regional commerce. Meanwhile, the retail space on the ground floor exceeded all expectations. Walnut counters, frescoed walls, and gaslight fixtures beckoned customers into separate departments that sold ladies' cloaks, shawls, men's suits or neckties, cardigans, and jackets. The overall arrangement hinted at the lavish department stores of the future.

Shoppers outside Marshall Field & Company, c. 1910.
The store and its famous clock anchored Chicago's retail
district on State Street, serving generations of shoppers.

Fashions of the Hour, published by Marshall Field &
Company, featured the latest trends in clothing for
women, men, and children. Its attractive covers
featured cutting-edge graphic design and set a new
standard for the advertising industry.

Before that occurred, however, Field pioneered several innovations of his own that set him apart from other merchants and made Field & Leiter's one of the country's leading retail stores. Following Palmer's footsteps, Field sent buyers abroad to purchase the latest European fashions, but he took the practice a step further in 1869 by establishing a permanent overseas office in Manchester, England, textile capital of the world. Closer to the source, Field & Leiter's buyer—Joseph Field, Marshall's older brother—had direct access to manufacturers and more opportunities to strike a better deal, giving the company a decided advantage over its competition.[5]

Shoppers at Marshall Field's could find top-quality merchandise from America and Europe, making the store an international crossroads of commerce.

Destroyed in the Great Fire of 1871, Field & Leiter's resumed operations less than two weeks later in a brick horse barn located at State and Twentieth streets. Initially, shoppers flocked to the store, but eventually the novelty of its unusual setting wore off and profits declined. Field & Leiter's moved back to State Street in 1873, occupying a new building on their former location constructed and owned by the Singer Sewing Machine Company as investment property. After this building burned in 1877, Field & Leiter's moved into temporary headquarters in the Inter-State Industrial Exposition building on North Michigan Avenue, then made arrangements with Singer to purchase, not rent, a new building at State and Washington streets that opened in 1879 to great acclaim. Once again, sales soared, reaching $25 million in 1880. The following year, Field bought out Leiter's share of the business for a mere $2.5 million renamed the firm Marshall Field & Company, and continued to provide shoppers with quality goods and impeccable customer service, reaping enormous profits in the process.[6]

Around this time, an energetic young man from Michigan named Henry Selfridge joined the firm, working first as a stock boy, then as a salesman. Selfridge introduced many new ideas, including annual sales to make room for new merchandise, a bargain basement or "Budget Floor" that eventually grossed $25 million in yearly sales, a children's clothing department, and a ladies' tearoom on the third floor that catered to thousands of hungry shoppers each day. Like Potter Palmer, Selfridge understood that attractive displays in department store windows would entice shoppers, and in 1895 he hired Arthur Valair Fraser, a talented young window dresser from Iowa, to create a new image for Field's. Fraser believed that window displays should make people think, and his elegant designs set a new standard that other merchants copied along State Street and across America.[7]

Capitalizing on Chicago's flourishing economy, an ever-expanding class of consumers, and an abundance of manufactured and hand-made goods from around the world, Marshall Field & Company continued to flourish under the famous adage "Give the lady what she wants!"—a directive uttered by Field when he witnessed a clerk arguing with a customer. When Field died in 1906, John Graves Shedd, head of the wholesale division, took charge and completed the construction of a twelve-story building designed by Daniel H. Burnham, chief architect of the 1893 World's Columbian Exposition. Completed in 1907, the new store had nearly forty acres of retail space and forty-five display windows that became the store's most famous feature under Fraser's stylish and witty direction. A magnificent Tiffany dome soared above the main floor, which featured a dazzling array of merchandise, as did every department in the store. Shoppers could find top-quality merchandise from America and Europe, making the store an international crossroads of commerce. Although there were competitors, such as Carson Pirie Scott and The Fair Store, Marshall Field's remained State Street's premier retail emporium for decades, attracting customers

Crate & Barrel developed a casual, yet urbane look that attracted younger customers.

Left: Crate & Barrel's original store at 1510 North Wells Street, 1968.

Right: Crate & Barrel's flagship store on Michigan Avenue, 2001.

from near and far, many of whom made shopping at Field's a family tradition. After World War II, Field's became a regional chain with several stores in nearby suburban malls and more distant cities such as Rockford, Illinois. Simultaneously, State Street declined as a shopping district, while North Michigan Avenue blossomed with a new Marshall Field's at Water Tower Place. Efforts to revive State Street in the 1990s proved successful, and Marshall Field's remained its anchor until Macy's of New York City purchased the store and announced plans to change the name in 2006, thus closing a legendary chapter in Chicago history.[8]

Chicago's contributions to American retail, however, are not restricted to Marshall Field's. Crate & Barrel has set new standards for the industry since owners Gordon and Carole Segal opened the first store on North Wells Street in 1962. Taking a fresh approach, the young couple sold modern European table goods, imported directly from small manufacturers, at reasonable prices. Their modest store displayed merchandise on open shelves, in white cubes, and inside wooden barrels, creating a casual, yet urbane look that attracted younger customers. The success of the Wells Street store prompted the Segals to open several more stores in Chicago and across the nation, eventually reaching 130 locations. In 1990, they opened a new forty-five-thousand square-foot store on North Michigan Avenue that embodies the company's modern approach to retail.[9]

Aiming for rural and small-town markets, Montgomery Ward & Company published catalogs with heartwarming imagery. Note the RFD (Rural Free Delivery) wagon in the background.

Aaron Montgomery Ward, c. 1900, founder of America's first mail-order company.

CHICAGO MAIL ORDER

In addition to the modern department store, Chicago pioneered the American mail-order industry. A revolutionary concept, mail order allowed consumers to shop for a wide variety of goods from the comfort of their homes. Moreover, mail order bridged America's urban and rural areas by offering a plethora of products manufactured in cities like Chicago to farmers and small-town residents who would otherwise lack access to them. Ultimately, Chicago's mail-order industry helped foster mass-consumerism while standardizing popular taste across the country. No matter where mail-order shoppers lived, they could buy the same products.

The history of Chicago mail order begins in 1872, shortly after the Great Chicago Fire, when a twenty-eight-year-old entrepreneur from New Jersey named Aaron Montgomery Ward and his brother-in-law, George R. Thorne, established the world's first mail-order business: Montgomery Ward & Company. Based on his experience as a store manager and traveling dry-goods salesman in the rural Midwest, Ward conceived of the notion of buying merchandise in large quantities from manufacturers for cash, then selling the goods through the mail directly to farmers, thus eliminating the "middleman" or small-town merchant. Of course, Ward was the ultimate middleman, but he branded his company "The Original Grange Supply House," a direct appeal to members of the Grange, a national association of farmers. Ward started in a livery-stable loft with twenty-four hundred dollars in capital and a single-sheet catalog listing a few dry goods. Borrowing a page from Potter Palmer, he reduced customers' risk with a money-back guarantee. After all, he was asking consumers to purchase goods based on trust; since they couldn't inspect items firsthand, all they had to go by were catalog illustrations and descriptive text. Eventually, Ward's catalogs featured thousands of items, including dry goods, clothing, shoes, toiletries, jewelry, watches, household furnishings, guns, and farming equipment—all warehoused in Chicago and shipped to customers via the railroad. Buying and selling in great volume, Ward's became a large and highly complex organization, employing scores of workers who processed and shipped thousands of orders each day. Selling on such a massive scale kept prices low and profits high, eventually reaching forty million dollars by 1913, the year Ward died.[10]

Ward's chief rival, Sears, Roebuck & Company, traces its origins to 1886 when Richard Warren Sears, a twenty-three-year-old telegraph operator and railroad agent for the Minneapolis & St. Paul Railroad in North Redwood, Minnesota, began selling watches to other railroad agents. An instant success, Sears formed the R. W. Sears Watch Company in 1887, moved to Chicago, and hired Alvah Curtis Roebuck, a watch repairman. The two men became partners and, in 1893, founded Sears, Roebuck & Company. At first, the company sold only watches, watch chains, diamonds, and other jewelry, but Sears soon expanded the line to include sewing

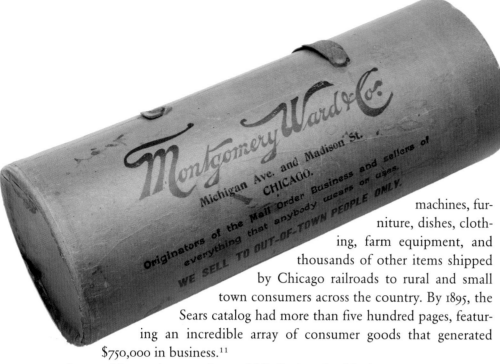

Montgomery Ward & Company mailing tube, c. 1900, carries the following notice: "We Sell to Out of Town People Only."

machines, furniture, dishes, clothing, farm equipment, and thousands of other items shipped by Chicago railroads to rural and small town consumers across the country. By 1895, the Sears catalog had more than five hundred pages, featuring an incredible array of consumer goods that generated $750,000 in business.[11]

A natural-born salesman who could "sell a breath of fresh air," Sears reaped the benefits of Rural Free Delivery (RFD), established by Congress in 1896 to provide mail service to rural Americans at no charge. In response, Sears flooded the market with catalogs and promotions that "waged war" against manufacturers and dealers with low prices and money-back guarantees on any product. In 1900, Sears developed the "Send No Money" sales campaign that allowed rural customers to receive and inspect goods without paying a penny. Although the campaign resulted in $900,000 worth of unclaimed merchandise at railroad depots across the country, it made Sears seem like a "real friend" of the farmer, and ultimately helped the company replace Ward's as the largest mail-order house in the country.[12]

While Ward's and Sears flourished, small-town merchants suffered. Understandably, they opposed mail order and pressured local newspapers to keep their advertisements out of circulation. In the early 1900s, when mail order was at its height, a newly formed association known as the Home Trade Leagues of America encouraged customers to patronize local merchants rather than purchase goods through the mail. In Chicago, Thomas J. Sullivan, a writer for the American Press Association, published *Merchants and Manufacturers on Trial*, in which he charged,

Richard W. Sears, c. 1900, the enterprising watch salesman from Minnesota who established the country's largest mail-order company in Chicago.

> War has been declared on the great catalog houses of Chicago and other cities by the 500,000 retail merchants. . . . The mammoth institutions, which employ thousands of workers, doing their business entirely through the medium of their bulky catalogs, spending no money in the community whence they derive annually millions of dollars of patronage are forcing increasing numbers of home merchants to the wall and, so their opponents claim, are making commercial graveyards of once prosperous towns.

The attack on mail order reached its peak in 1910 when Congress held hearings on parcel post, which allowed for the direct mailing of packages through regular mail, rather than by rail freight or mail express. As expected, farmers supported parcel post while small-town merchants and retail associations vigorously opposed it. Nevertheless, Congress approved parcel post, boosting the combined sales of Ward's and Sears to $300 million by 1918.[13]

Sears, Roebuck & Company sold many products made in Chicago, including alphabet blocks manufactured by Halsam Products Company, c. 1925.

Although mail order remained an important fixture of the national economy for the next twenty years, American shopping habits began to change dramatically after World War I. The advent of the automobile and the steady growth of cities such as Chicago signaled a profound change in American society. What was once a rural population had, by 1920, become predominately urban. Catalog sales began to decline and, in 1925, both Sears and Ward's opened their first retail stores. By 1929, they had a combined total of eight hundred stores; although Ward's tended to locate smaller stores in smaller cities than Sears, both companies had clearly shifted to urban markets. After a long and steady decline, both Ward's and Sears eventually phased out mail order.[14] The concept has survived however, with thousands of companies printing direct-mail catalogs that reach consumers around the world. Now online shopping has emerged as an important sector of the economy, and it surely will continue to grow as more people take advantage of a convenient system originally developed at the crossroads of Chicago.

In addition to selling goods to rural Americans, Sears purchased raw materials from them in the form of small animal pelts. This catalog provided instructions on how to ship them to special receiving stations across the country, including one in Chicago. During the Great Depression, Sears also sponsored a national fur contest with $5,000 in prize money, a substantial sum at the time.

"Minnesota" Model A sewing machine sold by Sears, Roebuck & Company, c. 1895. The sewing machine remained one of the company's all-time best-selling items.

Bes-Ben Hats

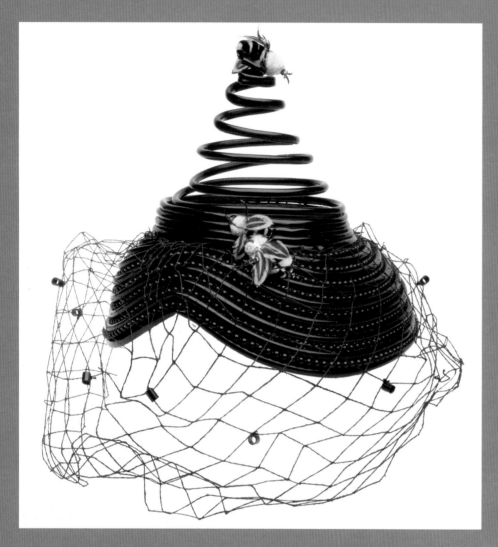

Women's hats designed by Benjamin Green-Field, c. 1950. The "bee in her bonnet" (left) and coin hats (above) illustrate the stylish wit of Chicago's "Mad Hatter."

Established by Benjamin B. Green-Field and his sister Bes in 1919, the Bes-Ben Shop acquired a national reputation for witty and sophisticated ladies' hats. Although Bes left the business after a few years, Benjamin continued to work as chief designer and promoter. During the 1940s, wartime shortages and fabric restrictions forced him to use different types of materials. As is often the case, constraint forced creativity, and in 1941, he and hat-maker Margit Amberg produced a new hat made with small leather Dalmatian dogs that created a fashion buzz. Over the next twenty years, Green-Field continued to make delightful hats for fashion-conscious women across the country, including New York socialites and Hollywood starlets. Featuring found items such as cigarettes and matchbooks or trinkets collected on world tours, the hats were often humorous, but always well made. While some hats provided social commentary, most were simply fun. As Green-Field explained, "These hats stimulate conversation, and what woman doesn't like to be the object of conversation." An astute businessman, Green-Field held an annual, invitation-only summer clearance sale that began at 2:15 A.M. with women lined up for blocks to take advantage of huge discounts. All hats, even those regularly selling for nearly five hundred dollars, were marked down to five dollars. After the doors opened, Green-Field would toss hats into the crowd for anyone to catch and buy. The party-like atmosphere added to the merriment and, after all the hats were gone, Green-Field closed the store until the fall.[15]

Benjamin Green-Field with hat-maker Margit Amberg, c. 1956.

Using new materials and methods while working under tight deadlines and limited budgets, Chicago architects developed a series of innovations that made high-rise construction possible.

William Le Baron Jenney, c. 1885. Trained as a Union Army engineer, Jenney developed the first metal-frame skyscraper, a revolutionary advance in architecture that allowed buildings to soar higher than ever before.

THE MODERN SKYSCRAPER

Like the department store and the mail order, the modern skyscraper evolved in Chicago during the late 1800s. At the time, many Chicago-based companies were expanding at a phenomenal rate and needed more office space for their workers. Most companies wanted to be located downtown, near public transportation and financial services, but the area was becoming increasingly congested. There was literally nowhere to go but up. Using new materials and methods while working under tight deadlines and limited budgets, Chicago architects developed a series of innovations that made high-rise construction possible. The first to do so was William Le Baron Jenney, who designed the Home Insurance Building at the northeast corner of LaSalle and Adams streets. Completed in 1885, the building used an interior skeletal-frame made of iron and steel to support its weight, rather than masonry walls made of brick and stone. The lightweight frame allowed Jenney's building to soar nine floors above street level, several stories higher than other buildings in Chicago. On account of their weight, masonry buildings could only reach six or seven stories before their walls began to buckle, but the skeletal frame solved that problem. Furthermore, skeletal-frame buildings cost less money and took less time to build than masonry buildings, and their simple forms created a new aesthetic that favored clean, structural lines rather than elaborate ornamentation.[16]

According to the architectural historian Carl Condit, the skeletal frame was the "most radical transformation in the structural art since the development of the Gothic system of construction in the twelfth century." Yet, some of Jenney's contemporaries continued to build masonry structures, such as the eleven-story Rookery Building by Daniel Burnham and John Root (1886), the ten-story Auditorium Building by Dankmar Adler and Louis Sullivan (1889), and the Monadnock Building (1891), Burnham and Root's sixteen-story structure that required six-foot base walls for support. To construct such massive buildings in the sandy, clay-like soil of Chicago, architects used a "floating raft" type of foundation comprising timber, concrete, and iron beams, first developed by Burnham and Root in 1882 for the Montauk Block.

The skeletal frame, however, eventually became the preferred method of high-rise construction in Chicago and around the world. But skyscrapers required more than skeletal frames and Chicago architects were quick to utilize innovations developed here or elsewhere that made their construction possible. Chief among them is the passenger elevator, originally developed in New York City and quickly adopted in Chicago. In addition, skyscrapers required better fireproofing; George H. Johnson of New York developed a new method and brought it to Chicago after the Great Fire of 1871. Johnson's technique of applying ceramic tiles to iron beams prevented them from melting and buckling in excessive heat. Taller buildings also needed a new type

The Home Insurance Building, 1926. Designed by William Le Baron Jenney the structure had an interior metal frame that supported its weight. Demolished in 1931, the building is considered the world's first modern skyscraper.

A stylized rosette from the entrance of the Home Insurance Building is one of the few remaining pieces of Jenney's historic structure.

of caisson foundation, originally developed by Adler & Sullivan for the Chicago Stock Exchange Building. Still used today, the caisson foundation consists of separate piles driven deep into bedrock to support tall buildings by evenly distributing their weight. Finally, skyscrapers required a new type of wind-bracing which was first developed by the engineer Louis E. Ritter while working with Jenney on the Manhattan Building, completed in 1891.[17]

Collectively, the innovative and pioneering architects working in the city during the late nineteenth century are known as "The First Chicago School." Among them, the firm of Adler & Sullivan ranks among the most influential. Dankmar Adler, born in Germany in 1844, excelled at engineering, a skill he learned while serving with the Union Army during the Civil War. His partner, Louis Henri Sullivan was born in Boston in 1856, and studied at the Massachusetts Institute of Technology and the Ecole des Beaux-Arts in Paris before moving to Chicago in 1875. After working

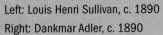

Left: Louis Henri Sullivan, c. 1890
Right: Dankmar Adler, c. 1890

As partners, architects Dankmar Adler and Louis Sullivan designed some of the most significant buildings in American history. Their structures combined engineering and artistic brilliance that revolutionized architectural practices while transforming the urban landscape. Unfortunately, many of their buildings have been demolished, but their legacy remains.

The firm's door light was designed by Sullivan in 1883 and executed by the Western Sand Blast Company of Chicago. Sullivan's organic design reflects the influence of the early Art Nouveau Movement, as well as his personal preference for natural forms and stylized harmony.

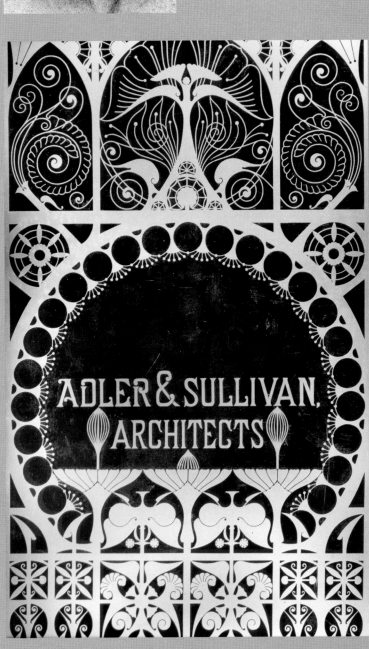

A magnificent elevator lintel from the Chicago Stock Exchange Building reflects Sullivan's preference for organic ornamentation that reminds urban dwellers of the natural world.

Watercolor rendering of the Carson Pirie Scott Building by Albert Fleury, 1903. Originally known as the Schlesinger & Mayer Store, this structure is considered Louis Sullivan's masterpiece. Its modern exterior is softened by an elaborate grillwork entryway that extends along both sides of the building.

An elaborate medallion from the Carson Pirie Scott Building is a superb example of Sullivan's genius for ornamental design.

as a draftsman for the office of Johnston and Edelman, Sullivan joined Adler's firm in 1879 and became his partner the following year. Complementing each other's strengths, they collaborated on a series of remarkable buildings. The Auditorium Building (1889), the Garrick Theater (1891), and the Chicago Stock Exchange (1894) rank among their finest efforts. After their partnership dissolved in 1895, Adler and Sullivan established separate firms. Sullivan's commissions included the Schlesinger & Mayer Store, now the Carson Pirie Scott Building (1899) (widely considered to be his best work) and several midwestern bank buildings.[18]

FRANK LLOYD WRIGHT AND THE PRAIRIE SCHOOL

Frank Lloyd Wright, c. 1950. One of the world's greatest architects, Wright pioneered the Prairie style home, a revolutionary form of residential architecture rooted in the midwestern landscape.

While one group of Chicago architects revolutionized commercial architecture, another transformed the American home. In 1887, a young man named Frank Lloyd Wright from Richland Center, Wisconsin, moved to Chicago where he became a draftsman for Joseph Silsbee, a noted midwestern architect. Shortly thereafter, Wright joined Adler & Sullivan, became their chief draftsman, and worked on the Auditorium and Stock Exchange buildings, two of the firm's most important commissions. Leaving Adler & Sullivan in 1893, Wright established his own firm in Oak Park where he developed a new form of residential architecture known as the Prairie School. Although uniquely American, the Prairie School style embodies the philosophy of the Arts and Crafts Movement, a social reform movement that originated in England during the mid-nineteenth century with the writings of Thomas Carlyle, John Ruskin, and William Morris. Briefly stated, the movement argued against the effects of industrialization, claiming that mechanization robbed workers of creativity and a sense of pride in their work. Transplanted to Chicago by British publications, lectures at the Art Institute, and social reformers such as Jane Addams of Hull-House, the Arts and Crafts Movement found fertile ground in the raw, industrial city that epitomized the machine age in America. The Chicago Arts and Crafts Society, founded in 1897 at Hull-House, included artists, writers, designers, potters, metalworkers, and reform-minded architects, including Wright. He articulated a radical departure in 1901 when he delivered his famous lecture "The Art and Craft of the Machine" at Hull-House, in which he professed that "in the Machine lies the only future of art and craft." Rather than a destructive force, Wright thought that the machine helped achieve "simplicity," which William Morris believed to be the basis of all true art.[19]

Using balloon-frame construction and simple, machine-cut forms, Wright developed low, horizontal structures that blended with the softly undulating midwestern landscape to create an organic appearance. Rather than a series of small,

Rather than a destructive force, Wright thought that the machine helped achieve "simplicity," which William Morris believed to be the basis of all true art.

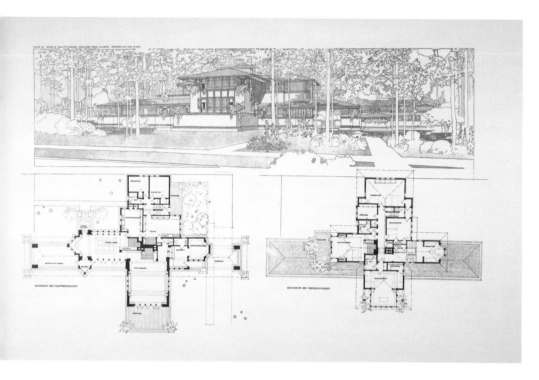

Elevation and floor plan of the Ward Willits House, designed by Frank Lloyd Wright in 1902. Considered Wright's first fully realized Prairie style home, the Willits House still stands in Highland Park, Illinois.

Frank Lloyd Wright's Prairie style sewing table designed for the Avery Coonley House, c. 1908, is a study in functional elegance with leaves that open to create more workspace, four accessory drawers, and an inlaid measuring tape on the top work surface.

separate rooms, Wright designed interior spaces that flowed into each other and opened outdoors through porches and terraces. He used dark woods and natural colors to create a sense of intimacy and warmth, and designed the furniture, windows, and all other decorative elements as integral parts of the whole space. Wright's most notable achievements include the Ward Willits House in Highland Park, Illinois (1902); the Susan Lawrence Dana House in Springfield, Illinois (1903); the Avery Coonley House in Riverside, Illinois (1908); and the Frederick G. Robie House in Chicago (1910).[20]

Although few people could afford his homes, Wright still had an enormous impact on residential architecture in America. Many architects and designers, primarily in the Midwest and western states, belonged to the Prairie School, including Walter Burley Griffin, Francis Barry Byrne, Marion Mahony, and William Drummond, who came out of Wright's studio, as well as George W. Maher, William Gray Purcell, and George Grant Elmslie. The Prairie style also influenced the bungalow, a low-cost housing type popular in the teens and twenties, and the ubiquitous suburban ranch house of the post–World War II era. Wright, as well as Purcell and Elmslie, were interested in developing well designed but affordable homes for the middle class, an attitude very much in keeping with the Arts and Crafts philosophy.[21]

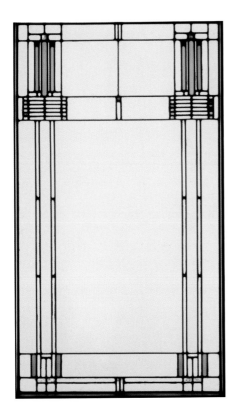

Left: Clear and opaque glass window from the Ward Willits House, designed by Frank Lloyd Wright and manufactured by Giannini and Hilgart, Chicago, 1902. The Willits House featured 115 art glass windows that created a transparent screen between the interior and exterior of the residence.

Below: Copper urn designed by Frank Lloyd Wright and produced by James A. Miller, c. 1900. Wright's urn is a Prairie School masterpiece with incised geometric lines and a warm, burnished tone that complements his residential interiors.

Oak side chair designed by Frank Lloyd Wright for the Sherman Booth House, c. 1912. Wright designed furniture as architecture and the results were striking but not very comfortable. Wright later confessed, "I have been black and blue in some spot, somewhere most of my life from too intimate contact with my own early furniture."

TECO POTTERY

Several Chicago designers were also expressing a democratic impulse. Gates Potteries (an offshoot of the American Terra Cotta & Ceramic Company, a manufacturer of drain tile, brick, and architectural terra cotta founded in 1881 by William Day Gates near Crystal Lake, Illinois) first began to market Teco pottery in 1901. Developed during the 1890s by Gates and two of his sons, Paul and Ellis, the line of Teco (named from the first two letters of the words "terra" and "cotta") featured simple, unadorned shapes and a cool green color in varying shades that became its hallmark. Unlike the fussy Victorian styles of the late nineteenth century, Teco ware had an earthier, more natural appearance. It echoed the midwestern landscape and provided a perfect complement to the emerging Prairie School aesthetic. Indeed, several Prairie School architects, including Frank Lloyd Wright, designed Teco ware, but Gates, along with the firm's chief modelers, Fritz Albert and Fernand Moreau, developed most of the early designs. While some were highly unusual with twisting, plant-like forms, most Teco pottery retained a graceful simplicity that appealed to modern tastes.

Reflecting the Arts and Crafts philosophy that good design should be available to everyone, Gates marketed Teco ware to "a large element of the public cultured of taste and in love with the beautiful who cannot afford to indulge in the luxury of high-price articles of a decorative nature." Attractive, well-made, and affordable, Teco ware sold well enough for the company to adapt mass-manufacturing techniques to keep up with customer demand without sacrificing quality. At the world's fair in St. Louis in 1904, Teco ware received the Grand Prize, a remarkable achievement for such a young company. In 1910, Gates Potteries introduced a new line of warm, autumn colors (red, gold, and blue) and continued to develop new forms until 1912, when an increased demand for architectural terra cotta left little time for the production of art pottery. Although the company ceased making Teco ware in 1922, the pottery became highly prized by private collectors and museums alike during the late twentieth century.[22]

Teco ware vase designed by Fritz Albert and made by Gates Potteries, c. 1905. The vase's swirling form reflects the influence of the Arts and Crafts and Art Nouveau movements, which emphasized the use of organic designs and natural colors for the home.

THE KALO SHOP

The Kalo Shop followed a similar path. Established in 1900 by Clara Barck Welles, the Kalo Shop became Chicago's premier maker of handwrought silver. Like Gates, Welles adhered to the Arts and Crafts philosophy and applied its principles to everyday life. Originally from Oregon, Welles moved to Chicago as a young woman to study decorative design at the School of the Art

This Teco ware vase made by Gates Potteries, c. 1915, suggests the influence of architect Louis H. Sullivan.

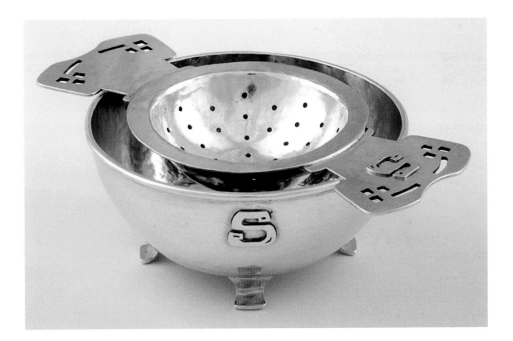

The Kalo Shop's early pieces, such as this sterling silver tea strainer (above) are more angular, reflecting the influence of the British Arts and Crafts Movement.

The handwrought surface and elegant simplicity of this sterling silver sugar bowl and creamer, c. 1910, typify the Kalo Shop style.

The Kalo workshop at 32 North Michigan Avenue, c. 1917, employed many highly skilled silversmiths under the careful direction of Clara Barck Welles.

Clara Barck Welles combined artistic talent and a keen sense of business to create the Kalo Shop, Chicago's largest producer of handwrought silver from 1900 until 1970.

Institute of Chicago. After graduation, she opened a small shop at 175 Dearborn Street where she and several young women made leather goods and some hand-woven items. Adapting the Greek word for beautiful, Clara named her shop "Kalo." After marrying George S. Welles, a metalworker, in 1905, she turned her attention to jewelry and metalwork. In addition to opening a larger shop in the Fine Arts Building on Michigan Avenue, Clara and George established the Kalo Art-Craft Community in their Park Ridge home where a group of artisans produced small pieces of jewelry and copper bowls, trays, and desk accessories. Soon, the shop was selling a complete line of handwrought silver table service designed by Clara. While some of her early pieces, such as a creamer and sugar bowl (c. 1908), clearly show the influence of the British Arts and Crafts Movement, Welles quickly developed a more unique, softly rounded style that became the Kalo hallmark. The company's motto — Beautiful, Useful, and Enduring — guided Welles and her team of artisans (both male and female) as they created an expanding line of products, including jewelry, hollow-ware, table services, special presentation pieces, and trophies. In 1914, Welles consolidated the artisans' workshop and store at 32 North Michigan Avenue, and opened a retail outlet in New York City. Although she rarely advertised, Welles developed a large and loyal clientele in both cities. A firm believer in fair employment practices and providing opportunities for women, Clara Barck Welles directed the Kalo Shop with great care until she retired in 1940. In 1959, she gave the shop to four employees, who maintained its operations until 1970. As described by a New York critic in 1937 when Welles exhibited several pieces of Kalo silver at the Metropolitan Museum of Art, her designs were "freshly creative" and "emphatically American," a fitting tribute to one of Chicago's most creative designers.[23]

A Kalo bowl made around 1913 demonstrates how the company developed a more softly rounded form that became its trademark.

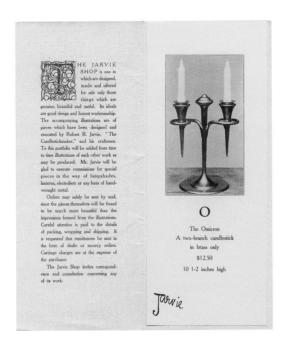

A rare catalog, c. 1905, contains photographic illustrations of Robert Jarvie's handwrought metalwork and a philosophical statement from the artisan: "The Jarvie Shop is one in which are designed, made and offered for sale only those things which are genuine, beautiful and useful. Its ideals are good design and honest workmanship."

ROBERT JARVIE

Chicago also claims Robert Jarvie, one of America's outstanding modern metalsmiths. Apparently self-taught, Jarvie worked out of his home on West Congress before establishing a shop in the Fine Arts Building on Michigan Avenue in 1904. Moving in 1909 to 1340 East Forty-seventh Street, then to the upper floor of the Old English Cottage building in the Union Stock Yard, Jarvie created an elegant line of candlesticks, bowls, vases, trays, trophies, desk sets, and other assorted items. Perhaps his most successful piece is a magnificent silver punch bowl commissioned by Art Institute president Charles L. Hutchinson as a presentation piece to the Cliff Dwellers Club, an association of artisans and writers to which both men belonged. Adhering to the Arts and Crafts philosophy to use natural forms, Jarvie modeled the bowl after an actual vessel used by cliff-dwelling Native Americans of the Southwest that he found in the collections of the Field Museum of Natural History. Another outstanding example of Jarvie's work is a silver trophy presented to the "Best Local Combination Horse" at the 1916 International Live Stock Exposition in Chicago. Exquisitely executed, the trophy features a simple, hemispherical bowl

A copper bowl made by Robert Jarvie, c. 1915, reflects the artisan's ideals and skill.

with chased floral band resting on a simple standard and base. Versatile as well as talented, Jarvie also worked in copper, brass, and gold, and adopted Colonial Revival styles when those became popular. Around 1915, Jarvie added furniture and wool rugs to his line, but he could not survive the difficult years of World War I. Sometime around 1918, Jarvie closed his shop and found employment as a metalworker for the C. D. Peacock Company of Chicago.[24]

ABEL FAIDY AND WOLFGANG HOFFMANN

By the end of World War I, Chicago's first era of innovative architecture and design had come to a close. Many of the early founders had either died or moved away. Furthermore, the war ushered in new design ideas, methods, and materials from Europe. Overall, design became more urbane and sophisticated to reflect life in the twentieth century. Instead of looking back to older forms, modern designers embraced machine-age technologies, man-made materials such as plastic and tubular steel, and favored bright, vivid colors that stood in sharp contrast to the earth tones of the earlier era. The new style, alternatively known as Art Moderne or Art Deco, reached American shores soon after the *Exposition Internationale des Arts Decoratifs et Industriels Modernes* held in Paris in 1925 focused worldwide attention on contemporary European designers.[25]

Several Chicago designers articulated the style, including Abel Faidy, a Swiss-born architect who studied in England and Germany before the war. Moving to Chicago in 1918, Faidy worked as a commercial interior designer, but after 1926, he became a freelance designer, creating interiors for stores, offices, and showrooms. In addition, Faidy designed for S. Karpen and the Howell Company, two of Chicago's leading furniture manufacturers. Faidy also had private clients, most notably Ruth and Charles Singletary, who commissioned him in 1927 to design a suite of furniture for their small penthouse apartment at 1244 North Stone Street. Strikingly modern in appearance, the suite comprises several case pieces with a trapezoid form, along with a leather settee and dining room chairs that feature a stepped-back shape associated with modern skyscrapers. Thus, the suite complements the urban landscape visible from the apartment windows. Elegantly compact, Faidy's furniture also provides additional storage space. Both the dining room and breakfast table have folding leaves and storage cabinets and drawers. A compact telephone-stand has a slide-out chair, while all of the upholstered pieces can be easily moved and re-grouped for social gatherings. Made in the shops of Marshall Field & Company,

Robert Jarvie's fine workmanship and attention to detail are evident in this sterling silver trophy made for the "Best Local Combination Horse" at the 1916 International Live Stock Exposition in Chicago.

Modern designers working in Chicago embraced new technology, man-made materials, and bright, vivid colors.

European-trained designer Abel Faidy achieved success in Chicago working for private and corporate clients from the 1920s through the 1950s.

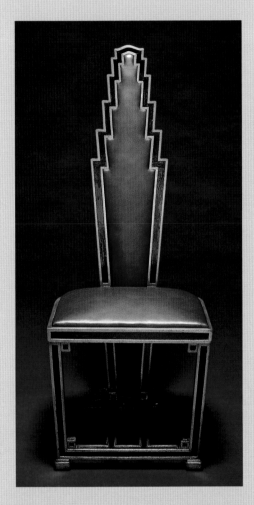

A stylish sketch of a dining room set by Abel Faidy for the W. W. Howell Company includes one of his trademark silhouette figures.

Maple armchair with leather upholstery from a suite of furniture designed by Abel Faidy for Ruth and Charles Singletary of Chicago, 1927.

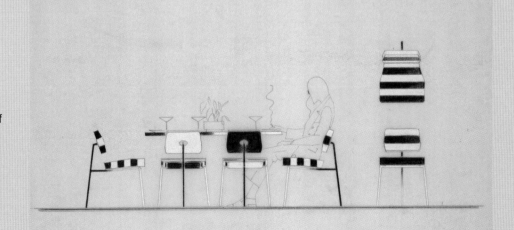

the Faidy suite of furniture is a marvel of modern style, practicality, and superb craftsmanship.[26]

On a broader scale, Chicago's A Century of Progress International Exposition of 1933–34 advanced modern design in America. Unlike the World's Columbian Exposition, Chicago's first world's fair held in 1893, A Century of Progress put more emphasis on the future rather than the past. Its many displays and buildings carried out the theme with sleek tubular forms, polished glass, and bright colors. Several of the fair's largest structures, most notably the Chrysler Motors, Travel and Transport, and General Motors buildings were masterpieces of modern design and dominated the fairgrounds. Meanwhile, smaller structures such as the House of Tomorrow featured fresh new designs for residential interiors.

The fair attracted many modern designers, such as Wolfgang Hoffmann, son of Josef Hoffmann, the well-known Viennese architect. For the fair, Hoffmann

Born in Austria, Wolfgang Hoffmann designed modern tubular steel furniture for the W. W. Howell Company of Geneva, Illinois, from 1934 until 1942.

Sketch of a chair by Wolfgang Hoffmann, c. 1935.

Prototype tubular steel serving cart designed by Wolfgang Hoffmann for the W. W. Howell Company, c. 1935. A similar model became one of the company's best-selling items.

Students at the New Bauhaus learned by doing, experimenting with different materials, methods, and colors to create simple design forms suitable for mass-production.

Walter Gropius (left) and Laszlo Moholy-Nagy at the Institute of Design, c. 1950.

helped the New York architect Joseph Urban develop a dramatic color scheme and he also designed all of the furniture and accessories for the Lumber Industries House. Hoffmann's work caught the eye of William McCredie, president of the Howell Company, a furniture manufacturer based in Geneva, Illinois. The Howell Company had been making tubular steel furniture since 1929, the first to do so in the United States, but as the effects of the Great Depression worsened, McCredie sought to produce affordable, modern designs for consumers on a tight budget. Between 1934 and 1942, Hoffmann worked exclusively for Howell, designing tables, desks, and chairs, including a simplified version of the "S" chair that the company paired with a small kitchen table to create a dinette set perfectly suited for small apartment kitchens or modern dining areas. Hoffmann also designed serving carts, folding chairs, and chaise lounges in a contemporary style that remains fresh and exciting.[27]

THE INSTITUTE OF DESIGN

Innovative yet practical, stylish but affordable, Hoffmann's furniture reflected the influence of the Bauhaus school of design established by architect Walter Gropius in Weimar, Germany, at the end of the World War I. Gropius hired leading painters, sculptors, architects, and designers as instructors; among others, they including the abstract artists Wassily Kandinsky, Paul Klee, Laszlo Moholy-Nagy, and Oskar Schlemmer. Offering more than methodology, the Bauhaus taught a philosophy about the integration of art and technology into a "New Unity," while preparing students for a practical, meaningful place in society as craftsmen or industrial designers. In terms of style, the Bauhaus stressed simple, unadorned forms in all fields, from architecture to household furnishings to graphic design—an aesthetic strongly influenced by the Arts and Crafts Movement and the Chicago School of Architecture, as well as Frank Lloyd Wright and the Prairie School.[28]

In 1933, the Nazi government closed the Bauhaus, dispersing its supposedly subversive teachers and students to various countries, including the United States. While Gropius became chairman of the department of architecture at Harvard University, the Chicago Association of Arts and Industries invited Moholy-Nagy to organize a new school in Chicago. Arriving in 1937, Moholy-Nagy established the New Bauhaus in an empty Prairie Avenue mansion owned by Marshall Field III. Moholy-Nagy recruited instructors and students from across the country, but financial difficulties forced the school to close in June 1938. Rescued by Walter Paepcke, president of the Container Corporation of America, the school reopened as the School of Design of Chicago in a large loft at 247 East Ontario Street. After a brief stay, the school moved to North State Street and, in 1946, to a building originally occupied by the Chicago

This miner's flashlight designed by Alfred Mell at the Institute of Design and manufactured by Justrite Manufacturing Company, c. 1955, exemplifies how good design can improve everyday products.

Students in a foundation course at the Institute of Design, c. 1949.

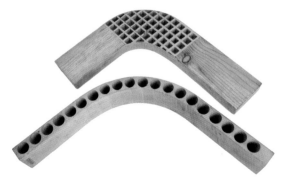

Wooden sculpture made by a student at the Institute of Design, c. 1960. The school encouraged students to experiment with materials and methods, taking some in entirely new directions.

Historical Society at the northwest corner of Ontario and Dearborn streets. Renamed the Institute of Design, the school continued to teach the Bauhaus philosophy while conducting classes that emphasized "total design": the equality of all creative design (furniture, fabrics, sculpture, etc.) within the master art of architecture. In class, students learned by doing, exploring new possibilities by experimenting with different materials, methods, and colors to create simple forms that could be mass-produced at low cost with a minimum of materials and labor. In addition, the school was a leading center of modern photography from the 1930s through the 1960s. In 1946, the school merged with the Illinois Institute of Technology and continues to train students in the philosophy and practice of modern design at a downtown location.[29]

Ludwig Mies van der Rohe, c. 1955, whose famous adage "less is more" defines modern architecture of the post–World War II period.

A Hedrich-Blessing photograph of Mies van der Rohe's apartment buildings at 860-880 North Lake Shore Drive under construction reveals the skeletal steel framing that forms the basis of modern architecture.

LUDWIG MIES VAN DER ROHE

During the 1940s, another member of the Bauhaus living in Chicago introduced a radical new form of architecture to the world. Ludwig Mies van der Rohe, a noted German architect and designer who was serving as the director of the Bauhaus when the Nazis closed its doors, fled to the United States in 1937. Persuaded by Chicago architect John A. Holabird, Mies moved to Chicago in 1938 to head the School of Architecture at the Armour Institute of Technology (later renamed the Illinois Institute of Technology). Mies planned a new campus for the school, designing twenty complementary buildings on either side of Thirty-third Street between State Street and the railroad tracks adjacent to Federal Street. Made of steel, brick, and glass, Mies's austere buildings clearly illustrate his belief that structure and space are the essential elements of architecture. Crown Hall, completed in 1956, is considered by many critics to be Mies's greatest work. Essentially a glass box, the building appears to float between the podium and roof, which is suspended from four plate girders that rise above its silhouette. Mies's famous axiom that "less is more" is fully realized in this building, which has a commanding presence despite its transparent appearance.[30]

The brilliance of Mies is further realized in the twin towers at 860–880 North Lake Shore Drive (1949–51). Developed from sketches originally drawn between 1919 and 1921, Mies's startling use of glass as an exterior curtain wall revolutionized modern architecture. Although many doubted their practical nature, Mies's "glass houses" became a new prototype of urban architecture adopted throughout the world. Chicago has several outstanding examples: 900–910 North Lake Shore Drive and Commonwealth Plaza at 330–340 West Diversey Parkway (both completed between 1953 and 1956), and three buildings at Chicago Federal Center: the Everett McKinley Dirksen Building (1959–64), the John C. Kluczynski Building (1966–74), and the U.S. Post Office (1966–74). Adhering to the Bauhaus practice of "complete design," Mies outfitted building lobbies with modernistic furniture made of steel, leather, and glass.[31]

Although Mies died in 1969, he remains one of the world's most influential architects. His legacy is visible in cities everywhere, but most notably in Chicago, which has the world's largest collection of Mies-designed buildings and several by his followers, including Lake Point Tower at 505 North Lake Shore Drive (1968). Designed by two of Mies's former students, George Schipporeit and John Heinrich, the building is based on the Glass Skyscraper, an undulating glass tower designed by Mies in 1922 but never built. Lake Point Tower, the world's first skyscraper with curving glass, is based on a Y-shaped plan that affords spectacular views of Lake Michigan while preserving residents' privacy.[32]

Left: Fazlur Khan, a brilliant engineer from Pakistan, developed new methods of construction that made super-high-rise structures such as the John Hancock Center and Sears Tower possible.

Right: Soaring high above Chicago and the surrounding prairie, Sears Tower remains the tallest building in the United States.

Opposite: The John Hancock Center, designed by Bruce Graham and Fazlur Khan of Skidmore, Owings & Merrill, makes a bold and dramatic statement in Chicago's skyline.

Two of Chicago's most famous buildings, the John Hancock Center (1969) and Sears Tower (1974), also owe a considerable debt to Mies. Rising one hundred stories above ground level, the Hancock Center briefly reigned as the world's tallest building until the completion of Sears Tower five years later. Designed by architect Bruce Graham and engineer Fazlur Khan of Skidmore, Owings & Merrill, the Hancock combines striking design with innovative engineering. The building is essentially a tapering tower of glass and steel with exterior cross bracing that forms a series of distinctive Xs. Like other skyscrapers, the Hancock overcomes urban density by using air space above and by combining several different functions within one structure; floors 1–5 are retail space, 6–12 are parking, 13–41 are offices, and 42–43 are for mechanical equipment. Private residences occupy floors 44–93, while the 94th floor houses a public observatory, bar, and restaurant popular with tourists and city dwellers alike; television, communication, and mechanical equipment occupy floors 95–100. Although the Hancock Center destroyed the small-scale environment of North Michigan Avenue, most Chicagoans embraced the building for making a bold statement. "Big John" is a fitting tribute to the city of Big Shoulders. Sears Tower, also designed by Graham and Khan, soars 110 stories above the city. While not as visually exciting as the Hancock, Sears Tower remains a marvel of engineering and one of Chicago's proudest accomplishments.[33]

REFORMING SOCIETY

Left: Jane Addams, social reformer and activist, c. 1892. Her progressive but practical ideas shaped modern social work and national attitudes toward the urban poor.

Right: Ellen Gates Starr, co-founder of Hull-House, 1914.

I n addition to shaping modern retail, architecture, and design, Chicago has been a pioneer in the arena of social reform. The city's many contributions include the settlement house, modern social work, visiting nurses, infant welfare, child labor laws, and the juvenile court. These innovative ideas emerged during the late-nineteenth and early-twentieth centuries in response to a host of problems created by rapid industrialization and explosive urban growth. Perhaps no city better illustrated the ills of modern urban society than Chicago. Within fifty years, the city had grown from an isolated frontier outpost into a major metropolis with a large population of working-class poor who lived in miserable conditions. Illiteracy, disease, and death rates soared as thousands of immigrants, primarily from Eastern Europe, streamed into the city, crowding into congested neighborhoods that had few if any support facilities other than local churches. Into the void stepped a group of reform-minded citizens who not only concerned themselves with the physical welfare of the poor, but wrestled with larger questions about society itself, particularly economic equality and how to sustain American democracy in the industrial age as old forms of community and civic involvement declined.

Leading Chicago's reform movement were two figures who achieved international fame: Jane Addams and John Dewey. Addams, born in Cedarville, Illinois, on September 6, 1860, grew up in the household of John H. Addams, a wealthy businessman and Republican state senator. Her father's friendship with Abraham Lincoln

The Hull-House complex at 800 South Halsted Street, c. 1910, included a kindergarten, daycare facility, classrooms, libraries, and meeting spaces for neighborhood residents.

A yellow-glazed ceramic bowl made in the Hull-House Kilns, c. 1930, reflects the continuing influence of the Arts and Crafts Movement.

Pottery from Hull-House, published in 1933, featured linoleum block illustrations depicting both process and products.

and his own deeply held convictions about American democracy, individual rights, and community service had a profound influence on Addams throughout her life. One of a small percentage of women to attend college at the time, Addams enrolled in Rockford Female Seminary in the fall of 1877. She excelled both in and out of the classroom, serving as class president, editing the school magazine, leading a science club and literary society, and graduating as class valedictorian in 1881. The death of her father and obligation to take care of her ailing stepmother, however, forced Addams to give up plans to attend Smith College in preparation for medical school. Enrolling in the Women's Medical College of Pennsylvania, Addams left after a semester for health reasons and spent the next few years traveling abroad.

Searching for a larger purpose in life and questioning the inequality between the rich and poor, Addams began to chart a new course. In 1888, she traveled to Europe with Ellen Gates Starr, a close friend from college, and the two began to discuss ways of helping the poor. Although their plans remained hazy, a visit to Toynebee Hall, a settlement house located in the London slums, showed Addams what could be done. Addams and Starr moved to Chicago in 1889 and established Hull-House, Chicago's first settlement house, using sixty thousand dollars of Addams's inheritance.[34]

Modeled after Toynbee Hall, Hull-House served thousands of working-class poor and destitute who lived in nearby neighborhoods. Wealthy donors, most notably Louise de Koven Bowen and Mary Rozet Smith, helped Addams expand Hull-House into a sprawling complex that covered an entire city block with thirteen additional buildings. Its extensive services included a kindergarten and daycare facilities for children of working mothers; classes in cooking, sewing, and citizenship; and free lending libraries. Adhering to the belief that cultural activities help the poor lift themselves up from degradation, Hull-House sponsored a full array of art and music classes that trained many young students, including Benny Goodman, who achieved international fame as a big band leader during the 1930s and 1940s. In addition, Hull-House Pottery sold students' work fashioned after popular styles of the time.[35]

Children painting in a Hull-House art class, 1924. The settlement house also provided classes in music, pottery, metalwork, and weaving.

A copper bowl, c. 1915, made by Olga Hunke at Hull-House reflects the influence of the Arts and Crafts Movement on Chicago's first settlement house.

Putting her youthful ideals into practice, Addams lived at Hull-House until her death in 1935. She believed her presence created a more democratic community, one that fostered participatory dialogue and one in which all parties recognized their mutual needs and responsibilities. Addams attracted a number of like-minded activists, most notably child-welfare reformer Julia Lathrop and Florence Kelley, who focused on child-labor reform. Together, they made Hull-House a center of important social discourse and influence. On a broader level, Addams wanted to convince more affluent Americans that a poor person's surroundings limited their ability to participate in a democratic society. At the time, most people believed that a person's moral character determined their standing in society, but Addams turned that notion on its head.[36]

To achieve her goal of a more equitable society, Addams became more involved in politics. She organized local residents to put pressure on City Hall to clean up city streets, lobbied for an eight-hour workday for women, and helped pass Illinois's first child-labor law and the nation's first juvenile-court law. A landmark piece of legislation, the latter required the separation of children from adults in correctional facilities and prohibited any child under twelve from being detained in jail. A staunch supporter of equal rights and pacifism, Addams also campaigned for women's suffrage and spoke passionately against America's involvement in World War I, a highly controversial stance. During the 1920s, Addams continued to work for world peace and social justice and received the Nobel Peace Prize in 1931 for her efforts. Hull-House however, remains Addams's most important legacy, inspiring the establishment of hundreds of similar institutions across the country and helping shape public policy toward the poor.[37]

John Dewey, 1929. Dewey's progressive theories of education, developed at the University of Chicago, revolutionized teaching by emphasizing student participation rather than rote memorization.

Ella Flagg Young, c. 1909. As superintendant of Chicago Public Schools from 1909 to 1915, Flagg put into place many of John Dewey's new theories of education.

LEARNING BY DOING

John Dewey, Addams's contemporary and friend, was born in Burlington, Vermont, in 1859. He graduated from the University of Vermont in 1879 and received a doctorate from Johns Hopkins University five years later. After teaching at the state universities of Minnesota and Michigan, Dewey accepted a position at the University of Chicago in 1894 where he chaired the departments of philosophy, psychology, and pedagogy from 1895 to 1904. In 1896, Dewey organized the University of Chicago Laboratory School as a testing ground for his educational theories, which emphasized "learning by doing," problem solving, and judgment rather than rote memorization and strict discipline. One of the most important educational theorists in American history, Dewey believed this kind of approach would allow schools to be "major agencies for the development of free personalities" who would better serve and sustain a modern democratic society.[38]

Dewey stressed preparing children for adult roles in society, advocating manual arts programs for the classroom in the belief that they provided children with the opportunity to learn the rudimentary tasks of civilization: raising food, building shelter, making clothing. At the time, European schools were offering manual arts classes on a regular basis, but most schools in America still stressed book learning. With the publication of *The School and Society* (1900), Dewey proposed a manual arts program that would help students developing social and historical awareness as well as manual skills. At Dewey's lab school, children under ten cleaned, carded, spun, dyed, and wove wool and flax into cloth. Eleven- and twelve-year-olds studied the transition of the textile industry from domestic to factory production, while thirteen-year-olds made a complete study of the factory system and its history. From this progressive study, children not only learned about cloth, but also about raw materials, geography, tools, machinery, manufacturing, and distribution.[39]

Thanks to Ella Flagg Young, Dewey's approach became an integral part of the Chicago public school curriculum. Young, who trained under Colonel Parker at the Chicago Normal School, served as Chicago's first woman school superintendent between 1909 and 1915. A pragmatic reformer, Young believed that manual arts would better prepare students for the future, not merely as industrial workers but as active, engaged citizens who would support and sustain democracy. In 1912, Young appointed Edward F. Worst as supervisor of manual training and construction work for the elementary schools. Under his direction, students in the first through third grades received instruction in simple construction projects from their regular teachers. Fourth and fifth graders advanced to basketry, pottery, folio making, and bookbinding; boys also took light woodworking while girls learned to sew. In the sixth, seventh, and eight grades, boys learned mechanical drawing while girls took cooking

Dewey believed the approach of "learning by doing" would allow schools to be "major agencies for the development of free personalities" who would better serve, and sustain, a modern democratic society.

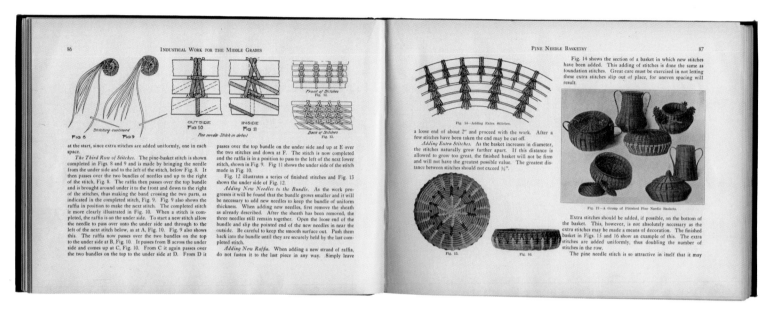

and sewing classes. Separate programs for the sexes remained standard practice throughout Worst's term, although he initiated a new, albeit temporary, program giving girls a chance to learn woodworking while boys took camp cooking.[40]

Worst believed that manual arts classes were more effective when they were linked to solving practical problems; he wrote, "in order to secure the child's best efforts, it is necessary that there should be a real motive back of the construction of each article." Manual arts remained an important part of Chicago's public school curriculum through the 1920s but its primary source of support shifted from educational reform to vocational training that stressed practical skills. Although Worst maintained his belief that manual arts were "pre-vocational and not trade training," he tried to meet the demand for vocational training by developing a two-tier manual arts program for the recently created junior high schools. While technical arts prepared students for vocational high schools, the "practical" division prepared other students for general studies. In addition to woodworking and mechanical drawing, Worst also introduced sheet metal, electricity, printing, and home economics to the grade schools. During the Great Depression of the 1930s, budget cuts and recommendations from Columbia University (where Dewey had gone after leaving the University of Chicago) to replace manual arts classes with technical classes, such as industrial chemistry and structural design, eliminated the manual arts program from the public schools.[41] Its basic premise, however, has survived to the present day with hands-on activities, self-directed learning, and research projects that require students to compile and interpret information on their own, rather than receiving it from an instructor. Although these methods come under attack from those who

Edward F. Worst's *Industrial Work for the Middle Grades,* 1919, included lessons on woodworking, basketry, pottery, and book-binding.

Edward F. Worst, craftsman, educator, and supervisor of manual arts in Chicago public schools for thirty years.

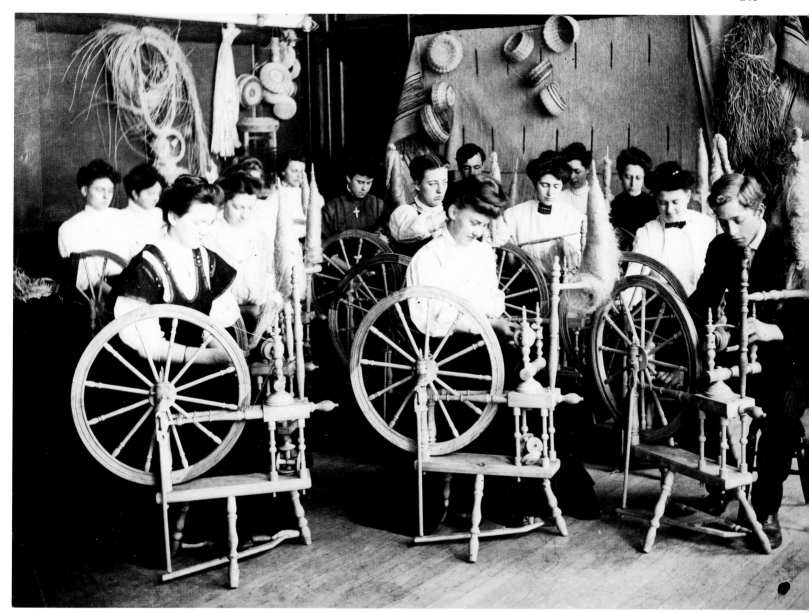

"Spinning Flax into Thread," one of the many steps involved in weaving, a manual arts class at the Chicago Normal School directed by Edward F. Worst in the early 1900s.

support more traditional methods that stress basic skills and the accumulation of knowledge, most public schools in America use progressive methodologies. Ultimately, John Dewey and his followers transformed American education into what we know today.

HERE WE ARE AGAIN!

A pioneer in early film and television, Chicago played a major role in shaping American popular culture. Once again, the city's position as a crossroads supported the effort by attracting creative minds, technical know-how, and ready capital, while its unparalleled distribution network resulted in broad reach and substantial profit. Although Chicago faced stiff competition from other cities and eventually lost both industries to the East and West coasts, its proud legacy

Left: George K. Spoor, c. 1910, cofounder of Essanay Studios in Chicago and pioneer of the early American film industry.

Right: Gilbert M. Anderson, c. 1910, cofounder of Essanay Studios in Chicago, also played Broncho Billy, cowboy star of the silver screen.

includes some of the most significant technical and creative achievements in celluloid history.

The history of Chicago's early film industry began in 1893 when Thomas Edison exhibited a new invention, the Kinetoscope, at the World's Columbian Exposition. Essentially a cabinet with a peephole on top, the Kinetoscope had revolving spools that ran a continuous strip of film (about fifty-feet long) over a lighted lens. The film contained still images, but as they passed over the light, they appeared to move. Although only one person at a time could peer through the peephole, the Kinetoscope astonished the public and inspired two Chicagoans to make "the flickers" a shared experience. In 1894, George K. Spoor, manager of the Waukegan Opera House who had seen a Kinetoscope in a Loop amusement parlor, began to experiment with projecting images on a wall so that a group of people could view them together. He discovered that a calcium lamp threw enough light through a lens to do the trick. Spoor sold his machine, known as the "Kinodrome," to vaudeville houses throughout the country and established a distribution company to supply them with rental films.[42]

About the same time, William N. Selig entered the picture. Born in Chicago in 1864, Selig grew up in California. As a young man, he worked as a magician with a touring minstrel show. Familiar with the Kinetoscope and "magic lantern" shows that delighted audiences, Selig saw the potential for something more. Returning to

Filming a Broncho Billy movie at Essanay Studios in Chicago, c. 1915. Broncho Billy, America's first cowboy hero of the silver screen, is the second figure from the left, wearing chaps and a white hat.

Chicago in 1895 or 1896, he opened a commercial photographic printing studio and developed a motion picture camera and projector based on the Lumiere machine, known as the Selig Standard Camera and Selig Polyscope projector, respectively. In 1897, he established the Selig Polyscope Studio, quite possibly the first commercial motion picture studio in America. At first, Selig shot industrial films, which brought in much-needed cash, but he gradually moved into feature films with plot lines and recognizable characters. His first such film, *The Tramp and the Dog*, lasted ninety seconds; by 1904, Selig was making longer melodramas that lasted as long as ten minutes. Although short by today's standards, these silent films thrilled audiences unaccustomed to seeing moving pictures on a large screen. Achieving success, Selig moved from a small studio south of the Loop on Peck Court to larger facilities at Irving Park Road and Western Avenue; he also established a branch in California where better weather permitted year round filming on location. In Chicago, Selig's company either filmed in the studio under flood lamps or outdoors on quiet back streets and empty lots. Melodramas, serial cliffhangers, and westerns remained the company's stock-in-trade for years, making actors such as Kathlyn Williams and Tom Mix household names across America.[43]

Like Selig, George K. Spoor moved into production. In 1907, he formed Essanay Studios with the popular actor Gilbert M. Anderson (the first letters of each man's last name — "S" and "A" — formed the studio's name). Anderson, whose real name was Max Aaronson, had starred in the Edison Company's classic film, *The Great Train Robbery*, shot in New York City. Essanay had offices on Clark Street in downtown Chicago and a large studio at 1333–45 West Argyle Street on the North Side. Under Spoor's direction, Anderson, a former vaudevillian who had never ridden a horse before, became "Broncho Billy," the first western movie star and one of the most popular characters in film history. Together, they produced more than three hundred westerns, making the genre an American standard. Typically, the films followed a simple plotline in which the hero battles a gang of outlaws while winning the affections of a pretty girl. Essanay also made hundreds of melodramas, employing dozens of actors, including Francis X. Bushman, America's first matinee idol; Gloria Swanson; and Wallace Beery, who also became major stars. Even Charlie Chaplin worked for Essanay, but shot only one film in Chicago, *His New Job* (1915),

Essanay Studios cameraman's button, c. 1910, featured a Plains Indian head logo that also appeared on company newsletters and correspondence.

During the early 1900s, Chicago moviemakers produced scores of silent melodramas, western adventures, and serial cliffhangers, shipping them across America via the railroad.

Opposite: As the February 27, 1915, edition of *Essanay News* reveals, the Chicago studio employed some of the silver screen's biggest stars, including Francis X. Bushman, Gilbert M. Anderson, and the legendary Charlie Chaplin.

Urban Bioscope movie camera used by Essanay Studios, c. 1910. Note the company's name across the upper side of the box.

before moving to California where he made several more movies for Essanay before joining another studio for more money.[44]

Normally shot in a few days for a minimal budget, movies made in Chicago reached a broad audience. After shooting ended, skilled technicians processed the film and spliced shorter strips together to create a continuous loop. Studios then rushed completed films to thousands of small theaters across the country known as nickelodeons (which charged a five-cent admission fee) via Chicago's extensive rail network that reached every section of the country. In addition, both studios advertised extensively with posters, broadsides, newspaper advertisements, and in the case of Essanay, a weekly illustrated newspaper that highlighted recent movies and well-known actors. Some advertising, like the movies themselves, appeared to glorify crime and immorality. Many people, including Jane Addams, considered the movies a threat to youth and demanded some form of control, which resulted in the City Council passing a resolution in 1906 banning movies that presented crime in a favorable light. The next year, an amendment passed requiring theaters to obtain a police permit before showing any movie at all.[45]

While Selig and Essanay remained the largest studios, other moviemakers worked in Chicago, including several African American firms. They included Foster Photoplay Company, established in 1913, and the Ebony Film Corporation, founded in 1917 by Luther Pollard, who focused on making slapstick comedies using black actors. Around 1915, Oscar Micheaux, the son of former slaves born in Metropolis, Illinois, who moved to Chicago at age seventeen to work as a Pullman Porter, established the Micheaux Film Corporation. He based his first production, *The Homesteader*, on his life as a farmer in South Dakota during the early 1900s. Prior to making the film, Micheaux had written and published a novel about his experience, but refused to sell the rights to an African American film company in Lincoln, Nebraska. Instead, he decided to make the film himself. An eight-reel film, *The Homesteader* portrayed African Americans as dignified people in real-life situations, a far cry from most productions of the time, including Selig's and Essanay's, which portrayed blacks as stereotypical buffoons. Premiering on February 20, 1919, at the 8th Armory Regiment on the South Side, *The Homesteader* won praise from audiences and critics alike. The *Chicago Defender*, the city's leading black newspaper, claimed the movie to be "the greatest of all Race productions." Later that same year, Micheaux released *Within Our Gates* in response to D. W. Griffith's racially charged *Birth of a Nation*. Micheaux's film contained a controversial lynching scene that some feared would inflame Chicago's black community, recently devastated by the 1919 Race Riot. Despite efforts to ban the film, *Within Our Gates* debuted in Chicago the following January to much acclaim, and while it played to packed houses, no rioting occurred. Over the next thirty years, Micheaux continued to make films that portrayed African Americans in a positive light, reflecting his belief that "the colored man can do anything." His many achievements include the technique of cross-cutting, first used in *Within Our Gates*, to create suspense; the "dream flash-back" technique; and the first all-talking film made by a black company, *The Exile*, released in 1931.[46]

Although Micheaux remained in Chicago, the local industry was in decline before World War I. Most companies moved to southern California, attracted by the new studios in Hollywood, a milder climate for year round shooting, and better scenery, a critical factor for making realistic films, especially the ever-popular westerns. A serious blow came in 1915 when several Chicago film producers lost an antitrust suit filed against Thomas Edison for controlling industry patents, a financial blow from which they never recovered. Compelled by this loss, and Chaplin's earlier departure, Gilbert Anderson sold his share of Essanay Studios to Spoor, who closed the studio in 1918 and moved to California. He continued to work in the industry, developing the Natural Vision System for widescreen 3-D films, which, in his words, added, "the vital touch—reality and life" to moving pictures. In 1948, both Spoor and Selig received an honorary Oscar from the Academy of Motion Pictures for their work, cited as belonging to a "small group of pioneers whose belief in a new medium and whose contribution to its development blazed the trail along which the motion picture has progressed, in their lifetime, from obscurity to worldwide acclaim."[47]

Although its film industry died, Chicago re-emerged as a hub of celluloid creativity after World War II, developing a unique style of broadcast communication known as the Chicago School of Television. Then as now, the television industry had three major networks based in New York City—NBC, CBS, and ABC—as well as a number of independent local stations scattered across the country. During the late 1940s, the major networks established affiliated stations in cities like Chicago to expand their audience. NBC's station, WNBQ, took television creativity to new heights under the direction of station manager Jules Herbuveaux and program manager Ted Mills.[48]

Contrary to the heavily scripted television shows produced in New York and Los Angeles—similar to theatrical or movie productions—those made at WNBQ used a different approach, one that recognized both the opportunities and limitations of a new medium, in particular its intimate nature that brought performers directly into viewers' homes. Working with original ideas, but small budgets and even smaller studios, WNBQ's players produced a distinctive style, characterized by creative camera-work and an extemporaneous, improvisational method of performance. As described by *Look* magazine in 1951, Chicago television had a "relaxed, intimate, friendly, natural, subtle" style, but most important, viewers did not know what to "expect next and next and next."[49]

During a brief "golden era" that lasted from 1948 until 1953, WNBQ produced a number of high-quality programs. The roster includes *Zoo Parade* with Lincoln Park Zoo curator Marlin Perkins; *Mr. Wizard*, an educational science program starring

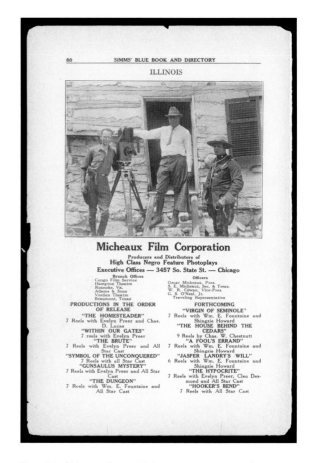

Based in Chicago, Oscar Micheaux became one of the nation's leading African American producers and remained active through the 1930s.

Chicago emerged as a hub of celluloid creativity after World War II, developing a unique style of innovative programming known as the Chicago School of Television.

A group shot of the NBC Studios casts and sets includes, from left to right: *Kukla, Fran, and Ollie* with Burr Tillstrom, *Studs' Place* with Studs Terkel, and Dave Garroway, reclining on the couch and raising his hand in trademark sign-off wave.

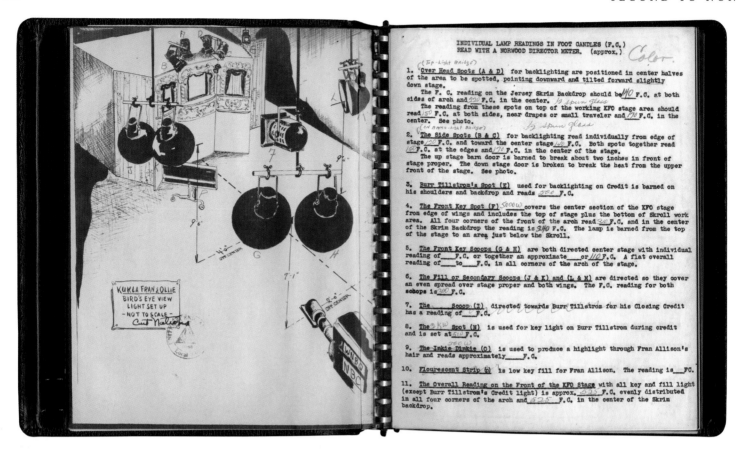

Stage and lighting directions for the *Kukla, Fran, and Ollie* show, c. 1950. The simplicity of the set allowed for the improvisational style preferred—and perfected—by Burr Tillstrom.

Don Herbert; *Ding Dong School*, aimed at preschool children with host Dr. "Miss Frances" Horwich; *Walt's Workshop*, a "how-to" home-repair program with Walt Durban; *Short Story Playhouse*, featuring Professor Robert Breen of Northwestern University and a local repertory troupe; and *Portrait of America*, which took viewers into the homes of Chicagoans to discuss family problems. Although short-lived, these path-breaking shows paved the way for later programs, such as *Wild Kingdom*, *Mister Rogers*, and today's reality shows. Three of WNBQ's most popular shows— *Studs' Place*, *Garroway at Large*, and *Kukla, Fran, and Ollie*— were all broadcast live (but without a studio audience) from the Merchandise Mart. A transmission cable between New York and Chicago, completed by American Telephone and Telegraph in 1948, allowed NBC to air these programs nationally. They attracted millions of viewers, making Chicago, not New York, "Television Town," according to radio legend Fred Allen.[50]

Similar to the latter-day *Cheers*, *Studs' Place* was set in a neighborhood tavern/ restaurant. It featured the well-known Chicago actor and radio personality Studs Terkel as the proprietor, Beverly Younger as Gracie the waitress, blues piano player Chet Roble, and folk singer Win Stracke in real-life situations. Essentially, they played themselves, working from a two-page outline rather than a script and improvising the dialogue. *Studs' Place* first aired in 1949 as part of a larger variety program, *Saturday Night Square*, and returned the following April as its own freestanding show. The low-key, offbeat show failed to attract a sponsor and ran on WNBQ for only one season. In 1951, ABC picked up the show, televised from the studios of WENR, located in the Civic Theater, but also canceled it after one season for lack of a national sponsor.[51]

One of the most influential programs in television history, *Garroway at Large* inspired later programs such as *That Was the Week That Was, Saturday Night Live,* and comedy skits on David Letterman's *Late Show.*

Two of the most creative minds in television history, Burr Tillstrom (above) and Dave Garroway (below) on the occasion of Garroway's guest appearance on *Kukla, Fran, and Ollie,* c. 1950.

Kukla and Ollie hand puppets made by Burr Tillstrom, c. 1950. Tillstrom's genius lay in his ability to give each puppet a distinct personality and unique charm.

Also debuting in 1949 on WNBQ, *Garroway at Large* featured Dave Garroway as the host of a musical variety show. Originally from Schenectady, New York, Garroway graduated from Washington University in St. Louis and attended NBC's school for announcers in New York City before moving to Chicago in 1939 to work as a late-night disc jockey for WMAQ radio. After serving in the navy during World War II, Garroway returned to Chicago and began his television career. Working with three other young writers (Charlie Andrews, producer Ted Mills, and director Bill Hobin, a former drummer), Garroway developed a basic concept for each program, rather than a detailed script. The approach allowed the cast to perform in an off-handed manner that looked totally spontaneous, but actually required eight hours of rehearsal. Broadcast at 10:00 p.m. on Sunday evenings, the program featured Garroway roaming around the set, discussing a variety of topics (some ludicrous), and introducing popular musical acts and humorous skits. Wacky visuals, such as

Burr Tillstrom with Kukla, Ollie, and Fran Allison greeting children, c. 1948. The long-running Chicago program entertained several generations of children and their parents.

cameras filming each other, or Garroway opening a small curtain in front of a painting to reveal a moving picture, kept the show lively and fun. Critically acclaimed at the time, *Garroway at Large* inspired later programs such as *That Was The Week That Was* and *Saturday Night Live*, as well as comedy skits on the David Letterman and Jay Leno late night shows. Although *Garroway at Large* attracted more than three million viewers, NBC ended its run in June 1951 after the show lost its sponsor.[52]

Kukla, Fran, and Ollie was the brainchild of Burr Tillstrom, a Chicago native. As a child, he had entertained family and friends with his own puppet shows and remarkable ability to mimic many different types of voices. After attending the University of Chicago for one year during the Great Depression, Tillstrom joined

160

the Chicago Park District's puppet theater, operated by the Works Progress Administration (WPA). In 1936, Tillstrom created a small puppet for a friend, but could not bear to part with him. By chance, a Russian ballerina saw the puppet and named it "Kukla," the Russian name for "doll" and a term of endearment. In 1939, Tillstrom appeared with Kukla and other puppets at the New York world's fair, serving as the warm-up act for a marionette show. In total, Tillstrom staged more than two thousand shows, but disliking repetition, he continuously improvised, creating a fresh show each time by interacting with the audience, as well as actresses and models working at the fair. Returning to Chicago, Tillstrom managed a puppet theater at Marshall Field's department store and performed at local hospitals for the USO during World War II. At a bond rally, he met Fran Allison, a popular radio star of Don McNeill's *Breakfast Club*, and asked her to join his act on a trial basis. The two became good friends and fruitful collaborators, creating a witty, warm show that delighted audience of all ages.[53]

Tillstrom and the Kuklapolitans began their television career on Chicago's local station, WBKB, in 1947 with a daily hour-long program. When NBC bought the station in 1948, *Kukla, Fran, and Ollie* became a national treasure. It featured a colorful cast of hand puppets, all worked by Burr and each radiating a distinct personality, interacting with the multitalented Fran. Led by the sweet-natured Kukla and the mischievous Oliver J. Dragon, the show's memorable cast featured Madame Ophelia Ooglepuss, Buelah Witch, Fletcher Rabbit, Cecil Bill, Mercedes, and Colonel Crackie, all voiced by Tillstrom. The program was originally intended for children, but it also appealed to adult viewers with its witty dialogue, references to current events, and simple lessons on human kindness. Loosely scripted by Burr, with help from Fran, director Lewis Gomavitz, musical director Jack Fascinato, costume designer Joe Lockwood, and producer Beulah Zachary, the show featured humorous skits and musical numbers, including its popular theme song, "Here We Are (Again)!"[54]

The program aired nightly, attracting legions of viewers and critical acclaim. the *New York Times* described the show as "the most charming and heart-warming excursion into pure make-believe that is to be found in television today" while *Life* magazine featured the program in a three-page article in its May 23, 1949, issue. By its third season, the program boasted six million viewers and an avalanche of fan mail. However, in 1951, NBC cut the program to fifteen minutes because it lacked a commercial sponsor and eventually moved the program to Sunday afternoons. When ABC picked up the show in 1954, it returned to a daily broadcast and remained on the air until 1957. Nominated for excellence on numerous occasions, *Kukla, Fran, and Ollie* won an Emmy Award for Best Children's Program in 1949. An enduring presence, the Kuklapolitans remained on television in various formats until 1979.[55]

Although Chicago played a major role in shaping early television, the city's influence quickly waned. As early as 1950, the major networks began to shorten or cut

The Vast Wasteland

In a memorable and oft-quoted address delivered on May 9, 1961, Newton N. Minow, chairman of the Federal Communications Commission, challenged the National Association of Broadcasters "to sit down in front of your television set . . . until the station signs off. I can assure you that you will observe a vast wasteland." Appointed by President John F. Kennedy, Minow, a prominent Chicago attorney and civic leader, believed that television had shirked public service in favor of escapist entertainment that dulled viewers' intellect and understanding of the world. Minow's speech articulated a growing concern about television's impact on society and played a role in establishing a public television network (PBS) in 1969. Decades later, when viewers have access to hundreds of stations with round-the-clock programming, Minow's critique still packs a punch.[56]

Newton N. Minow, chairman of the Federal Communications Commission, 1961.

The Birth of the Atomic Age by Gary Sheahan. Oil on board, 1957.

No cameras or artists were present at the event, but Chicago artist Gary Sheahan worked from eyewitness accounts to depict the world's first nuclear chain reaction, the first step in developing the atomic bomb for use in World War II.

Chicago shows from the schedule, replacing them with programs filmed in New York City. Not only did New York have more advertising dollars than Chicago, its position as the industry's headquarters gave networks more control over the creative process and final product. Simultaneously, key personnel left Chicago for more lucrative careers elsewhere, including such notable figures as Dave Garroway, who moved to New York to host the *Today* show. Finally, the extension of a coast-to-coast cable in 1953 allowed New York stations to broadcast their programs nationwide. By 1955, the major networks did not carry any Chicago-produced programs, signaling the end of one of the most creative chapters in television history.[57]

THE FIRST NUCLEAR CHAIN REACTION

On December 2, 1942, at 3:25 P.M. a small team of scientists at the University of Chicago achieved the world's first self-sustaining nuclear chain reaction: a truly momentous accomplishment with enormous consequences. In 1939, shortly after the outbreak of World War II, Albert Einstein warned President Franklin D. Roosevelt about German efforts to build an atomic bomb. Greatly alarmed by prospects of the Nazi government having such a powerful weapon, Roosevelt authorized the National Defense Research Committee (NDRC) to study the feasibility of making atomic weapons for the war effort. Officially known as the Manhattan Project, the highly secretive effort ultimately resulted in the development of the atomic bomb that ended World War II and ushered in the nuclear age.

Headed by Vannevar Bush, president of the Carnegie Institution, the NDRC included a Committee on Uranium charged with achieving a controlled nuclear

On December 2, 1942, a team of scientists led by Enrico Fermi achieved the world's first self-sustaining nuclear chain reaction under the stands of the Stagg Field football stadium at the University of Chicago.

reaction. The committee, reorganized in June 1941 as part of the Office of Scientific Research and Development (OSRD), became known as OSRD Section One, or S1. Six months later, on December 6, 1941, one day before the Japanese attack on Pearl Harbor, S1 came under the direction of Arthur H. Compton, a physics professor at the University of Chicago. Compton oversaw the research at several universities, including Columbia and Princeton, but in mid-January 1942, he decided to bring the entire project to the Metallurgical Laboratory (Met Lab) at the University of Chicago.[58]

As the nation's rail center, Chicago provided easy access to other parts of the country, and its distance from either coast provided the top-secret project with an extra measure of protection from enemy attack. Among those heading to Chicago from Columbia University was Enrico Fermi, an Italian physicist who had received the Nobel Prize in 1938 for his work on uranium. Shortly after receiving the prize, Fermi and his family fled Europe for America. The Italian press had harshly criticized Fermi for not wearing a Fascist uniform to the ceremony and for failing to give the Fascist salute when he received the award. In addition, Fermi and his Jewish wife, Laura, felt increasingly uncomfortable staying in Europe as the German Nazis expanded their power.[59]

Described by his colleagues as "completely self-confident but wholly without conceit," Fermi directed the project in Chicago. Under his guidance, two construction crews built an "atomic pile" known as CP-1 in an abandoned squash court beneath the west stands of Stagg Field football stadium. Braced with wooden timbers, the large oval pile consisted of uranium pellets embedded in a matrix of machine-planed graphite blocks. What happened next is best explained by Fermi himself:

Enrico Fermi, left in the front row, and the team of scientists responsible for the first sustained nuclear chain reaction, 1946.

> With sufficient uranium in the pile, the few neutrons emitted in a single fission that may accidentally occur strike neighboring atoms, which in turn undergo fission and produce more neutrons. These bombard other atoms and so on at an increasing rate until the atomic "fire" is going full blast.
>
> The atomic pile is controlled and prevented from burning itself to complete destruction by cadmium rods, which absorb neutrons and stop the bombardment process. The same effect might be achieved by running a pipe of cold water through a rubbish heap; by keeping the temperature low the pipe would prevent the spontaneous burning.
>
> The first atomic chain reaction experiment was designed to proceed at a slow rate. In this sense, it differed from the atomic bomb, which was designed to precede at as fast a rate as was possible. Otherwise the basic process is similar to that of the atomic bomb.[60]

Essentially the world's first nuclear reactor, Fermi's structure served as the model for nuclear reactors subsequently built at Oak Ridge, Tennessee, and Hanford, Washington, which produced the necessary materials (i.e., plutonium) for atomic weapons.

A photograph of the world's first nuclear pile taken during its construction shows dozens of uranium pellets embedded in graphite blocks. Note the "No Smoking" sign against the far wall.

In 1943, a new laboratory for the actual building of the bomb opened in Los Alamos, New Mexico, under the direction of J. Robert Oppenheimer. The first test explosive occurred on July 16, 1945, at the White Sands Missile Range near Alamogordo, New Mexico. On August 6, 1945, the United States dropped the first atomic bomb on Hiroshima, Japan, killing seventy thousand people, injuring another seventy thousand and devastating five square miles. Three days later, the United States dropped a second bomb on Nagasaki, killing forty thousand people and injuring sixty thousand. On August 14, the Japanese surrendered, ending World War II.[61]

A stunning achievement, the atomic bomb changed world history. During the Cold War, a dangerous nuclear arms race between Russia and the United States threatened world survival while Germany, France, and Israel developed their own nuclear weapons. More recently, India and Pakistan joined the nuclear league and nations such as Korea and Iran strive for the same goal. In addition to weapons use, atomic power is used for peaceful means. During the 1960s and 1970s, nuclear power plants were built throughout North America and Europe. Although they are a good source of renewable energy, accidents at Three Mile Island and Chernobyl dimmed industry prospects, and what to do with plant waste remains a challenge.[62]

Frank Colton working in the Searle laboratory, c. 1952.

THE BIRTH CONTROL PILL

I n 1960, G. D. Searle and Company helped launch the sexual revolution with the introduction of the birth control pill. This story also illustrates how Chicago serves as a crossroads of ideas and resources from many different sources. Searle, a pharmaceutical company established by Civil War veteran Gideon D. Searle, moved from Omaha, Nebraska, to the North Side of Chicago in the late 1890s. Between 1925 and 1941, Searle occupied a building in the Ravenswood neighborhood on the city's North Side. In 1942, Searle moved to new state-of-the-art facilities in Skokie, a suburb located about ten miles north of Chicago.

In 1951, a young scientist named Frank Colton joined the company. Born in Poland in 1923, Colton immigrated to the U.S. in 1934, and obtained advanced degrees in chemistry from Northwestern University and the University of Chicago. While working for Searle, Colton developed a synthetic progesterone compound, norethynodrel. Originally intended to treat gynecological disorders, the drug, actually a steroid taken in oral form, also inhibited ovulation. In its natural form, progesterone is secreted by a woman's ovary prior to the implantation of a fertilized ovum. Synthetic progesterone "tricks" the body with a signal that conception has occurred; the body then suppresses ovulation, which prevents a real pregnancy from occurring.

Margaret Sanger (top) and Katharine McCormick (above), whose efforts and financial support made the birth control pill possible.

Searle's development of the birth control pill in the late 1950s helped launch the sexual revolution and women's liberation movement while stirring controversy among those who opposed its use on moral grounds.

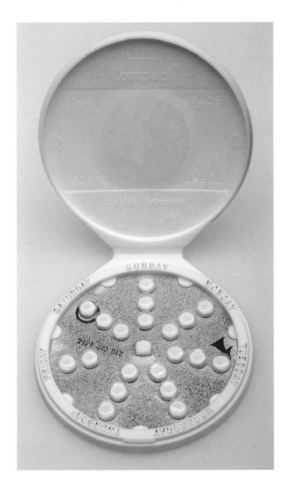

Ovulen Compack birth control pill dispenser manufactured by Searle and Company, c. 1977.

Simultaneously, Gregory Pincus, head of a Shrewsbury, Massachusetts lab, had been working to develop a new form of birth control. He was supported by the feminist Margaret Sanger and funded by Katharine Dexter McCormick, wealthy heiress to the reaper fortune. Pincus found that the hormone progesterone impedes ovulation in rabbits, but needed a synthetic hormone to manufacture a birth control pill.[63]

When Pincus approached Searle about developing a synthetic birth control pill that could be used in human trials, he discovered Colton had already done so. The company, however, did not want to pursue birth control products. Thirty states had anti–birth control laws on the books, and the Roman Catholic Church, which had a sizeable membership in the United States, took a firm stance against all forms of contraceptions except the officially sanctioned rhythm method. In addition, many people doubted that women would take a daily drug that did not cure or control a disease.[64]

Searle decided to supply Pincus and Dr. John Rock, a New York gynecologist, with enough pills to conduct human trials with fifty women but they did not go public with the news. Pincus and Rock actually tested pills from Searle and from Syntex, a company based in Mexico City. In the end, they selected Searle's product, named Enovid. In 1956, Pincus and Rock conducted the first large-scale clinical trials using Enovid in San Juan, Puerto Rico, which did not have anti–birth control laws.[65]

Further testing conducted in Haiti and Mexico City paved the way for the Food and Drug Administration's (FDA) approval of Evonid in 1957 as a treatment for menstrual disorders but with the warning that it suppressed ovulation. Evonid's soaring popularity prompted Searle to apply to the FDA for a license to market the pill as a contraceptive. By 1960, Evonid sales reached thirty-seven million dollars. Searle marketed the pill to women around the world, and, for a brief time, retained a monopoly. During the 1960s, however, several other companies developed their own versions of the pill. Despite increased competition and reports that Evonid caused serious side effects, including blood clots and heart attacks, Searle reaped handsome profits (twenty-four million dollars alone in 1964).

By giving women control over their reproductive cycles, the Pill transformed society. It helped launch the sexual revolution of the 1960s, when many traditional restrictions regarding sex fell away, and the women's liberation movement. The Pill also stirred controversy, especially in the Catholic Church, which took a strong stance against its use on the grounds that it interfered with God's natural order. Some Catholics disagreed, however, and the issue remains controversial.

"But, Wait! There's More!"

Reflecting the city's diverse economic base, Chicago has produced a wide array of innovative products for everyday use. Mass marketed and distributed nationwide and overseas, many of these products have become icons of the American experience, part and parcel of the modern landscape of consumer goods that shape our lives and memories. Some of the best-known Chicago products include Lincoln Logs, Tinkertoys, Schwinn bicycles, Weber Grills, Rand McNally maps, Morton Salt, Quaker Oats, and Wrigley Gum. Other well-known Chicago products include Radio Flyer wagons, Sunbeam appliances, Lava Lamps, Playskool educational toys, Bell & Howell cameras, Brunswick bowling balls, Zenith remote controls, World Book Encyclopedia, *Ebony* and *Jet* magazines, and last, but not least, handy household gadgets developed by the Popeil Family, including the Veg-o-Matic and Pocket Fisherman. While most of these products are no longer manufactured in Chicago, many have joined the ranks of popular collectibles and can be found in museum collections, recognized as telling reminders of the American past.

Chicago innovators have developed some of the most familiar products in American history. They include: Tinkertoys, Lincoln Logs, Schwinn bicycles, Yakkity-Yak Talking Teeth, the Mousetrap Game, Veg-o-Matic, the remote control, and Weber Grills.

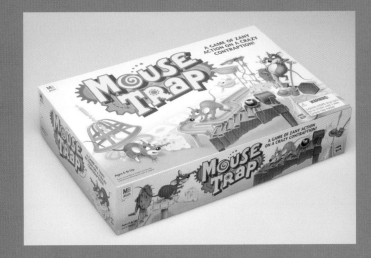

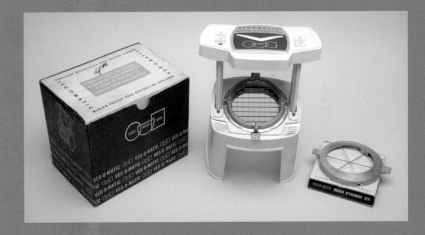

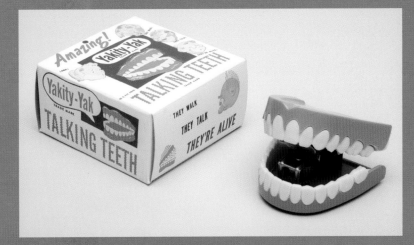

"Chicago is one town
that won't let you down."

Sammy Cahn and James VanHeusen, 1964

Chapter Five

MY KIND OF TOWN

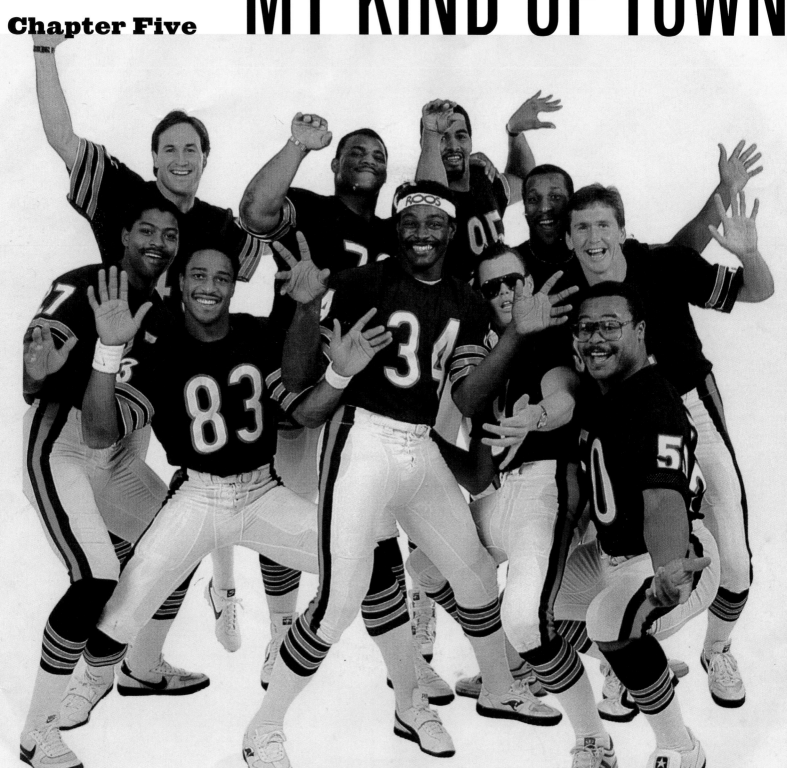

Immortalized in song as "My Kind of Town," Chicago has been a vibrant crossroads of the cultural arts and popular entertainment throughout its history. As Chicago grew from a raw frontier settlement into a bustling metropolis, civic leaders, who wished to edify the public, along with ambitious entrepreneurs who pursued profit, established a wide variety of cultural institutions and recreational facilities throughout the city. By 1850, Chicago had several downtown theaters, including those operated by John B. Rice and James H. McVickers. Crosby's Opera House, opening in 1865, quickly established itself as a leading venue for touring musicals. The following year, a group of local artists established the Chicago Academy of Design, precursor of the Art Institute of Chicago. Citizens led the movement to establish the South, West, and Lincoln Park Commissions in 1869, and in the spring of 1871, the Chicago White Stockings debuted as the city's first professional baseball team.

Largely destroyed by the Great Fire of 1871, Chicago's nascent cultural scene exploded during the aftermath. Scores of theaters, music and dance halls, hotels, and restaurants sprang up, primarily in the downtown area, which enjoyed the benefits of converging transportation systems. In 1891, the Chicago Symphony Orchestra played its first concert at the Auditorium Theater, a watershed moment in the city's cultural development. Together, these venues and institutions signaled Chicago's arrival as a leading cultural hub, certainly of the Midwest but also of the nation, as East Coast and European artists, crisscrossing the country by rail, made frequent stops in Chicago to appreciative audiences.

Directors, artists, and sculptors of the World's Columbian Exposition, 1892. The fair's chief of construction and director of works, Daniel Burnham, is on the far left.

The 1893 World's Columbian Exposition greatly enhanced Chicago's position as a cultural crossroads. Scores of people from throughout the country and around the world visited Chicago during the run of the fair and left with vivid memories of the host city being a much more interesting and refined place than its reputation as a "porkopolis" had led them to believe. Indeed, the 1893 fair made Chicago a cultural mecca, attracting increasing numbers of American and foreign visitors who wished to see the much-heralded city. Chicago's cultural attractions fostered the growth of a new industry—tourism—that played an increasingly significant role in fueling the city's economy.

THE 1893 WORLD'S COLUMBIAN EXPOSITION

Chicago's first world's fair drew more than twenty million people to the city. A spectacular event, the fair attracted attention around the world, reinforcing Chicago's position as a national and international crossroads and a cultural hub. A product of its time, the fair embodied a set of cultural values that ultimately delivered a powerful message about American achievement and superiority. Staged at a time when the United States was just beginning to emerge as a global power, the fair helped form a national identity and sense of purpose that persisted long after the fairgrounds closed.

Indeed, fair organizers had national goals in mind all along. Talk of a fair to commemorate the four-hundredth anniversary of Christopher Columbus's journey to the New World in 1492 began in the early 1880s. Americans had just celebrated the centennial of the nation's birth with the Philadelphia Exposition of 1876, and it

Ivory and gold scepter created by Spaulding and Company of Chicago and presented to Daniel Burnham in honor of his work on the 1893 World's Columbian Exposition.

The Electricity Building, World's Columbian Exposition of 1893, by Childe Hassam.

The extensive use of electricity at the fair astonished visitors, many of whom were from rural areas or small towns with little or no electricity.

seemed logical to stage another grand event. Furthermore, Paris was readying for an international exposition in 1889 and those plans prompted Americans to think along similar lines. Staging a world's fair in the New World would give the young nation an opportunity to demonstrate its accomplishments to the Old World. Having survived the Civil War and a five-year recession during the 1870s, the United States was enjoying a period of sustained growth and prosperity. On a local level, Chicago fared well during the 1880s. Its industries and transportation networks boomed, swelling the city's population to more than one million by 1890.[1]

Thus, when talk of a world's fair began to circulate, Chicago threw its hat into the ring of contenders that also included St. Louis, New York City, and Washington, D.C. These cities vied for the fair, not only for the prestige it would bring but for the economic boon it would create. In the end, the contest came down to New York and Chicago and the two cities waged a fierce debate in the daily newspapers. To settle the dispute, Congress held public hearings in April 1890 for each city to plead its case. Chicago Mayor De Witt C. Creiger made a strong argument for his city based on its central location; simply put, more people living in the Midwest and Great Plains would be able to reach a fair held in Chicago rather than in New York. In the end, Congress awarded the prize to Chicago, not only because of its location, but also because its financial backers, led by banker Lyman J. Gage, had raised more money than New York's supporters. In making their decision, Congress defined a three-fold purpose for the fair: to celebrate the four-hundredth anniversary of Columbus's landing in America, to exhibit America's vast resources, and to demonstrate the

The World's Columbian Exposition of 1893, by Lawrence Carmichael Earle, captures the glowing luminosity of the Grand Basin with the towering statue of the Republic facing the Administration Building.

progress of Western civilization in the New World. Finally, Congress pushed the fair's date back to 1893 to allow more time for preparation.[2]

Harlow N. Higinbotham, fair president, and Daniel H. Burnham, chief of construction (later he was appointed director of works), oversaw the massive project. After much debate, organizers selected Jackson Park, adjacent to Lake Michigan on the South Side, as the fair's site. Previous world's fairs in Philadelphia (1876) and Paris (1889) inspired their efforts, but they imagined a far grander event, one that would prove their sprawling city could host an international event of such magnitude. Burnham's approach to the fair reflected these lofty ambitions. After convincing authorities that it would be better to invite the best American architects to design the fair, rather than hold a competition, Burnham selected several prominent East Coast firms, including Richard Morris Hunt and McKim, Mead, and White of New York City, widely considered to be America's leading architects. Criticized by some for not selecting any Chicago firms, Burnham explained that his choices gave the fair a national, rather than a regional scope. He agreed, however, to select five Chicago firms, including Adler & Sullivan, to design buildings outside the central Court of Honor, which he reserved for the East Coast architects. In designing the fair, Burnham and his team adopted a neoclassical style that resulted in a harmonious suite of palatial buildings resembling those found in European cities. Although the fair's buildings were temporary structures made of steel and wooden frames with applied plaster, their style, massive scale, and chalky color created the illusion of an imperial "White City" set within Frederick Law Olmsted's landscape of interlocking canals, placid lagoons, and lush gardens.[3]

Unlike previous world's fairs, which primarily focused on comparing industrial machinery and products to determine their marketability, Chicago's fair sought to teach visitors about the progress and beneficial effects of Western civilization as compared to more "primitive" societies. Burnham's plan supported this message with five majestic buildings—Manufactures and Liberal Arts, Agriculture, Machinery Hall, Mines and Mining, and Electricity—in a central Court of Honor. They surrounded the Grand Basin, a large pool of water with a colossal, gold leaf Statue of the Republic, designed by Daniel Chester French. It stood sixty-five-feet tall on a forty-

One of many guidebooks to the 1893 world's fair, the International Guide emphasized attractions from other countries with an emphasis on the exotic. The "peaceable kingdom" is suggested by the lion and lamb figures below the Statue of Liberty.

Debuting at the 1893 World's Columbian Exposition, the Ferris Wheel had thirty-six cars that held more than two thousand passengers. Not surprisingly, the ride became the fair's most popular attraction and inspired a host of smaller imitators across the country.

foot base, exuding a sense of strength and power befitting a nation poised to assume a larger role in global affairs. On the opposite side stood the Administration Building, official headquarters of the fair, and the magnificent Columbian Fountain, designed by Frederick MacMonnies.[4]

Each building on the Court of Honor housed extensive displays of machinery, inventions, and products intended to showcase Western civilization's accomplishments. Outside the court, buildings such as Fine Arts and Transportation featured similar displays and provided a sharp contrast to those found in the Anthropology Building on the far southeast side of the fairgrounds. There, visitors found displays of anthropological objects collected from indigenous people in North and South America and archaeological artifacts retrieved from Native American sites. These exhibitions conveyed a deliberate message about the cultural inferiority of native people to European and American whites represented elsewhere at the fair.[5]

The Midway Plaisance, a mile-long avenue of entertainment located off the main fairgrounds, repeated the same message of cultural superiority. In addition to the world's first Ferris Wheel, a spectacular attraction, the Midway featured numerous ethnic villages and street scenes arranged in a manner that allowed visitors to trace human evolution. Like those at European fairs, these displays included a "primitive" African village, "exotic" streets of Cairo, and "more advanced" Irish and German folk villages.[6]

Although present on the Midway, African Americans were absent from the main fairgrounds. The exclusion reflected, and reinforced, the nation's increasing adherence to racial segregation. In the South, Jim Crow practices cast blacks into a separate, unequal world from whites. Although fewer blacks lived in the North, they, too, faced racial discrimination on a daily basis and, for the most part, lived in separate communities. The fair's exclusion of blacks came under attack from the noted

African American civil rights leader Ida B. Wells. Born into slavery in Holly Springs, Mississippi, in 1862, Wells attended Shaw University before teaching school in Memphis, Tennessee. While in Memphis, Wells became co-owner of a black militant newspaper, *Free Speech and Headlight*, for which she wrote extensive articles about civil rights issues, focusing on the growing number of black lynchings in the South. In 1892, after whites destroyed her office and threatened her life, Wells moved to New York City where she continued her anti-lynching campaign on a national level. By 1893, Wells had attained national and international stature, giving her a platform to protest the exclusion of blacks from the fair. Together with the noted abolitionist Frederick Douglass and Ferdinand L. Barnett, a black lawyer from Chicago with militant views, Wells published the pamphlet *The Reason Why the Colored American Is Not in the World's Columbian Exposition*. Wells also encouraged blacks to boycott the fair on Colored American Day (August 25), a position not shared by Douglass, who believed blacks should be part of the public festivities and visited the fairgrounds on numerous other occasions.[7]

White women received slightly better treatment. In awarding the fair to Chicago, Congress mandated the creation of a Board of Lady Managers to include women in the planning. Bertha Honoré Palmer, a wealthy socialite from Chicago,

Ida B. Wells, c. 1892, civil rights activist and author of *The Reason Why the Colored American Is Not in the World's Columbian Exposition*, which criticized the exclusion of African Americans from the fair's planning and exhibits.

On the Midway, fair-goers enjoyed a wide array of activities, including camel rides at the Hindoo Village. More amusing than educational, these kinds of activities nonetheless exposed Americans to other lands and cultures.

Bertha Honoré Palmer, c. 1893, Chicago's leading socialite and president of the 1893 world's fair Board of Lady Managers.

For assisting the 1893 world's fair federal legislation committee, Bertha Honoré Palmer received this sterling silver medal inset with rubies made by Tiffany & Company.

served as board president. Unlike some women who argued for incorporating women's exhibits alongside men's, she supported the notion of a separate woman's building. Palmer devoted herself to making the Woman's Building a showcase of women's talents and contributions, although she, like her male counterparts, excluded African Americans from the planning phase and eventual exhibitions. While Boston architect Sophia Hayden designed the structure, numerous women artists led by Mary Cassatt and Mary Fairchild MacMonnies painted its interior murals and many panels. Although women did not achieve equal status with men at the fair, the Woman's Building presented women's capabilities in a positive light, thus helping advance the long struggle for equality.[8]

The World's Columbian Exposition had several other far-reaching effects. Most tangibly, the fair announced a new age of mass consumerism in America. The staggering amount of manufactured goods on view not only demonstrated the country's ability to mass-produce goods, but also to mass consume them. At its most basic level, the fair showcased an increasingly affluent nation, but beyond the material goods, the fair also gave rise to new forms of American popular culture. Ragtime musician Scott Joplin, motion pictures, and entertainers such as Buffalo Bill Cody and Harry Houdini made their national debut at the fair, as did Cracker Jack, Juicy Fruit gum, Cream of Wheat cereal, postcards, the penny-press, and a host of other well-known products. The fair's magical qualities inspired L. Frank Baum, a Chicago window dresser, to write *The Wizard of Oz*, one of the most popular books in American history. The fair may have influenced Walt Disney, whose father worked as a carpenter at the event, to create Disneyland. Fulfilling its obligation to celebrate America, the fair also introduced new forms of patriotism, including John Philip Sousa's music for marching bands, the Pledge of Allegiance, and designating Columbus Day as a national holiday.[9]

CHICAGO AMUSEMENT PARKS

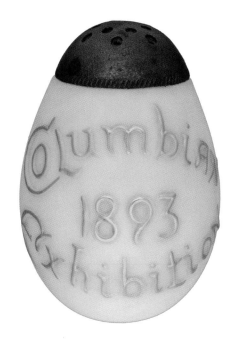

n addition, the enormously popular Midway gave rise to the American amusement park. Within a year of the fair's closing, on July 4, 1894, Paul Boyton, who
had performed as a swimmer and showman at the fair, opened the city's first
modern urban amusement park at Sixty-third and Drexel streets on the city's
South Side. Featuring Shoot-the-Chutes, Boyton's park was the first to rely solely on
mechanical rides for public entertainment. Inspired by its success, Boyton opened a
second amusement park at New York's Coney Island in 1895. The following year, the
original Ferris Wheel from the 1893 fair resumed operations in Lincoln Park at Clark
and Wrightwood streets on the city's North Side. Subsequently, two of Chicago's
most famous amusement parks, Riverview and White City, opened for business.[10]

Located at Belmont and Western avenues, Riverview debuted in 1904 as a
neighborhood shooting range and picnic grounds known as German Sharpshooter
Park. When owner Wilhelm Schmidt installed swings and rides for families, the setting
took on a carnival-like quality. Schmidt's son, George, subsequently expanded the
park along the lines of Tivoli Gardens in Europe, Coney Island in New York, and,
of course, the Midway at the World's Columbian Exposition. Occupying seventy-
three acres, the new Riverview Park featured numerous rides and attractions, including
Shoot-the-Chutes, the world's first suspended roller coaster, and a magnificent, hand-

Clockwise from top: A pickle fork, porcelain egg, and
enameled bowl are among the countless souvenirs
purchased at the 1893 World's Columbian Exposition
by visitors wishing to preserve and share their
memories of the grand event.

Riverview Park, one of many legendary venues that
made Chicago a vibrant hub of leisure-time activities
and entertainment. The park remained opened from
1904 to 1967.

carved carousel. In later years, Riverview added the Bobs roller coaster, the Pair-O-
Chutes, and the Water Bugs. Although mechanical rides remained the main draw,
other attractions added to the fun. During the 1920s, park owners installed a ballroom and roller rink to attract customers during the winter season.

Reflecting widespread racist attitudes, Riverview Park informally excluded
blacks but featured them in derogatory concessions. During the 1940s, "Dunk the
Clown" turned into "Dunk the Nigger" (later renamed the "African Dip"). One of
the most profitable concessions in Riverview's history, the "Dip" continued to
operate until pressure from the National Association for the Advancement of Colored
People (NAACP) forced its closing in the late 1950s. During the turbulent 1960s,
tensions between the races and different ethnic groups often erupted in fights,
forcing the park to hire its own police force, and the threat of violence kept many
people away. Moreover, the park lost customers as more middle-class families moved
to the suburbs. Increasing costs reduced profits, prompting the Schmidt family to
sell the property and close Riverview Park in 1967.[11]

Its chief rival, White City opened on the South Side in 1905. Named after the
1893 world's fair, the park drew working-class families with wholesome entertainment.
It featured vaudeville shows and concerts in addition to many rides, including the
ever-popular roller coasters and water rides. Tiny lights illuminated the park at night,
creating a fairy-tale effect. A 250-foot Jewel Tower, taller than any other structure
south of the Loop, featured 20,000 light bulbs and could be seen from miles away. A
fire in 1927 and the hard times of the Great Depression drove the park into bank-
ruptcy and closure in 1934.[12]

A spirited, hand-carved horse evokes fond memories of Riverview Park. It belonged to a magnificent carousel made by Leo Zoller of the Philadelphia Toboggan Company and was installed at Riverview in 1908.

THE CITY BEAUTIFUL MOVEMENT AND THE 1909 PLAN OF CHICAGO

Among the greatest legacies of the 1893 world's fair are the City Beautiful Movement and the 1909 *Plan of Chicago*. Both are the creation of Daniel Hudson Burnham, chief architect of the White City who led a nation-wide effort to beautify American cities along the lines of older European capitals. In the process, he helped establish urban planning as a profession and left his mark on cities throughout the world. Working from his Chicago office, Burnham developed plans for Washington, D.C. (1902), Cleveland (1903), Manila (1904), and San Francisco (1905), gaining international recognition for his efforts.[13]

Closer to home, Burnham faced an urban nightmare. In contrast to a lovely outer perimeter of parks and boulevards, Chicago's central district had become an ugly knot of congestion, dirt, and noise. The daily crush of people, horse-drawn vehicles, and trains impeded the flow of traffic and stifled the future growth of commerce. In response, the Commercial Club of Chicago, an elite group of civic-minded business-men, commissioned Burnham to develop a new concept for the city. In collabora-tion with architect Edward H. Bennett, editor Charles Moore, and artist Jules Guerin, Burnham produced the *Plan of Chicago*. Its ambitious scope expressed Burnham's per-sonal motto to "Make no little plans. They have no magic to stir men's blood." He suggested: (1) developing Chicago's lakefront as open public space; (2) creating a high-way system outside the city; (3) establishing more city parks; (4) improving railway and shipping networks; (5) widening the streets; and (6) re-aligning the business dis-trict on a new Congress Street axis, creating a government center where radial streets converge at Halsted and Congress streets, and establishing a cultural center at the foot on Congress Street in Grant Park overlooking what is now Monroe Harbor.[14]

Over the next twenty years, Chicago implemented many of the plan's recom-mendations, including the development of Municipal Pier (Navy Pier), Grant Park, Northerly Island, and a recreational lakefront with cultural institutions (the Field Museum, Adler Planetarium, and Shedd Aquarium). In addition, many streets were

Children on the Riverview Park carousel, 1946. One of the largest ever made, the Riverview Park carousel continues to operate at Six Flags Over Georgia and joined the National Register of Historic Places in 1995.

Published in 1909, the *Plan of Chicago* expressed Daniel Burnham's personal motto: "Make no little plans. They have no magic to stir men's blood."

A miniature portrait of Daniel H. Burnham captures the architect at the height of his powers, shortly after completing the 1909 *Plan of Chicago*.

widened, Wacker Drive was built, and a new Union Station helped consolidate some of the city's rail traffic. And, thanks to the plan, an extensive system of forest preserves encircles the city.

Inspiration for these preserves came from the Municipal Science Club of Chicago, whose members included noted architects Dwight D. Perkins and Jens Jensen. After studying the natural areas of Cook County in 1904, the club concluded: "The bluffs and beaches along the Lake Shore, the Skokie, the North Chicago river valley, the Des Plaines Valley, Salt Creek, Flag Creek, Mt. Forest, the Sag Valley, Palos Heights, Blue Island Ridge, the Calumet River and Lake . . . should be preserved for the benefit of the public in both the city and its suburbs." Burnham agreed, and the preservation of forestlands became a major component of the plan. Formed in 1911, the Forest Preserve District Association campaigned for the passage of a Forest Preserve District Act, which Cook County residents approved in November 1914. The district has expanded to include 68,000 acres of land with educational and recreational centers, biking and hiking trails, picnic groves, fishing ponds, lakes and streams, swimming pools, golf courses, and 4,400 acres of habitat for native birds and wildlife.[15]

Despite falling short of all of its goals, the 1909 plan remains a visionary masterpiece. Indeed, Millennium Park, Chicago's newest park, is an extension of Burnham's plan. Its site formerly belonged to the Illinois Central Railroad and,

Ice skating at Humboldt Park, c. 1938. Chicago's many parks have provided generations of residents with recreational opportunities throughout the year.

The 1909 *Plan of Chicago* by Daniel H. Burnham and
Edward H. Bennett called for a "well-ordered and
convenient city" that would also be beautiful. Exquisite
watercolor renderings by the artist Jules Guerin helped
promote their ideas to the public.

As a result of the 1909 plan, Chicago's lakefront has
remained open to the public. Swimmers in 1921
enjoying Clarendon Beach, created as part of landfill
into the lake in the Uptown neighborhood on the city's
North Side.

Debuting in 2004, Millennium Park has become a modern urban crossroads of the post-industrial era.

bowing to its importance, Burnham left the company's dense network of tracks intact while developing Grant Park around it. The tracks and nearby parking lots, however, remained an eyesore despite efforts by concerned citizen groups to have them removed. Finally, in 1997, Mayor Richard M. Daley directed his staff to develop plans for a new musical venue to be built over the tracks. From this effort emerged expanded plans to build Millennium Park. Despite many delays and cost overruns, Millennium Park opened to great fanfare on July 24, 2004. The twenty-four-and-a-half-acre park features an innovative music pavilion and winding bridge designed by architect Frank Gehry; an interactive fountain by Jaume Plensa; *Cloud Gate*, a reflecting sculpture by Anish Kapoor affectionately known as "the bean"; and contemporary landscape gardens by Kat Gustafson, Piet Oudolf, and Robert Israel. Innovative, yet accessible to people from all walks of life, Millennium Park demonstrates Chicago's penchant for bringing ideas to fruition, enhances the city's position as a tourist destination, and ushers in a new era of urban leisure and entertainment at the crossroads of America.[16]

The Chicago Symphony Orchestra

Created by an unknown craftsman around 1895, a working model of the proscenium arch of the Auditorium Theater includes a fully articulated miniature Chicago Symphony Orchestra. The CSO made its debut at the Auditorium in 1891 and played there until moving to Orchestra Hall in 1904.

Widely considered to be one of the world's premier orchestras, the Chicago Symphony Orchestra (CSO) made its debut at the Auditorium Theater in 1891. Its conductor, the nationally renowned Theodore Thomas, had been lured away from New York City by wealthy businessman Ferdinand Peck, a member of Chicago's influential Commercial Club. Both Peck and Thomas strove to make high culture available to the general public, believing that it would improve civic life. With that goal in mind, Thomas exposed Chicago audiences to complex, classical works in addition to simpler—and more popular—waltzes and polkas. In 1892, for example, Thomas and the CSO performed the American premier of Tchaikovsky's *Nutcracker Suite*, which has remained a perennial favorite in Chicago. The following year, Thomas initiated a series of "People's Concerts" that remained popular for decades. That same year, as music director of the World's Columbian Exposition, he exposed audiences to innovative European composers such as Wagner and Strauss. Thomas, however, had his share of controversy. Critics charged that he did not hire enough local talent, and he often complained that the cavernous Auditorium Theater was too large for a young orchestra to fill acoustically and too difficult to sell out. The CSO, however, continued to play at the Auditorium Theater until 1904, when it moved to Orchestra Hall on Michigan Avenue shortly before Thomas's death. Subsequently, the CSO had several notable conductors, including Fritz Reiner, Sir George Solti, and Daniel Barenboim, who led the orchestra to international acclaim.[17]

Left: The Original Creole Orchestra, one of the first New Orleans jazz bands to tour the North, played on Chicago's South Side before World War I and helped make the city a hotbed of cutting-edge music.

Right: Saxophone used by James Palao of the Original Creole Orchestra and King Oliver's Creole Jazz Band, c. 1920.

CHICAGO JAZZ AND BLUES

Perhaps no story better reflects Chicago's role as a cultural crossroads than that of jazz and blues. In both cases, musicians from other places brought new forms of music to Chicago. Here, they were transformed into more urban sounds that audiences across the country and around the world embraced. Chicago's connections to jazz are actually rooted in the syncopated rhythms of ragtime music, introduced to the American public by Scott Joplin at the 1893 world's fair. Ragtime's close association with African Americans and new styles of dance alarmed many whites, but its popularity, particularly among the youth, continued to grow nationwide. In Chicago, audiences could hear ragtime in many clubs on the South Side, home to the city's small but growing black community. These establishments included the Pekin Inn, established in 1904 by the African American entrepreneur Robert T. Motts. Located at 2700 South State Street, the club featured vaudeville acts, gambling, and musical entertainment that drew upper-class white as well as black customers. Other clubs of the era included the Café de Champion operated by heavyweight boxer Jack Johnson and the Pompeii Café under the direction of Ferd LaMenth "Jelly Roll" Morton, who introduced a looser, jazzier style of playing that took music in a new direction.[18]

During the 1910s, Chicago's early jazz scene blossomed as more African American musicians arrived from the South. They were part of the Great Migration, the mass movement of southern blacks to northern cities like Chicago. Seeking

Cornet given by legendary jazz musician Bix Beiderbecke to Jimmy McPartland, member of the Austin High Gang, 1929.

employment opportunities and freedom from the repressive Jim Crow practices, these migrants joined Chicago's older black communities on the South and West Sides. Most of the musicians moving North at this time came from New Orleans, the birthplace of jazz and a city directly connected to Chicago via the Illinois Central Railroad. As a result, New Orleans musicians had an easy route to the city's lively jazz scene, appreciative audiences, and better pay.

The Original Creole Orchestra of New Orleans was among the earliest groups to arrive. Led by Freddie Keppard on the cornet, bass player Bill Johnson, and James (Jimmie) Palao on violin, the band started touring the North in 1912. They were one of the first jazz bands to play outside the Crescent City, making a wide circuit from California to Chicago. Weary of traveling, they settled in Chicago in 1918 and replaced Keppard with cornet player Joseph "King" Oliver the following year. A giant of early jazz who also came from New Orleans, King Oliver gradually assumed control of the band and changed its name to King Oliver's Creole Jazz Band. One of the most influential jazz bands in history, Oliver's group featured Johnny Dodds on clarinet, Lil Hardin on piano, and the young Louis Armstrong on cornet. Jimmie Palao, who played banjo and saxophone in addition to the violin, also worked with the band for a brief time. Oliver, who once described his band as "eight men playing fifteen instruments," emphasized playing as an ensemble rather than solo artistry, and his band delivered a hot, powerful sound that defined the Jazz Age.[19]

Although Oliver led the band, Armstrong was its biggest star. Born in New Orleans, he grew up in poverty and, according to legend, learned to play cornet while in reform school after firing a gun in the air on New Year's Eve. After his release, Armstrong frequented the clubs of Storyville (the city's bordello district), forming a close friendship with King Oliver, who became his mentor. Between 1917 and 1921, Armstrong played in several different jazz bands in New Orleans and St. Louis before King Oliver invited him to join his Creole Jazz Band then at Lincoln Gardens in Chicago. Armstrong's brilliant musicianship thrilled audiences, and he remained with Oliver for two years before his wife, Lil, concerned that he would remain in Oliver's shadow, convinced him to start his own band. After spending time in New York playing with Fletcher Henderson's Orchestra, Armstrong returned

Louis Armstrong, c. 1930. Recognized as one of the greatest jazz musicians of all time, Armstrong played with King Oliver's Creole Jazz Band on the South Side of Chicago for about seven years before moving to New York to establish his own orchestra.

Noted jazz musicians including Duke Ellington made the Regal Theater on Chicago's South Side an important venue during the 1940s.

A native of Chicago, Benny Goodman achieved international stardom during the late 1930s with a distinctive sound played by his integrated swing band.

Duke Ellington, c. 1935.

to Chicago in 1925 and joined his wife's band at the Dreamland Café at 3520 South State Street. That same year, Armstrong began recording under his own name for Okeh Records, a New York company with studios in Chicago. Between 1925 and 1928, Louis Armstrong and the Hot Five, later the Hot Seven, made a series of notable recordings. Although the band never played in front of a live audience, the records made Armstrong a national star. After returning to New York in 1930, Armstrong assembled a new band that toured the world with occasional stops in Chicago.[20]

Chicago also produced many white jazz musicians. Some, like Benny Goodman and Gene Krupa, grew up in city neighborhoods, while members of the Austin High Gang—Jimmy and Richard McPartland and Bud Freeman—hailed from the suburbs. Others, such as Wild Bill Davison and Bix Beiderbecke moved to Chicago from other parts of the Midwest. Frequenting South Side clubs, they heard Armstrong and dozens of other talented African American jazzmen. Immersing themselves in the intoxicating music and high-spirited atmosphere of the Roaring Twenties, Chicago's white jazzmen established their own bands that achieved local, and in some cases, national, stardom.[21]

Topping the list is Benny Goodman, the King of Swing. Born on the West Side of Chicago in 1909, Goodman grew up in a large, impoverished family. His father, a Russian Jewish immigrant who worked in the stockyards and slaughterhouses, encouraged his son's musical talents by sending him to the local synagogue and Hull-House for clarinet lessons. Well-grounded in classical technique, Goodman stressed perfectionism and rigorous rehearsals throughout his career. During the 1920s, Goodman played with bands on Great Lakes excursion boats and frequented South Side clubs where he listened to Oliver, Armstrong, and other early jazz greats. In 1934, Goodman moved to New York City and eventually formed his own band. Between November 1935 and May 1936, Goodman's band attained national fame playing at the Congress Hotel in Chicago. Billed for the first time as a swing band, Goodman's group created a national sensation with an up-tempo style of jazz that remained popular through World War II. Undoubtedly influenced by his experience

Nightclubs such as the Blue Note Café gave Chicago a
national reputation for innovative jazz during the 1950s
and 1960s.

on the South Side, where blacks and whites mingled freely, Goodman broke racial
barriers by hiring African American pianist Teddy Wilson and vibes player Lionel
Hampton. Goodman's appearance at Carnegie Hall in 1938 with Wilson, Hampton,
and drummer Gene Krupa remains one of the outstanding events in jazz history.[22]

Goodman's decision to remain in New York reflected a larger shift in the
American music scene. While Chicago had flourished during the Jazz Age, New York
dominated during the Swing Era. Not only did New York have a larger market in
terms of paying customers, it also served as the headquarters of the musical recording
industry, which boomed during the 1930s and 1940s, drawing the best talent away
from smaller markets like Chicago. Unable to compete, Chicago lost its position as
the premier city for cutting-edge jazz, although the city has remained a leading venue
for local and imported talent for decades.[23]

Like jazz, the blues moved from the South to Chicago with the Great
Migration. Historically, the blues developed from traditional African American work
songs and field hollers. While the blues often expressed the anguish of enslaved

Legendary blues guitarist Muddy Waters, c. 1960, revolutionized American music and paved the way for rock 'n' roll.

Chuck Berry, c. 1960, bestselling recording artist for Chess Records of Chicago. His hit single, "School Day" topped the charts in 1959. Berry's innovative guitar work broke new ground in the early days of rock 'n' roll.

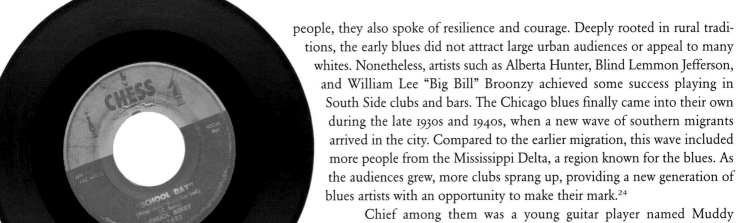

people, they also spoke of resilience and courage. Deeply rooted in rural traditions, the early blues did not attract large urban audiences or appeal to many whites. Nonetheless, artists such as Alberta Hunter, Blind Lemmon Jefferson, and William Lee "Big Bill" Broonzy achieved some success playing in South Side clubs and bars. The Chicago blues finally came into their own during the late 1930s and 1940s, when a new wave of southern migrants arrived in the city. Compared to the earlier migration, this wave included more people from the Mississippi Delta, a region known for the blues. As the audiences grew, more clubs sprang up, providing a new generation of blues artists with an opportunity to make their mark.[24]

Chief among them was a young guitar player named Muddy Waters. Born McKinley Morganfield in 1915, Waters grew up in Rolling Fork, Mississippi, deep in the heart of the Delta. After learning how to play harmonica, Waters taught himself how to play the bottleneck guitar, a style unique

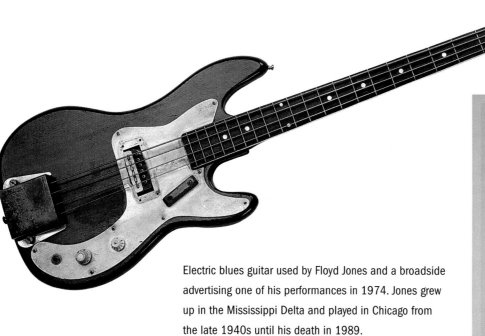

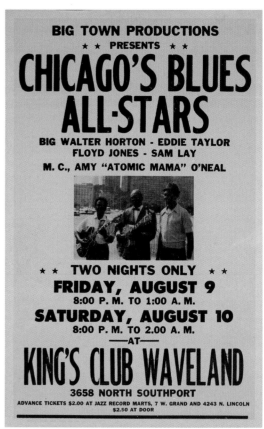

Electric blues guitar used by Floyd Jones and a broadside advertising one of his performances in 1974. Jones grew up in the Mississippi Delta and played in Chicago from the late 1940s until his death in 1989.

to the region. Deeply influenced by the brilliant Robert Johnson, Waters mastered the jagged, pulsating rhythms of the bottleneck guitar and developed a powerful singing style that took the Delta blues to a new level. In 1943, Waters moved to Chicago and launched a career that revolutionized popular music.[25]

In addition to playing the club scene, Waters began to record. Although his first records for Columbia were never released, Chicago's Chess Records made Waters a star with a string of hits including "I Can't Be Satisfied/I Feel Like Going Home," "Louisiana Blues," "I Just Want to Make Love to You," "Hoochie Coochie Man," and "Got My Mojo Working." In addition to Waters, Chess Records issued hit recordings by Willie Dixon, Little Walter, Howlin' Wolf, John Lee Hooker, Bo Diddley, and Chuck Berry, their bestselling artist. Highly influential in the development of rock 'n' roll, Chess Records was owned and operated by Leonard and Phil Chess, immigrant brothers from Poland. Starting in 1963, the entrepreneurial brothers also operated their own radio station, WVON. In addition to playing their own records, the Chess brothers had a special arrangement to play Motown Records on WVON. Not surprisingly, WVON quickly became the most popular black radio station in Chicago.[26]

The blues remained popular through the 1950s and greatly influenced the development of early rock 'n' roll. As rock became more popular during the 1960s, however, the popularity of the blues declined. Major record companies and radio stations relegated the genre to second-class status, although Chicago artists such as Buddy Guy and Koko Taylor maintained a lively presence in local clubs and at the annual blues festival. Since the 1990s, the Chicago blues scene has experienced a revival with the establishment of new clubs, the independent blues label Alligator Records, and interest from people around the world who want to experience Chicago blues.[27]

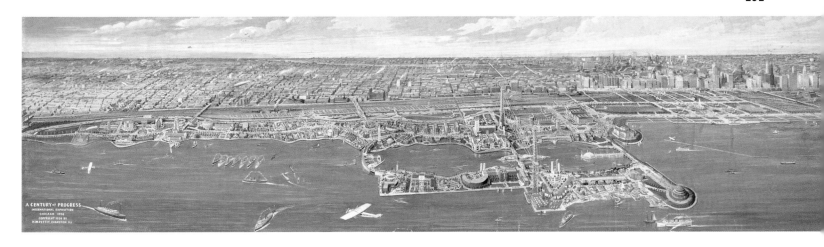

A panoramic watercolor representation of the Century of Progress fair by Harry M. Pettit captures the magical quality of Chicago's second world's fair in remarkable detail.

A souvenir ticket booklet from the Century of Progress fair illustrates how the use of bold colors conveyed a sense of optimism and hope during the Great Depression.

THE 1933–34 A CENTURY OF PROGRESS INTERNATIONAL EXPOSITION

Forty years after the 1893 World's Columbian Exposition, Chicago hosted the 1933–34 A Century of Progress International Exposition. Ostensibly held to celebrate the one-hundredth anniversary of Chicago's incorporation and the city's many achievements, the fair actually focused more on the future of America. Staged in the midst of the Great Depression, when millions of people had lost their jobs as well as their faith in the American dream, the fair became a beacon of hope and optimism for people across the nation.

Talk of a second Chicago fair began in the wake of World War I, but local disturbances, particularly the 1919 Race Riot and gangland wars, threatened the city's social order as well as its reputation. Inspired by several recent fairs including Chicago's own Pageant of Progress (1921) and Philadelphia's Sesquicentennial International Exposition (1926), a group of local business and civic leaders launched a campaign to secure a world's fair. Chicago executive Rufus C. Dawes served as exposition chairman, while his brother, former United States senator and vice-president Charles G. Dawes, served as chairman of the finance committee. When hopes dimmed after the 1929 stock market crash, Julius Rosenwald, the wealthy and influential head of Sears, Roebuck & Co., secured twelve million dollars in gold notes to finance the fair's initial construction costs, giving planners enough leverage to convince Congress to authorize the construction of a government building and invite foreign governments to participate.[28]

The resulting fair, located on Northerly Island (just west of Monroe Harbor), delivered a carefully crafted message to millions of visitors. Although much smaller than its predecessor, the exposition highlighted American progress, with a special emphasis on the benefits of modern science, technology, and consumerism. In sharp contrast to the White City, it featured modern, streamlined buildings and bold colors, but harkened back to the past with a whirling logo that represented the star Arcturus, whose light took forty years to reach Earth (the span of time since the 1893 fair). Displayed throughout the fairgrounds and on countless souvenirs, the stylish motif captured the fair's modern spirit with a slight nod to the past that probably escaped most visitors.

Appropriately, the Hall of Science anchored the fairgrounds, while nearly two dozen private corporations erected pavilions to showcase their own products,

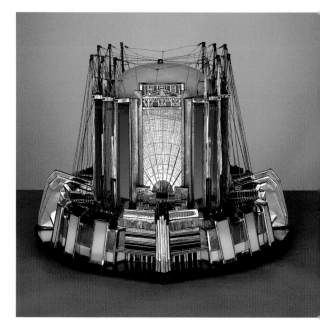

Left: A colorful Avenue of Flags greeted visitors as they entered the fairgrounds. Originally planned to be open for six months in 1933, the popular fair enjoyed an extended run in 1934.

Right: A scale model of the Travel and Transport Building captures the overall look and feel of Chicago's second world's fair: modern, sleek, and futuristic.

including General Motors, Chrysler, and Havoline Motor Oil. Smaller structures included the House of Tomorrow and Design for Living Home, both equipped with the latest technological advancements, such as dishwashers and air conditioning. Like its predecessor, the Century of Progress fair had a carnival-like Midway where visitors could find the Odditorium, a new version of the old-time "freak-show" the Midget Village; the Darkest Africa Show; and the Streets of Paris, where Sally Rand, a Chicago striptease artist, caused a sensation with an "artistic" fan dance. Other attractions included the Enchanted Isle for children and the Sky Ride with futuristic rocket cars transporting visitors high above the fairgrounds.[29]

A Century of Progress International Exposition souvenirs collected and saved for sixty years in an old cigar box by Chicagoan Walter H. Schwebke typify the small, inexpensive items sold at the fair.

Despite its optimistic view of America's future, the Century of Progress fair failed to promote gender or racial equality. Unlike the 1893 fair, the 1933 event did not include women in the planning, or provide them with many exhibitions or a building of their own. The fair also shortchanged African Americans in hiring practices and had few exhibitions about their history other than a recreated cabin of Jean Baptiste Point DuSable, Chicago's first permanent settler. Meanwhile, the Darkest Africa Show on the Midway featured degrading performances of half-naked dancers in native-like costume.[30]

Despite its flaws, the Century of Progress fair succeeded on a financial level, a remarkable achievement given the country's economic straits. It stimulated Chicago's economy with employment opportunities for local residents who worked as concessionaires, guards, and entertainers. More than forty million people attended the fair, including tens of thousands of out-of-town visitors whose spending helped stimulate the transportation and tourism industries (railroads, hotels, and restaurants). The fair's success prompted President Franklin D. Roosevelt to request that the fair be

A souvenir button from the Century of Progress fair features the official logo: swirling light from the star Arcturus reaching Earth forty years after the 1893 World's Columbian Exposition.

A bold poster for the fair's Skyride promoted the attraction as a futuristic space-age adventure. The ride cost $1.4 million to build, and its twin 628-feet tall towers soared higher than any other structure in the city.

Like its predecessor in 1893, the Century of Progress fair featured displays of native people as a way to promote the notion of American progress and cultural superiority. This group of African tribesmen was part of the Darkest Africa Show.

Among the many attractions on the Midway, visitors encountered ethnic dancers at the Swiss Village. Ironically, such traditions were dying out in Europe at the time.

extended into 1934, but when the Illinois state legislature met in Springfield, black legislators refused to agree until fair management agreed to wording in the legislation that forbade racial discrimination, either in hiring practices or serving patrons.[31]

Ultimately, the exposition reinforced Chicago's position as a regional, national, and international crossroads. Its ability to successfully stage a world's fair in the midst of a major economic crisis cheered the nation and encouraged other cities, including San Diego, San Francisco, and New York, to subsequently stage similar events. Moreover, the fair provided Chicago with an opportunity to promote itself as a national center of major league sports, an emerging, and increasingly important, American industry.

CHICAGO B. B. C., 1871.
Fred Treacy, *L.F.*, J. Simmons, *C.F.*, E. Pinkham, *R.F.*
E. Duffy, *S.S.*,   M. McAtee, *1st B.*
C. Hodes, *3d B.*,   JAS. WOOD, *2d B.*   Mart. King, *C.*
E. P. Atwater, *Sub.*, G. Zettlein, *P.*   T. J. Foley, *Sub.*

The Chicago White Stockings Base Ball Club, the city's first professional baseball team later known as the Chicago Cubs. In 1871, second baseman Jimmy Woods (center) managed the team to a second-place finish in the National Association of Professional Base Ball Players league.

CHICAGO SPORTS

During the 1933 run of the fair, Chicago hosted the first Major League Baseball All-Star Game, the first Negro League East-West baseball game, and the first College All-Stars football game. The idea for an all-star baseball game originated with Arch Ward, sports editor of the *Chicago Tribune*, as a means to revive fan interest during the bleak days of the Great Depression when attendance dropped to its lowest point in decades. The Century of Progress fair, then drawing thousands of people each day, provided a perfect opportunity for outstanding players from the American and National Leagues to meet. Played on July 6, 1933, in Comiskey Park, the game drew 49,200 fans who watched the American League post a 4–2 victory. Similarly, the Negro League East-West All-Star Game at Comiskey Park on September 10 drew 20,000 people. Finally, the College All-Stars football game, another suggestion from Arch Ward and sponsored by the *Chicago Tribune* to support local charities, pitted the best college graduate football players against the National Football League (NFL) champions, in this case, the Chicago Bears. The game, played on August 31, 1934, at Soldier Field, adjacent to the fairgrounds, ended in a scoreless tie, but established an annual tradition that lasted forty-two years.[32]

More than local attractions, these games confirmed Chicago as a leading center of American sports. As a major American city, Chicago had the financial resources and a large enough fan base to support professional sports on a mass scale. Its position as the nation's transportation crossroads also helped, providing home and visiting teams, as well as fans, easy access to and from the city, a key element in the formation of national leagues. In addition, Chicago's media—newspaper, radio, and eventually television—played a key role by disseminating sporting news to fans in the city, suburbs, and beyond. As in other arenas of Chicago history, the story of sports often reveals complex issues at play, primarily those related to race, class, and gender, which have not only shaped the teams themselves, but their fans' loyalties as well.

Although Chicago has supported professional sports teams of all kinds, its greatest contributions are found in the worlds of baseball and football. Chicago's first professional sports team was a baseball club, the Chicago White Stockings, who made their debut in 1870. The following year, the White Stockings joined the Philadelphia Athletics, Boston Red Stockings, New York Mutuals, and several other teams to form the National Association of Professional Base Ball Players, the first professional baseball league in America. Previously, baseball had been played on an amateur level but its increasing popularity transformed the game into a business with club owners and investors seeking profitable returns at the gate. The players, however, ran the league by controlling their contracts.[33]

In February 1876, William A. Hulbert, president of the Chicago White Stockings, met with representatives from midwestern and eastern baseball clubs and convinced them to adopt a plan that reseulted in the National League.

The White Stockings played in a newly built seven-thousand-seat wooden park on the West Side. During the 1871 season, they led the league until their stadium burned down in the Great Chicago Fire. They had to play the remainder of their games on the road, finishing a close second to Philadelphia, but the fire's devastation forced them to drop out of the league for two seasons. When the team returned in 1874, its officers included William A. Hulbert, a Chicago grain dealer who transformed the game. Born in 1832 in upstate New York, Hulbert moved with his family to Chicago at age two and grew up during the city's boomtown era. After attending Beloit College in Wisconsin, Hulbert returned to Chicago and developed a successful coal dealership. He took great pride in his home, often telling people that he'd "rather be a lamppost in Chicago than a millionaire elsewhere."[34]

By 1875, Hulbert had become the White Stockings' president, a position that allowed him to hire away star players from competing teams, including ace pitcher Albert Spalding of the Boston Red Stockings and Adrian "Cap" Anson of the Philadelphia Athletics. Fearing reprisals from other teams, including possible expulsion from the league for contract violations, Hulbert moved to form a new league with other business-minded investors. In February 1876, he met with representatives from midwestern and eastern clubs in New York City and convinced them to adopt a thirteen-point organizational plan that resulted in the National League of Professional Base Ball Clubs. Hulbert's plan put club owners, not players, in control.

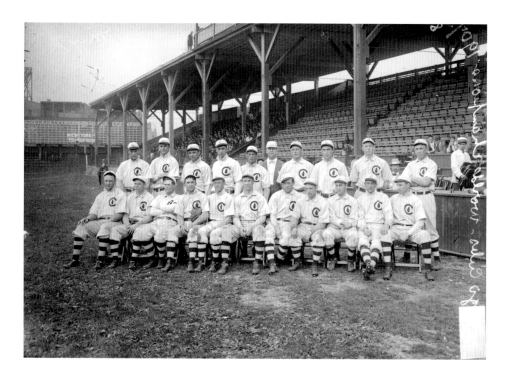

The 1908 Chicago Cubs won the World Series with a talented roster that included ace pitcher Mordecai "Three Finger" Brown and the legendary infield combination of "Tinker to Evers to Chance."

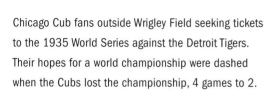

Chicago Cub fans outside Wrigley Field seeking tickets to the 1935 World Series against the Detroit Tigers. Their hopes for a world championship were dashed when the Cubs lost the championship, 4 games to 2.

Each team had to be financially sound, pay membership dues, and agree to play each league team ten times per season or be expelled for failing to do so. Hulbert also banned gambling, liquor sales, and Sunday games, and ordered tighter contracts to prevent players from jumping teams.[35]

In addition to Chicago, the National League included teams in St. Louis, Louisville, Cincinnati, Philadelphia, Boston, New York, and Hartford. Its inaugural year witnessed Hulbert's White Stockings, led by player-manager Albert Spalding, finish in first place, six games ahead of St. Louis. Hulbert's organizational genius put the league on firm footing, helping it survive the first four years of flagging attendance, a gambling scandal in Louisville, and competition from a rival league. Unfortunately, Hulbert died in 1882, just as baseball began to surge in popularity, but he lived long enough to see his beloved White Stockings win the National League pennant in 1880 and 1881.[36]

Thereafter, the team, under the direction of player-manager Cap Anson, dominated baseball, capturing three more pennants (1882, 1885–86) and four second-place finishes. Anson, major league baseball's biggest star, helped to popularize the game with powerful hitting (he was the first player with three thousand hits). He also pioneered the hit-and-run, signals, pitching rotations, and spring training. Unfortunately, Anson's refusal to compete against teams with African American players stopped the movement toward integrating the sport. At the time, dozens of black athletes played on the professional level for various teams scattered across the county, but not for the National League, whose owners had a "gentlemen's agreement" barring blacks. Anson's stance effectively shut the door on black players for decades.[37]

A program and tickets to the World Series are every Cubs fan's dream. These are from the 1935 fall classic, when the Cubs played the Detroit Tigers.

The White Stockings next winning era occurred in the early 1900s. By then, they had acquired a new nickname—the Cubs—for their youthful ineptitude. In 1906, however, they fielded one of the best teams in baseball history with shortstop Joe Tinker, second baseman Johnny Evers, first baseman Frank Chance, and pitchers Orval Overall, Jack Pfiester, and Mordecai "Three Finger" Brown. At age seven, Brown had cut the top two-thirds of his right index finger off in a farming accident, giving him a natural knuckle ball. Under manager Frank Chance, the Cubs compiled a 116–36 record, the best in the major leagues, and faced their crosstown rivals, the Chicago White Sox, in the World Series. Chicago's first and, so far, only city series went to the White Sox, 4 games to 2.[38]

The Cubs repeated as pennant winners in 1907 and 1908 and beat the Detroit Tigers for back-to-back World Series championships. After winning the NL pennant in 1910, and again in 1918, the Cubs entered a long championship drought. Years passed before Lewis "Hack" Wilson, Rogers Hornsby, and "Gabby" Hartnett led the Cubs to four NL championships (1929, 1932, 1935, 1938), but, alas, no World Series championship. In 1945, the Cubs won another pennant but lost the World Series to Detroit in seven games.[39]

For the next twenty-three years, the Cubs remained out of pennant competition. Then in 1969, they fielded a talented team that included Ernie Banks, Ron Santo, Don Kessinger, Ferguson Jenkins, and Billy Williams under the colorful and crafty manager Leo Durocher. After leading most of the season, the Cubs collapsed late in the season and wound up eight games behind the New York Mets. Although they won division titles in 1984, 1989, and 2003, the Cubs failed to advance to the World Series, leaving their fans broken-hearted.[40]

Over the years, the Cubs have attracted a large and loyal fan base. For decades, they have been one of the top drawing teams in the major leagues, an accomplishment partially owed to playing in Wrigley Field, one of baseball's crown-jewel stadiums. Additionally, the Cubs exploited Chicago's media resources to their advantage. In 1925, the Cubs started broadcasting their games live on the radio, the first major league baseball team to do so. Thirty years later, they launched television broadcasts on WGN, reaching fans throughout the region. Over the years, announcers such as Vince Lloyd, Lou Boudreau, Jack Brickhouse, and Harry Caray helped make baseball a favorite American pastime. The result has been generations of loyal Cubs fans across the country who patiently "wait 'til next year" for a long overdue trip to the World Series.[41]

The Cubs' crosstown rivals, the Chicago White Sox, have an equally devoted fan base. They were established in 1900 by Charles A. Comiskey as a charter member of the American League, an upstart rival to the National League. Comiskey, a Chicago native, played first base for the St. Louis Browns of the American Association between 1882 and 1889; beginning in 1883, he also managed the team, leading them to four straight pennant flags (1885–88). A mediocre hitter but a good fielder, Comiskey is credited with revolutionizing his position by letting the pitcher cover ground balls wide of the bag. As a manager, Comiskey pioneered moving fielders around for different hitters, adding a new layer of strategy to the game. In 1893, Comiskey and Bancroft "Ban" Johnson, a former sports writer, took over the Western League, a strong minor league based in the Midwest. When the National League

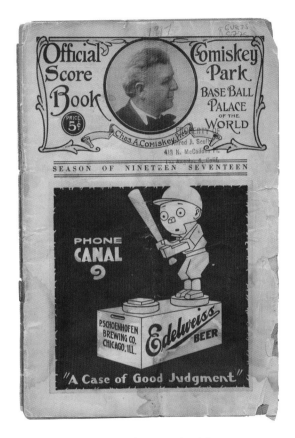

A 1917 Chicago White Sox score book features a portrait of owner Charles A. Comiskey above an advertisement for a local brewery. That year, the White Sox won their first World Series championship.

The 1917 Chicago White Sox included the outstanding outfielder "Shoeless" Joe Jackson (bottom row, second from the left), who led the franchise to its first World Series championship.

Baseball fans in Peoria, Illinois, keeping tabs on a 1917 World Series game between the Chicago White Sox and New York Giants. Before the days of radio and television coverage, major league baseball "broadcast" games by telegraphing reports to saloons and pool halls, despite team owners' concern that "free baseball" would drive down attendance. Note the man's hand in the window relaying a fresh report to the scorekeeper standing on the balcony next to the scoreboard.

eliminated four teams in 1899, Comiskey and Johnson seized the opportunity to upgrade their league. They signed surplus players, moved to Chicago, and declared themselves the American League. Comiskey renamed his team the Chicago White Stockings after the city's first major league baseball team that dominated the game in the early years.[42]

Comiskey's White Stockings originally played at a stadium on Thirty-ninth Street on the city's South Side, not far from their current home. They had an auspicious debut, winning the American League pennant in 1900 and 1901, but in 1902, the team, now called the White Sox, slid to fourth, then seventh the following year. In 1906, however, the White Sox rebounded with a pennant victory behind superb pitching, but the team's weak bats earned them the dubious nickname, the "hitless wonders." In a rare crosstown World Series, the White Sox defeated the heavily favored Chicago Cubs 4 games to 2. Despite fielding some competitive teams, the White Sox did not return to the World Series until 1917. That year, manager Clarence H. "Pants" Rowland, veteran pitcher Eddie Cicotte, second baseman Eddie Collins, and outfielder "Shoeless" Joe Jackson led the team to one hundred victories, the club's best record to date. In the World Series, they defeated the New York Giants, 4 games to 2.[43]

Two years later, the White Sox were at the center of the greatest scandal in baseball history. The 1919 team, loaded with talented players like Jackson and Cicotte,

Row 1: L.Aparicio-J.Sala, Bat Boy-J.Roscich, Bat Boy-J.Heinsen,Bat.Prt.Cth.,
Row 2: S.Lollar-B.Goodman-D.Gutteridge,Coach-T.Cuccinello,Coach-A.Lopez,Mgr.-J.Cooney,Coach-R.Berres,Coach-S.Esposito-J.Romano
Row 3: E.Colledge,Sox Equipt.Mgr.-B.Snyderworth,Trvl.Sec.-D.Donovan-O."Turk"Lown-B.Shaw-G.Staley-B.Latman-K.McBride-A.Smith-
         T.Kluszewski
Row 4: J.Rivera-E.Battey-R.Arias-N.Cash-J.Landis-E.Froelich,Trnr.-A.Colledge,Visiting Equipt.Mgr.
Row 5: E.Wynn-E.Torgeson-J.Stanka-R.Moore-J.McAnany-N.Fox-B.Pierce-J."Bubba"Phillips

The 1959 "Go-Go" Chicago White Sox won the American League pennant but lost the World Series to the Los Angeles Dodgers, 4 games to 2.

A ticket and program from Game 1 of the 2005 World Series are treasured keepsakes of the Chicago White Sox's first baseball championship since 1917.

won eighty-eight games, enough to advance to the World Series against an inferior Cincinnati Reds team. When the Sox lost the championship, rumors started about a possible fix. Nothing came to light until the following year when a grand jury indicted eight White Sox players, including Jackson and Cicotte, for throwing the series. Although acquitted, the players were banned for life from professional baseball by commissioner Kenesaw Mountain Landis. In recent years, some of the blame for the scandal has shifted from the players to Comiskey, who kept players' salaries low, making the temptation of gambling hard to resist. Still, the scandal rocked America, disillusioning many fans, especially youngsters who looked up to major league players as heroes and role models.[44]

The 1919 Black Sox Scandal, as it became known, sent the team into a decades-long funk. Although players like the talented shortstop Luke Appling sparked the White Sox during the 1930s, the franchise did not return to postseason play until 1959. The "Go-Go" White Sox of the 1950s featured good pitching, sharp defense, and speed on the base path. After finishing second to the New York Yankees in 1957 and 1958, they captured the pennant in 1959 under manager Al Lopez with a 94–60 record. Key players included pitcher Early Wynn, shortstop Louis Aparacio, the first Latino player to reach baseball's Hall of Fame, and second baseman Nellie Fox. Like the "hitless wonders" of 1906, the 1959 White Sox lacked firepower, winning 35 games by just one run. In the first game of the World Series against the Los Angeles Dodgers, the White Sox surprised everyone with an 11–0 victory, but wound up losing the fall classic, 4 games to 2.[45]

Long-suffering fans were finally rewarded in 2005 when the White Sox won the World Series. Led by second-year manager Ozzie Guillen, a former White Sox

shortstop from Venezuela, the team featured superb pitching and airtight defense that overcame a low-scoring offense throughout the season. After leading their division wire to wire, the White Sox defeated the Boston Red Sox in the American League Division Series, 3 games to 0, and the Los Angeles Angels in the American League Championship Series, 4 games to 1, before knocking off the Houston Astros, 4 games to 0 for the World Series Championship. Players including Mark Buehrle, Freddy Garcia, A.J. Pierzynski, Paul Konerko, Juan Uribe, Joe Crede, and Jermaine Dye captured fans' hearts with their hard work, unselfish attitude, and, in the words of one sportscaster, a "relentless" style of baseball that gave Chicago its first World Series championship in eighty-eight years.[46]

As the city of Chicago celebrated the White Sox's achievement with a joyous ticker-tape parade up LaSalle Street, many fans recalled former owner Bill Veeck, who also endeared himself to fans. One of baseball's most colorful characters, Veeck owned the Cleveland Indians and St. Louis Browns before purchasing a controlling interest in the White Sox from the Comiskey family in March 1959. Veeck learned the game of baseball from his father, who had been general manager of the Cubs between 1919 and 1933, and understood the game from the fans' perspective. To make games more interesting and fun, Veeck put players' names on their uniforms, invented the exploding scoreboard, and tried numerous gimmicks to attract and amuse fans, including sending a midget to bat for the St. Louis Browns. More importantly, Veeck

Pinwheel from Comiskey Park's Monster Scoreboard, 1982–90. Always eager to please fans, Chicago White Sox owner Bill Veeck installed major league baseball's first exploding scoreboard in 1960. Every time a White Sox player hit a home run, eight red and white pinwheels flashed on and off while a shower of fireworks exploded overhead. This pinwheel is from the park's second Monster Scoreboard installed in 1982 and salvaged when Comiskey Park fell to the wrecker's ball in 1990. The team's current stadium, U.S. Cellular Field, has a similar scoreboard.

Barred from major league baseball on racial grounds, ace pitcher Rube Foster played for black teams in Chicago and formed the Negro National League in 1920.

Chicago-Style Softball

Sixteen-inch softball is unique to Chicago. The game was born in November 1887 inside the gymnasium of the Farragut Boat Club at 3018 Lake Park Avenue, where a group of Yale and Harvard alumni had gathered to await the results of a Yale-Harvard football game. When news came that Yale had won, one fan jokingly threw an old boxing glove at another, who tried to hit it back with a stick. The action prompted George Hancock, of the Chicago Board of Trade, to initiate a game of indoor baseball. After tying the glove's laces together and marking off a field on the gym floor, Hancock and his friends played a 41–40 game. That spring, Hancock took his game outdoors with a modified set of baseball rules and the game quickly caught on. Although twelve- and fourteen-inch softball eventually became the national standard, Chicagoans continued to play with a larger, softer, sixteen-inch "mush" ball. Numerous teams and organized leagues sprang up across the city, providing a relaxing, and inexpensive, form of entertainment. Often described as a working-man's game, sixteen-inch softball also is played by women and children; indeed, anyone can play.[47]

Chicago companies, neighborhood parks, and park districts have a long tradition of sponsoring competitive softball teams that play for local honors. This sixteen-inch softball is inscribed "Metropolitan / Champs 1972 / American Rivet Co."

Judge Zuris's All-Star Softball Team, c. 1937, one of the many amateur softball teams that have played in Chicago since the game's inception in 1887.

Women's Baseball

Although baseball remains a male-dominated sport, Chicago broke the gender barrier during the 1940s and created a legendary chapter in the annals of American sports. The All-American Girls Baseball League, founded by Chicago Cubs owner, Philip K. Wrigley, debuted in 1943. Wrigley hoped the experiment would sustain fans' interest during World War II, when many players were serving in the armed forces. The league had teams scattered throughout the Midwest, including the Kenosha Comets, Racine Belles, Rockford Peaches, South Bend Blue Sox, Milwaukee Chicks, and Chicago Colleens, a team that didn't make its appearance until 1948. Initially, the women played a version of softball, using a large ball and underhand pitching, but as the game evolved, they adopted a smaller ball and overhand pitching, which made the game faster and livelier. The league's popularity peaked in 1948 when ten teams attracted nearly one million fans.

The National Girls Baseball League, a smaller, rival organization also based in Chicago, preferred to play a softball version of the game. The league had six teams, including the Queens and the Music Maids of Chicago, sponsored by the Rock-Ola Juke Box Company. Teams played games at Thillen's Park, a small field on the city's far North Side constructed by a check-cashing company for amateur players.

After reaching its peak in the late 1940s, both forms of women's baseball declined, largely because of internal organizational problems and the rising popularity of Major League Baseball created by increased television coverage. Years later, the popular movie, *A League of Their Own* retold the story of the All-American Girls Baseball League.[48]

The June 1948 edition of National Girls Baseball League featured a member of the Music Maids team, sponsored by the Rock-Ola Juke Box Company of Chicago.

Founded by Andrew "Rube" Foster, the American Giants of Chicago dominated black baseball during the 1910s, winning more than eleven championships.

Held every summer at Comiskey Park during the 1930s and 1940s, the East-West All-Star Game showcased top players from the National and American Negro Leagues.

integrated the American League by signing twenty-three-year-old Larry Doby to play for Cleveland in July 1947, several months after Jackie Robinson broke the color barrier in Major League Baseball by signing with the Brooklyn Dodgers.[49]

Both Doby and Robinson had played for the Negro Leagues, successor to the Negro National League established by Andrew "Rube" Foster of Chicago in 1920. Known as the "Father of Black Baseball," Foster hailed from Texas and moved to Chicago in 1902 to play for Frank Leland's Union Giants, one of the city's early black baseball teams. At the time, dozens of black teams across the country provided African Americans, who were barred from major league baseball on account of race, a chance to play baseball on the professional level. Foster, a fearsome pitcher, emerged a skillful manager as well, leading the 1910 Union Giants to a 123–6 record with an emphasis on speed and pitching. In 1911, Foster and white saloonkeeper John Schorling, son-in-law of White Sox owner Charles Comiskey, formed the Chicago American Giants. With Schorling's financial backing and regular playing dates at the White Sox's South Side Park, the American Giants earned enough revenue to attract outstanding players. For the next decade, Foster's team dominated black baseball, but white booking agents remained in charge of stadium dates, and thus, revenue streams. To break the stranglehold, Foster created the National Association of Professional Baseball Clubs, better known as the Negro National League, consisting of six midwestern teams (Chicago, St. Louis, Detroit, Kansas City, Dayton, and Indianapolis). Foster insisted on black ownership, with the exception of the Kansas City Monarchs, owned by J. L. Wilkinson, who eventually became Foster's trusted ally and the league's secretary.[50]

Under their direction the Negro National League flourished, proving there was a market for black baseball in America. This was particularly true in northern cities, like Chicago, where the African American community was growing as a result of the Great Migration. Overall, however, the league remained somewhat chaotic, with many teams skipping regular games for more lucrative exhibition games, players jumping from one team to another, and poor officiating. In 1926, Foster, who worked

Amos Alonzo Stagg coaching the University of Chicago football team, 1904. Stagg's many innovations shaped the modern game.

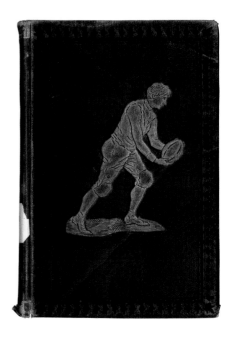

Published in 1894, *A Scientific and Practical Treatise on American Football* by Amos Alonzo Stagg and Henry L. Williams contains general descriptions of the game as well as specific plays, many of which are still used today.

grueling fifteen-hour days without a regular salary, suffered a nervous breakdown, leaving the league without strong leadership.

After the first league's collapse in 1931, a second Negro National League emerged in 1933 with eight teams, including the Chicago American Giants, in two leagues. On Sunday, September 10, the league staged the first East-West All-Star Game at Comiskey Park. The event drew twenty-thousand fans to watch players they had elected by casting ballots published in black newspapers, including the *Chicago Defender*. Held every September at Comiskey Park until 1950, the East-West game was black baseball's premier event. It drew a biracial crowd, often larger than its white counterpart, and, some say, contributed to the eventual integration of major league baseball by showcasing the talent and skill of black players.[51]

In addition to major league baseball, Chicago played a key role in making football a new American pastime. Chicago's contributions to the gridiron begin with the legendary Amos Alonzo Stagg, who coached at the University of Chicago between 1892 and 1933. Often called the father of American football, Stagg pioneered the use of numbered jerseys, the huddle, the bowl game, and most important, the forward pass, which transformed a running and kicking game into its modern form. Under Stagg's direction, the U of C's football teams dominated collegiate play for decades. At the time, they played in the Big Ten Conference, which they helped establish in 1896 at a meeting of midwestern colleges at the Palmer House Hotel in Chicago. With the advent of radio, college football grew in popularity, and Stagg's teams remained competitive until the 1920s when the university began to de-emphasize athletics. In addition to football, Stagg also coached the school's track, baseball, and basketball teams, and he is credited with developing the five-man team for basketball.[52]

The rise of collegiate football inspired another Chicagoan, George Halas, to develop the game on a professional level. Halas, a graduate of the University of

During the 1890s, the University of Chicago dominated collegiate football. A leather pigskin from 1896 commemorates the team's victory over archrival Northwestern University located in Evanston, Illinois.

Chicago Bears official program, 1928.

Illinois and Most Valuable Player in the 1919 Rose Bowl, established the Decatur Staleys in 1920 as a charter member of the American Professional Football Association, later renamed the National Football League (NFL). One year later, Halas moved the team to Chicago, where they played at Cubs Park (Wrigley Field), and renamed them the Bears in 1922. As owner, coach, and defensive end until 1929, Halas developed the Bears into a formidable team, changing the game of football in the process. Together with coach Ralph Jones, Halas perfected the T-formation with a man-in-motion, revolutionizing the game by opening up the offense. Halas also instituted daily practices and the use of films to prepare for next week's opponent. Along with his coaching skills, Halas had a salesman's touch when it came to promoting the game he loved. In 1925, he signed the well-known University of Illinois running back Red Grange, known as the "Galloping Ghost," and took him on a whirlwind tour to promote the upcoming season. As another first, Halas put the Bears games on radio, reaching a vast audience throughout the Midwest and beyond.[53]

Under Halas's guidance, the Bears dominated league play during the 1930s and 1940s, earning the nickname, "Monsters of the Midway," a moniker borrowed from

Head coach "Papa Bear" George Halas with members of the Chicago Bears football team, 1935.
By then, Halas had retired from playing and devoted himself full-time to coaching.

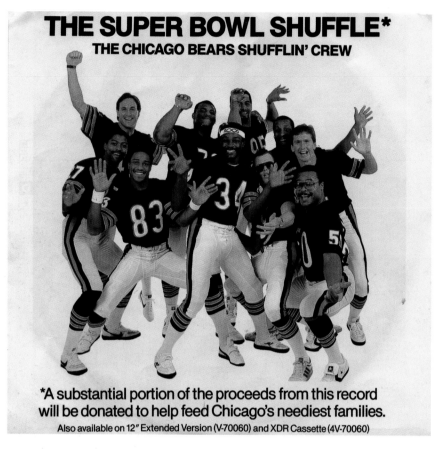

THE SUPER BOWL SHUFFLE*
THE CHICAGO BEARS SHUFFLIN' CREW

***A substantial portion of the proceeds from this record will be donated to help feed Chicago's neediest families.**
Also available on 12" Extended Version (V-70060) and XDR Cassette (4V-70060)

Months before reaching the NFL playoffs, the Chicago Bears released "The Super Bowl Shuffle," a humorous recording that topped the charts. The Bears made good on their bravado, winning Super Bowl XX in convincing fashion.

Chicago Bears football helmet worn by linebacker Mike Singletary during the 1985 championship season. An outstanding player, Singletary was inducted into the NFL Hall of Fame in 1994.

the defunct University of Chicago football team. During this golden era, the Bears won five NFL championships (1932–33, 1940–41, 1946). Their 73–0 victory over the Washington Redskins in 1940 still stands as the greatest margin of victory in any NFL championship game. Although the Bears' fortunes declined during the 1950s, Halas fielded competitive teams in the 1960s, winning the 1963 championship with a talented roster of players that included quarterback Bill Wade, running backs Joe Marconi and Willie Galimore, wide receiver Johnny Morris, tight end Mike Ditka, and linebacker Joe Fortunato.[54]

After Halas retired in 1968, the Bears struggled despite having a number of top players, such as Dick Butkus, Gale Sayers, and Walter Payton. They did not win another championship until the 1985 team coached by Ditka, posted a 15–1 record during the regular season. The team featured running back Walter Payton, linebacker Mike Singletary, defensive tackle William "The Fridge" Perry, and quarterback Jim McMahon. Their spirited play and colorful personalities attracted national attention, enhanced by their popular hit recording, "The Super Bowl Shuffle," which helped raise funds for needy Chicago families. After defeating the New York Giants and Los Angeles Rams during the playoffs, the Bears advanced to Super Bowl XX in New Orleans, where they demolished the New England Patriots 46–10. To date, the Bears have not made another Super Bowl appearance, much to the disappointment of their many fans.[55]

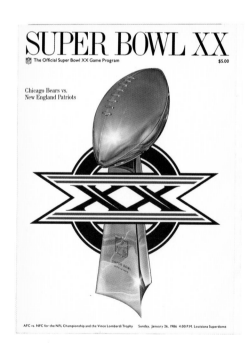

SUPER BOWL XX
The Official Super Bowl XX Game Program $5.00

Chicago Bears vs.
New England Patriots

AFC vs. NFC for the NFL Championship and the Vince Lombardi Trophy   Sunday, January 26, 1986 4:00 P.M. Louisiana Superdome

Super Bowl XX Official Program, 1986. Played in New Orleans at the Louisiana Superdome, the game pitted the Chicago Bears against the New England Patriots.

The Chicago Bulls

A familiar sight at the United Center during the 1990s has Michael Jordan of the Chicago Bulls (23) making a shot, with Scottie Pippen (33) and Steve Kerr (25) in supporting roles.

Established in 1966, the Chicago Bulls featured some good players, including Bob Love, Norm Van Lier, and Jerry Sloan, but the team remained a mediocre franchise for many years. All that changed when Michael "Air" Jordan arrived in 1984. A top college player from the University of North Carolina, Jordan developed into one of the greatest basketball players of all time. During his reign, Jordan and the Bulls, coached by Phil Jackson, captured six National Basketball Association (NBA) championships during the 1990s, a series that included two "three-peats": 1991, 1992, 1993, and 1996, 1997, and 1998. In addition to Jordan, players included Scottie Pippen, Toni Kukoc, and Dennis Rodman. After the 1997–98 season, however, the championship team broke up, closing a glorious chapter in Chicago—and American—sports history.[56]

Chicago Bulls fan helmet, 1998. Although the Bulls' name refers to the city's long history as a center of livestock trading, fans, especially those born after the closing of the Union Stock Yard in 1971, may not understand the connection.

The Harlem Globetrotters

Founded in 1926 by Abe Saperstein, a Jew from Chicago's North Side, the Harlem Globetrotters consisted of African American players from Wendell Phillips High School on the South Side. Like other blacks, they were barred from playing in the newly formed National Basketball Association. Under Saperstein, they originally played for an American Legion post and later as an attraction to boost attendance at the Savoy Ballroom, a South Side dance hall. The team's popularity encouraged Saperstein to take them on the road. He named them the Harlem Globetrotters after the famous black neighborhood in New York City as a way to draw attention and identify their race. The Globetrotters played wherever they could find a willing opponent and established themselves as worthy competitors.

During the 1930s, the team adopted a comedic style of playing that became their trademark, but it also brought criticism from African Americans who considered it demeaning. The team's fast-break style of playing, however, influenced professional basketball and helped create the modern game. During the height of the Cold War during the 1950s and 1960s, the Globetrotters toured extensively throughout Europe on goodwill tours sponsored by the U.S. State Department. In 1976, they moved from Chicago to New York City, where they remain.[57]

The Second City attracted a young, well-educated audience that enjoyed the troupe's biting satire and daring improvisational style that broke the norms of American theater.

Second City's "sold out" sign disappointed many would-be customers but thrilled the company's talented cast.

In addition to fairs, parks, beaches, and sporting events, Chicago developed a lively theater and nightclub scene that has entertained generations of residents, conventioneers, and tourists alike. Over the years, Chicago has had countless such establishments, but only a few can claim to have had national influence. Among the select few are the Second City and the Playboy Club.

Brash, immediate, and above all, irreverent, the Second City has shaped the face of American comedy. The company, established in 1959 by Paul Sills, Bernard Sahlins, and Howard Alk, took its name from a series of derogatory articles in the *New Yorker* about Chicago as a second-rate city. The Second City traces its origins to the Compass, an improvisational comedy group that performed in Chicago between 1955 and 1957. That group's talented roster included Sills, Elaine May, Mike Nichols, and Barbara Harris, who studied the art of improvisation with Viola Spolin, a gifted actress, teacher, and mother of Paul Sills.

Opening in a small, 125-seat theater at 1842 North Wells Street, the Second City staged two-act satirical revues with scripted scenes, parodies, musical numbers, and a series of improvisational skits based on suggestions from the audience. Fast-paced and funny, the Second City attracted a young, well-educated audience that enjoyed the troupe's biting satire and daring improvs that broke the accepted norms of

Second City cast with producer Bernard Sahlins and director Paul Sills in the foreground, 1960. The company's improvisational style reflected and suited the temperament of Chicago audiences.

American theater with skits about formerly taboo subjects, in particular sex and politics. A breeding ground of talent, the Second City launched the careers of major film and television stars such as Alan Arkin, Del Close, John Belushi, John Candy, Bill Murray, Dan Aykroyd, Gilda Radner, George Wendt, and Chris Farley. In addition to its home base in Chicago (now at 1616 North Wells Street), the Second City has companies in Toronto and Las Vegas.[58]

Established in Chicago, *Playboy* magazine and the Playboy Club helped launch America's sexual revolution. In 1953, Hugh Hefner of Chicago, then twenty-seven years old, published the first issue of *Playboy*, which featured articles, short fiction, naughty jokes, and, most startling, nude pictures of Marilyn Monroe. Although scantily clad pinup girls had appeared on calendars throughout World War II, none had been completely undressed. Within two weeks, 72,000 thousand copies of the magazine had sold, and its continued success led to the establishment of the first Playboy Club in Chicago in 1960. The club, restricted to dues-paying members, featured Playboy Bunny waitresses dressed in revealing costumes, complete with "bunny" ears and a fluffy cottontail. Although some feminists decried the work as sexually demeaning, many Bunnies felt liberated by the experience.

Hefner's marketing genius made Playboy a household name. During the early 1970s, *Playboy* had more than seven million subscribers, and Hefner, who had moved to Los Angeles, starred on his own television program, *Playboy after Dark*. As the sexual revolution took hold, however, the intrigue of *Playboy* faded. Other magazines, with more sexually explicit photographs, surpassed *Playboy*. The clubs began to shut down, including Chicago's own in 1988.[59]

Beginning in 1980, Chicago's cultural and recreational scene expanded in another direction. That year, Mayor Jane Byrne's office staged the first Taste of Chicago. Held on the Fourth of July, the one-day festival featured local food vendors on North Michigan Avenue, just south of the river. An instant success, the "Taste" moved to Grant Park the following year and featured more vendors with live music in a ten-day event that drew millions of people to the crossroads city from near and far. The free festival also featured fireworks on the evening of July 3 in honor of the nation's Declaration of Independence and soon became the world's largest food festival.[60]

Byrne's successor, Richard M. Daley, followed suit with the redevelopment of Navy Pier on Chicago's lakefront. Originally built as Municipal Pier No. 2 in 1916, the three-thousand-foot-long structure received a steady stream of freight and passenger traffic during the 1920s. It served as a naval training facility during World War II and then as the Chicago branch of the University of Illinois between 1946 and 1965. Used for civic and cultural events during the late 1970s, Navy Pier reopened as a major tourist attraction in 1994 with restaurants, a theater, a children's museum, a musical carousel, and a 148-foot Ferris Wheel modeled after the one at the 1893 world's fair. Despite its critics, who complain about the attraction's commercial

Above: Hugh Hefner at the Playboy Mansion in Chicago, c. 1965. Hefner's commercial empire included the well-known monthly magazine for men and numerous clubs across the country.

Below: Bunny and customers at the Playboy Club in Chicago, c. 1960.

Navy Pier recalls a legendary chapter in Chicago history with a modern version of the original Ferris Wheel that debuted at the 1893 World's Columbian Exposition. While the contemporary wheel is 148' tall with a 240 person capacity, its predecessor soared 264' into the air and held up to 2,160 people in thirty-six rail-size cars.

nature, Navy Pier draws an average of eight million people a year and anchors Chicago's tourism industry.[61]

Indeed, tourism is now one of Chicago's leading enterprises. Like other post-industrial American cities, Chicago must find new sources of tax revenue, and there has been a growing awareness at City Hall that cultural attractions, sporting events, and leisure activities provide that opportunity. Chicago's 2006 budget, for example, projected $125 million in recreational taxes or more than 6 percent of the total. Meanwhile, the budget allocates $10 million to the Office of Cultural Affairs and $26 million to the Mayor's Office of Special Events, which sponsors Taste of Chicago, Venetian Night, neighborhood festivals, and many other popular activities that attract residents and tourists alike. Additionally, the Chicago Park District allocated $33 million in financial support to several museums (including the Field Museum, the Art Institute, the Chicago History Museum, and the DuSable Museum) that draw thousands of visitors to the city each year.

While these figures pale in comparison to allocations for public safety or Streets and Sanitation, the dollar amounts are significant. Moreover, they point to an interesting trend in Chicago's recent efforts to maintain itself as a viable city. The fact that City Hall has shown interest in cultural affairs should come as no surprise. After all, Chicago has always been an enterprising and innovative city, determined to be—and remain—the crossroads of America.[62]

CHECKLIST

The following is a checklist of objects and documents in the Chicago History Museum's long-term exhibition *Chicago: Crossroads of America*. The organization reflects the major galleries of the exhibition: the Introduction, 'L' Car No. 1 Platform, City on the Make, City in Crisis, Sweet Home Chicago, Second to None, and My Kind of Town. Each entry contains basic information about the artifact or document, while those for photographs also include image reference numbers (ICHi). Please note that not all of the artifacts and documents listed here appear in this catalogue; page numbers are noted for those that do.

GALLERY 1
INTRODUCTION

Lithograph, *A Bird's Eye View of Chicago*
Charles Inger, after a drawing by J. T. Palmatary
1857
Reproduction
ICHi-05656
CHS
endsheets

Photograph, Looking west on Randolph Street from Wabash Avenue
1901
ICHi-04653
Gift of Rand McNally & Company

Engraving, *View of Chicago, from the Prairie*
Published in Sears' Pictoral Description of the United States
1849
Reproduction
ICHi-14374
Gift of Dr. Otto L. Schmidt

Photograph, Downtown Chicago and Lake Michigan
Joseph Sohm
1997
Corbis JS006682
© Joseph Sohm; ChromoSohm Inc./CORBIS

Photograph, Telephone operators boarding an elevated train
Chicago Daily News
1907
DN-0005074
CHS

Photograph, Chicagoans waiting for a train on the Chicago Avenue Brown Line platform
Jay Crawford
2005
ICHi-40063
CHS

International Glove Workers Union of America convention badge
1902–40
Metal, plastic
X.3055.2005
CHS

A Century of Progress International Exposition souvenir bank
American Can Company
1934
Tin
1994.143.11
Gift of Walter H. Schwebke

World's Columbian Exposition souvenir toothpick holder
Libbey Glass Works
1893
Pressed glass
1925.93
Gift of Mr. John H. Weber

Chicago White Sox drinking glass
1988
Glass
1988.648.2
Gift of Robert & Vivian Van Brundt

Pendant
A. Fogliati
1904
Gold, opal
1977.87.2
Gift of Mrs. Charles Batchelder

Can of Chopped Ham & Cheese
Oscar Mayer & Company
c. 1960
Metal
1992.185.14
Gift of Oscar Mayer & Company

Bowl with floral design
Madeline Wynne
c. 1885
Copper, enamel
1997.29.3
CHS Purchase

Red-glazed Teco vase
Gates Potteries
c. 1910
Pottery
1985.40.30
Gift of Chase Gilmore

Green-glazed Teco vase
Gates Potteries
c. 1910
Pottery
1969.1092
Gift of Mrs. John R. Weiss

Cowbell from drum set
Sargent
c. 1920
Metal
1995.232.24
Gift of Howard F. Kapso & Charles R. Keebler

Playboy Club drinking glass
c. 1960
Glass
2001.268.5
Gift of Edward R. Weed

Wrigley Field *Diamond Dust*
2003
Glass, paper, metal
2004.76.4
Gift of Kathy Horky

City peddler badge
Late 19th century
Metal
939-1H
Gift of Edna Schwartzmann

Native American stemmed point marked *Park Ridge*
Late Archaic Period
Flint
X.282
CHS

Vase damaged in Great Chicago Fire
1871
Ceramic
X.2308.2004
CHS

GALLERY 2
'L' CAR NO. 1 PLATFORM

Photograph, A traffic jam on Dearborn Street, looking south from Randolph Street
Frank M. Hallenbeck
1909
ICHi-04191
CHS

Photograph, Elevated train crossing the Lake Street Bridge
1924
ICHi-40000
CHS

Thornton Old Fashioned Lager Beer advertising sign
Owl Sign Company
Late 19th century
Glass, wood
1953.371
Gift of Mr. J. H. Weber

Tailor, Cleaner and Dyer advertising sign
J. H. Weber Sign Company
Late 19th century
Glass, wood
1953.639
Gift of Mr. J. H. Weber

Lincoln Turner Hall Café advertising sign
J. H. Weber Sign Company
Late 19th century
Glass, wood
1953.368
Gift of Mr. J. H. Weber

Atlas Prager Beer advertising sign
J. H. Weber Sign Company
Late 19th century
Glass, wood
1953.367
Gift of Mr. J. H. Weber

Car 1, Chicago and South Side Rapid Transit Railroad Company
Jackson & Sharp Company
1892
Mixed materials
Courtesy of the Chicago Transit Authority
p. 103

Photograph, Detail of World's Columbian Exposition Ferris Wheel
1893
ICHi-02434
CHS

Photograph, Ida B. Wells
c. 1892
Courtesy of University of Chicago Library
p. 176

Photograph, Mabel Treseder
c. 1890
Courtesy of Vernon County Historical Society, Viroqua, Wisconsin

Photograph, South Side Elevated Road
c. 1893
ICHi-05396
CHS

Photograph, Construction of 'L' tracks on Lake Street, north of Rockwell Street
1893
ICHi-05376
Gift of Chicago Transit Authority via George Krambles

Postcard, Chicago's Union Loop
Franklin Postcard Company
1917
Reproduction
ICHi-40001
CHS

Photograph, Charles Tyson Yerkes
c. 1895
ICHi-13104
Gift of Walter S. Brewster

Photograph, Woman with
Children on El Platform
Jay Wolke
1983
ICHi-40002
Gift of Jay Wolke

Fare card
Chicago Transit Authority
c. 2000
Plastic, paper
2006.1.1
CHS

Fare tokens
Chicago Transit Authority
1922–98
Metal
1999.76
Gift of Loretta Blank

Photograph, Elevated trains in
the Loop
Jay Crawford
2005
ICHi-40064
CHS

Map, Chicago's rapid transit
system
Dennis McClendon
2004
Reproduction
Courtesy of the Newberry
Library

GALLERY 3
CITY ON THE MAKE

CHECAGOU
Indian Homelands

Illustration, People of the
Archaic Period
Andy Buttram
2001
Reproduction
Courtesy of the Dickson
Mounds branch of the Illinois
State Museum
p. 2

Grooved ax head
Archaic Period
Polished stone
Acc. No. 500
CHS

Grooved ax head
Archaic Period
Polished stone
X. 271
CHS
p. 2

Knife or dart point
Early Archaic Period
Chipped stone
X.3264.2005
CHS

Knife or dart point
Early Archaic Period
Chipped stone
X.3265.2005
CHS

Celt
Woodland Period
Polished stone
X.3267.2005
CHS

Celt
Mississippian Period
Polished stone
X.3266.2005
CHS

The French Explorers

Bas-relief panel, *Arrival of
Marquette at the Chicago River*
Herman A. MacNeil
1894
Plaster
1895.25
Gift of Herman A. MacNeil
p. 3

Book, *Decouverte de quelques pays
et nations de l'Amerique,* or
*Discovery of Several Countries and
Nations of America*
Jacques Marquette
Published in Recueil de
Voyages de M. Thevenot, Paris
1681
Ink on paper
69519
CHS Purchase

Holy Water font
1752
Brass
1948.64
Gift of Mr. John Gerten
p. 4

Cross
c. 1696
Brass, wood
1929.47
Gift of Mr. James A. Hammill

Map of New France and
Canada
1755
Reproduction
ICHi-15570
CHS
p. 5

Fort Dearborn

Logs from the Second Fort
Dearborn, Officer's Quarters
1816
Oak
1912.23
Gift of The Board of
Commissioners, South Parks,
Chicago

Model of Fort Dearborn
Albert L. Van den Berghen
1898
Mixed materials
1898.2
Gift of Mrs. Charlotte
Whitehead Pitkin, in memory
of Rebecca and Jesse
Whitehead

Plan of Fort Dearborn
Adapted from pencil drawing
by Kate Bacon Bond
Published in Frederic William
Bond's *A Little History of a Great
City/Chicago*
1934
ICHi-40234
Gift of Fred Bond

Signal gun used at Fort
Dearborn
c. 1820
Wood, iron
X.1182
CHS

Trunk belonging to Rebekah
Heald
1811
Wood, hide, iron, felt
1912.13
Gift of Mrs. Wright Johnson

Daguerreotype, Rebekah Wells
Heald
c. 1845
ICHi-13957
CHS

Ladle given as a wedding gift to
Rebekah Wells and Nathan
Heald
Best & Deterly
1811
Silver
1912.10
Gift of Mrs. Wright Johnson

Teaspoon given as a wedding
gift to Rebekah Wells and
Nathan Heald
Best & Deterly
1811
Silver
1912.11
Gift of Mrs. Wright Johnson

Teaspoon given as a wedding
gift to Rebekah Wells and
Nathan Heald
1811
Silver
1912.12
Gift of Mrs. Wright Johnson

Comb given as a wedding gift
to Rebekah Wells
1811
Tortoise shell, gold
1912.14
Gift of Mrs. Wright Johnson

Sword belonging to Captain
Nathan Heald
c. 1810
Steel, brass
1914.11
Gift of Mrs. L. M. Ottofy

Painting, William Wells
c. 1810
Watercolor on paper
X.269
CHS

Lithograph, *Me-Te-A, A
Pottawatomie Chief*
Published by F. W. Greenough,
Philadelphia
c. 1830
Ink on paper
X.3172.2005
CHS
p. 7

Shot dredged from the Chicago
River at the site of Fort
Dearborn
c. 1812
Iron
1906.9a-e
Gift of George W. Lemar

Bullets found at site of the Fort
Dearborn attack
c. 1812
Ferrous metal
1925.109ab
Gift of Frank T. Andrews

Bullet mold found at site of
Fort Dearborn attack
c. 1812
Ferrous metal
X.285
CHS

Loyalty medal presented by the
British to Chief Blackbird
1815
Silver
1946.28
Gift of Colonel Robert R.
McCormick and the *Chicago
Tribune*
p. 7

The Fur Trade

Painting, *The Kinzie Home and
Fort Dearborn*
Artist unknown
c. 1900
Oil on canvas
1967.405
Gift of The Guild of the
Chicago Historical Society
p. 6

Engraving, *Jean Baptiste Point
DuSable*
Moss Engraving Company,
New York
1920
Reproduction
ICHi-34559
CHS
p. 6

Painting, *Ne-Sa-Au-Quot,* or *The
Bear in the Fork of the Tree*
Charles Bird King
1837
Oil on wood
X. 513
CHS

Safe used by the American Fur
Company
c. 1825
Iron
X. 120
CHS

Flint lock gun used by the
American Fur Company
W. Chance & Son, London
c. 1825
Wood, steel, brass
1920.707
CHS Purchase, Charles F.
Gunther Collection

Tomahawk head
17th century
Iron
X.1240
CHS

Trade beads
c. 1750
Glass
X. 1219
CHS

Armlet engraved with the
British coat of arms
C. F. London
c. 1812
Silver
1920.696
CHS Purchase, Charles F.
Gunther Collection

Cross
Robert Cruickshank, Montreal,
Canada
c. 1775
Silver
X.255
CHS

Cross
Nathaniel Richardson,
Philadelphia
c. 1775
Silver
1938.71
Gift of Miss Mary L. Stevenson

Earrings
c. 1800
Silver
1920.697
CHS Purchase, Charles F.
Gunther Collection
Cross
John Kinzie
c. 1820
Silver
1982.72.1
CHS Purchase

Miniature portrait, *Gurdon
Saltonstall Hubbard*
Attributed to Anson Dickinson
1828
Oil on ivory
1923.56
Gift of Mr. Henry E. Hamilton
p. 8

Miniature portrait, *Jean-Baptiste
Beaubien*
c. 1825
Watercolor on ivory
1980.249
Gift of Aline Brandseth
p. 8

Photograph, Shabbona
c. 1850
Ambrotype
1952.234
Gift of Mrs. Joseph M. Cudahy
p. 8

Didn't Expect No Town

Painting, *Wolf's Point 1833*
Justin Herriott
c. 1902
Reproduction
ICHi-05946
Gift of Mr. William H. Gale
p. 9

Lithograph, *Wa-Baun-See, A
Pottawatimie*
Published by F. W. Greenough,
Philadelphia
c. 1842
Ink on paper
X.3319.2005
CHS
p. 12

Photograph, Mark Beaubien
c. 1850
Daguerrotype
1918.56
Gift of Frank Beaubien and
Mrs. Emily Beaubien Le Beau
p. 9

Fiddle reportedly used by Mark
Beaubien
c. 1860
Wood
1980.226
Gift of Bernice K. Hicks
p. 9

Teapot, sugar bowl, and pitcher
presented to Mark Beaubien
c. 1830
Britanniaware
1929.61b, c, d
Gift of Mrs. Anton Bernard

Earrings worn by Monique
Nadeau Beaubien
c. 1830
Gold
1920.700ab
Bequest of Mrs. Emily
Beaubien Le Beau

Cabinet card, William Butler
Ogden
C. D. Mosher
c. 1868
ICHi-32561
CHS
p. 10

Gavel used by Chicago's
Common Council
1837
Wood
X.10
CHS
p. 10

Map of Chicago
J. S. Wright
1834
Reproduction
ICHi-34590
CHS

Engraving, *Chicago in 1845, from
the West*
Published in Sears' Pictoral
Description of the United
States
1849
Reproduction
ICHi-14374
Gift of Dr. Otto L. Schmidt

Model of 19th-century Chicago
warehouses
Dennis F. McCarthy
c. 1950
Mixed materials
X.438
CHS

Surveyor's compass used by
James Thompson
Thomas Whitney, Philadelphia
1830
Brass
1920.665
CHS Purchase, Charles F.
Gunther Collection

Drafting instruments used by
James Thompson
1830
Brass, steel, wood
1920.664
CHS Purchase, Charles F.
Gunther Collection
p. 10

A Map of the Town of Chicago,
1830
Copy created from map by
James Thompson
1840
Ink on paper
0296
Gift of P. W. Kunning
p. 11

Club with studs
c. 1835
Wood, brass
1904.23
Gift of Stephen F. Gale
p. 12

BIG SHOULDERS
TRANSPORTATION CROSSROADS
Water Crossroads

Photograph, Steamboat on the
Chicago River passing under
bridge
Kaufmann & Fabry
1928
ICHi-40229
CHS

Whistle from the S. S. Shelter
Bay
1922
Metal
1956.482
Gift of the *Chicago Tribune*

Stack and Flag Chart
Port of Chicago
c. 1965
Ink on paper
X.3280.2005
Gift of the Better Government
Association
p. 32

Carved bowsprit from the
schooner *Mary A. Gregory*
John Gregory
1875
Wood, paint
1925.43
Gift of Paul Strayer
p. 14

Carved eagle figurehead from
the schooner *Mary A. Gregory*
John Gregory
1875
Wood, paint
1935.98
Gift of the daughters of
Captain John Harry Woltman

Megaphone from the schooner
Mary A. Gregory
Stentor Megaphone
1899
Metal
1935.102
Gift of the daughters of
Captain John Harry Woltman

Broadside, Buffalo, Chicago &
Lake Huron Tri-Weekly Line
Daily Courier Job Printing
House
1861
Ink on paper
X.2922.2005
CHS

Photograph, *Continental Grain
Silos*
Jay Wolke
1984
ICHi-40071
Gift of Jay Wolke
p. 32

Photograph, Barge traffic on
the North Branch of the
Chicago River
R. F. Stibal
1958
ICHi-40072
Gift of R. F. Stibal

Photograph, Construction of
the Sanitary and Ship Canal
c. 1895
ICHi-40068
CHS

Photograph, Workers hauling
rocks
William M. Christie
1898
ICHi-40084
CHS

Set of seven caulking chisels
Wilcox & Crittenden & Co.,
Middletown, Connecticut
c. 1900
Steel
1991.556.1–.7
Gift of Donald W. Burns

Photograph, The schooner
Edward Blake
c. 1890
ICHi-40069
CHS

Broadside, Illinois & Michigan
Canal tolls
William Gooding, Secretary
1857
Ink on paper
X.3320.2005
CHS

Engraving, *The Illinois and
Michigan Canal*
Copcutt
c. 1848
Reproduction
ICHi-40067
CHS
p. 13

Rail Crossroads

Photograph, The Pennsylvania
Limited arriving at Union
Station
Barnes-Crosby
c. 1910
ICHi-19132
Gift of the Barnes-Crosby
Company
p. xv

Photograph, Women and child
boarding a train assisted by a
Pullman porter
c. 1915
ICHi-26271
CHS
p. 17

Tail drum sign from the Santa
Fe Railroad's train *The Chief*
c. 1970
Glass, metal
1973.150
Gift of the Atchison, Topeka
and Santa Fe Railway Company

Quarter-scale working model of
a Pullman sleeping car berth
The Pullman Company
c. 1930
Mixed materials
1970.137
Gift of the Pullman Company
p. 17

Menu, Chicago Rock Island
and Pacific Railroad
Printed by Cosack & Co.
1885
Ink on paper
1943.169
Gift of Mrs. James Ward
Thorne

Illinois Central Railroad syrup
pitcher
Reed & Barton
c. 1930
Silver
1966.376
Gift of Illinois Central Railroad

Illinois Central Railroad syrup
pitcher
Reed & Barton
c. 1920
Silver
1966.374ab
Gift of Illinois Central Railroad

Menu, Colorado Flyer
Chicago and North Western
Railway
1932
Ink on paper
X.3268.2005
CHS

Postcard, Broadway Limited
c. 1915
Ink on paper
X.3278.2005
CHS

Railroad ticket punch
Railway Register Manufacturing
Co., Buffalo
c. 1855
Brass, nickel-plated
1920.40
CHS Purchase, Charles F.
Gunther Collection

Postcard, Denver Zephyr
Burlington Railway
c. 1936
Ink on paper
X.3269.2005
CHS

Crofutt's New Overland Tourist
and Pacific Coast Guide
George A. Crofutt
Published by the Overland
Publishing Company
1878
Ink on paper
2001.222.1NA
Gift of Joseph Kelly

Photograph, International
Convention of the
Brotherhood of Sleeping Car
Porters
1938
ICHi-40065
Gift of The Brotherhood of
Sleeping Car Porters

Broadside, Brotherhood of
Sleeping Car Porters Chicago
Division meeting
1927
Ink on paper
66:571
Gift of Illinois State & Chicago
Federations of Labor

Detail of broadside, Chicago,
Rock Island & Pacific Railroad
Printed by G. W. & C. B.
Colton & Co.
1870
ICHi-31192
CHS
p. 16

Pioneer locomotive engine
Matthias W. Baldwin (Baldwin
Locomotive Works),
Philadelphia
c. 1840
Mixed materials
1972.42
Gift of the Chicago and North
Western Railway

Pioneer locomotive bell
c. 1840
Copper alloy
2001.264.1
Gift of the Estate of Robert L.
Williams

Photograph, The Pioneer at the
National Railway Appliance
Exposition, Chicago
1883
ICHi-40636
CHS
p. 15

Trainman's hand lantern,
Galena & Chicago Union
Railroad
J. F. Griffin
c. 1863
Silver plate, glass
1950.149
CHS Purchase

Lamp wick trimmer, Chicago
and North Western Railway
c. 1900
Steel
1960.304
Gift of E. W. McBride

Timetable, Chicago & Aurora
Railroad
Walter S. Johnson,
Superintendent
1854
Ink on paper
1924.121
Gift of Mrs. Charles Henry
Chappell

Railway Timekeeper watch
and chain
James Brindle
c. 1855
Gold
1934.9
Gift of William J. Chalmers

Photograph, Rail shipment of
iron ore to a Chicago steel mill
C. J. Horecky
1951
ICHi-40073
Gift of C. J. Horecky

Broadside, Tariff and Eastward
Classification
Pittsburgh, Fort Wayne &
Chicago Railway
1864
Reproduction
ICHi-40124
CHS Purchase

Photograph, Illinois Central
Railroad freight yards
c. 1950
ICHi-40070
Gift of the Illinois Central
Railroad

Photograph, Coupling freight
cars at the Santa Fe Railroad
yard
Stephen Deutch
c. 1965
ICHi-40108
Gift of Stephen Deutch

Photograph, Railroad freight
cars waiting for engines in the
Chicago train yards
c. 1985
© Corbis

Photograph, Chicago and
North Western Railway ticket
office
1886
ICHi-29809
CHS

Broadside, Chicago and North
Western Railway
Geo. L. Dunlap,
Superintendent
Printed by Dunlop, Sewell &
Spalding
1862
Ink on paper
X.3281.2005
Gift of the Chicago and North
Western Railway

Chicago and North Western
Railway sign
c. 1875
Glass, wood
X.2910.2005
CHS
p. 14

Meatpacking

Photograph, Packinghouse
workers trimming pigs
Stephen Deutch
c. 1945
ICHi-40111
Gift of Stephen Deutch
p. 23

Reproduction of terra cotta
arch from entrance of the
National Live Stock Bank
Designed by Burnham and
Root
1984.726.1
Gift of Prince Charitable Trust

Killing floor light fixture from
the Hygrade Foods packing
plant
c. 1900
Metal, paint
1995.52.8
Gift of Chiappetti Wholesale
Meat Company

Meat hooks
c. 1920
Steel
X.3270.2005.1–.11
CHS

Swift's *Silverleaf* Brand Pure
Lard container
c. 1920
Metal
X.3271.005
CHS

Chiappetti Packing Co. storage
buckets
Airlite, Omaha, Nebraska
c. 1990
Plastic
1995.52.2, 1995.52.4
Gift of Chiappetti Wholesale
Meat Company

Texas longhorn hat rack
c. 1900
Horn, wood, metal
X.3272.2005
CHS

Meat cleaver used by the
Chiappetti Wholesale Meat
Company
c. 1930
Steel, wood
1995.52.6
Gift of Chiappetti Wholesale
Meat Company

Set of five skinning knives used
at the Lincoln Meat Company
c. 1920
Steel, wood
1978.154.5a-e
Gift of Lincoln Meat Company

Lithograph, *Interior Views of a
Modern First Class Pork Packing
& Canning Establishment of the
United States of America*
Shober & Carqueville, Litho
Co., Chicago
1880
Ink on paper
0995
CHS Purchase

Bull's head from the east gate
of the Union Stock Yard,
Chicago
1865
Cast bronze
1999.123
Gift of Mrs. Charles S. Potter
(Barbara Ogden McClurg) in
memory of Charles S. Potter
p. 20

Hatch Live Stock Commission
Company pen sign
c. 1966
Wood
2003.251.5
Gift of Eldon Hatch

Whip used at the Union Stock
Yard
c. 1971
Nylon
2003.251.12
Gift of Eldon Hatch

Cane used by cattle dealer Fred
Hatch Jr.
1919–69
Wood
2003.251.1
Gift of Eldon Hatch

Photograph, Livestock pens and
workers herding sheep at the
Union Stock Yard
Barnes-Crosby
c. 1910
ICHi-19106
Gift of the Barnes-Crosby
Company
pp. xv (detail), 18

Photograph, Ceremony celebrating the arrival of the billionth animal at the Union Stock Yard
J. Sherwin Murphy
1954
ICHi-04101
CHS
p. 19

Hatch Live Stock Commission Company alley and gate number sign
c. 1900
Wood
2003.251.4
Gift of Eldon Hatch

Livestock scale bell used at the Union Stock Yard
c. 1900
Metal, wood
2003.251.9
Gift of Eldon Hatch

Painting, *Scene at the International Live Stock Exposition at the International Ampitheater*
Gary Sheahan
1947
Oil on canvas
1977.109
Gift of Charles S. Potter

Football
Wilson Sporting Goods Company
c. 2005
Leather
2005.69.1
Gift of Wilson Sporting Goods Company

Photograph, Chicago leather workers
Ed Stratton
c. 1900
ICHi-40228
Gift of Elaine Friedman

Trade card, A. Kahn: Dealer of fine calfskin and kid boots and shoes
Calvert Litho Co., Detroit
1880
Ink on paper
X.3279.2005
CHS

Women's slippers
N. B. Holden, Chicago
c. 1900
Bronze kid
1956.554ab
Gift of Mr. Charles Gelis

Men's gloves
c. 1920
Leather
X.3321.2005NA
CHS

Women's leather gloves
c. 1920
Leather
X.3322.2005NA
CHS

Broadside, *Vote for Agnes Nestor*
1928
Ink on paper
58:123
Gift of the Estate of Mary Nestor

Delegate ribbon badge worn by Agnes Nestor
1940
Mixed materials
(1958.629
Gift of the Estate of Mary Nestor

Photograph, Worker making hot dogs at an Oscar Mayer plant
Arthur Siegel
c. 1955
ICHi-40062
Gift of Irene Siegel

Wienermobile toy
c. 1965
Plastic
1992.155.1
Gift of Oscar Mayer & Co.

Can of Oscar Mayer wieners
Oscar Mayer & Co.
c. 1960
Tin
1992.185.17
Gift of Oscar Mayer & Co.

Book, *The Jungle*
Upton Sinclair
1906
Ink on paper
26681
Gift of Otto Schmidt
p. 24

Photograph, Stockyards Strike Parade
Chicago Daily News
1904
DN-0000999
CHS
p. 24

Meat stamp used at the Lincoln Meat Company
c. 1920
Brass, iron, wood
1978.154.4
Gift of Lincoln Meat Company

Halftone, *Making Final Inspection*
Published in *The Evolution of a Vast Industry* by Charles Winans
1906
Reproduction
ICHi-40113
Gift of *Chicago Daily News*

Photograph, Bidding on Champion Carload feeder cattle
J. F. Abernathy
1947
ICHi-27025
Gift of CMD Realty Management Co.
p. 21

Illustration, *Standard Breeds of Cattle*
Published in *The Livestock Producer* and *Armour* by Armour & Co.
1920
Ink on paper
38106
Gift of Armour & Co.

Comptometer used in the office of John Clay and Company
Felt & Tarrant Manufacturing Co., Chicago
c. 1914
Metal, wood, plastic
2003.251.6
Gift of Eldon Hatch

International Live Stock Exposition badge.
c. 1900
Mixed materials
(2001.257
Gift of Elizabeth Lewis
p. 19

Loving cup presented to William H. Thompson Jr.
Hyman, Berg & Co., Chicago
1902
Silver
2001.257.1a
Gift of Elizabeth Lewis
p. 19

Halftone, *Trimming*
Published in *Views in the Chicago Stockyards and Packing Industry*
1892
Reproduction
ICHi-34356
Gift of William S. R. Mitchell

Photograph, Disassembling pigs at the Oscar Mayer plant
Arthur Siegel
c. 1955
ICHi-40005
Gift of Irene Siegel

Photograph, Philip Danforth Armour
C. D. Mosher
c. 1885
ICHi-09424
Gift of Gerald Grant

Trade card, Armour and Co. breakfast sausages
1880–1920
Ink on paper
X.3166.2005
Gift of Staples & Charles

Trade card, Swift and Company Packers Refrigerator Line Display
c. 1893
Ink on paper
X.3167.2005
CHS
p. 23

Halftone, Gustavus F. Swift
Published in *Yankee of the Yards*
c. 1885
Reproduction
ICHi-34834
Gift of Swift & Co.

Halftone, *Fig. 89—Hoisting hogs on a Hurford revolving wheel*
Published in *The Modern Packing House*
1905
Reproduction
ICHi-40078
CHS Purchase
p. 20

Halftone, *Fig. 90—Sticking and bleeding hogs*
Published in *The Modern Packing House*
1905
Reproduction
ICHi-40079
CHS Purchase

Photograph, Back of the Yards neighborhood
c. 1905
ICHi-22431, ICHi-40003
Gift of Chicago Commons Association

Photograph, Skimming the *Bubbly Branch* of the Chicago River
1905
ICHi-23820
Gift of Chicago Commons Association

Photograph, Slovak June Bride of the stockyards
1921
ICHi-22982
Gift of Chicago Commons Association

Photograph, Slovak June Bride of the stockyards with wedding party
1921
ICHi-40004
Gift of Chicago Commons Association

Photograph, Cattle dealer Fred Hatch Sr. at the Union Stock Yard
c. 1890
ICHi-36829
Gift of Eldon Hatch

Photograph, Fred Hatch Jr. at the Union Stock Yard
c. 1935
ICHi-36825
Gift of Eldon Hatch
p. 21

Photograph, Eldon Hatch and his son Gavin at the Union Stock Yard
c. 1966
ICHi-36827
Gift of Eldon Hatch

Map of the Union Stock Yard of Chicago showing Railroads & Connections
Published by Rand McNally & Company
1891
Reproduction
ICHi-27741
CHS
p. 20

Photograph, Panorama of the Union Stock Yard
Kaufmann & Fabry
1901
ICHi-40085
Gift of Kaufmann & Fabry

Photograph, International Live Stock Exposition's Grand Champion Wether
1954
ICHi-40075
Gift of Chiappetti Wholesale Meat Company

Photograph, Winners of the Angus Steer competition at the International Live Stock Exposition
1954
ICHi-40074
Gift of CMD Realty Management Company
p. 22

Photograph, International Live Stock Exposition's Stockyard Princess and companion
1954
ICHi-40076
Gift of CMD Realty Management Company

Broadside, *International Live Stock Exposition and Horse Show*
1949
Ink on paper
ICHi-40057
CHS
p. 22

Furniture

Furniture leg patterns
Montalbano-Majestic Wood Carving Co.
1912–70
Wood
1984.252.5b, 4a, 5d
Gift of Richard Montalbano

Furniture leg patterns
Montalbano-Majestic Wood Carving Co.
1912–70
Plywood
1984.252.2a, g
Gift of Richard Montalbano

Furniture drawer patterns
Montalbano-Majestic Wood
Carving Co.
1912–70
Wood
1984.252.2h, m
Gift of Richard Montalbano

Bentwood chair
Great Northern Chair Co.
1939
Oak
1977.43b
CHS Purchase
p. 26

Headboard from the Palmer
House Hotel bridal suite
W. W. Strong Furniture Co.
1873
Black walnut
1979.55.1a
CHS Purchase
p. 26

S. Karpen & Bros. Upholstered
Furniture, 26th Annual Catalog
Published by The Campbell
Company, Chicago
1906
Ink on paper
X.3273.2005
CHS Purchase
p. 27

Glue pot used at the
Montalbano-Majestic Wood
Carving Company
STA-WARM Electric Company,
Ravenna, Ohio
c. 1940
Metal, copper
1984.1.2ab
Gift of Richard Montalbano

Chair made for Dr. John
McGowan from the horns of
his cows
c. 1890
Horn, wood, textiles, metal
1986.358
CHS Purchase
p. 25

Photograph, Looking northwest
from the lighthouse
John W. Taylor
c. 1885
ICHi-29531
CHS Purchase

Broadside, Logs Wanted
C. M. Covell, Hart
c. 1870
Ink on paper
58:95
Bequest of Carrie E. Mears

Photograph, Valley Lumber
Company train hauling logs
c. 1930
ICHi-40086
Gift of Dorothy and William
Worst

Photograph, Wood trimming
room
1906
ICHi-40087
Gift of Agnes J. Ranseen

Photograph, Goodrich
Steamship Dock
John W. Taylor
c. 1888
ICHi-05408
CHS Purchase

Photograph, Furniture store at
905 State Street
1868–69
ICHi-12014
Gift of the Estate of Potter
Palmer
Furniture Workers' (Moebel
Arbeiter) Union No. 1 silk ban-
ner
c. 1877
Reproduction
1981.51.1
Gift of Mill Division of
Carpenter's District Council

Photograph, Tonk
Manufacturing Company
employees
Waterman Photo Company
1893
ICHi-34809
Gift of Mr. and Mrs. Hampton
E. Tonk and Doris A. Tonk
p. 25

Photograph, Tonk
Manufacturing Company
worker
c. 1925
ICHi-40081
Gift of Mr. and Mrs. Hampton
E. Tonk and Doris A. Tonk

Automatic carving machine
blades used by Montalbano-
Majestic Wood Carving
Company
c. 1910
Steel
1984.1.4abc
Gift of Richard Montalbano

Catalog, Tonk Manufacturing
Company
Published by Geo. L. Marshall
& Co.
1884
Ink on paper
1984.535
Gift of Mr. and Mrs. Hampton
E. Tonk and Doris A. Tonk

Breweries

Photograph, Bottling beer at
Seibel's Brewing Academy
1909
ICHi-25667
Gift of J. E. Seibel Co. and
Sons
p. 30

Photograph, Birk Brothers
Brewing Company delivery
wagon
c. 1895
ICHi-40231
Courtesy of Mr. James Madden
p. 30

Photograph, Andy Cashore
Tavern
c. 1895
ICHi-40230
Courtesy of Mr. James Madden

Brewery refrigeration panel and
gauges
Fred W. Wolf Company,
Chicago
c. 1900
Cast iron, brass
1998.120.2
Gift of Wolfe-Linde, Inc.

Chromolithograph, Wacker &
Birk Brewing Company
c. 1894
Ink on paper
1988.55
Gift of Frank L. Flay
p. 30

Beer bottles
c. 1900
Glass
1979.17
Gift of Ed Lace

Birkenhead lager beer bottle
Ambrosia Brewing Co.
c. 1945
Glass
1979.40
Gift of Mr. and Mrs. Nick J.
Poolos & Family

P. Schoenhofen beer bottle
S B & C Co.
c. 1900
Glass
1972.58
Gift of Mr. Robert Natke

Birk Brothers Brewing
Company beer case
c. 1920
Wood, tin
1984.337
Gift of Joseph B. Zywicki

Keeley Brewing Company beer
case and bottles
c. 1950
Wood, glass
X.3274.2005
CHS

Keeley Brewing Company
serving tray
c. 1910
Tin
1988.55
Gift of Frank L. Flay

Anti-prohibition button
J. L. Lynch Company, Chicago
1919
Metal
X.1899.1996
CHS

Beer growler
c. 1900
Tin
1979.19
Gift of Perry Duis

Beer stein
Mettlach, Germany
c. 1910
Ceramic, pewter
1972.115
Gift of Miss Helen M. Lange

Beer seidel
The Steuer Glass Company,
Chicago
c. 1910
Glass, pewter, enamel
1954.354
CHS Purchase

Steel

Photograph, Men at work,
Allied Structural Steel
Companies
c. 1948
ICHi-40082
CHS
p. xvi

Photograph, Open hearth fur-
nace at U.S. Steel's South
Works mill
c. 1950
ICHi-40192
Gift of United States Steel
Corporation
p. 28

Locomotive wheel
Made by the Griffin Wheel and
Foundry Company, Chicago
1888
Cast iron
1979.37
Gift of Griffin Wheel Company

Letters from the Wisconsin
Steel Works
c. 1970
Iron alloy, enamel
2000.68.2–.4
Gift of International Truck &
Engine Corporation
p. 29

Broadside, *The Steel Mills by
South Shore Line*
Printed by Wm. R. Crawford,
Chicago
1928
Ink on paper
X.3323.2005
CHS Purchase
p. 27

Safety glasses
c. 1975
Plastic
2001.30.1a
Gift of Mr. Frank Valadez Sr.

Hard hat
Mine Safety Appliances
Company, Pittsburgh
c. 1970
Fiberglass
2000.116.1–.2ab
Gift of Mr. Herbert H. Post

Steel-toed work boots
Hytest Safety Footwear
c. 1970
Leather
2000.116.1–.2ab
Gift of Mr. Herbert H. Post
p. 28

Photograph, Men and women
having a picnic in South
Chicago
John Becker
c. 1910
ICHi-20521
Gift of Nicholas Pemmer

Photograph, Families at South
Chicago's annual sidewalk sale
Antonio Perez
1987
ICHi-40080
Gift of the Focus/Infinity Fund

Photograph, Valley Mould and
Iron Company blast furnace
William Siegel
1956
ICHi-37735
Gift of William Siegel
p. 29

Photograph, Aerial view of U.S.
Steel's North Works
Hugh W. Celander
1954
ICHi-40083
Gift of Hugh W. Celander

Photograph, Police confronting
strikers during the Memorial
Day Massacre
Chicago Daily News
1937
DN-C-8769
CHS

Subpoena issued to George A.
Patterson
Coroner of Cook County
1937
Ink on paper
82:41
Gift of George A. Patterson

Republic Steel Strike Bulletin
Steel Workers Organizing
Committee Women's Auxiliary
1937
Ink on paper
80:5
Gift of United Steelworkers of
America, District 31

Photograph, Women picketing
City Hall during the Republic
Steel Strike
Chicago Daily News
1937
DN-C-8805
CHS

THE NEW ECONOMY
Modern Trading

Photograph, Traders at the
Chicago Board of Trade
c. 2004
Courtesy of the Chicago Board
of Trade
p. xvii

Photograph, Trading at the
Chicago Mercantile Exchange
2005
Courtesy of the Chicago
Mercantile Exchange

Trader's jacket from the
Chicago Board of Trade
ASG Custom Jackets
c. 2000
Natural and synthetic fiber
textiles
2005.66.1
Gift of Mr. Michael A. Pesoli
p. 37

Platform shoes from the
Chicago Board of Trade
Work America
c. 2000
Leather, rubber
2005.65.1ab
Gift of Mr. Norbert A.
Klucikowski
p. 37

Photograph, Chicago Board of
Trade Building
Hedrich-Blessing
1954
HB-17513A
CHS, Hedrich-Blessing collec-
tion
p. 36

Model of Ceres for the Chicago
Board of Trade Building
John Storrs
1930
Electro-plated plaster, marble
1991.202
Gift of Edwin Cole in memory
of John W. Root and John
Storrs
p. 36

iPAQ pocket computer
c. 2005
2005.43.1
Gift of the Chicago Mercantile
Exchange

Trader's buttons
c. 2005
2005.43.2–.7
Gift of the Chicago Mercantile
Exchange
p. 37

Cellular One telephone
Motorola
c. 1988
Plastic, metal
Courtesy of Motorola, Inc.

T720 cell phone
Motorola
2004
Plastic, metal
Courtesy of Motorola, Inc.

M68690 microprocessor
Motorola
1974
Metal
Courtesy of Motorola, Inc.

Modern Transportation

Photograph, *Pilsen Skyline*
Jay Wolke
1984
ICHi-40066
Gift of Jay Wolke
p. 33

U.S. Interstate 57 sign
c. 1980
Metal
X.3275.2005
CHS

U.S. Interstate 94 sign
c. 1980
Metal
X.3276.2005
CHS
p. 33

Photograph, Congress Street
Expressway under construction
Chicago Daily News
1954
DNP-9935
CHS
Photograph, Dedication of
O'Hare International Airport
1963
ICHi-32484
Gift of the Department of
Public Works
p. 34

Photograph, United Airlines
Terminal at O'Hare
International Airport
Neal Callahan
1978
ICHi-26528
Gift of Neal Callahan
pp. xiv (detail), 35

GALLERY 4
CITY IN CRISIS

GREAT CHICAGO FIRE

Model of the Chicago Water
Tower
Rex Petty
c. 1940
Plaster
1942.16
Gift of Rex Petty

Photograph, Looking southeast
and southwest from
Washington and LaSalle streets
Alexander Hesler
1858
ICHi-05728, ICHi-05730
CHS

Chicago fire alarm box
Gamewell & Company
1871
Iron
1959.399
Gift of Fire Commissioner
Robert J. Quinn

Half-model of balloon-frame
house
Richard Rush Studios, Inc.
1963
Wood
1963.570
CHS Purchase

Photograph, Fire Engine
Company #2
1879
ICHi-40040
Gift of Harry C. Irons

Fire marshall helmet used
during the Great Chicago Fire
Cairns & Bros., New York.
c. 1870
Leather, metal
1972.132
Gift of Mrs. Robert Biggert
p. 45

Speaking trumpet used during
the Great Chicago Fire
c. 1870
Brass
1928.62
Gift of Mrs. Margaret A. Cook

Photograph, Mary A.
Livermore
c. 1865
ICHi-22144
CHS

Photograph, George M.
Pullman
c. 1865
ICHi-40036
CHS

Photograph, Leonard W. Volk
c. 1865
ICHi-22107
CHS

Photograph, Cyrus H.
McCormick
c. 1865
ICHi-40050
CHS

Lithograph, *Corner of Lake and
Wells Streets, 1861*
Reproduction published by
Jevne & Almini
1866
ICHi-40005
Reproduction
Gift of Mr. W. A. Hamel
p. 42

Photograph, Chicago White
Stockings
O. F. Weaver
1871
ICHi-19572
CHS
p. 195

Photograph, Young man
Henshel
c. 1865
ICHi-40037
Gift of J. Busse

Photograph, Young woman
C. D. Mosher
c. 1865
ICHi-40039
CHS

Photograph, Child
H. Rocher
c. 1865
ICHi-40038
Gift of Frederick E. Olinger

Photograph, John Jones
Mosher & Baldwin
1882
ICHi-22362
Gift of Michelle Madison and
Grace Mason

Photograph, Mary Jones
Baldwin & Drake
c. 1883
ICHi-22363
Gift of Michelle Madison and
Grace Mason

Photograph, Emma Jane
Atkinson
c. 1865
ICHi-22392
Gift of Michelle Madison

Painting, *Memories of the Chicago
Fire in 1871*
Julia Lemos
1912
Oil on canvas
1918.10
Gift of Mr. and Mrs. Dennis D.
O'Keefe
p. 43

Drawing, *Trying to Save a
Wagonload of Goods from the Fire*
Alfred R. Waud
1871
Pencil and white chalk on paper
1962.761
CHS Purchase
p. 45

Drawing, *Fleeing the Burning City*
Alfred R. Waud
1871
Pencil and white chalk on paper
1962.767
CHS Purchase

Carte-de-visite, Alfred R. Waud
c. 1863
ICHi-40041
CHS

Carriage bolts melted in the fire
1871
Iron
1921.6
Gift of Mrs. L. B. Doud
p. 46

Billiard ball picked up on Clark
Street during the fire
1871
Ivory
X.1323
CHS

Pencils fused together in the
fire
1871
Slate
1925.4
Gift of Mr. W. Gregg

Photograph, Panoramic view of
the ruins between Wabash and
Michigan avenues
1871
ICHi-02797
Gift of the Buffalo Historical
Society
pp. ii (detail), 46

Photograph, New buildings
under construction after the
Great Chicago Fire
1871
ICHi-34529
CHS
pp. 38 (detail), 49

Map of Chicago Showing the
Burnt District
Published by Rufus Blanchard,
Chicago
1871
Reproduction
ICHi-40046
Gift of Miss Mary Julia Chase

Manuscript, Personal account
of the Great Chicago Fire
Justin
October 14, 1871
Reproduction
Gift of Frederick M. Bradley

Toy dog
1871
Terra cotta
X.2316.2004
CHS

Toy wheel fused to chunk
of glass
1871
Glass, tin
X.2314.2004
CHS

Melted marbles
1871
Glass
X.1331.6
CHS

Beaded necklace damaged in
the fire
1871
Glass, metal
X.2313.2004
CHS

Jar damaged in the fire
1871
Ceramic
1957.673
Gift of Ruth Meyers

Doll head
1871
Ceramic
495-2H
CHS

Melted toy dishes
1871
Ceramic
X.2276.2004
CHS
p. 51

Melted bottle
E. Burnham & Son Wholesale
Druggists
1871
Glass
1949.197
Gift of David and Gordon Lake

Doll in chair
1871
Ceramic
X.2315.2004ab
CHS

Doll in bathtub
1871
Ceramic
1948.458.2
Gift of Mrs. D.C. Behrle

Melted coins
1871
Silver
1947.10
Gift of Mrs. Charles G. Long

Photograph, Joseph Hudlun
c. 1870
ICHi-22375
Gift of Michelle Madison and
Grace Mason

Key found "in the heart of the
city" after the fire
1871
Metal
X.2317.2004
CHS

Charred pocket watches
1871
Silver
1925.7
Gift of Mr. Adolph Felsenthal
p. 47

Fused pennies
1871
Copper
1934.12
Gift of Mrs. August Von Glahn

Photograph, Mayor Roswell
B. Mason
Brisbois
c. 1885
ICHi-40044
Gift of the *Chicago Daily News*
p. 44

Manuscript, Draft of order
written by Mayor Roswell B.
Mason to release prisoners
from jail
October 9, 1871
Reproduction
1998.137
Gift of Elizabeth Trowbridge
Wild

Key reportedly to the
Chicago jail
1871
Iron
1961.35
Gift of the Estate of E. May
Dixon

Constable badge found after
the fire
1871
Tin
X.1319
CHS

Toy bird's nest with three eggs
1871
Ceramic
1947.76
Gift of Mrs. A. Mead Van Law

Toy bird
1871
Stone
X.2279.2004
CHS

Fused clump of marbles
1871
Glass
1919.9
Gift of Miss Maretta Twitty

Doll's head damaged in the fire
1871
Ceramic
X.1335
CHS

Bust burned in the fire
1871
Marble
1496-1H
Gift of Mr. Henry J. Ullner

Washers melted in the fire
1871
Iron
1942.15
Gift of Dr. Charles W. Olsen

Statuary hands damaged in
the fire
1871
Marble
1920.199
CHS Purchase, Charles F.
Gunther Collection
p. 47

Doll carried by Elizabeth
Richardson through the fire
1871
Porcelain, cloth
1930.86
Gift of Mrs. Albert W.
Chatterton (Elizabeth
Richardson
p. 51

.44 caliber U.S. military rifle
Ball and Williams, Worcester,
Massachusetts
c. 1865
Steel, walnut
1938.184
Gift of Dr. Clifford Mitchell

Broadside, Proclamation of
Mayor Roswell B. Mason
October 10, 1871
Ink on paper
X.3285.2005
CHS
p. 45

Broadside, Proclamation of the
General Relief Committee
October 10, 1871
Ink on paper
X.3286.2005
CHS

Broadside, Proclamation of the
Rockford Relief Committee
October 10, 1871
Ink on paper
1356
Gift of Lewis A. Williams

Engraving, *The Fire—A Day
Scene in Grace Church—
The Pastor and Assistants Serving
Out Rations For the Destitute*
From a sketch by Joseph Becker
Published in *Frank Leslie's
Illustrated Newspaper*
November 4, 1871
Reproduction
ICHi-02885
CHS
p. 47

Application and plan for two-
room shelter
Chicago Relief and Aid Society
1871
Reproduction
ICHi-40047, ICHi-40048
Gift of the United Charities of
Chicago

Broadside, Proclamation by
Mayor Roswell B. Mason
October 11, 1871
Reproduction
742
CHS

Photograph, Lieutenant
General
Philip H. Sheridan
C. D. Mosher
c. 1876
ICHi-34798
CHS

Sign, *Wm. D. Kerfoot is at 59
Union Park Place*
William D. Kerfoot
1871
Wood
1918.32
Gift of the William D. Kerfoot
Estate

Painting, *W. D. Kerfoot's Block*
W. J. Burton
1872
Oil on canvas
1918.4
Gift of the William D. Kerfoot
Estate
p. 48

Photograph, William D.
Kerfoot
John Carbutt
c. 1871
ICHi-40049
Gift of E. R. Shoenberger
p. 48

Photograph, Boy sitting in
remains of the Chicago
Courthouse bell
Shaw
1871
ICHi-40051
CHS
p. 50

Fragment of Chicago
Courthouse bell
1871
Bronze
X.84
CHS

Box of souvenir bells made
from the Chicago Courthouse
bell
Everhart & Company, Chicago
c. 1871
Bronze, wood, satin
X.1130
CHS
p. 50

Lithograph, *The Cause of the
Great Fire, October 9th, 1871*
Published by The Kellogg &
Buckley Company, Hartford,
Connecticut
1871
Ink on paper
1913.55
Gift of Dr. Otto Schmidt
p. 44

Bell reportedly worn by
Catherine O'Leary's cow
c. 1871
Iron
1945.4
Gift of Miss Mary Jane Lynch

Piece of charred wood reportedly from the O'Leary barn
c. 1871
Wood
798-2H
Gift of Miss Bertha Stewart
Ludlam

Melted opera glasses
1871
Glass, metal
X.2312.2004
CHS

Burned ginger cookies
1871
Food product
X.76
CHS

Melted pins
1871
Ferrous metal
1918.11
Gift of Dr. Gustav H.
Moldenhauer

Fused buttons
1871
Glass, shell, metal
CHS

HAYMARKET

Photograph, Monument to
Chicago laborers and free
speech
Jay Crawford
2005
ICHi-40013
CHS

Photograph, Monument to the
police who marched on
Haymarket Square
Jay Crawford
2005
ICHi-40012
CHS
p. 57

Photograph, Monument to the
Haymarket martyrs
Jay Crawford
2005
ICHi-40011
CHS
p. 57

Headline, *Hanged!*
Published in the *Chicago Daily
News*
November 11, 1887
Reproduction
ICHi-40010
CHS

Wood engraving, *The Law
Vindicated: Four of the Chicago
Anarchists pay the penalty of their
crime*
Published in *Frank Leslie's
Illustrated Newspaper*
November 19, 1887
Reproduction
ICHi-19645
CHS
p. 56

Wood engraving, *The Anarchist
Riot in Chicago*
Thure de Thulstrup
Published in *Harper's Weekly*
May 15, 1886
Reproduction
ICHi-03665
Bequest of Joseph T. Ryerson
p. 53

Headline, *Dynamite*
Published in the *Chicago Times*
May 5, 1886
Reproduction
ICHi-40009
CHS

Bomb casing introduced as
evidence during the Haymarket
trial
1886
Lead
1979.154ab
Gift of Robert Brayton
p. 53

Pipe bombs introduced as
evidence during the Haymarket
trial
1886
Lead
1887.2, 1943.167
Gift of Inspector John Bonfield
Gift of Carter H. Harrison

Photograph, Randolph Street,
showing the police monument
in Haymarket Square
Interstate Photo Service
c. 1893
ICHi-16155
Gift of Arthur J. Connor

Flag to the Veterans of the
Haymarket Riot
1886
Reproduction
1933.229
Gift of Capt. Frank P. Tyrell

Haymarket souvenir tokens
c. 1887
Brass
X.12ab
CHS

Gallows-shaped lapel pin
1887
Brass
1958.420
Gift of Mrs. Olive Sprogle
Herne

Photograph, Imprisoned
Anarchists: Fielden; Schwab;
Neebe
S. W. Wetmore
1889
ICHi-31335
Gift of Estelle S. Burton

Wood engraving, *The Doom of
Anarchy*
Published in *Frank Leslie's
Illustrated Newspaper*
November 19, 1887
Reproduction
ICHi-03662
CHS

Telegram from publisher Joseph
Pulitzer to Cook County
Sheriff Canute Matson
November 7, 1887
Reproduction
ICHi-31365
Gift of Isabelle Matson
Hofmann (Mrs. Frank P.
Hofmann

Manuscript, *Dynamite*
People's Exhibit 39, Illinois vs.
August Spies et al. trial
evidence book
Written by T. Lizius,
Indianapolis
Published in *The Alarm*
February 21, 1885
Ink on paper
16152
Gift of the Estate of Ernst
Schmidt

Photograph, Judge Joseph E.
Gary
C. D. Mosher
c. 1886
ICHi-18750
CHS

Photograph, Julius S. Grinnell
c. 1886
ICHi-10570
Gift of Mrs. Julius A. Grinnell

Photograph, George Engel
c. 1886
ICHi-03703
CHS

Photograph, Louis Lingg
c. 1886
ICHi-03693
CHS
p. 54

Photograph, William Perkins
Black
James S. Windeatt
c. 1895
ICHi-31330
Gift of G. A. R. Memorial
Association

Photograph, Michael Schwab
c. 1886
ICHi-30018
CHS
p. 55

Photograph, Adolph Fischer
c. 1886
ICHi-03692
CHS
p. 54

Photograph, Oscar Neebe
c. 1886
ICHi-03704
CHS
p. 55

Police officer's handcuffs
owned by Captain Michael J.
Schaack
c. 1886
Steel
1976.98.1
Gift of Mrs. Walter McDonough

Chicago Police Department
badge worn by Officer Timothy
Flavin
1886
Silver
1968.400
Gift of John E. Flavin
p. 53

Police officer's .38 caliber
revolver owned by Officer John
Schermann and purportedly
carried by him at the
Haymarket meeting
Smith & Wesson
c. 1882
Steel, nickel
1968.403a
Gift of Charles Schermann

Police baton carried by
Captain William Ward at the
Haymarket meeting
1886
Wood
1887.1
Gift of Captain William Ward
p. 53

Photographs, First Division
who charged the mob at the
Haymarket riot
C. D. Mosher
1886
ICHi-03676
CHS

Photograph, Samuel Fielden
c. 1886
ICHi-03705
CHS
p. 54

Photograph, August Theodore
Vincent Spies
c. 1886
ICHi-30017
CHS
p. 52

Photograph, Albert R. Parsons
c. 1886
ICHi-14950
CHS
p. 52

Flier, *Attention Workingmen*
Defense Exhibit 1, Illinois vs.
August Spies et al. trial
evidence book
1886
Ink on paper
16152
Gift of the Estate of Ernst
Schmidt

Flier, *Attention Workingmen*
People's Exhibit 5, Illinois vs.
August Spies et al. trial
evidence book
1886
Ink on paper
16152
Gift of the Estate of Ernst
Schmidt

Photograph, Horn Brothers
Furniture Company workers
1886
ICHi-20069
Gift of Carol Hendrickson
p. 52

Revenge circular
August Spies
May 3, 1886
Ink on paper
1952.478
CHS Purchase
p. 55

1919 RACE RIOT

Photograph, White children
raiding African American home
during Chicago Race Riot
Jun Fujita
1919
ICHi-40052
Gift of Mrs. Jun Fujita
(Florence Carr Fujita)
p. 65

Fragment from the Knights of
Pythias Temple
Walter T. Bailey
1928
Terra cotta
1994.274
CHS Purchase, Anna Hasburg
Memorial Fund

Photograph, Whites stoning an
African American man during
the Chicago Race Riot
Jun Fujita
1919
ICHi-22430
Gift of Mrs. Jun Fujita
(Florence Carr Fujita)
p. 64

Photograph, Mob with bricks
and stones chasing African
American man
Jun Fujita
1919
ICHi-31915
Gift of Mrs. Jun Fujita
(Florence Carr Fujita)
p. 63

Photograph, Beginning of the
Chicago Race Riot at the
Twenty-ninth Street Beach
Jun Fujita
1919
ICHi-30315
Gift of Mrs. Jun Fujita
(Florence Carr Fujita)
p. 62

Photograph, National guards-
men question an African
American man during the race
riot
Jun Fujita
1919
ICHi-25571
Gift of Mrs. Jun Fujita
(Florence Carr Fujita)
p. 65

Photograph, South Park
Avenue
Published in *The Negro in
Chicago*
c. 1925
ICHi-40055
CHS Purchase
p. 92

Photograph, Members of Olivet
Baptist Church
c. 1925
ICHi-26767
CHS
p. 66

Photograph, Liberty/Supreme
Life Insurance Building
Kaufmann & Fabry
c. 1935
ICHi-40125
Gift of Mrs. Earl A. Dickerson

Photograph, The Knights of
Pythias Temple
1928
ICHi-19351
CHS

Advertisement for Binga State
Bank
Published in *The Light* and
Heebie Jeebies
February 1927
Reproduction
ICHi-40054
Gift of Mrs. Etta Moten Barnett

Book, *The Negro in Chicago*
The Chicago Commission on
Race Relations
Published by University of
Chicago Press
1922
Ink on paper
68539
CHS Purchase

Map, The Chicago Riot, July 27
to August 8, 1919
1919
Reproduction
ICHi-40053
CHS
p. 66

Book, *Rhea's New Citizen's
Directory of Chicago*
1908
Ink on paper
30266
CHS Purchase

Photograph, Eighth Illinois
Regiment and Directory
1918
ICHi-07559
CHS

Photograph, Oscar Stanton
DePriest
R. D. Jones
c. 1930
ICHi-10015
CHS

Photograph, Reverdy and Mrs.
Ransom
Chicago Daily News
c. 1910
ICHi-31112
CHS

Photograph, Claude Barnett
Rembrandt
c. 1905
ICHi-25363
Gift of Mrs. Etta Moten Barnett

Photograph, African American
migrants
Published in *The Negro in
Chicago*
c. 1918
ICHi-28567
CHS Purchase
p. 61

GANGLAND CHICAGO

Map outlining Chicago gang
territories, c. 1925
Created by the *Chicago Tribune*
Published in *The Gem of the
Prairie*
1940
Reproduction
ICHi-40200
CHS
p. 70

Photograph, Johnny Torrio
1925
ICHi-40203
Gift of Mrs. Geraldine Damon
p. 68

Photograph, Dion O'Banion
1921
ICHi-40205
Gift of Mrs. Geraldine Damon
p. 70

Photograph, George "Bugs"
Moran
1925
ICHi-40206
Gift of Mrs. Geraldine Damon
p. 70

Photograph, Earl "Hymie"
Weiss
1925
IChi-40207
Gift of Mrs. Geraldine Damon
p. 71

Photograph, St. Valentine's Day
Massacre
Jun Fujita
February 14, 1929
ICHi-14406
Gift of Mrs. Willard Loarie
p. 72

Photograph, Al Capone's
mugshot
Chicago Detective's Bureau
Published in the *Chicago Daily
News*
1931
DN-0094945
CHS
p. 69

Still and bucket for making
alcohol
c. 1920
Copper, metal
1956.537–538
Gift of Mr. and Mrs. Thomas
Ducey
p. 68

Booklet, *Life of Al Capone in
Pictures!* and *Chicago's Gang
Wars*
Published by Lake Michigan
Publishing Company
1931
Ink on paper
X.3287.2005
CHS
p. 73

Booklet, *X Marks the Spot*
Published by Spot Publishing
Company
1930
Ink on paper
1987.221
Gift of Mrs. Geraldine Damon
p. 73

Comic book, Dick Tracy no.
136, *Mystery of the Iron Room*
Published by Harvey Comics
October 1959
Ink on paper
2005.70.1
CHS Purchase

Illustration, *The Underworld
Language*
Published in *Life of Al Capone
in Pictures!*
1931
Reproduction
ICHi-40233
CHS

Gangs of Chicago movie poster
1940
Reproduction
ICHi-40058
CHS

Photograph, Eliot Ness
c. 1938
Courtesy of the Cleveland
Public Library
p. 72

Headline, *List 28 as 'Public
Enemies'*
Published in the *Chicago Tribune*
April 24, 1930
Reproduction
ICHi-40118
CHS

Photograph, Al Capone in a
Chicago courtroom
Chicago Daily News
1931
DN-95038, ICHi-23954
CHS

Court transcript, *United States of
America vs. Alphonse Capone*
June 16, 1931
Ink on paper
J03690 (1984:28
Gift of Alfred B. Teton

1968

Photograph, Fire raging during
Chicago's West Side riots
Declan Haun
April 1968
ICHi-40020
Gift of the Estate of Declan
Haun
pp. 40 (detail), 77

Photograph, Lawndale neighborhood building and residents
c. 1960
ICHi-40015
Gift of Greater Lawndale
Conservation Commission
p. 75

Photograph, Lawndale commu-
nity march commemorating a
church bombing in Alabama
James H. Hall
1963
ICHi-40016
Gift of Greater Lawndale
Conservation Commission

Photograph, Destroyed build-
ings in Lawndale following the
West Side riots
Declan Haun
April 1968
ICHi-40021
Gift of the Estate of Declan
Haun

Photograph, National Guard
officers policing a street in
Lawndale
Declan Haun
April 1968
ICHi-40022
Gift of the Estate of Declan
Haun

Photograph, Nighttime rally in
Grant Park during the
Democratic National
Convention
August 28, 1968
ICHi-18354
Gift of Chicago Seed

Broadside, *Bring the Troops
Home Now*
Nancy Coner, Student
Mobilization Committee, New
York City
1968
Ink on paper
1970.55
Gift of John S. Tris

Broadside, *Hello! Democrats
Welcome to Chicago*
1968
Ink on paper
X.3290.2005.1
Gift of Ralph G. Newman
p. 80

Broadside, *A Closed Convention
in a Closed City*
Students for a Democratic
Society
1968
Ink on paper
X.3290.2005.2
CHS Purchase
p. 81

Broadside, *Festival of Life*
Youth International Party
1968
Ink on paper
X.3290.2005.3
Gift of Ralph G. Newman
p. 82

Broadside, Rally and speech by
Dr. Martin Luther King Jr.
Illinois Rally for Civil Rights
June 21, 1964
Ink on paper
1966.573
Gift of Independent Voters of
Illinois
p. 74

Bust of Dr. Martin Luther
King Jr.
Sara S. Miller
1994
Bronze
1998.176
Gift of Ms. Judy P. Thornber
p. 75

Photograph, Martin Luther
King Jr. and his wife, Coretta
Scott King
January 26, 1966
© Corbis
Image donated by Corbis-
Bettman

Photograph, Tenement apart-
ment in North Lawndale
c. 1965
ICHi-40018
Gift of Greater Lawndale
Conservation Commission

Newspaper, *West Side Torch*.
Vol. III, no. 16
Published by the West Side
Organization
April 12-26, 1968
Ink on paper
X.3167.2005
CHS
p. 76

Photographs, Three views of
looted businesses on Chicago's
West Side
Sister Julia of Marillac House
April 1968
ICHi-40025, ICHi-40026,
ICHi-40027
Gift of Marillac House

Political protest buttons
c. 1968
Metal
1986.436.5-7
Gift of Shirley Lens
p. 80

Yippie button
1968
Metal
X.1993.199
CHS

On to Chicago button
1968
Metal
1989.220.2
Gift of Brooks McCormick Jr.
p. 81

Car sign, *Going to Chicago*
Published in The Fifth Estate,
Detroit
September 4, 1968
Reproduction
ICHi-40028
CHS

Photograph, Democratic
National Convention
Oscar & Associates, Inc.
August 26-29, 1968
ICHi-40029
Gift of CMD Realty
Management Co.
p. 82

Book, *The Guide*
August 22, 1968
Ink on paper
X.3288.2005
CHS

Photograph, Aerial view of
crowd surrounding the Chicago
Hilton
Declan Haun
August 28, 1968
ICHi-40032
Gift of the Estate of Declan
Haun
p. 83

Photograph, Demonstrators
near Grant Park
Declan Haun
August 28, 1968
ICHi-40033
Gift of the Estate of Declan
Haun
p. 39 (detail)

Photograph, Boy marching in
support of Chicago police
Jack Lenahan
September 5, 1968
ICHi-40019
Gift of *Chicago Sun-Times*

Chicago police officer's riot
helmet worn by Max O. Ziegler
1968
Plastics, rubber, metal
2004.73.2
Gift of Mr. Keith W. Ziegler
p. 83

EASTLAND DISASTER

Headline, *919 Bodies Recovered, Total Eastland Victims May Reach 1,200*
Published in the *Chicago Sunday Tribune*
July 25, 1915
Reproduction
ICHi-40239
CHS

Steering wheel from the Eastland
Barnes Tool Company
1903
Brass, wood
1969.1
Gift of Mr. and Mrs. Everett B. Michaels
p. 58

Photograph, The capsized steamer Eastland on its side in the Chicago River
Jun Fujita
July 1915
ICHi-40126
Gift of Mrs. Jun Fujita (Florence Carr Fujita)
p. 59

Whistle from the Eastland
1903
Iron
1953.388
Gift of Reverend William J. Ohan

Photograph, Rescue worker in diving bell at the Eastland disaster site
Jun Fujita
July 1915
ICHi-30724
Gift of Mrs. Jun Fujita (Florence Carr Fujita)
p. 60

Photograph, Fireman Leonard E. Olson carrying a child from the Eastland
Jun Fujita
July 1915
ICHi-30783
Gift of Mrs. Jun Fujita (Florence Carr Fujita)

Folding chair from the Eastland
c. 1903
Wood
1955.176
Gift of Mr. Walter Bergeon in memory of his wife, Mrs. Ruby Bergeon

Postcard, The Eastland
Photograph by D. J. Lewis
c. 1903
X.3289.2005
CHS
p. 58

Stateroom key from the Eastland
1915
Metal
1988.386
Gift of Mrs. Lorraine Cumming

Hand-baggage tag from the Eastland
c. 1903
Metal
2765
Gift of Mr. Louis F. Birnbaum

Button from the Eastland
c. 1903
Metal, enamel
N650
CHS

Diagram illustrating the Eastland's instability
Published in the *Chicago Sunday Tribune*
July 25, 1915
Reproduction
ICHi-40119
CHS

Letter, St. Joseph-Chicago Steamship Company to local inspectors
July 2, 1915
Reproduction
Courtesy of the National Archives

Cartoon, *Inspection–Afterward.*
Published in the *Chicago Daily News*
July 28, 1915
Reproduction
ICHi-40120
CHS

Photograph, Secretary of Commerce William C. Redfield during the Eastland inquiry
Samuel A. Marrs
1915
ICHi-15793
Gift of Judge Robert L. Marrs

Photograph, Police officers holding back spectators at the scene of the Eastland disaster
Jun Fujita
July 1915
ICHi-40121
Gift of Mrs. Jun Fujita (Florence Carr Fujita)

Photograph, Crowd outside the Second Regiment Armory
Jun Fujita
July 1915
ICHi-40122
Gift of Mrs. Jun Fujita (Florence Carr Fujita)

Badge awarded to August Holdorf for his efforts during the Eastland disaster
C. H. Hanson, Chicago
1919
Metal
1982.118.1
Gift of Nedra Woods
p. 60

Report, Eastland Disaster Relief, 1915–18
Published by the American Red Cross
1918
Ink on paper
37143
Gift of the Chicago Chapter American Red Cross

GALLERY 5
SWEET HOME CHICAGO

Photograph, Maxwell Street market
Barnes-Crosby
c. 1905
ICHi-14059
Gift of the Barnes-Crosby Company
pp. 84 (detail), 94

Photograph, East Indian women walking down Devon Avenue
Mukul Roy
1984
ICHi-26014
Gift of Mukul Roy

Photograph, The Morris Williams Family
c. 1920
ICHi-26565
Gift of J. LeVelle Williams
p. 89

Photograph, View of Dan Ryan Expressway northeast from 51st Street
1964
ICHi-23505
CHS
p. 86

Photograph, Lithuanian-American children
J.P. Rashinski
1910
ICHi-40949
Gift of Ann Markin
p. 88

Photograph, View of the Indian Independence Day parade on Devon Avenue
Vasile Bouleanu
1998
ICHi-40880
Gift of Vasile Bouleanu
p. 89

Photograph, Mandel family
c. 1900
ICHi-31721
Gift of Mrs. Oscar G. Foreman
p. 90

Photograph, Harlow N. Higinbotham
J.H. Moyston
c. 1893
ICHi-31730
CHS
p. 90

Photograph, Reverend and Mrs Reverdy Ransom
Chicago Daily News
c. 1910
ICHi-31112
CHS
p. 90

Photograph, View of Illinois Central Railroad looking north of Thirty-fifth Street
c. 1895
ICHi-21429
CH
p. 91

Photograph, 2700 block of West Devon Avenue
Howard B. Anderson
1977
ICHi-40953
Gift of Howard B. Anderson
p. 101

Photograph, Two men standing in front of an electronics store on Devon Avenue
Vasile Bouleanu
1998
ICHi-40881
Gift of Vasile Bouleanu
p. 102

Photograph, Children dressed for their First Holy Communion
Antonio Perez
1987
ICHi-24902
Gift of the Focus/Infinity Fund

Photograph, West Ridge bungalow
Jay Crawford
2005
ICHi-40611
CHS
Map, Chicago Neighborhoods
Big Stick, Inc.
2001
Reproduction
Courtesy of Big Stick, Inc., Naperville, Illinois

Map showing the boulevards and park system and twelve miles of lake frontage of the city of Chicago
Rand, McNally & Co.
1886
Reproduction
ICHi-31337
CHS

Map, Community settlement in 1900
Published by the City of Chicago Department of Development and Planning
1976
Reproduction
ICHi-40505
CHS
p. 89

Map, Chicago's Ethnic Mosaic in 2000
Michael P. Conzen
2004
Reproduction
Courtesy of the Newberry Library

Photograph, South Chicago neighborhood residents
John Becker
c. 1910
ICHi-20520
Gift of Nicholas Pemmer
p. 85 (detail)

Photograph, Prarie Avenue north of Twenty-second Street
1893
ICHi-31691
CHS

Photograph, Hattie Sanger Pullman
Cox
1896
ICHi-40702
Gift of Mrs. C. Phillip Miller

Photograph, George M. Pullman
Steffens
c. 1885
ICHi-34271
Gift of Mrs. C. Phillip Miller

Photograph, Pullman residence at 1729 South Prairie Avenue
c. 1887
ICHi-21936
CHS

Photograph, Interior view of the Pullman residence
c. 1895
ICHi-24688
Gift of Mrs. C. Phillip Miller

South Park Avenue
c. 1925
ICHi-40055
CHS Purchase

Slum conditions in the 500 block of 37th Street
Mildred Mead
1951
ICHi-00809
Gift of Mildred Mead
p. 93

Aerial view of Chicago's south-west side, from Damen Avenue and West 18th Street
c. 1955
ICHi-05803
CHS
p. 94

Three of the Chicago youth served by Hull-House
c. 1920
ICHi-01544
CHS
p. 95

Baptismal certificate for Christina Kozik
Pilger Publishing House
1910
Ink on paper
ICHi-40848
Gift of Mrs. Ellen M. Stortz
p. 96

Confirmation class at Saints Peter and Paul Slovak Church on the West Side
Vicelik
1921
ICHi-40851
Gift of Mrs. Ellen M. Stortz
p. 96

Our Lady of Guadalupe straw figure
c. 1999
Straw, cloth, plastic
2000.95.3
CHS Purchase
p. 97

Christ on Cross straw figure
c. 1999
Straw, textiles, plastic
2000.95.2
CHS Purchase
p. 97

Poster for Fiesta de Sol
1994
Ink on paper
1996.129.27
Gift of Roger Tobolt
p. 97

Photograph, Schmidt Metzgerei, butcher shop at 1800 North Hudson Street
c. 1978
ICHi-40696
Gift of William Schmidt
p. 99

Carrying case used by Nanni Helena Korolainen, immigrant from Finland
1921
Wood, leather, brass
1984.248.1
Gift of Mrs. Nanni Laitinen
p. 100

Finnish Passport for Nanni Helena Korolainen
1921
Ink on paper
1984.248
Gift of Mrs. Nanni Laitinen
p. 100

Photograph, Carter H. Harrison
C. D. Mosher
c. 1883
ICHi-19662
Gift of Thomas George Fischer
p. 105

Photograph, Mayor Carter H. Harrison I making a speech at the World's Columbian Exposition
1893
ICHi-40700
CHS
p. 105

Chicago ballot box
c. 1890–1932
Wood, glass, brass
1984.330
Gift of the Board of Election Commissioners
p. 104

Chicago flag
c. 1893
Cotton
1946.75
Gift of Miss Florence Cadwaller

Chicago flag
1947
Cotton
1947.7
Gift of Honorable Martin H. Kennelly

Photograph, Chicago aldermen in session
c. 1900
ICHi-40815
CHS
p. 104

Photograph, Campaign trucks for Anton J. Cermak
1931
ICHi-19481
Gift of Lauren Crawford
p. 106

Campaign broadside for Anton J. Cermak
1931
Ink on paper
58:128
Gift of Maureen Sullivan
p. 107

Campaign pamphlet for Anton J. Cermak
1931
Ink on paper
67:694
Gift of Arthur W. Mitchell
p. 107

Campaign button for Anton J. Cermak
Geraghty Company
1931
Metal
X.1984.1996
CHS
p. 107

Campaign poster for Richard J. Daley
Allied Printing
1955
Ink on paper
1955.596
Gift of Daley Headquarters
p. 108

Photograph, Mayor Richard J. Daley delivering a speech at City Hall
R. E. Murphy
1959
ICHi-40701
Gift of Mrs. Ira J. Beck
p. 109

Photograph, Women of Chicago's 11th Ward carrying banners for Richard J. Daley
Bud Daley
1959
ICHi-34722
CHS
p. 109

Broadside, mocking Richard J. Daley control of Chicago politics
c. 1970
Ink on paper
X.3325.2005
CHS
p. 109

Photograph, Harold Washington campaigning
Richard Gordon
1983
ICHi-40826
Gift of Richard Gordon
p. 111

Campaign poster for Harold Washington
E. Rodriguez
1983
Ink on paper
1983.195.45
Gift of Archie Motely
p. 110

Campaign pamphlet for Richard M. Daley
Allied Printing
1989
Ink on paper
2004.42.1NA
Gift of Kevin Leonard
p. 111

Campaign button for Richard M. Daley
1989
Metal
1989.878
Gift of Clarence Clark
p. 111

GALLERY 6
SECOND TO NONE

MODERN RETAIL
Marshall Field's

Evening dress with turquoise and brass brooches
Created by an unknown Parisian designer
c. 1925
Chiffon, sequins
1981.104.1
Gift of Mrs. John A. Holabird

Women's black velvet and gold brocade opera cape with green satin lining
c. 1925
Velvet, brocade, satin
1962.545
Gift of Mrs. Nathaniel Leverone

Gold and silver glass beaded evening gown
c. 1925
Silk
1982.167.4
Gift of Mrs. E. F. Swift

Photograph, Potter Palmer
J. Carbutt
Published in *Biographical Sketches of the Leading Men of Chicago*
1868
ICHi-27395
CHS
p. 116

Photograph, Shoppers on State Street outside Marshall Field & Co.
William T. Barnum
c. 1925
ICHi-15608
Gift of Lake Bluff Public Library
p. 118

Photograph, Marshall Field
Matzene
c. 1900
ICHi-10281
Gift of Northwestern University School of Commerce
p. 117

Fashions of the Hour magazine, Exposition Number 1924
Published by Marshall Field & Co.
1924
Ink on paper
1963.776.3
Gift of Helen C. Wills

Fashions of the Hour magazine, Autumn Number 1922
Published by Marshall Field & Co.
1922
Ink on paper
1963.776.2
Gift of Helen C. Wills
p. 118

Fashions of the Hour magazine, Exposition Number 1923
Published by Marshall Field & Co.
1923
Ink on paper
1963.776.1
Gift of Helen C. Wills
p. 119

Fashions of the Hour magazine, Spring Number 1924
Published by Marshall Field & Co.
1924
Ink on paper
1963.776.4
Gift of Helen C. Wills
p. 119

Fashions of the Hour magazine, June Number 1924
Published by Marshall Field & Co.
1924
Ink on paper
1963.776.5
Gift of Helen C. Wills

Bes-Ben

Woman's hat featuring coils and multicolored pillows
Bes-Ben
c. 1955
Fabric, plastic
1989.562.1.117
Gift of Benjamin Benedict Green-Field Foundation

Woman's hat featuring three bumblebees with feather wings
Bes-Ben
c. 1950
Plastic, net
1982.19.9
Gift of Mr. Kendall Lingle
p. 124

Woman's woven hat
Bes-Ben
c. 1950
Straw, net
2001.172.1
Gift of Mrs. Peter Wolkonsky

Woman's hat featuring gold coins and beads
Bes-Ben
c. 1960
Wool, metal
1978.5.1
Gift of Mrs. George H. Rezek
p. 124

Woman's hat featuring embroidered fish
Bes-Ben
1965
Wool, cotton, net
1976.203.2
Gift of Mrs. Charles H. Brown

Photograph, Crowd jumping to catch a hat at a Bes-Ben sale
Life magazine
1962
ICHi-40268
Gift of Benjamin Benedict Green-Field Foundation

Photograph, Benjamin Green-Field with assistant Margit Amberg in the workshop
c. 1956
ICHi-31750
Gift of Benjamin Benedict Green-Field Foundation
p. 124

Crate & Barrel

Marimekko Unikko design, 1954
Designed by Maija Isola
2003
Reproduction
Courtesy of Marimekko

Nortica flatware
WMF Cromargan, Japan
2005
Stainless steel
2005.80.2.1–.5
Gift of Crate & Barrel

Chambourd French press
Bodum, Portugal
2005
Glass, stainless steel
2005.80.7a
Gift of Crate & Barrel

Krouvi beer mugs
IITTALA, Europe
2005
Glass
2005.80.6
Gift of Crate & Barrel

Teapot and warmer
Arzberg, Germany
2005
Porcelain
2005.80.8a-d
Gift of Crate & Barrel

Ona pitcher
2005
Glass
2005.80.9
Gift of Crate & Barrel

Madison dinnerware set
Kahla, Germany
2005
Porcelain
2005.80.1.1–.4ab
Gift of Crate & Barrel

Working glasses
2005
Glass
2005.80.4–.5
Gift of Crate & Barrel

Photograph, Gordon and Carole Segal
c. 2005
Courtesy of Gordon and Carole Segal

Photograph, Exterior view of Crate & Barrel store at 1510 N. Wells Street
Hedrich-Blessing
1968
HB-31384
CHS, Hedrich-Blessing collection
p. 120

Photograph, Interior view of Crate & Barrel store at 1510 N. Wells Street
Hedrich-Blessing
1968
HB-31384-3
CHS, Hedrich-Blessing collection

Photograph, Crate & Barrel's Michigan Avenue flagship store
Steve Hall
October 2001
Courtesy of Crate & Barrel
p. 120

Catalog, Crate & Barrel Best Buys
Published by Crate & Barrel
2003
Ink on paper
X.3326.2006
CHS

Catalog, Crate & Barrel Spring Living
Published by Crate & Barrel
2005
Ink on paper
2005.80.10NA
Gift of Crate & Barrel

Catalog, Crate & Barrel Best Buys
Published by Crate & Barrel
2005
Ink on paper
CH_04235 (2005.80.10NA
Gift of Crate & Barrel

Mail Order

Photograph, Richard W. Sears
c. 1900
ICHi-29811
CHS Purchase
p. 122

Photograph, Sears, Roebuck & Co. railroad yards
c. 1900
ICHi-40298
CHS Purchase

Photograph, Clerks in Sears, Roebuck & Co.'s billing section
1947
ICHi-40292
Gift of Sears, Roebuck & Co.

Fall and Winter catalog
Published by Montgomery Ward & Co.
1935-36
Ink on paper
X.3215.2005
CHS

Spring and Summer catalog
Published by Sears, Roebuck & Co.
1935
Ink on paper
X.3216.2005
CHS

Montgomery Ward & Co. mailing tube
c. 1900
Paper, cloth
2001.163
Gift of Montgomery Ward & Co.
p. 122

Photograph, Aerial view of Montgomery Ward & Co.'s Chicago Avenue property
1940
ICHi-40288
Gift of Montgomery Ward & Co.

Photograph, Montgomery Ward & Co. telephone sales department
1950
ICHi-40289
Gift of Montgomery Ward & Co.

Engraving, *A. Montgomery Ward Campbell, NY, 1926*
Published in *Historical Encyclopedia of Illinois*, Munsell Publishing Co.
c. 1900
Reproduction
ICHi-40269
CHS
p. 121

Radio catalog
Published by Sears, Roebuck & Co.
1927
Ink on paper
X.3225.2005
Gift of Harold R. Nestor, Inc.

Cameras and Photo Supplies catalog
Published by Sears, Roebuck & Co.
1907
Ink on paper
X.3227.2005
CHS

Automobile Supplies catalog
Published by Sears, Roebuck & Co.
c. 1910
Ink on paper
X.2327.2004
CHS

Ladies' automobile goggles
c. 1900
Glass, metal screen
1971.141
Gift of Mrs. Ethel A. Thomas

Sample Book of Ready to Wear Clothes for Men and Young Boys
Published by Sears, Roebuck & Co.
1918
Ink on paper, fabric
X.3224.2005
Gift of Harold Skramstad

Ideal Patterns catalog
Published by Montgomery Ward & Co.
1916-17
Ink on paper
X.2328.2004
CHS

Tips to Trappers catalog
Published by Sears, Roebuck & Co.
1931
Ink on paper
X.3223.2005
Gift of Van Norman
p. 123

Stock and Poultry Feed catalog
Published by Sears, Roebuck & Co.
1917
Ink on paper
X.3217.2005
CHS Purchase

Broadside, *Free Windmill Catalogue*
Sears, Roebuck & Co.
c. 1904
Ink on paper
X.3226.2005
CHS

Catalog cover
Montgomery Ward & Co.
1904-05
Reproduction
ICHi-40411
CHS
p. 121

Advertisement, Shirley Temple dolls
Published in the Sears, Roebuck & Co. catalog
1939–40
Reproduction
ICHi-40415
CHS

Advertisement, Round corner safety blocks
Published in the Sears, Roebuck & Co. catalog
1927
Reproduction
CH_03816 (ICHi-40324
CHS

Advertisement, Columbia Graphophone
Published in the Sears, Roebuck & Co. catalog
1908
Reproduction
ICHi-40325
CHS

Advertisement, Decorated parlor or reception lamps
Published in the Montgomery Ward & Co. catalog
1908
Reproduction
ICHi-40326
CHS

Advertisement, The Blick typewriter
Published in the Sears, Roebuck & Co. catalog
1930
Reproduction
ICHi-40416
CHS Purchase

Advertisement, The Apex All Metal Gravity Washer
Published in the Montgomery Ward & Co. catalog
1915-16
Reproduction
ICHi-40414
CHS

Advertisement, Kitchen ranges
Published in the Montgomery Ward & Co. catalog
1940
Reproduction
ICHi-40413
CHS

Advertisement, Star Brand Barn & Fence Paint
Published in Montgomery Ward & Co. catalog
1904–05
Reproduction
ICHi-40412
CHS

Sled
c. 1900
Wood, iron
1966.184
Gift of Mr. Elmer P. Renstrom Jr.

Shirley Temple doll
Designed by Bernard Lipfert
Manufactured by Ideal Novelty and Toy Co.
c. 1933
Composition, mohair
1985.768.2
Gift of Mrs. Lee W. Alberts

Buddy L toy dump truck
Moline Pressed Steel Co., East Moline, Illinois
c. 1925
Sheet metal, steel
X.1257
CHS

Alphabet safety blocks
Halsam Products Company, Chicago
c. 1926
Wood, cardboard
1983.349.1a-u
Gift of William R. Goss
p. 123

Cylinder graphophone
Columbia Phonograph
Company
c. 1900
Wood, steel
1971.171a, c
Gift of Mrs. Richard Bentley

Kerosene lamp with gilt floral
decoration
The Haida
c. 1890
Glass, brass
1972.315
CHS Purchase

Blickensderfer No. 6 typewriter
The Blickensderfer
Manufacturing Co.
c. 1910
Metal, hard rubber
1961.372
Gift of Mr. Jevne A. Rhenisch

Carved clock with glass front
E. Ingraham
c. 1905
Wood, glass
1962.315
Gift of Mr. And Mrs. Warren I.
Doonan

Wall-mounted telephone
Chicago Telephone Supply Co.,
Chicago
1901
Wood, metal
1989.660.36
Gift of Illinois Bell

Washing machine
Apex Appliance Company
c. 1910
Steel, iron
1956.338
Gift of Commonwealth Edison
Company

"Minnesota" Model A sewing
machine
Sears, Roebuck & Co.
c. 1895
Oak, cast iron
1976.205
CHS Purchase
p. 123

Interchangeable tattoo for
livestock, poultry, and pets
O. M. Franklin Serum Co.,
Denver
1937–63
Metal
X.2325.2004a
CHS

Coot duck decoy
Evan's Decoy Company
c. 1935
Wood
1971.206
Gift of Mr. Ralph M. Loeff

Mallard hen duck decoy
Dahlstrem, Burlington, Iowa
c. 1935
Wood
1971.189
Gift of Mr. Ralph M. Loeff

Rifle
Winchester Repeating Arms
Co., New Haven, Connecticut
c. 1886
Nickel steel, walnut, iron
1981.68.6
Gift of Donald E. Weiss, M.D.

Potato scoop
c. 1890
Wood, iron
1971.359
CHS Purchase

BUT WAIT, THERE'S MORE
Publishing

Map of the United States
Rand McNally & Co.
2005
Ink on paper
2006.72.22NA
CHS Purchase

Easy Finder map of Chicago
and vicinity
Rand McNally & Co.
2005
Ink on paper
2006.72.22NA
CHS Purchase

Rand McNally Pioneer globe
Replogle Globes Inc.
2005
Paper, plastic, metal
2006.72.2
CHS Purchase

SBC Yellow Pages
Published by R. H. Donnelley
February 2005
Ink on paper
2006.72.23NA
CHS

Life magazine
Printed by R. R. Donnelley
September 6, 1968
Ink on paper
2006.72.26NA
CHS Purchase

Time magazine
Printed by R. R. Donnelley
March 15, 1963
Ink on paper
X.3292.2005
CHS

Photograph, Meeting of the
Ebony magazine staff
Stephen Deutch
c. 1945
ICHi-40405
Gift of Stephen Deutch

Ebony magazine,
50th anniversary issue
Published by Johnson
Publishing Company
November 1995
Ink on paper
X.3291.2005
CHS

Jet magazine
Published by Johnson
Publishing Company
September 22, 1966
Ink on paper
1982.24
Gift of Mr. Luis Kutner

Encyclopædia Britannica,
Volume 2 *Annual Register to
Baltic Sea*
1938
Ink on paper
2006.72.25NA
CHS Purchase

World Book Encyclopedia,
2006 *Spinescape* edition
2005
Ink on paper
2006.73.1
Gift of World Book, Inc.

Toys

Advertisement, Ride Schwinn-
Built Bicycles
Published by Arnold, Schwinn
& Co.
1941
Ink on paper
X.2332.2004
CHS

Starlet girl's bicycle
Arnold, Schwinn & Co.
1955
Steel, rubber
1986.231
Gift of Ms. Susan Brady
p. 166

Schwinn Sting-Ray Fair Lady
bicycle
1972
Mixed materials
2003.233.1
Gift of Richard and Cathryn
Nauman for Vickie Nauman

Lincoln Logs set
J. L. Wright, Inc., Chicago
c. 1940
Wood, cardboard
1981.166.1
Gift of Robert Furhoff
p. 166

Advertisement, Tinkertoys and
Lincoln Logs
Published by Montgomery
Ward & Co.
1958
Reproduction
ICHi-40406
CHS

Tinkertoys set
The Toy Tinkers, Evanston
c. 1955
Wood, cardboard, tin
1984.332.5
Gift of Don Miller
p. 166

Photograph, Marvin Glass
c. 1965
ICHi-40329
Gift of Marvin Glass &
Associates

Talking Teeth toy and box
Designed by Marvin Glass
Made by H. Fishlove and Co.
c. 1950
Plastic, paper, cardboard
1982.99.1abc
Gift of Howard Fishlove
p. 167

Drawing, U.S. Patent No.
3,298,692, *Game with Action
Producing Components*
Designed by Marvin Glass
1967
Reproduction
ICHi-40440
Gift of Marvin Glass &
Associates

Mousetrap board game
Designed by Marvin Glass
Made by Milton Bradley
1999
Plastic, cardboard
2005.100.1
Gift of Michael Nash

Photograph, Mousetrap game
c. 1970
ICHi-40328
Gift of Marvin Glass &
Associates
p. 167

Mr. Machine toy
Designed by Marvin Glass
Made by Ideal
c. 1960
Plastic, metal, wood
1989.657.203
Gift of Marvin Glass &
Associates

Wagon
Radio Flyer
2004
Painted metal, rubber, plastic
2004.137.1
Gift of Radio Flyer, Inc.

Photograph, Radio Flyer
exhibit at A Century of
Progress International
Exposition
1933–34
ICHi-40327
Gift of William Hellyer

Cobblers Bench pounding toy
Playskool, Inc.
1960
Wood
1984.729.3ab
Gift of Playskool, Inc.

Colorol Wagon pull toy
Playskool, Inc.
c. 1950
Wood, cotton cord, masonite
1984.729.16
Gift of Playskool, Inc.

Advertisement, Playskool toys
Published in the F. A. O.
Schwarz Children's World cata-
log
1966
Ink on paper
X.3293.2005
CHS

Household Goods

Ironmaster electric iron
Sunbeam Corporation
c. 1928
Steel, plastic, cloth
1990.613
Gift of Scott La France

Mixmaster stand mixer
Sunbeam Corporation
1948
Metal, glass, plastic
2001.206.1
Gift of Mrs. Annette Kaplan

Instruction booklet, *How to Get
the Most Out of Your Sunbeam
Mixmaster*
Published by Sunbeam
Corporation
1948
Ink on paper
2006.72.27NA
CHS Purchase

Coffee maker
Sunbeam Corporation
1947
Chrome and nickel-plated
copper, plastic
1994.193
Gift of Mrs. Eleanor Mellick

Tennis balls
Wilson Sporting Goods Co.
c. 1950
Metal, plastic, rubber
CH_04179 (2006.72.3
CHS Purchase

Advertisement, Wilson sporting
goods
1951
Ink on paper
2006.72.1
CHS Purchase

Filmo Auto Master 16mm
home movie camera
Bell & Howell Company
c. 1945
Metal, glass, plastic
1992.382.49
Gift of Marvin and Charlotte
Zandberg

134 8mm home movie camera
Bell & Howell Company
c. 1950
Metal, glass, plastic
1989.401.2ab
Gift of Elmer P. Renstrom

Pamphlet, Bell & Howell Filmo
8 movie projector
Bell & Howell Company
1936
Ink on paper
X.3294.2005
CHS

Kettle grill
Weber-Stephen Products Co.
c. 1975
Steel, teak
1986.198.1
Gift of Robert S. Jacobs
p. 167

Photograph, Ron Popeil
c. 1990
ICHi-40441
Gift of Ron Popeil

Donut Maker
Popeil Brothers
c. 1960
Plastic, metal
1997.69
Gift of Ms. Barbara Odette

Veg-o-Matic
Popeil Brothers
c. 1961
Plastic, metal
1985.490.1
Gift of Sharon Darling
p. 167

Space Command 600 television
remote control
Zenith Corporation
c. 1960
Plastic, metal
2004.147.1
Gift of Courtney Collie
p. 167

Advertisement, Zenith Space
Command remote controlled
TV
c. 1955
Ink on paper
X.2331.2004
CHS

Black Beauty bowling ball
Brunswick
c. 1970
Mixed material
2004.125.6
Gift of Mr. Fred Fagenholz

Advertisement, *Bowl Better*
1934
Ink on paper
X.3295.2005
CHS

Food

Poster, Vienna Beef hot dogs
Illustration by Timothy
Spindler
c. 1985
Ink on paper
1989.834
Gift of Archie Motley

Booklet, *The Story of Salt: A
Century of Progress in Salt Making*
Published by the Morton Salt
Company
1933
Ink on paper
X.3297.2005
CHS

Salt canister
Morton Salt Company
2005
Cardboard, metal
2006.72.10
CHS Purchase

Juicy Fruit gum package
Wrigley Company
2005
Paper
2006.72.6
CHS Purchase

Doublemint gum package
Wrigley Company
2005
Paper
2006.72.7
CHS Purchase

Advertisement, Wrigley
Doublemint gum
c. 1965
Reproduction
ICHi-40499
Gift of O'Ryan and Batchelder,
Inc.

Photograph, Cracker Jack plant
in Chicago
Hedrich-Blessing
1958
HB-21557
CHS, Hedrich-Blessing collection

Horse and wagon toy
Cracker Jack
c. 1935
Tin
X.3296.2005
CHS

Assorted toys
Cracker Jack
c. 1950
Plastic, metal, paper
1978.153
Gift of Mr. C. Carey Cloud

Cracker Jack
2005
Cardboard
2006.72.9
CHS Purchase

Macaroni & Cheese dinner
Kraft
2005
Cardboard
2006.72.8
CHS Purchase

Advertisement, Kraft Deluxe
Macaroni & Cheese
Published in McCall's maga-
zine
October 1961
Reproduction
ICHi-40410
Gift of Kenneth A. Harris

Oatmeal canister
Quaker Oats
2005
Cardboard, plastic
2006.72.11
CHS Purchase

FORM FOLLOWS FUNCTION
Evolution of the Skyscraper

Rosette from Home Insurance
Building entrance
Designed by William Le Baron
Jenney
1885
Bronze
1934.113
Gift of Charles Rubens
p. 126

Photograph, The Montauk
Block, 1881–82
Published in *History of Chicago*,
A.T. Andreas
1886
ICHi-40396
CHS

Photograph, John Wellborn
Root
Max Platz
c. 1880
ICHi-30622
Gift of Mr. Lawrence B. Perkins

Photograph, The Home
Insurance Building
Chicago Architectural
Photographic Company
1885
ICHi-37731
Gift of George Richardson
p. 126

Photograph, William Le Baron
Jenney
c. 1885
ICHi-18887
CHS
p. 125

Photograph, Dankmar Adler
c. 1890
ICHi-09386
CHS
p. 127

Photograph, Louis Henri
Sullivan
Alexander Hesler
c. 1890
Sullivaniana Collection,
Ryerson & Burnham Archives,
The Art Institute of Chicago
p. 127

Photograph, Chicago Stock
Exchange Building
W. T. Barnum
c. 1907
ICHi-19456
CHS

Engraving, *Freight and Passenger
Cars Combined*
Ellithorpe Air-Brake Co.,
Chicago
c. 1887
Reproduction
ICHi-40353
CHS Purchase

Photograph, The Reliance
Building
Kaufmann & Fabry
1926
ICHi-24215
CHS

Photograph, Detail of the
Reliance Building
Richard Nickel
c. 1970
ICHi-16339
Gift of the Chicago
Architecture Foundation
p. xvii

Photograph, Daniel Hudson
Burnham
Harrison & Coover
c. 1890
ICHi-27044
Gift of Mr. Lawrence B. Perkins

Photograph, Construction of
860–880 North Lake Shore
Drive
Hedrich-Blessing
c. 1950
HB-13809-L4
CHS, Hedrich-Blessing
collection
p. 141

Photograph, Aerial view of
860–880 North Lake Shore
Drive
Hedrich-Blessing
c. 1960
HB-13809-S6
CHS, Hedrich-Blessing
collection

Photograph, Ludwig Mies
van der Rohe
Arthur Siegel
c. 1955
ICHi-40317
Gift of Irene Siegel
p. 141

Photograph, The John Hancock
Center
Hedrich-Blessing
1972
HB-31216-E3
CHS, Hedrich-Blessing
collection
p. 142

Photograph, Fazlur Khan
Reprinted from *Engineering-
News Record*
February 10, 1972
Copyright The McGraw-Hill
Companies, Inc. All rights
reserved.
p. 143

Photograph, Sears Tower
Hedrich-Blessing
1974
HB-37734-E
CHS, Hedrich-Blessing
collection
p. 143

Photograph, Sears Tower model
in wind tunnel
c. 1970
Courtesy, Skidmore, Owings &
Merrill

Photograph, Sears Tower wind
testing model with Nick
Isuymov
c. 1970
Courtesy, Skidmore, Owings &
Merrill

Sears Tower model
c. 1970
Mixed material
Courtesy of Skidmore, Owings
& Merrill

Lake Point Tower model
Designed by Schipporeit-
Heinrich
c. 1968
Mixed material
1996.280
Gift of Mr. George Schipporeit

Adler & Sullivan

Painting, *Carson Pirie Scott
Building*
Albert Fleury
1903
Watercolor and pencil on paper
1979.223
Gift of John Dern, Jr.
pp. 113 (detail), 128

Medallion from the Carson
Pirie Scott Building
Designed by Louis H. Sullivan
1898-99
Copper-plated cast iron
2000.23.2
Gift of Ms. Margaret Keck
pp. 112, 128

Fragment from the Chicago
Stock Exchange Building
Designed by Louis H. Sullivan
1894
Terra cotta
2003.154.1
Gift of Stuart Grannen and
Richard Rasnick

Elevator lintels from the
Chicago Stock Exchange
Building
Designed by Louis H. Sullivan
1894
Copper-plated cast iron
1991.522ab
Gift of Lawrence Booth
p. 128

Elevator grilles from the
Chicago Stock Exchange
Building
Designed by Louis H. Sullivan
1894
Iron
1987.608.1–2
Gift of Mr. and Mrs. Philip M.
Burno

Newel post from the Chicago
Stock Exchange Building
Designed by Louis H. Sullivan
1893–94
Copper-plated cast iron
1977.207.2
Gift of D. Coder Tayor

Door light from the office of
Adler & Sullivan
Designed by Louis H. Sullivan
Made by the Western Sand
Blast Mfg. Co., Chicago
1883
Sandblasted plate glass
1979.80
CHS Purchase from Drehobl
Glass Co., Chicago
p. 127

Photograph, Chicago Stock
Exchange
Institute of Design
c. 1970
ICHi-40319
Gift of the Estate of Ray
Pearson

Photograph, Entrance to
Chicago Stock Exchange
Aso Doi
c. 1970
ICHi-40318
Gift of the Estate of Ray
Pearson

Photograph, Detail of the
Chicago Stock Exchange
Richard Nickel
c. 1970
ICHi-40346
Gift of the Chicago
Architecture Foundation

Photograph, Schiller
Building/Garrick Theater
c. 1917
ICHi-20440
CHS

Photograph, Schiller
Building/Garrick Theater
proscenium arch
Richard Nickel
c. 1960
ICHi-40321
Gift of the Estate of Ray
Pearson

Photograph, Schiller/Garrick
Theater during demolition
Richard Nickel
1960
ICHi-40320
Gift of Irene Siegel

Photograph, Schiller/Garrick
Theater demonstration
Arthur Siegel
1960
ICHi-40390
Gift of Irene Siegel

Photograph, The Auditorium
Building
Copelin
c. 1890
ICHi-26943
CHS Purchase

Postcard, Auditorium Hotel
c. 1890
Reproduction
ICHi-40492
CHS

Photograph, The Auditorium
Theatre stage
c. 1890
ICHi-14707
Gift of Kovler Gallery

Photograph, View from The
Auditorium Theatre stage
J. W. Taylor
c. 1895
ICHi-00593
Gift of Arthur S. Cummings

Prairie School

Sewing table
Designed by Frank Lloyd
Wright
c. 1907
Walnut
1978.233
Gift of Mr. and Mrs. Wilbert
Hasbrouck
p. 130

Side chairs with cane backs
and seats
Designed by Frank Lloyd
Wright
c. 1912
Oak
1978.40ab
Gift of Mr. and Mrs. Julius
Abler
p. 131

Clear and opaque white glass
windows from the Ward Willits
House
Designed by Frank Lloyd
Wright

Produced by Giannini &
Hilgart, Chicago
1902
Glass, copper
1985.423
Gift of Willits-Robinson
Foundation
p. 131

Textured opalescent and cathe-
dral glass lunette window from
the Patrick J. King House
Designed by George W. Maher
Fabrication attributed to Louis
Millet, Chicago
1901
Glass
1985.170.1
CHS Purchase

Book, *The House Beautiful*
William C. Gannett
Designed by Frank Lloyd
Wright
Printed by the Auvergne Press,
River Forest, Illinois
1897
Ink on paper
1963.777
Gift of Mrs. George Langhorne

Urn
Designed by Frank Lloyd
Wright
Produced by James A. Miller
and Brothers
c. 1900
Copper
1998.41
Gift of Emilie H. Anderson and
Joy Brown Atwood
p. 131

Photograph, Frank Lloyd
Wright
Jun Fujita
c. 1950
ICHi-12960
Gift of Mrs. Jun Fujita
(Florence Carr Fujita)
p. 129

Elevation and floor plan of the
Frank Lloyd Wright Home and
Studio
Frank Lloyd Wright
Published by Horizon Press,
New York
1963
Reproduction
ICHi-40395
Gift of Mrs. George Langhorne

Elevation and floor plan of the
Ward Willits House
Frank Lloyd Wright
Published by Horizon Press,
New York
1963
Reproduction
ICHi-40315
Gift of Mrs. George Langhorne
p. 130

Floor plan and interior view of
the Avery Coonley House
Frank Lloyd Wright
Published by Horizon Press,
New York

1963
Reproduction
ICHi-40316
Gift of Mrs. George Langhorne

Robert Jarvie

Candlesticks
Robert Jarvie
c. 1905
Brass
1975.53ab
CHS Purchase

Sauce bowl and ladle
Robert Jarvie
c. 1910
Sterling silver
1973.156ab
Gift of Mr. Eugene Kimball
Morsman

Bowl
Robert Jarvie
c. 1905
Copper
1977.89.1
Gift of Miss Jessie Dobson
p. 135

Trophy
Robert Jarvie
1916
Sterling silver
1974.151
Gift of Mr. and Mrs. Charles S.
Potter
p. 136

Catalog, *The Book of
The Jarvie Shop*
c. 1905
Ink on paper
2005.27.1
Gift of Glen and Katharine
Elsasser
p. 135

Photograph, The Jarvie Shop at
the Union Stock Yards
c. 1912
Courtesy of the International
Live Stock Exposition

Teco Pottery

Vase with green matte glaze
Gates Potteries
c. 1905–25
Ceramic
1975.134.3
CHS Purchase

Creamer with green matte glaze
Gates Potteries
c. 1905–25
Ceramic
1975.134.9
CHS Purchase

Double-bellied vase with green
matte glaze
Gates Potteries
c. 1915
Ceramic
1975.134.2
CHS Purchase

Planter with green matte glaze
Gates Potteries
c. 1910
Ceramic
1985.40.45
Gift of Chase Gilmore

Jardiniere with green matte
glaze
Designed by Hugh M. Garden
Made by Gates Potteries
c. 1905
Ceramic
1980.71
Gift of Violet Wyld and Philip
Maker

Vase
Designed by Fritz Albert
Made by Gates Potteries
c. 1905
Ceramic
1980.161.3
CHS Purchase
p. 132

Lamp base
Designed by M. P. White
Made by Gates Potteries
c. 1907
Ceramic
1976.97
CHS Purchase

Vase
Gates Potteries
c. 1915
Ceramic
1976.107
CHS Purchase
p. 133

The Kalo Shop

Sugar bowl and creamer
The Kalo Shop
c. 1910
Sterling silver
1975.218ab
CHS Purchase
p. 133

Sugar tongs
The Kalo Shop
c. 1910
Sterling silver
1991.344.1
Gift of Mrs. Frank D. Mayer

Bowl
The Kalo Shop
c. 1913
Sterling silver
1976.187.1
CHS Purchase
p. 134

Tea strainer
The Kalo Shop
1908
Sterling silver
1976.20.3ab
CHS Purchase in honor of
Theodore Tieken by his
children
p. 133

Salad servers
The Kalo Shop
1909
Sterling silver
1972.43ab
Gift of Mrs. Jessie Orton Jones

Photograph, Clara Barck Welles
1906
ICHi-40389
Courtesy of Stanley W. Hess
p. 134

Photograph, Kalo-Art Craft
Community, Park Ridge
c. 1910
ICHi-40333
Gift of Robert R. Bower

Photograph, The Kalo Shop
workroom
c. 1917
ICHi-40332
Gift of Robert R. Bower
p. 134

Photograph, The Kalo Shop at
222 South Michigan Avenue
c. 1940
ICHi-40334
Gift of Robert R. Bower

**Abel Faidy and Wolfgang
Hoffmann**

Armchair
Designed by Abel Faidy
Fabrication attributed to
Marshall Field & Co.
1927
Maple, leather
1977.191.2
CHS Purchase
p. 137

Drawing, black and white
dining set
Abel Faidy
1954
ICHi-40276
Gift of Renor Faidy
p. 137

Drawing, green plaid armchair
with red enamel frame
Wolfgang Hoffmann
c. 1936
ICHi-40286
Gift of Mr. Murray Moxley

Prototype serving cart
Designed by Wolfgang
Hoffmann
Produced by W. H. Howell
Company, Geneva, Illinois
c. 1935
Tubular steel, formica, rubber
1981.81.2
Gift of the William McCredie
Estate
p. 138

"S" chair
Made by W. H. Howell
Company, Geneva, Illinois
c. 1935
Tubular steel, vinyl
1981.81.7
Gift of the William McCredie
Estate

Photograph, Wolfgang
Hoffmann
c. 1955
ICHi-40331
Gift of Murray Moxley
p. 138

Photograph, Abel Faidy
Hedrich-Blessing
1968
HB-31189
CHS, Hedrich-Blessing collection
p. 137

Institute of Design

Dove soap prototype
Made by a student at the
Institute of Design
c. 1955
Wood
X.2349.2004
CHS

Miner's flash light
Designed by Alfred Mell at the
Institute of Design
Manufactured by Justrite
Manufacturing Co.
c. 1955
Plastic
1985.714
Gift of Mrs. Alfred Mell
p. 140

Boomerang sculpture with
lattice cut-outs
Made by a student at the
Institute of Design
c. 1960
Wood
X.2346.2004
CHS
p. 140

Woven sculpture
Made by a student at the
Institute of Design
c. 1960
Metal
X.2343.2004
CHS

Sculpture
Made by a student at the
Institute of Design
c. 1960
Plastic
X.2624.2004
CHS

Photograph, Students in a
foundations course at the
Institute of Design
c. 1949
ICHi-40342
Gift of the Estate of Ray
Pearson
p. 140

Advertisement, Courses at the
Institute of Design
Designed by Frank Barr
1944
Ink on paper
1982.88
Gift of James Prestini

Photograph, Walter Gropius
and Laszlo Moholy-Nagy at the
Institute of Design
c. 1950
ICHi-40341
Gift of the Estate of Ray
Pearson
p. 139

WE'RE COOKIN'
The Birth Control Pill

Photograph, Ovulen Compack,
c. 1977
John Alderson
2005
ICHi-40420
CHS

Photograph, Frank Colton
working in the laboratory
c. 1952
Courtesy of G. D. Searle & Co.
p. 164

Research chart, *Anti-Fertility
Tests in Rabbits*
Created by Dr. Gregory Pincus
1959
Ink on paper
Courtesy of G. D. Searle & Co.

Bottle containing 100 Enovid
5mg birth control pills
Manufactured by G. D. Searle
& Co.
c. 1960
Plastic, paper
Courtesy of G. D. Searle & Co.

Ovulen Compack birth control
pill dispenser and instruction
booklet
Manufactured by G. D. Searle
& Co.
c. 1977
Plastic, paper
Courtesy of G. D. Searle & Co.
p. 165

Photograph, Technician at
Abbott Labs analyzing
penicillin samples
1958
ICHi-40314
Gift of Irene Siegel

Photograph, Technician at
Abbott Labs measuring liquid
into beakers
Stephen Deutch
c. 1945
ICHi-40313
Gift of Stephen Deutch

Advertisement, Enovid-E birth
control pill
Published by G. D. Searle &
Co.
1971
Ink on paper
Courtesy of G. D. Searle & Co.
Photograph, Dr. Gregory
Pincus
c. 1960
Courtesy of G. D. Searle & Co.

Photograph, Katharine
McCormick
c. 1910
Courtesy of G. D. Searle & Co.
p. 164

Photograph, Margaret Sanger in
Chicago
Chicago Daily News
1917
DN-0067907
CHS
p. 164

**The First Sustained Nuclear
Chain Reaction**

Photograph, Explosion of the
atomic bomb at Nagasaki,
Japan
August 9, 1945
Courtesy of the National
Archives

Painting, *The Birth of the
Atomic Age*
Gary Sheahan
1957
Oil on board
1964.521
Gift of Mr. Gary Sheahan
p. 161

Scientists' notebook recording
the first sustained nuclear chain
reaction
1942
Ink on paper
Courtesy of the National
Archives

Booklet, *Atoms to Kilowatts*
Published by Commonwealth
Edison
c. 1957
Ink on paper
X.3218.2005
CHS

Headline, *Atom Bomb Dooms
Japs*
Published in the *Chicago Daily
News*
August 6, 1945
Reproduction
ICHi-40300
Chicago Daily News

Photograph, Overhead view of
Chicago Pile 1
November 1942
ICHi-40299
Courtesy of Argonne National
Laboratory
p. 163

Photograph, Scientists responsible for the first sustained
nuclear chain reaction
December 2, 1946
Courtesy of the National
Archives
p. 162

Drawing, Overhead plan of
Chicago Pile 1
1942
Reproduction
Courtesy of the National
Archives

REFORMING SOCIETY

Photograph, Neighborhood
scene showing a woman hang-
ing wash
The Visiting Nurse Association
c. 1910
ICHi-21345
Gift of the Visiting Nurse
Association of Chicago

Photograph, Grade Four
classroom at Cook County
Normal School
c. 1900
ICHi-17874
Gift of Mrs. Cyrus Hall (Nettie
Fowler) McCormick

Hull-House

Photograph, Jane Addams
Allen, Gordon, Schroeppel and
Redlich, Inc.
c. 1892
ICHi-09378
Gift of Hull-House
p. 144

Photograph, Ellen Gates Starr
Chicago Daily News
1914
DN-0062288
CHS
p. 144

Photograph, Children sitting
and kneeling on the ground
and painting at Hull-House
Chicago Daily News
1924
DN-0076595
CHS
p. 114 (detail), p. 146

Photograph, Hull-House complex at 800 South Halsted Street
Barnes-Crosby
c. 1910
ICHi-19288
Gift of the Barnes-Crosby Company
p. 145

Pedestal candy dish made in a Hull-House class
Martha Meis
1934
Ceramic
1995.105
Gift of Roberta Reb Allen

Green-glazed sugar bowl and creamer made in the Hull-House Kilns
c. 1930
Ceramic
1992.116.1–.2
Gift of Mr. and Mrs. Rod Zamotin

Yellow-glazed bowl made in the Hull-House Kilns
c. 1930
Ceramic
1994.288
Gift of Lois Waller
p. 145

Photograph, Welcome to our family
c. 1900
ICHi-01544
Gift of Hull-House Association

Booklet, *Pottery from Hull House*
Published by Hull-House
1933
Ink on paper
1963.778
Gift of Newberry Library

Bowls made in the metal shop at Hull-House
Olga Huncke
c. 1915
Copper
1979.22, 1979.138
Gift of Miss Ada Huncke in memory of Olga Huncke
p. 146

Progressive Education

Textile of the type made in Edward Worst's manual arts classes, c. 1925
1985.335
Gift of Dorothy and William Worst

Book, *The School and Society*
Written by John Dewey in 1899
Published by the University of Chicago Press in 1936
Ink on paper
X.3327.2005
CHS

Photograph, Professor John Dewey
Chicago Daily News
1929
DN-0087487
CHS
p. 147

Book, *Industrial Work for the Middle Grades*
Edward Worst
1919
Ink on paper
1985.335
Gift of Dorothy and William Worst
p. 148

Doll bed made in a manual arts class at Garfield School
c. 1917
Wood
1978.52.1
Gift of Miss Marie C. Friedline

Book, *Constructive Work*
Written by Edward Worst in 1900
Published by A. W. Mumford and Company in 1905
Ink on paper
1985.335
Gift of Dorothy and William Worst

Photograph, Edward Worst
Harrington
c. 1905
ICHi-40136
Gift of Dorothy and William Worst
p. 148

Photographs, Creating linen from flax at the Chicago Normal School
1907
ICHi-40135– 40139
Gift of Dorothy and William Worst
p. 149

Photograph, Ella Flagg Young
Jarvis Weed
c. 1909
ICHi-13108
CHS
p. 147

Beyond the Settlement House Doors

Broadside, *Benefit concert for the Juvenile Court*
Illustration by John McCutcheon
1905
Reproduction
ICHi-40295
Gift of Mrs. John McCutcheon

Photograph, Mother doing "homework"
c. 1910
ICHi-21086
Gift of the Visiting Nurse Association of Chicago

Photograph, Mary McDowell with the Filipiak children
c. 1910
ICHi-40129
Gift of Mary McDowell Settlement

University of Chicago Settlement fundraising pamphlet
1909
Ink on paper
X.3220.2005
CHS

Chicago Commons Association fundraising pamphlet
1915
Ink on paper
X.3219.2005
CHS

Photograph, Graham Taylor with children on the settlement house's playground
1910
ICHi-40133
Gift of Chicago Commons Association

Photograph, Cleanliness inspection at Parker Practice School
Kaufmann & Fabry
1927
ICHi-40131
Gift of Chicago Community Trust

Photograph, Open Air School on the roof of the Mary Crane Nursery
c. 1915
ICHi-18485
Gift of Chicago Community Trust

Public Housing

Photograph, Slum conditions in the 500 block of 37th Street
Mildred Mead
1951
ICHi-00809
Gift of Mildred Mead

Photograph, Family in their living room in Jane Addams Homes
Mildred Mead
1954
ICHi-29572
Gift of Mildred Mead

Photograph, Family in their home in the Brooks Homes public housing complex
Mildred Mead
1954
ICHi-24661
Gift of Mildred Mead

Photograph, Children use the playground at Francis Cabrini Homes
Mildred Mead
1951
ICHi-40127
Gift of Mildred Mead

Photograph, Trumbull Park Homes
Photograph by Hedrich-Blessing.
1949
HB-12520B
CHS, Hedrich-Blessing collection

Photograph, Donald and Betty Howard barricade their windows
1953
ICHi-15102
Gift of Etta Moten Barnett

Photograph, Donald Howard watches his family approach their home
1953
ICHi-36837
Gift of Etta Moten Barnett

Photograph, A Chicago police officer holds a door open for Donald Howard
1953
ICHi-15103
Gift of Etta Moten Barnett

Letter protesting the CHA's dismissal of Elizabeth Wood
Emergency Committee on Public Housing
October 16, 1954
Ink on paper
X.3221.2005
CHS

Chicago Housing Authority Annual Report
1954
Ink on paper
X.3222.2005
CHS

Broadside, *Remember the Housing Projects?*
1950
Ink on paper
1966.574
Gift of Archibald J. Carey, Jr.

Photograph, Elizabeth Wood
Published in Chicago Housing Authority Annual Report
1948
ICHi-40296
CHS

Photograph, Studs Terkel
Stephen Deutch
c. 1970
ICHi-25638
Gift of Stephen Deutch

JAZZ

Photograph, Entrance to the Blue Note Café, Chicago
c. 1955
ICHi-18511
Gift of Mr. Frank H. Holzfeind
pp. 169 (detail), 188

Photograph, Cool Breeze and the Four Breezes
c. 1950
ICHi-40631
Gift of Mr. Scotty Piper

Photograph, The Palm Tavern
Gordon Coster
1940
ICHi-29772
Gift of Peter Coster

Photograph, King Oliver's Creole Jazz Band at Lincoln Gardens
1923
Courtesy of Howard-Tilton Memorial Library, Tulane University

Photograph, Benny Goodman in Chicago with Howard Baumgarten
Chicago American
1938
ICHi-24453
CHS

Photograph, Dizzy Gillespie
c. 1955
ICHi-40432
Gift of Mr. Scotty Piper

Photograph, Gene Krupa
c. 1955
ICHi-18645
Gift of Mr. Frank H. Holzfeind

Photograph, Cab Calloway
c. 1955
ICHi-40433
Gift of Mr. Scotty Piper

Photograph, Ella Fitzgerald
c. 1955
ICHi-40429
Gift of Mr. Frank H. Holzfeind

Photograph, Louis Armstrong
c. 1930
ICHi-13194
Gift of Mr. Scotty Piper
p. 186

Photograph, Dinah Washington
c. 1960
ICHi-40430
Gift of Mr. Scotty Piper

Photograph, Lionel Hampton
c. 1950
ICHi-40431
Gift of Mr. Scotty Piper

Photograph, Duke Ellington
c. 1935
ICHi-23883
Gift of Mr. Scotty Piper
p. 187

Photograph, Charlie Parker
c. 1950
ICHi-4042
Gift of Mr. Frank H. Holzfeind

Cornet given by Bix
Beiderbecke to Jimmy
McPartland
Vincent Bach Corporation,
New York
1929
Gold-plated brass
1985.451
Gift of James D. McPartland
p. 186

Saxophone used by James Palao
C. G. Conn, Ltd., Elkhart,
Indiana
c. 1920
Silver plate, brass plate
1990.387.3ab
Gift of Clotile Palao Wilson
p. 185

Banjo used by James Palao
c. 1920
Wood, metal, wire
1990.387.2ab
Gift of Clotile Palao Wilson

Drum set used by Michael F.
Kapso
Bass drum made by
Slingerland, Chicago
Snare drum made by Frank
Holton
c. 1925
Wood, metal, calfskin
1995.232
Gift of Howard F. Kapso and
Charles R. Keebler

Broadside, *Duke Ellington and
his Famous Orchestra*
c. 1945
Ink on paper
1995.89
CHS Purchase
p. 187

Sign from Gerri's Palm Tavern
c. 1965
Paint on cardboard
2004.117.1
Gift of Ms. Gerri Oliver

Photograph, The Original
Creole Orchestra
c. 1918
Courtesy of Clotile Wilson
p. 185

Photograph, King Oliver's
Creole Jazz Band
c. 1920
Courtesy of Tulane University

Record album, Benny
Goodman Sextet
c. 1945
Reproduction
Private Collection

Record Album, *Flying Home*
Benny Goodman Sextet
c. 1945
Reproduction
Private Collection

Record album, *Grand Slam*
Benny Goodman Sextet
c. 1945
Reproduction
Private Collection

Record album, 1938 Carnegie
Hall Jazz Concert
Benny Goodman
c. 1960
Reproduction
Private Collection
p. 187

DownBeat magazine
May 2005
Reproduction
Courtesy *DownBeat* Magazine

Blue Note Café photograph
envelope
c. 1960
Reproduction
ICHi-40633
Gift of Mr. Frank H. Holzfeind

Photograph, Bob Kelly Band
performing at Club Silhouette
Henry D. Green
c. 1950
ICHi-25580
CHS Purchase

BLUES

Electric bass guitar used by
Floyd Jones
c. 1960
Wood, metal, cloth
1990.818.1
Gift of Justin B. O'Brien
p. 190

Amplifier used by Floyd Jones
Peavey Electronics Corp.,
Meridian, Mississippi
c. 1960
Vinyl, plastic, metal
1990.818.2
Gift of Justin B. O'Brien

Broadside, *Chicago's Blues
All-Stars*
1974
Ink on paper
1990.818.3
Gift of Justin B. O'Brien
p. 190

Broadside, *Celebrate Chicago
Blues*
1980
Ink on paper
1982.003.1
Gift of Barry Dolins

Broadside *Checkerboard Lounge*
c. 1980
Ink on paper
1983.756
Gift of Mr. Paul Petraitis

Broadside, *B.B. King*
1972
Ink on paper
1973.244
Gift of Mr. Paul Petraitis

Broadside, *Atomic Mama's
Wang-Dang-Doodle Blues Show*
c. 1975
Ink on paper
X.2334.2004
CHS

Photograph, Muddy Waters
c. 1960
ICHi-31738
Gift of *Chicago* magazine
p. 189

Photograph, McKie Fitzhugh
performing with Willie Dixon
on bass
c. 1955
ICHi-24317
Gift of Scotty Piper

Photograph, Chuck Berry
c. 1960
ICHi-40345
Gift of Scotty Piper
p. 189

Record album, *School Day*
Chuck Berry
1957
Reproduction
Courtesy of Bill Riordan
p. 189

PLAYBOY CLUB

Photograph, Playboy bunny
walking through a crowd at the
Playboy Club
Stephen Deutch
c. 1960
ICHi-23629
Gift of Stephen Deutch
p. 212

Playboy Bunny costume
1972
Nylon-antron satin
1972.239
Gift of Playboy Enterprises,
Inc.

Photograph, Two Playboy
bunnies at work
Stephen Deutch
c. 1960
ICHi-40392
Gift of Stephen Deutch

Playboy Club swizzle sticks
c. 1960-86
Plastic
2001.268.6–7
Gift of Edward R. Weed

Playboy Club ashtray
c. 1970
Glass and enamel
1996.294.16
Gift of Howard E. Hight

Playboy Club key card issued
to Howard E. Hight
c. 1970
Metal
1996.294.18b
Gift of Howard E. Hight
Playboy magazine
December 1959
Ink on paper
CH_03822 (1986.210.2)
Gift of Don McCoy

Advertisement, *What sort of man
reads Playboy?*
Published on the back cover of
Playboy magazine
January 1959
Ink on paper
1986.210.1
Gift of Don McCoy

Photograph, Playboy founder
Hugh Hefner at the Playboy
Mansion in Chicago
Declan Haun
c. 1965
ICHi-40391
Gift of the Estate of Declan
Haun
p. 212

HERE WE ARE AGAIN
Film

Essanay News
February 27, 1915
Ink on paper
X.2329.2004
CHS
p. 152

Photograph, Filming a Broncho
Billy movie at Essanay Studios
c. 1916
ICHi-16886
CHS Purchase
p. 151

Urban Bioscope movie camera
used by Essanay Studios
Charles Urban Trading Co.,
Ltd.
1902
Wood, metal, leather
1975.187.1
CHS Purchase
p. 153

Light meter
Watkins, England
c. 1910
Metal, glass
1957.411
Gift of Burke & James, Inc.

Essanay Studios cameraman's
button
c. 1910
Metal
1975.187.3
CHS Purchase
p. 152

Essanay Studios printing block
c. 1910
Wood, metal
1975.187.4
CHS Purchase
Photograph, Selig cameraman
Chicago Daily News
c. 1905
DN-0062406
CHS

Photograph, Movie still from
Selig production *Fort Dearborn
Massacre*
c. 1910
ICHi-40393
CHS

Photograph, George K. Spoor
Moffat
c. 1910
ICHi-12538
CHS
p. 150

Photograph, Gilbert M.
Anderson
c. 1910
ICHi-20120
CHS Purchase
p. 150

Photograph, Movie still with
Wallace Beery, Francis
Bushman, and Gloria Swanson
c. 1910
ICHi-20134
CHS Purchase

Advertisement, Micheaux Film
Corporation
1924
Reproduction
ICHi-40394
CHS Purchase

Television

Photograph, WNBQ
performers
1949–50
ICHi-05013
Gift of Sarajane Wells
pp. 155, xiv (detail)

Kukla hand puppet
Burr Tillstrom
c. 1955
Nylon, leather, felt
1985.549.64
Gift of the Estate of Burr
Tillstrom
p. 158

TV Forecast magazine
February 14, 1953
Ink on paper
1985.549

Gift of the Estate of Burr
Tillstrom
Photograph, Children meeting
Burr Tillstrom, Fran Allison,
Kukla, and Ollie
c. 1948
ICHi-40338
Gift of the Estate of Burr
Tillstrom
p. 159

Burr Tillstrom's *KFO*
production notebook
1947–48
Ink and pencil on paper
1985.549
Gift of the Estate of Burr
Tillstrom

Burr Tillstrom's "KFO Setup"
notebook
1948
Leather, plastic, paper
1985.549
Gift of the Estate of Burr
Tillstrom
p. 156

Drawing of Kukla and Ollie by
Donald Iwanski, New Jersey
c. 1948
Pencil on paper
1985.549
Gift of the Estate of Burr
Tillstrom

Photograph, Dave Garroway
with Burr Tillstrom, Kukla, and
Ollie
c. 1950
ICHi-40347
Gift of the Burr Tillstrom
Estate
p. 157

Photograph, Studs Terkel, Win
Strake, Big Bill Broonzy, and
Larry Lane
Stephen Deutch
c. 1948
ICHi-26824
Gift of Stephen Deutch

Photograph, Newton N.
Minow, Chairman, Federal
Communications Commission
1961
Courtesy of Josephine B. Minow
p. 160

EDGEWATER BEACH HOTEL

Photograph, Carload of guests
arriving at the Edgewater Beach
Hotel
Chicago Architectural
Photography Company
c. 1920
ICHi-24489
Gift of John McCutcheon

Painted sign from the
Edgewater Beach Hotel
1916–67
Wood
2000.161.1
Gift of Mr. Marshall M. Holleb

Postcard, The Edgewater Beach
Hotel from Lake Michigan
Max Rigot Selling Co., Chicago
c. 1920
Ink on paper
X.3228.2005
CHS

Postcard, The Edgewater Beach
Hotel from Sheridan Road
Photograph by Koehne Photo
c. 1920
Ink on paper
2002.39
Gift of Mr. Wayne Makel

Edgewater Beach Hotel
candy box
CANCO
1924
Tin
1973.110
Gift of Miss Margaret Diers

Postcard, The beach promenade
at the Edgewater Beach Hotel
Commercial Colortype Co.
Chicago
c. 1920
Ink on paper
X.3229.2005
CHS

Postcard, The Edgewater Beach
Hotel's amenities
Curt Teich & Company,
Chicago
c. 1920
Ink on paper
1985.263.53
Gift of Mrs. Robert Jones
Coppoch

Photograph, Guests lounging
on the beach at the Edgewater
Beach Hotel
Acme Newspictures, Inc.
c. 1920
ICHi-40312
Gift of Mrs. Thomas M. Hoyne
III

Photograph, Porter helping a
guest out of a car at the
Edgewater Beach Hotel
Chicago Architectural
Photography Company
c. 1920
ICHi-24486
Gift of John McCutcheon

Photograph, View of the
Edgewater Beach Hotel from
Lake Michigan
Chicago Architectural
Photography Company
c. 1920
ICHi-34567
Gift of John McCutcheon

Postcard, The Edgewater Beach
Hotel's dining room
Photograph by Brooks Photo
c. 1920
Ink on paper
1974.207.2
Gift of Thomas C. Loggie

Postcard, The Edgewater Beach
Hotel's hydro-aeroplane
Photograph by Brooks Photo
c. 1920
Ink on paper
1974.207.1
Gift of Thomas C. Loggie

Edgewater Beach Hotel bever-
age menu
c. 1950
Ink on paper
1971.377
Gift of Martin A. Kaye

AMUSEMENT PARKS

Painting, *Parachutes ride at
Riverview Park*
H. P. Zwengel
1937
Watercolor on board
1987.367.4
Gift of William Schmidt

Photograph, Aerial shot of
Riverview Park
Chicago Aerial Survey
Company
1931
ICHi-40356
Gift of Mr. William B. Schmidt
p. 179

Carousel horse from Riverview
Park
Carved by Leo Zoller
c. 1908
Wood, paint
2003.54
Gift of Robert Buehler
p. 180

Photograph, Children on the
Riverview Park carousel
1946
ICHi-40303
CHS
p. 180

Postcard, Aerial view of White
City
Schmidt & Co.
c. 1906
Ink on paper
X.3328.2006
CHS

Postcard, West Boardwalk at
White City
V. O. Hammon Publishing Co.,
Chicago
1910
Ink on paper
1986.9
Gift of Jeffrey Haynes

Photograph, Crowds lined up
outside White City
Harry A. Atwell
c. 1925
ICHi-24749
Gift of Mrs. Harold M. Gilden

Photograph, Women eating hot
dogs on the White City
boardwalk
c. 1925
ICHi-24739
CHS

1893 WORLD'S
COLUMBIAN EXPOSITION

Lunette painting, *The World's
Columbian Exposition of 1893*
Lawrence Carmichael Earle
1900
Oil on canvas
1933.51
Gift of Central Republic Bank
and Trust Company
p. 174

Photograph, Art studio in the
Horticulture Building
C. D. Arnold
1892
ICHi-02492
Gift of Otto L. Schmidt

Pay Gate sign
1893
Wood
1923.123
Gift of Marshall Field &
Company

Painting, *The Sunset Hour on the
West Lagoon*
William LeRoy Metcalf
1893
Oil on canvas
1943.30
Gift of Chicago Public Library

Folding chair marked, *World's
Fair Chairs—For Rent*
1893
Wood
1943.70a
Gift of Miss Edith Patterson

Painting, *The Electricity Building*
Childe Hassam
1893
Watercolor on paper
1948.26
Gift of Chicago Public Library
p. 173

Photograph, The Ferris Wheel
on the Midway Plaisance
C. E. Waterman
1893
ICHi-02440
CHS
pp. iv (detail), 175

I Will bust
Sculpted by J. Fielde from a
drawing by Charles Holloway
1893
Plaster
1947.103
Gift of Mrs. Andrew H. Burgess

Scepter presented to Daniel
Burnham
Spaulding & Company,
Chicago
c. 1895
Ivory, gold
X.749
Gift of the Burnham Family
p. 172

Medal presented to Bertha
Honore Palmer
Tiffany & Company
1893
Sterling silver, enamel, ruby
1930.128a
Gift of Mrs. Potter Palmer II
p. 177

Surveyor's instrument
Eugene Dietzgen Co.
c. 1890
Brass, glass
1992.127.1
Gift of Norman Moore and
daughter Anya C. Moore

Egg-shaped souvenir salt shaker
Libbey Cut Glass Company
1893
Glass, metal
1993.135
Gift of Billie Logeman in
memory of Dr. Joseph and Dr.
Ada Blesh Chandler
p. 178

Souvenir bowl featuring a
nighttime view of the
Administration Building
1893
Metal, glass, paper
1985.27.8
Gift of Elizabeth Barbour and
Estate of Lillian Barbour
p. 178

Oversize souvenir cup with
drawings of fair buildings
1893
Ceramic
1981.107a
Gift of Margaret Huebner

Souvenir box featuring an
image of fair buildings
1893
Wood
X.3299.2005
CHS

Souvenir sailboat inscribed
*World's Columbian Exposition
Chicago 1893*
1893
Mother-of-pearl, metal, cork
1996.144
Gift of Mr. and Mrs. Donald
W. White

Castanets from the Italian
exhibit
1893
Wood
1956.24ab
Gift of Miss Cornelia Conger

Christopher Columbus World's
Fair official souvenir pin
1893
Metal
XG.6.2
CHS

Souvenir pickle fork
Distributed by Wichert's Pickles
1893
Enamel, metal
CH_01872 (1993.76.1
Gift of Mrs. George Shiller
p. 178

State of Illinois and Abraham
Lincoln souvenir teaspoon
R. Wallace & Sons
Manufacturing Co.,
Wallingford, CT
1893
Sterling silver
1980.31.2a
Gift of Mrs. Patricia Morgan

Official World's Fair souvenir
teaspoon
Alister & Co.
1893
Sterling silver
1972.323a
Gift of the North Carolina
Museum of History

Souvenir match case featuring a
relief of the Ferris Wheel
1893
Metal
N.517
CHS

Acorn advertising Acorn Stoves
& Ranges
1893
Wood
X.3298.2005
CHS

Program, *Buffalo Bill's Wild
West and Congress of Rough Riders
of the World*
Published by the Blakely
Printing Company, Chicago
1893
Ink on paper
X.3300.2005
CHS

Book, *The Wonderful Wizard of
Oz: 100th Anniversary Edition*
Authored by L. Frank Baum
Illustrated by W. W. Denslow
2000
Ink on paper
2005.38.1NA
CHS Purchase

Photograph, Daniel H.
Burnham
Harrison and Coover
c. 1893
ICHi-27044
Gift of Mr. Lawrence B. Perkins

Photograph, John Wellborn
Root
Max Platz
c. 1880
ICHi-30622
Gift of Mr. Lawrence B. Perkins

Photograph, Frederick Law
Olmsted
c. 1893
Daniel H. Burnham Collection,
Ryerson & Burnham Archives,
The Art Institute of Chicago

Photograph, Henry Sargent
Codman
c. 1893
Daniel H. Burnham Collection,
Ryerson & Burnham Archives,
The Art Institute of Chicago

Photograph, Bertha Honoré
Palmer
Steffens
c. 1893
ICHi-25223
CHS
p. 177

Photograph, Group portrait of
the Department of Surveys and
Grades
1893
ICHi-40309
Gift of Norman Moore and
daughter Anya C. Moore

Photograph, Construction of
the lagoon, looking east
C. D. Arnold
1891
ICHi-02394
Gift of Otto L. Schmidt

Photograph, Construction of
the Manufacturer's Building
C. D. Arnold
1892
ICHi-40310
CHS

Photograph, Construction of
the dome of the Horticultural
Building
C. D. Arnold
1892
ICHi-02359
Gift of Otto L. Schmidt

Photograph, Construction of
the Manufacturer's Building
C. D. Arnold
1892
ICHi-25072
Gift of Otto L. Schmidt

Book, *The International Guide to
the World's Columbian Exposition*
Published by International
Guide Syndicate
1893
Ink on paper
X.3242.2005
CHS
p. 174

General admission tickets to
the World's Columbian
Exposition
Published by the American
Bank Note Company, New
York
1893
Ink on paper
1961.750.2, .4
Gift of John P. Wilson

General admission tickets to
the World's Columbian
Exposition
Published by the American
Bank Note Company, New
York
1893
Ink on paper
X.3243.2005
CHS

Photograph, View from the
Manufacturer's and Liberal Arts
Building's
C. D. Arnold
1893
ICHi-02525
Gift of Mrs. Joseph Leiter

Photograph, Palace of Fine Arts
Building viewed across the
Grand Basin
Harrison
1893
ICHi-02227
Gift of William A. R. Mitchell

Photograph, View of the
moveable sidewalk
C. D. Arnold
1893
ICHi-25107
Gift of B. Pace

Photograph, Looking south
across the west end of the
Grand Basin
C. D. Arnold
1893
ICHi-02520
Gift of Mrs. Joseph Leiter

Map, 1893 World's Fair
Published by Lake Shore and
Michigan Southern Railway
1893
ICHi-40311
CHS

Photograph, *The Wonder of the
Age*
B. W. Kilburn
1893
ICHi-27808
Gift of Miss Florence Maynard

Handbill, Authentic Daily
Programme of the Midway
Plaisance
1893
Ink on paper
X.3236.2005
CHS

Tickets to various events and
villages on the Midway
Plaisance
1893
Ink on paper
X.3245.2005–X.3248.2005,
X.3251.2005–X.3253.2005
CHS

Photograph, Alaskan Indian
exhibit outside the
Anthropological Building
C. D. Arnold
1893
ICHi-04564
Gift of Pictorial Art Studios,
Inc.

Photograph, Men in traditional
costume entering the South Sea
Island Theater
1893
ICHi-25747
Gift of Mrs. Robert Alrich

Photograph, Irish Village and
Blarney Castle
C. D. Arnold
1893
CH_02396 (ICHi-22941
CHS

Photograph, Two female
visitors take a camel ride in the
Hindoo Village
1893
ICHi-25102
CHS
p. 176

Booklet, *Part One of Chicago
Times Portfolio of the Midway
Types*
Published by American
Engraving Co.
1893
Ink on paper
X.3237.2005
CHS

1933 A CENTURY OF
PROGRESS INTERNATIONAL
EXPOSITION

Painting, *The Fair at Night*
Frank Raymond
c. 1933
Watercolor on paper
1962.720
Gift of Mr. and Mrs. Thorne
Donnelley

Painting, *General Motors
Building*
Frank Raymond
c. 1933
Watercolor on paper
1962.719
Gift of Mr. and Mrs. Thorne
Donnelley

Broadside, *The Skyride*
1933
Ink on paper
X.2333.2004
CHS
p. 193

Painting, *Panoramic Overview of
A Century of Progress
International Exposition*
Harry M. Pettit
1934
Watercolor, pencil on paper
1976.49
Gift of Miss Lillian Woodworth
p. 191

Photograph, Dancers at the
Swiss Village
Kaufmann & Fabry
1934
ICHi-40307
CHS
p. 194

Photograph, Duke Kwesi Kuntu
and his ceremonial tribesmen
Frank D. Shean
Published in *Darkest Africa*
1933
ICHi-40308
CHS Purchase
p. 194

Photograph, Participants from
the Mexican Village on opening
day
O. L. Cook
1934
ICHi-40306
Gift of O. L. Cook

Sombrero-shaped souvenir
ashtray
1933
Ceramic
(1984.274.1
Gift of Jane and William
Hallett

Policeman toy from the
Czechoslovak Exhibit
1933
Wood
1984.274.2
Gift of Jane and William
Hallett

Souvenirs from the Century of
Progress Exhibiton
1933
1994.143
p. 193

Fort Dearborn sentinel house
souvenir model
1933
Metal
X.1189
CHS

Souvenir box from the
Egyptian Pavilion
1933–34
Wood
X.3299.2005
CHS

World Champion Log Rollers
souvenir button
1933
Metal
X.3241.2005
CHS

Midget City souvenir button
1934
Metal
X.2281.2004
CHS

Tickets to Midway attractions
1933–34
Ink on paper
X.3254.2005-X.3261.2005
CHS

Photograph, An Independence
Day crowd on the Midway
D. Ward Pease
1933
ICHi-40305
Gift of D. Ward Pease

Nuts removed from the Sky
Ride towers
1933
Nickel-plated steel
1970.89ab
Gift of Mrs. Adolph H. Lubin

Nut removed from one of the
Sky Ride towers
1933
Nickel-plated steel
X.2134.2004
CHS

Souvenir money clip featuring
Sky Ride tower
1933
Metal
X.2282.2004
CHS

Postcard featuring the Sky Ride
Max Rigot Selling Co., Chicago
1933
Ink on paper
X.3329.2006
CHS

Pamphlet, *See the World's Fair*
1933
Ink on paper
1985.752
Gift of John S. Darling

Admission ticket for the Sky
Ride
1933–34
Ink on paper
X.3240.2005
CHS

Photograph, Visitors looking
down from a Sky Ride tower
observation deck
O. L. Cook
1934
ICHi-40304
Gift of O. L. Cook

The World's Fair in a Nutshell
souvenir
Gale Specialty Company,
Chicago
1933
Paper, nutshell
1983.436.3
Gift of Joan Phillips

I Was There button
Geraghty & Co., Chicago
1933
Metal
1994.143.34
Gift of Walter H. Schwebke
p. 193

Souvenir box camera
Kodak
1933
Plastic, metal
X.3238.2005
CHS

Booklet, *World's Fair Time Saver
and Guide*
1934
Ink on paper
1967.535.2
Gift of M. Estelle Angier

Souvenir ticket booklet
1933
Ink on paper
1985.75a
Gift of Anne Kenney
p. 191

Photograph, *The Avenue of Flags*
Fred G. Korth
1934
ICHi-23852
Gift of Fred G. Korth
p. 192

Scale model of the Travel and
Transport Building
1933
Aluminum, wood, glass
1978.46d
Gift of the Evanston Historical
Society
p. 192

Child's Century of Progress
Junior Police uniform
1933
Cotton
1963.539
Gift of Mr. Joseph S. Nowicki

Black printed gown with
black belt
Blums-Vogue
1935
Silk, suede
1959.127
Gift of Mrs. James M. Hopkins

Avenue of Flags souvenir
playing cards
1934
Paper, cardboard
1983.440.7
Gift of Betty George

Souvenir salt and pepper
shakers
1934
Glass, plastic
1997.72ab
Gift of Betty J. Blum

U.S. Government Building
souvenir paperweight
1933–34
Glass, paper
X.3234.2005
CHS

Armour Building souvenir
ashtray
1934
Metal
X.3235.2005
CHS

Blix Wonder Block souvenir toy
1933–34
Wood, paper
1994.143.12a–k
Gift of Walter H. Schwebke

Souvenir toy Greyhound bus
Arcade Manufacturing Co.,
Freeport, Illinois
1933
Metal
1994.143.10ab
Gift of Walter H. Schwebke

Souvenir box of mineral speci-
mens distributed at the Ford
Exposition building
1934
Paper, plastic, minerals
1996.294.11
Gift of Howard E. Hight

CHICAGO THEATER
Contemporary Theater

Neon sign from the Second
City
c. 1995
Courtesy of the Second City
p. 211

Photograph, Second City cast
with producer Bernard Shalins
and director Paul Sills
Arthur Siegel
1960
ICHi-40436
Gift of Irene Siegel
p. 211

Photograph, Steppenwolf
Theatre
Michael Brosilow
c. 2005
Courtesy of Steppenwolf
Theatre Company

Photograph, The Goodman
Theatre
Jeff Goldberg
2004
Courtesy of the Goodman
Theatre

Program, Lookingglass Theatre
presents *The Jungle*, 1990
1992.290
Gift of the *Chicago Reader*

Program, The Goodman
Theatre presents *Glengarry Glen
Ross*
1984
Ink on paper
1984.186
Gift of Judy Weisman

Program, Steppenwolf Theatre
Company presents *Balm in
Gilead*
1981
Ink on paper
1984.107
Gift of Lucy Arnold

Photograph, Lookingglass
Theatre
Steve Hall, Hedrich-Blessing
c. 2005
Courtesy of Lookingglass
Theatre Company

AUDITORIUM THEATRE

Working model of the
proscenium arch of the
Auditorium Theatre
c. 1895
Wood, metal
1980.28
Gift of Lumbermens Mutual
Casualty Co.
p. 184

Program, Auditorium Theatre,
Chicago Grand Opera Co.
1913
Ink on paper
X.3232.2005
CHS

Postcard, Auditorium Hotel
lobby
Empire Art Co., Chicago
c. 1920
Ink on paper
X.3231.2005
CHS

Postcard, The Auditorium
Hotel's Summer Restaurant
Max Rigot Selling Co., Chicago
c. 1920
Ink on paper
X.3230.2005
CHS

Embroidered Empire-style
evening dress with train
Created by an unknown
American designer
c. 1910
Satin damask
L1974.30
Gift of Mrs. Martin A. Ryerson.
Courtesy of the Art Institute of
Chicago

Nosegay with candy-striped
glass handle
c. 1870
Gilt, glass
1961.632
Gift of Mrs. Robert D. Graff

Cigar case
c. 1890
Tortoise-shell, mother-of-pearl,
gold
1953.242
Gift of Mrs. Charles S. Dewey
Jr.

Opera glasses
Manufactured in Paris, France
1902
Mother-of-pearl, gold
1953.250
Gift of Mrs. Charles S. Dewey
Jr.

Chain mail handbag
c. 1870
Silver, amethyst
1985.156.1
Gift of Mrs. Charles W. Bryan
Jr.

WAIT 'TIL NEXT YEAR
Baseball

Pinwheel from Comiskey Park's
Monster Scoreboard
1982–90
Metal, glass
2004.108.1
Gift of the Chicago White Sox
p. 202

Photograph, Jim Landis of the
Chicago White Sox scores
during the World Series
1959
ICHi-16227
Gift of Marshall Field, Jr.

Photograph, Chicago White
Sox
1959
ICHi-35659
Gift of Chicago White Sox
p. 201

Section of foul pole from
Comiskey Park
c. 1990
Metal
2004.108.2
Gift of the Chicago White Sox

Photograph, Baseball fans in Peoria, Illinois, keeping tabs on the World Series
1917
ICHi-40451
Gift of Mrs. Frank D. Stafford
p. 200

Broadside, *Chicago White Sox Chicago Sunday Herald*
September 23, 1917
Ink on paper
1984.024.1
Gift of Frances Kendall
p. 199

Program, World Series at Wrigley Field, Chicago Cubs vs. Detroit Tigers
1935
Ink on paper
L.53.78h
p. 198

World Series championship tie clip worn by Chicago White Sox pitcher Joe Benz
1917
Gold
1988.470.11ab
Gift of Rita Benz

Chicago White Sox Official Score Book
1917
Ink on paper
CH_02780 (1954.618
Alfred J. Scully Baseball Collection, Gift of Mrs. Josephine and Theodore A. Nesbit
p. 199

Photograph, "Shoeless" Joe Jackson
c. 1917
ICHi-19569
CHS

Tickets, World Series at Wrigley Field, Chicago Cubs vs. Detroit Tigers
1935
Ink on Paper
L.53.87c
p. 198

Photograph, Crowd at Wrigley Field box office seeking World Series tickets
1935
ICHi-24313
CHS
p. 197

Photograph, Chicago White Sox celebrating World Series victory
October 26, 2005
Gift of Olivia Mahoney

World Series program, Chicago White Sox vs. Houston Astros
2005
Ink on paper
2005.57.16NA
Gift of Mike and Kathy Charlton Firth
p. 201

Ticket, Chicago White Sox vs. Houston Astros World Series Game 1
2005
Ink on paper
2005.57.16NA
Gift of Mike and Kathy Charlton Firth

Photograph, Gary Charlton (left) and Mike Firth (right) at World Series Game 1
2005
ICHi-40628
Gift of Mike and Kathy Charlton Firth

World Series baseball
Rawlings
2005
Leather
Courtesy of Mike and Kathy Charlton Firth

Chicago White Sox earrings
c. 2000
Plastic, metal
Courtesy of Mike and Kathy Charlton Firth

Chicago White Sox flag, T-shirts and caps
2005
[Material]
Courtesy of Mike and Kathy Charlton Firth

Photograph, Gary Charlton with Aaron Rowand
2005
Courtesy of Mike and Kathy Charlton Firth

Baseball from the ALCS play-off
Rawlings
2005
Leather
2005.57.7
Gift of Mike and Kathy Charlton Firth.

Photograph, Rube Foster
Chicago Daily News
1909
SDN-055355
CHS
p. 202

Photograph, The American Giants
Chicago Daily News
1911
SDN-009529
CHS
p. 205

Program, East-West Baseball Classic
1945
Ink on paper
X.3330.2006
CHS
p. 205

Photograph, Wrigley Field
c. 1965
CH_04113 (ICHi-24457
Gift of The Fair Store
Scorecard, Chicago Cubs vs. New York Giants playoff game
October 8, 1908
Reproduction
ICHi-40449
CHS

Photograph, Chicago Cubs
Chicago Daily News
1908
SDN-006934A
CHS
p. 196

Photograph, Gabby Hartnett with Cubs coaches
1938
ICHi-40340
Gift of Marshall Field Jr.

Gabby Hartnett's homerun bat and ball
September 28, 1938
Wood, leather
1938.146d-e
Gift of Chicago National League Baseball Club

Program, 1938 World Series
1938
Ink on paper
66148
Gift of the Chicago Cubs

National League Championship belt buckle and ring given to Chicago Cubs bat boy Vince Garrity
1938
Metal, enamel; gold, diamond
2003.153.1–2
CHS Purchase

Official Chicago Cubs batting order
October 15, 2003
Reproduction
ICHi-40459
Gift of Dusty Baker

Chicago Cubs promotional booklet
1985
Ink on paper
X.3304.2005
CHS

Unopened bottle of champagne
1984
Glass, cork, paper
2003.235.1
Gift of David and Susan Spitzer

Magazine, *National Girl's Baseball League*
June 1948
Ink on paper
X.3302.2005
CHS
p. 204

Program, Chicago Queens
1947
Ink on paper
X.3301.2005
CHS

16-inch softball
Tober, Rockville, Connecticut
1972
Leather
1978.235
CHS
p. 203

Photograph, Judge Zuris's All-Star Softball Team
Casey Prunchunas
c. 1937
ICHi-40339
Gift of Casey Prunchunas
p. 203

Football

Soldier Field seats
c. 2000
Plastic, metal
2006.30.1–.2NA
Mr. Fred Jacobs

Photograph, Chicago Bears vs. Chicago Cardinals at Comiskey Park
1957
ICHi-40438
CHS

Photograph, Amos Alonzo Stagg coaching the University of Chicago football team
Chicago Daily News
1904
SDN-4995
CHS
p. 206

Photograph, Passing play during University of Chicago football game
Chicago Daily News
1907
SDN-006128
CHS

Football used in game between the University of Chicago and Northwestern University
November 14, 1896
Leather
1978.109.3
Gift of Mr. Harold Metcalf, Director of Athletics, University of Chicago
p. 206

Book, *A Scientific and Practical Treatise on American Football*
Amos Alonzo Stagg and Henry L. William
Published by D. Appleton & Company, New York
1894
Ink on paper
X.3307.2005
CHS Purchase
p. 206

Program, NFL World Championship Game
1943
Ink on paper
X.3306.2005
CHS Purchase

Program, Chicago Bears
1928
Ink on paper
X.3305.2005
CHS
p. 207

Photograph, Chicago Bears football players with Coach George Halas
Chicago Daily News
SDN-076921
CHS
p. 207

John Fitzgerald Kennedy Memorial Trophy presented to the Chicago Bears
1963
Metal, wood
Courtesy of the Chicago Bears

Record album, *The Super Bowl Shuffle*
The Chicago Bears Shufflin' Crew
1985
Vinyl, paper
Courtesy of the Bouleanu Family
pp. 170 (detail), 208

Program, Super Bowl XX
1986
Ink on paper
1986.127
Gift of Nancy Machura
p. 208

Chicago Bears football helmet worn by Mike Singletary
Riddell
1985
Plastic
1986.178.1
Gift of Ray Earley
p. 208

Photograph, Walter Payton rushing against the Green Bay Packers
c. 1980
ICHi-40421
Gift of the Chicago Bears

Walter Payton Man of the Year
Trophy
1999
Bronze, marble
2004.77.1
Gift of Connie Payton

Basketball

Section of Chicago Stadium
floor
1998
Wood
1998.8
Gift of United Center Joint
Venture

Photograph, Chicago Bulls at
the United Center
Betty Kubis
1998
ICHi-40439
Gift of Betty Kubis
p. 209

Photograph, Chicago Bulls
1997–98
ICHi-40439
Gift of the Chicago Bulls

Magazine, *Bullpen: The Official
Game Program of the Chicago
Bulls*
1997–98
Ink on paper
X.3331.2006
CHS

Chicago Bulls fan helmet
1998
Plastic
1998.93abc
Gift of Jennifer Mindel
p. 209

Basketball shoes worn by
Michael Jordan during the
NBA playoffs
Nike
1989
Leather, rubber, nylon
1990.83ef
Gift of Michael Jordan

Photograph, The Harlem
Globetrotters
1931
ICHi-40465
Gift of Potter Palmer
p. 210

Hockey

Photograph, Chicago Blackhawks
vs. Detroit Red Wings at the
Chicago Stadium
Chicago Daily News
1966
ICHi-40612
CHS

Broadside, *Chicago Blackhawks,
Stanley Cup Winners*
1937–38
Ink on paper
1995.96
Gift of Virgil Charles Johnson

Chicago Blackhawks hockey
puck
c. 1970
Rubber
2004.116.14
Gift of Lloyd Kadish

Hockey stick used by Stan
Mikita, Chicago Blackhawks
Northland
c. 1970
Wood
1991.558
Gift of Albert P. Macejak

CITY IN A GARDEN

Embroidered bathing suit
Tina Leser
1956
Cotton
1962.230
Gift of Mrs. Solomon B. Smith

Ladies' blue wing-shaped
sunglasses with blue lenses
The House of Vision, France
c. 1955
Plastic
1979.198.1a
Gift of Mrs. Gardner Stern

Ladies' beaded beach sandals
with hut detail on heel
c. 1950
Straw
1989.959.66a-b
Gift of Cochran B. Suplee

Beach bag with flowers
c. 1955
Straw, raffia
1982.222.33
Gift of Laurance H. Armour
III, Steven S. Armour, and Miss
Brooks Armour

Photograph, Swimming and
wading at Clarendon Beach
Chicago Daily News
1921
DN-0073295
CHS
pp. 168 (detail), 182

Broadside, *Wooded Island,
Jackson Park by the Elevated Lines*
Printed by National Printing &
Engraving Co.
c. 1934
Ink on paper
X.3308.2005
CHS

Broadside, *25 Miles of Beach Via
South Shore Line*
Oscar Rabe Hanson
1925
Ink on paper
X.3309.2005
CHS Purchase

Book, *Plan of Chicago*
Daniel H. Burnham and
Edward H. Bennett
Published by the Commercial
Club of Chicago
1908
Ink on paper
1964.1051
Gift of Mrs. Philip K. Wrigley

Painting, *Daniel H. Burnham*
Gerald S. Hayward
1910
Oil on ivory
1964.316
Gift of Mr. Gerhardt F. Meyne
p. 181

Photograph, Segway tour
pausing at Buckingham
Fountain in Grant Park
Jay Crawford
2005
ICHi-40463
CHS

Photograph, Boy building a
snowman in Lincoln Park
Chicago Daily News
1915
DN-0065401
CHS

Photograph, Picnic in
Humboldt Park
Jay Crawford
2005
ICHi-40461
CHS

Photograph, Ice skating in
Humboldt Park
c. 1938
ICHi-29287
CHS
p. 181

Photograph, Father and sons
fishing at the 100th Street
breakwater
Ted Farrington
1952
ICHi-40423
Gift of Ted Farrington

Photograph, Beach volleyball
game at North Avenue Beach
John McCarthy
1994
ICHi-40424
Gift of John McCarthy

Photograph, Walkers, joggers,
and cyclists on path along Lake
Michigan
Jay Crawford
2005
ICHi-40462
CHS

MILLENNIUM PARK

Photograph, Millennium Park
Scott MacDonald
2005
HB-60907T
Gift of Hedrich-Blessing
pp. iii (detail), 183

Maquette, *Cloud Gate*
Created by Anish Kapoor for
Millennium Park
2003
Mixed materials
Courtesy of Chicago
Convention & Tourism Bureau

NOTES

CHAPTER ONE: CITY ON THE MAKE

1. Nelson Algren, *Chicago: City on the Make* with an introduction by Studs Terkel; newly annotated by David Schmittgens and Bill Savage (Chicago: University of Chicago Press, 2001); Witold Rybczynski, *City Life* (New York and London: Simon & Schuster, 1995), 116.

2. Alice Berkson, Michael D. Wiant, eds., *Discover Illinois Archaeology* (Springfield: Illinois Association for Advancement of Archaeology, 2001), 4–17.

3. Harold M. Mayer and Richard C. Wade, *Chicago: The Growth of a Metropolis* (Chicago: University of Chicago Press, 1969), 6; Milo Milton Quaife, *Chicago and the Old Northwest 1673–1835* (Urbana and Chicago: University of Illinois Press, 2001), 22–24.

4. Donald L. Miller, *City of the Century: The Epic of Chicago and the Making of America* (New York: Simon & Schuster), 46.

5. Raymond E. Hauser, "Illinois," and Bradley J. Birzer, "Miamis," in *The Encyclopedia of Chicago*, ed. Grossman, Keating, and Reiff, op. cit., 406, 534–35.

6. R. David Edmunds, "Chicago in the Middle Ground" in *The Encyclopedia of Chicago*, ed. James R. Grossman, Ann Durkin Keating, and Janice L. Reiff (Chicago and London: University of Chicago Press, 2004), 138.

7. Inventory and deed of property sold by Jean Baptiste Point DuSable to Jean Lalime, May 7, 1800, photostat copy in the Archives & Manuscript Collection, Chicago Historical Society; John F. Swenson, "Jean Baptiste Point Du Sable, The Founder of Modern Chicago" *Early Chicago*, ed. Ulrich Danckers and Jane Meredeth (River Forest: Early Chicago, Incorporated, 2000), 388–392.

8. Ibid., 394.

9. Arthur H. Frazier, "The Military Frontier: Fort Dearborn," *Chicago History* (Chicago: Chicago Historical Society, Summer 1980), 80–82.

10. Ibid., 84; Mayer and Wade, op. cit., 10.

11. Paul Gilbert and Charles Lee Bryson, *Chicago and Its Makers* (Chicago: Felix Mendelsohn, 1929), 604; Danckers and Meredeth, op. cit., 191.

12. Danckers and Meredeth, op.cit., 69.

13. Ibid., 69–70; Gilbert and Bryson, op. cit., 605.

14. Harold M. Meyer, "The Launching of Chicago: The Situation and the Site," *Chicago History*, Volume IX, Number 2, Summer 1980, 74–75.

15. Ibid., 78.

16. Helen Hornback Tanner, "Black Hawk War" *The Encyclopedia of Chicago*, ed. Grossman, Keating, and Reiff, op. cit., 80.

17. James A. Clifton, Chicago, "September 14, 1833: The Last Great Indian Treaty in the Old Northwest," *Chicago History*, op. cit., 91–96.

18. Mayer and Wade, op. cit., 28; John Lamb, "Illinois & Michigan Canal" in *The Encyclopedia of Chicago*, ed. Grossman, Keating, and Reiff, op. cit., 406–407.

19. Mayer and Wade, 28.

20. Miller, op. cit., 94–95.

21. A. T. Andreas, *History of Chicago, From the Earliest Period to the Present Time in Three Volumes* (Chicago: A. T. Andreas, 1884), Volume I, 248.

22. Olivia Mahoney, *Go West! Chicago and American Expansion* (Chicago: Chicago Historical Society, 1999), 16–25.

23. Andreas, op. cit., Volume III, 209, 213; Mahoney, ibid., pp. 41–48.

24. Andreas, ibid., 202, 213.

25. Mahoney, op. cit., 102–104.

26. Mahoney, ibid., 71–72, 81; Louise C. Wade, *Chicago's Pride: The Stockyards, Packingtown, and Environs in the Nineteenth Century* (Urbana, Illinois: University of Illinois Press, 1987), 48–57.

27. Wade, ibid., 188–190; interview with Eldon Hatch, Chicago livestock trader, conducted by Olivia Mahoney at the Chicago Historical Society, June 25, 2004.

28. Wade, op. cit., 88–89; Mahoney, op. cit., 85; authority file for Chicago Live Stock Exchange presentation trophy, 2001.257, Chicago History Museum.

29. Mahoney, op. cit., 85; *Official Catalog, International Live Stock Exposition* (Chicago: P. F. Pettibone & Co., 1901), 10–11.

30. Wade, 63; William Cronon, *Nature's Metropolis: Chicago and the Great West* (New York and London: W. W. Norton & Company, 1991), 228–235.

31. Louise Carroll Wade, "Meatpacking" in *The Encyclopedia of Chicago*, ed. Grossman, Keating, and Reiff, op. cit., 515–516.

32. Ibid., 516.

33. Ibid.

34. Ibid.

35. Sharon Darling, *Chicago Furniture: Art, Craft, and Industry: 1833–1983* (Chicago: Chicago Historical Society in association with W. W. Norton & Company, New York, 1984), 45.

36. Ibid., 45–52.

37. Ibid., 53–57.

38. Ibid., 296, 340.

39. Andreas, op. cit., Volume III, 477.

40. Ibid., Volume II, 674 and Volume III, 478.

41. David Bensman and Mark R. Wilson, "Iron and Steel," in *The Encyclopedia of Chicago*, ed. Grossman, Keating, and Reiff, op. cit., 425.

42. Ibid., 426–427.

43. Ibid.; Michael P. Conzen and Christopher P. Thale, "The Chicago Area's Iron and Steel Industry," ibid., 425.

44. William Julius Wilson, *When Work Disappears: The World of the New Urban Poor* (New York: Vintage Books, A Division of Random House, Inc., 1996), 29–30.

45. Adam Cohen and Elizabeth Taylor, *American Pharaoh, Mayor Richard J. Daley, His Battle for Chicago and the Nation* (Boston, New York, London: Little, Brown and Company, 2000), 174–178, 224–233.

46. Mayer and Wade, op. cit., 432–438; David M. Young, *Chicago Maritime: An Illustrated History* (De Kalb: Northern Illinois University, 2001), 207–211.

47. Denis McClendon, "Expressways," in *The Encyclopedia of Chicago*, ed. Grossman, Keating, and Reiff, op. cit., 286–287; Cohen and Taylor, op. cit., 188–189.

48. Cohen and Taylor, op. cit., 233–237.

49. David Brodherson, "O'Hare International Airport," in *The Encyclopedia of Chicago*, ed. Grossman, Keating, and Reiff, op. cit., 586.

50. "Airport Update," http://www.elk-grove-village.il.us; John Hilkevitch, "O'Hare Expansion in Holding Pattern," *Chicago Tribune*, May 17, 2006, http://www.chicagotribune.com.

51. Chicago Board of Trade, "Our History," http://www.cbot.com; Chicago Mercantile Exchange, "CME at a Glance," http://www.cme.com.

CHAPTER TWO: CITY IN CRISIS

1. "Chicago Metropolitan Population," *The Encyclopedia of Chicago*, ed. James R. Grossman, Ann Durkin Keating, and Janice L. Reiff (Chicago and London: University of Chicago Press, 2004), 1005.

2. Carl Smith, "A Bird's-Eye View of Pre-Fire Chicago," in *The Great Chicago Fire and the Web of Memory* Web site (Chicago: Chicago Historical Society and the Trustees of Northwestern University, 1996).

3. Ibid.

4. Smith, "The Great Conflagration" and "The Ruined City," in *The Great Chicago Fire*, ibid.

5. Justin's letter, October 14, 1871, Archives & Manuscript Collection, Chicago Historical Society; Smith, "The Ruined City," ibid.

6. Roswell B. Mason, *Proclamation* (Chicago: October 10, 1871); Smith, "Rescue and Relief," in *The Great Chicago Fire*, op. cit.

7. A. T. Andreas, *History of Chicago From the Earliest Period to the Present Time in Three Volumes* (Chicago: A. T. Andreas, 1884), Volume II, 770–771.

8. Smith, "Rescue and Relief," in *The Great Chicago Fire*, op. cit.

9. Harold M. Mayer and Richard C. Wade, *Chicago: Growth of a Metropolis* (Chicago and London: University of Chicago Press, 1969), 120–122.

10. Andreas, op. cit., Volume III, 62.

11. Mason, *Proclamation*, op. cit; *Chicago Tribune*, October 11, 1871.

12. Andreas, op. cit., Volume III, 59–61; Smith, "Queen of the West Once More," in *The Great Chicago Fire*, op. cit.

13. Mayer and Wade, op. cit., 122.

14. Mayer and Wade, ibid., 124; Smith, *"Queen of the West Once More"* in *The Great Chicago Fire*, op. cit.

15. "Mrs. O'Leary's Cow," *What We All Know: Icons of Memory/How Chicagoans Remember Their History,* http://www.encyclopedia.chicagohistory.org/pages/410070.html

16. Carl Smith, "Prologue: Whiter America?" in *The Dramas of Haymarket* Web site (Chicago: Chicago Historical Society, 2000).

17. Paul Avrich, *The Haymarket Tragedy* (Princeton, New Jersey: Princeton University Press, 1984), 26–35, 181–187.

18. Ibid., 3–38.

19. Ibid., 39–52.

20. Ibid., 68–118, 160–177.

21. Ibid., 186.

22. Ibid., 190.

23. Ibid., 206–210; Carl Smith, "Let Your Tragedy Be Enacted Here," in *The Dramas of Haymarket*, op. cit.

24. Avrich, op. cit, 215–259; Smith, "Toils of the Law," in *The Dramas of Haymarket*, op. cit.

25. Avrich, op. cit., 260–278; Smith, "Toils of the Law," ibid.

26. Avrich, op. cit., 279–293; 381–394.

27. Smith, "Drama Without End" in *The Dramas of Haymarket*, op. cit.

28. Ibid.

29. Ibid.

30. Allan H. Spear, *Black Chicago: The Making of a Negro Ghetto, 1890–1920* (Chicago and London: University of Chicago Press, 1967), 11–16; 201–212.

31. William M. Tuttle, Jr., *Race Riot: Chicago in the Red Summer of 1919* (New York: Atheneum, 1985), 3–7.

32. Ibid., 8–9; St. Clair Drake and Horace R. Cayton, *Black Metropolis: A Study of Negro Life in a Northern City* (Chicago: University of Chicago Press, 1993), 65–66.

33. Chicago Commission on Race Relations, *The Negro in Chicago* (Chicago: University of Chicago Press, 1922), 5–6; Tuttle, op. cit., 32–34.

34. Tuttle, ibid., 35–44.

35. Ibid., 46–55.

36. Ibid., 57–63.

37. Ibid., 64–65.

38. Chicago Commission on Race Relations, op. cit., 643–648; Drake and Cayton, op. cit., 69–73.

39. Norman H. Clark, "Prohibition and Temperance," and Ellen Carol DuBois, "Frances Willard," in *The Reader's Companion to American History*, ed. Eric Foner, and John A. Garraty (Boston: Houghton Mifflin Company, 1991), 871–874; 1151–1152.

40. Kenneth Allsop, *The Bootleggers: The Story of Chicago's Prohibition Era* (New Rochelle, New York: Arlington House, 1961), 42–43; Dennis McClendon, "Near South Side," in *The Encyclopedia of Chicago*, ed. Grossman, Keating, and Reiff, op. cit., 562–563.

41. Allsop, ibid., 13, 42–44.

42. Ibid., 43.

43. Ibid., 40–45.

44. Ibid., 81–83.

45. Ibid., 89–90.

46. Ibid., 111–120.

47. Ibid., 275–292.

48. Ibid., 133–142.

49. *Chicago Herald Examiner*, February 15, 1929; David E. Ruth, "Untouchables," in *The Encyclopedia of Chicago*, ed. Grossman, Keating, and Reiff, op. cit., 847.

50. David E. Ruth, "Chicago Crime Commission," ibid., 133–134; Allsop, op. cit., 317–329.

51. James R. Ralph Jr., *Northern Protest: Martin Luther King, Jr., Chicago, and the Civil Rights Movement* (Cambridge, Massachusetts, and London, England: Harvard University Press, 1993), 7–42; Adam Cohen and Elizabeth Taylor, *American Pharaoh: Mayor Richard J. Daley, His Battle for Chicago and the Nation* (Boston, New York, London: Little, Brown and Company), 326–356.

52. Ralph, ibid., 45–49; Cohen and Taylor, ibid., 357–360.

53. Ralph, ibid., 105–109.

54. Ralph, ibid., 109–113; Cohen and Taylor, op. cit., 383–387.

55. Ralph, ibid., 114–130.

56. Cohen and Taylor, op. cit., 400–429.

57. Ibid., 452–457; "Chicago and Richard J. Daley, 1960–1975," http://www.roosevelt.edu/chicagohistory/mod3-chap4.htm.

58. Cohen and Taylor, 453–454.

59. Ibid.

60. Ibid., 455; "Chicago and Richard J. Daley, 1960–1975," http://www.roosevelt.edu/chicagohistory/mod3-chap4.htm

61. Cohen and Taylor, op. cit., 469–471.

62. Ibid., 459–463.

63. Ibid., 466–468.

64. Ibid., 469–477.

65. Ibid., 481–482.

66. Ibid., 484–485.

CHAPTER THREE: SWEET HOME CHICAGO

1. Harold M. Mayer and Richard C. Wade, *Chicago: Growth of a Metropolis* (Chicago and London: University of Chicago Press, 1969), 18–24; Richard Jensen, "Yankees," in *The Encyclopedia of Chicago*, ed. James R. Grossman, Ann Durkin Keating, and Janice L. Reiff (Chicago and London: University of Chicago Press, 2004), 904.

2. Dominic A. Pacyga and Ellen Skerrett, *Chicago: City of Neighborhoods, Histories and Tours* (Chicago: Loyola Press, 1986), 3.

3. Ibid., 53–55, 209–211, 313.

4. St. Clair Drake and Horace R. Cayton, *Black Metropolis: A Study of Negro Life in a Northern City* (Chicago: University of Chicago Press, 1993), 58–64.

5. Pacyga and Skerrett, op. cit., 110–111.

6. Ibid., 112; Peter T. Alter, "Global Communities: Chicago Immigrants and Refugees," http://www.chicagohistory.org/immigration.html

7. Glen E. Holt and Dominic A. Pacyga, *Chicago: A Historical Guide to the Neighborhoods: The Loop and South Side* (Chicago: Chicago Historical Society, 1979), 49–52; Drake and Cayton, op. cit., 77–83.

8. Drake and Cayton, ibid., 83–89.

9. Arnold R. Hirsch, *Making the Second Ghetto: Race & Housing in Chicago 1940–1960* (Cambridge University Press, 1983), 260–263.

10. Ibid., 30, 265; Pacyga and Skerrett, op.cit., 318.

11. Pacyga and Skerrett, ibid., 199–210.

12. Ibid., 216–218.

13. Ibid., 238.

14. Ibid., 239, 257–258.

15. Ibid., 250; "Global Communities: Chicago's Immigrants and Refugees," http://www.chicagohistory.org/immigration.html.

16. Pacyga and Skerrett, op.cit., 61–64.

17. Ibid., 64–65.

18. Ibid., 67.

19. Ibid., 128–135.

20. Patricia Mooney-Melvin, "West Ridge," http://www.encyclopedia.chicagohistory.org/pages/1341.html

21. Ibid.

22. Ronald Dale Karr, "Rapid Transit System," http://www.encyclopedia.chicagohistory.org/pages/1042.html

23. Paul Gilbert and Charles Lee Bryson, *Chicago and Its Makers: A Narrative of Events from the Day of the First White Man to the Inception of the Second World's Fair* (Chicago: Felix Mendelsohn, 1929), 609.

24. Bessie Louise Pierce, *A History of Chicago 1848–1871* (New York and London: Alfred A. Knopf, 1940), 211, 437–438.

25. Ibid., 267–269.

26. Carter Harrison I biographical clipping file, Research Center, Chicago History Museum.

27. Ibid.

28. Ibid.

29. Adam Cohen and Elizabeth Taylor, *American Pharaoh: Mayor Richard J. Daley, His Battle for Chicago and the Nation* (Boston, New York, London: Little, Brown and Company, 2000), 48–50.

30. Ibid., 50–53.

31. Ibid., 19–21.

32. Ibid., 315–320.

33. Ibid., 234–238.

34. Ibid., 333–334, 452–457, 480–481.

35. Harold Washington biographical clippings file, Research Center, Chicago History Museum.

36. Ibid.

37. Richard M. Daley biographical clippings file, Research Center, Chicago History Museum.

CHAPTER FOUR: SECOND TO NONE

1. Harold K. Skramstad, Jr., Preface to Perry Duis, *Chicago: Creating New Traditions* (Chicago: Chicago Historical Society, 1976), 11.

2. Lloyd Wendt and Herman Kogan, *Give the Lady What She Wants!* (Chicago: Rand McNally & Company, 1952), 16–39.

3. Ibid., 56–62.

4. Ibid., 67, 82–83.

5. Ibid., 91–99.

6. Ibid., 114–116. 146–147, 165–166.

7. Ibid., 225, 304–305.

8. Ibid., 259–273.

9. Crate & Barrel, "About Us," www.crateandbarrel.com.

10. Boris Emmet and John E. Jueck, *Catalogs and Counters: A History of Sears, Roebuck and Company* (Chicago: University of Chicago Press), 19–22.

11. Ibid., 59–61.

12. Ibid., 74.

13. Olivia Mahoney, *Go West! Chicago and American Expansion* (Chicago: Chicago Historical Society, 1999), 95–96; Emmet and Jueck, op. cit., 150–158.

14. Emmet and Jueck, ibid., 345.

15. Various newspaper articles and clippings in Chicago History Museum authority file for the Benjamin Green-Field donation, 1989.562.

16. Carl W. Condit, *The Chicago School of Architecture: A History of Commercial and Public Building in the Chicago Area 1875–1925* (Chicago and London: University of Chicago Press, 1964), 79–87.

17. Ibid., 24, 49, 91–92, 137.

18. David Van Zanten, "Sullivan to 1890," in *Louis Sullivan: The Function of Ornament*, ed. Wim De Wit (New York and London: W. W. Norton & Company, 1986), 13.

19. Robert Judson Clark and Wendy Kaplan, "Arts and Crafts: Matters of Style" and Edward S. Cooke, Jr., "Frank Lloyd Wright," in *"The Art That is Life:" The Arts & Crafts Movement in America 1875–1920*, ed. Wendy Kaplan (Boston: Boston Museum of Fine Arts, 1987), 78–80; 391–392.

20. Duis, op. cit., 32.

21. Ibid., 3–37.

22. Sharon S. Darling, *Chicago Ceramics & Glass, An Illustrated History from 1871 to 1933* (Chicago: Chicago Historical Society, 1979), 54–70.

23. Sharon S. Darling in association with Gail Farr Casterline, *Chicago Metalsmiths* (Chicago Historical Society, 1977), 45–55.

24. Ibid., 55–61.

25. Sharon S. Darling, *Chicago Furniture: Art, Craft & Industry 1833–1983* (Chicago: The Chicago Historical Society in association with W. W. Norton & Company, New York and London, 1984), 270.

26. Ibid., 277.

27. Ibid., 314–316.

28. Ibid., 288.

29. Ibid., 288–290.

30. Ibid., 338.

31. Ibid., 338.

32. American Institute of Architects Chicago, Chicago Architecture Foundation, Landmarks Preservation Council of Illinois with special assistance from the Commission on Chicago Landmarks; Alice Sinkevitch, ed., *AIA Guide to Chicago* (New York, San Diego, London: Harcourt Brace & Company), 117–118.

33. Blair Kamin, "John Hancock Center," ibid., 108–110; Michael Bordenaro, "Sears Tower," ibid., 90–91.

34. Jane Addams, *Twenty Years at Hull-House* (New York and Scarborough, Ontario: New York Library, 1960), 60–74; Duis, op. cit., 61.

35. Addams, ibid., 101–117; Duis, ibid., 61.

36. Duis, op. cit., 61.

37. Ibid., 78.

38. Olivia Mahoney, *Edward F. Worst: Craftsman and Educator* (Chicago: Chicago Historical Society, 1985), 16.

39. Mahoney, ibid.; John Dewey, *The School and Society* (New York: McClure, Phillips & Co., 1900), 22.

40. Mahoney, ibid.

41. Ibid., 16–17.

42. Charles A. Jahant, "Chicago: Center of the Silent Film Industry," *Chicago History*, Vol. 3, No. 3, (Spring–Summer 1974), 54; "History of Edison Motion Pictures: Origins of Motion Pictures—the Kinetoscope," http://memory.loc.gove/ammem/edhtml/edmvhist.html

43. Jahant, ibid., 44–45.

44. Ibid., 47–48, 51.

45. Essanay News, January 2 and February 27, 1915 (Chicago: Essanay Studios, 1915).

46. "Oscar Micheaux," http://shorock.com/arts/micheaux

47. Jahant, op. cit., 53; "Academy Honorary Award," http://en.wikipedia.org/wiki/Academy_Honorary_Award

48. Joel Steinberg, "Television Town," *Chicago History*, vol. IV, no. 2 (Summer 1975), 112.

49. Rich Samuels, "The Chicago School of Television," http://www.richsamuels.com/nbcmm/chschool.html

50. Steinberg, op. cit., 112–113.

51. Ibid., 114–117.

52. Ibid.; Rich Samuels, "Dave Garroway," http://www.richsamuels.com/nbcmm/garroway/index.html

53. Steinberg, op. cit., 114; Burr Tillstrom Archives, Chicago History Museum, 1985.549.

54. Burr Tillstrom Archives, Chicago History Museum, 1985.549.

55. Ibid.

56. Newton N. Minow biographical clipping file, Research Center, Chicago History Museum.

57. Rich Samuels, "Chicago School of Television" in *The Encyclopedia of Chicago*, ed. James R. Grossman, Ann Durkin Keating, and Janice L. Reiff (Chicago and London: University of Chicago Press, 2004), 147.

58. Richard Rhodes, *The Making of the Atomic Bomb* (New York and London: Simon & Schuster, 1986), 305–309, 312–314, 399.

59. Emilio Segre, *Enrico Fermi: Physicist* (Chicago: University of Chicago Press, 1987), 94–130.

60. Enrico Fermi, *Fermi's Own Story*, in *The First Reactor*, U.S. Atomic Energy Commission (Oak Ridge, Tennessee: USAEC Division of Technical Information Extension, 1967), 30.

61. Corbin Allardice and Edward R. Trapnell, *The First Pile* (Oak Ridge, Tennessee: Technical Information Service, United States Atomic Energy Commission, 1955), 2–7.

62. WGBH, *American Experience: The Pill*. "People & Events." Public Broadcasting Service. http://www.pbs.org/wgbh/amex/pill/peopleevents/index.html

63. Ibid.

64. Ibid.

65. Ibid.; Searle Laboratory Archives, Chicago History Museum.

CHAPTER 5: MY KIND OF TOWN

1. Jeanne Madeline Weiman, *The Fair Women* (Chicago: Academy Chicago, 1981), 21–24.

2. Wim de Wit, "Building an Illusion: The Design of the World's Columbian Exposition," in *Grand Illusions: Chicago's World's Fair of 1893*, ed. Neil Harris, Wim de Wit, James Gilbert, and Robert W. Rydell (Chicago: Chicago Historical Society, 1994), 51.

3. Ibid., 57–58.

4. Ibid., 54–58.

5. Ibid., 62–64.

6. Robert W. Rydell, "A Cultural Frankenstein? The Chicago World's Columbian Exposition of 1893," in *Grand Illusions: Chicago's World's Fair of 1893*, op. cit., 158–164.

7. Ibid., 144–150.

8. Ibid., 152–156; Weiman, op. cit., 141–153, 193–213.

9. Julie K. Rose, "The Legacy of the Fair," in *The World's Columbian Exposition: Idea, Experience, Aftermath*, http://xroads.virginia.edu/ ~MA96/WCE/title.html, August 1, 1996.

10. Stan Barker, "Amusement Parks," in *The Encyclopedia of Chicago*, ed. James R. Grossman, Ann Durkin Keating, and Janice L. Reiff (Chicago and London: University of Chicago Press, 2004), 20–21.

11. "Riverview Park," http://history.amuseument-parks.com/riverviewmain.html, Amusement Park History, 2002; Scott A. Newman, "Riverview Park," in *Jazz Age Chicago 1893–1945*, http://chicago.urbanhistory.org/sites/parks/rivervie.htm, 1998.

12. Scott A. Newman, "White City," in *Jazz Age Chicago 1893–1945*, http://chicago.urbanhistory.org/sites/parks/rivervie.htm, 1998.

13. Thomas S. Hines, "The City Beautiful Movement," in *The Encyclopedia of Chicago*, Grossman, Keating, and Reiff, op. cit., 30–31; Lawrence Christmas, "Planning, City and Regional," ibid., 617–618.

14. Daniel H. Burnham, *Plan of Chicago* (Chicago: Commercial Club, 1909); Thomas S. Hines, ibid., 30–31.

15. Stephen Packard, "Forest Preserves," in *The Encyclopedia of Chicago*, Grossman, Keating, and Reiff, op. cit., 312.

16. "Millennium Park, Chicago," www.millenniumpark.org.

17. Robert J. Brubaker, *Making Music Chicago Style* (Chicago: Chicago Historical Society, 1985), 37–39.

18. William Howard Kenney, *Chicago Jazz: A Cultural History 1904–1930* (New York and Oxford: Oxford University Press, 1993), 5–8, 62–63.

19. Ibid., 21, 130–134.

20. Ibid., 58–60, 137–138; "Who is Louis Armstrong?" in *Louis Armstrong House & Archives*, Queens College, New York, 2002–2003, www.satchmo.net/bio.

21. Brubaker, op.cit., 16, 21; Kenney, op. cit., 87–102.

22. Brubaker, ibid., 23; Kenney, ibid., 93.

23. Keeney, ibid., 148–161.

24. Brubaker, op. cit., 48–51; Adam Green, "Blues," in *The Encyclopedia of Chicago*, ed. Grossman, Keating, and Reiff, op. cit., 83–84.

25. Brubaker, ibid., 52; Pete Welding, excerpted from "Gone to Mainstreet," Bluesland, E.P. Dutton, 1992, www.muddywaters.com.

26. "Chess Records," www.history-of-rock.com/chess_records.htm.

27. Green, op. cit., 85.

28. Robert W. Rydell, "Century of Progress Exposition," in *The Encyclopedia of Chicago*, ed. Grossman, Keating, and Reiff, op. cit., 124.

29. Ibid., 125.

30. Ibid., 126.

31. Ibid.

32. Frederick Ivor-Campbell, "The All-Star Game," *Total Baseball*, ed. John Thorn and Pete Palmer (New York: Warner Books, Inc., 1989), 243–244; John Odell, "Curator's Corner: The All-Stars Are Not the Only All-Stars," http://www.baseballhalloffame.org/, 2003; "Pro Football Firsts," http://www.pro-footballhof.com/history/, 2006.

33. David Q. Voigt, "The History of Major League Baseball," Thorn and Palmer, ibid., 9.

34. Ibid., 10; Perry Duis, "Whose City? Public and Private Places in Nineteenth Century Chicago," *Chicago History*, vol. XII, no. 1 (1983), 23.

35. Ibid., 10.

36. Ibid., 11.

37. Jules Tygiel, "Black Baseball," Thorn and Palmer, op. cit., 548.

38. Frederick Ivor-Campbell, "Chicago Cubs," Thorn and Palmer, ibid., 59–60.

39. Ibid., 60–61.

40. Ibid., 61; "Cubs History" on http://chicago.cubs.mlb.com, MLB Advanced Media, L.P. 2001–2006; author's personal experience.

41. Paul D. Adomites, "Baseball on the Air," Thorn and Palmer, op. cit., 671–673.

42. John B. Holway and Bob Carroll, "Charles Comiskey," Thorn and Palmer, ibid., 326.

43. Campbell, "Chicago White Sox," ibid., 61–62.

44. Ibid., 62.

45. Ibid.

46. "Sweep Dreams: After 88 Years, Sox Win Series," http://chicagowhitesox.mlb.com, 2006.

47. Jacob Austen, "Softball, 16-Inch," in *The Encyclopedia of Chicago*, ed. Grossman, Keating, and Reiff, op. cit., 765.

48. Debra A. Shattuck, "Women in Baseball," Thorn and Palmer, op. cit., 623–625.

49. Campbell, "Chicago White Sox," Thorn and Palmer, op. cit., 62; Holway and Carroll, "Larry Dolby," Thorn and Palmer, op. cit., 332.

50. Jules Tygiel, "Black Baseball," Thorn and Palmer, ibid., 548–551.

51. Ibid., 552–553.

52. Robin Lester, *Stagg's University: The Rise, Decline & Fall of Big-Time Football at Chicago* (Urbana and Champaign: University of Illinois Press, 1999), 101–105.

53. Elliott J. Gorn, "Creation of Chicago Sports," in *The Encyclopedia of Chicago*, ed. Grossman, Keating, and Reiff, op. cit., 217; "Chicago Bears History," http://www.chicagobears.com/history, 2001–2006.

54. "Chicago Bears History," http://www.chicagobears.com/history, 2001–2006.

55. Ibid.

56. "Bulls Six Titles a Gold Standard," http://www.nba.com/bulls/history/index.html

57. "History," www.harlemglobetrotters.com/history, 1996–2006.

58. Sheldon Patikin and Robert Klein, *The Second City: Backstage at the World's Greatest Comedy Theater* (Naperville, Illinois: Sourcebooks, 2000); Richard Christiansen, "Second City Theater," *The Encyclopedia of Chicago*, ed. Grossman, Keating, and Reiff, op. cit., 744.

59. Max Grinnell, "Playboy," in *The Encyclopedia of Chicago*, ed. Grossman, Keating, and Reiff, op. cit., 621.

60. "Taste of Chicago," http://en.wikipedia.org/wiki/Taste_of_Chicago.

61. "Navy Pier," http://en.wikipedia.org/wiki/Navy_Pier; Douglas Bukowski, "Navy Pier," http://www.encyclopedia.chicagohistory.org.

62. City of Chicago, 2006 Proposed Budget, http://egov.cityofchicago.org.

BIBLIOGRAPHY

This bibliography cites sources used to develop the exhibition *Chicago: Crossroads of America*, as well as this book. It therefore includes sources for several topics that are included in the exhibition but not the catalogue. Generations of historians and curators have researched, and collected, Chicago's past, and I am indebted to their efforts.

Abu-Lughod, Janet L. *New York, Chicago, Los Angeles: America's Global Cities*. Minneapolis: University of Minnesota Press, 1999.

Achilles, Rolf. *Made in Illinois: A Story of Illinois Manufacturing*. Chicago: Illinois Manufacturing Association, 1993.

Adams, Rosemary K. "Here We Are Again: Kukla, Fran and Ollie." *Chicago History* 26:3 (Fall 1997): 32–51.

——. *What George Wore and Sally Didn't: Surprising Stories from America's Past*. Chicago: Chicago Historical Society, 1998.

Addams, Jane. *Twenty Years at Hull House*. New York: New American Library, 1960.

"Airport Update." http://www.elk-grove-village.il.us.

Algren, Nelson. *Chicago: City on the Make*. Chicago: University of Chicago, 2001.

Allardice, Corbin and Edward R. Trapnell. *The First Pile*. Oak Ridge, Tennessee: Techinical Information service, United States Atomic Energy Commission, 1955.

Allsop, Kenneth. *The Bootleggers: The Story of Chicago's Prohibition Era*. New Rochelle, N.Y.: Arlington House, 1970.

"American Environmental Photographs: Ecology and the Preservation of the Indiana Dunes." Library of Congress. http://memory.loc.gov/ammem/award97/icuhtml/aepsp7.html.

American Institute of Architects Chicago, Chicago Architecture Foundation, Landmarks Preservation Council of Illinois with special assistance for the Commission on Chicago Landmarks, Alice Sinkevitch, ed., *AIA Guide to Chicago*. New York, Harcourt Brace & Co., 1993.

Andreas, A. T. *History of Chicago: From the Earliest Period to the Present Time*. Chicago: A. T. Andreas Company, 1886.

Applebaum, Stanley. *The Chicago World's Fair of 1893: A Photographic Record*. New York: Dover, 1980.

Asbury, Herbert. *Gem of the Prairie: An Informal History of the Chicago Underworld*. DeKalb: Northern Illinois University Press, 1986.

Avrich, Paul. *The Haymarket Tragedy*. Princeton, N.J.: Princeton University Press, 1984.

Bach, Ira J. "A Reconsideration of the 1909 'Plan of Chicago.'" *Chicago History* 2:3 (Summer 1973): 132–141.

Baker, Robert M. "A Brief History of the Blues." The Blue Highway, Curtis Hewston. http://www.thebluehighway.com/history.html.

Barker, Stan. "Paradises Lost," *Chicago History* 22:1 (March 1993): 26–49.

Barrett, James R. *Chicago's Packinghouse Workers, 1894–1922*. Urbana: University of Illinois Press, 1987.

Basketball Hall of Fame. "Hall of Famers: Harlem Globetrotters Biography." Naismith Memorial Basketball Hall of Fame. http://www.hoophall.com/halloffamers/harlem_globetrotters.htm.

Bates, Beth Tompkins. "The Brotherhood." *Chicago History* 25:3 (Fall 1996): 4–23.

Beecher, W. J. "Why Save the Indiana Dunes?" *Chicago History* 3:3 (Winter 1974–75): 141–150.

Bellis, Mary. "Selling the Cell Phone: History of Cellular Phones." About, Inc. http://inventors.about.com/library/weekly/aa070899.htm.

Berkson, Alice and Michael D. Wiant, eds. *Discover Illinois Archaeology*. Springfield: Illinois Association for Advancement of Archaeology, 2001.

Bird, Stewart, Dan Georgakas, and Deborah Shaffer. *Solidarity Forever: An Oral History of the IWW*. Chicago: Lake View, 1985.

Brubaker, Robert L. *Making Music Chicago Style*. Chicago: Chicago Historical Society, 1985.

——. "130 Years of Opera in Chicago." *Chicago History* 8:3 (Fall 1979): 156–159.

"Bulls.com: The Official Site of the Six-Time NBA Champions." National Basketball Association Media Ventures. http://www.nba.com/bulls/.

Burnham, Daniel H. and Edward H. Bennett, *Plan of Chicago*. Chicago: The Commercial Club, 1909.

Bushnell, George D. "When Chicago Was Wheel Crazy." *Chicago History* 4:3 (Fall 1975): 167–175.

Cahan, Cathy and Richard. "The Lost City of the Depression." *Chicago History* 5:4 (Winter 1976–77): 233–242.

Cain, Louis P. "The Creation of Chicago's Sanitary District and Construction of The Sanitary and Ship Canal." *Chicago History* (Summer 1979).

Carrier, Lois A. *Illinois: Crossroads of a Continent.* Urbana: University of Illinois Press, 1993.

"Chess Records." www.history-of-rock.com/chess_records.htm.

"Chess Records Office & Recording Studio." Save America's Treasures. http://www.saveamericastreasures.org/profiles/chess.htm.

"Chicago and Richard J. Daley, 1960–1975." http://www.roosevelt.edu/chicagohistory/mod3-chap4.htm.

Chicago Commission on Race Relations. *The Negro in Chicago.* Chicago: University of Chicago Press, 1992.

Chicago Herald Examiner, February 15, 1929.

Chicago Historical Society. http://www.chicagohistory.org/global/ialter.html.

——. Authority file, Burr Tillstrom collection. Accession No. 1985.549.

——. Authority file, Benjamin Green-Field. Accession No. 1989.562.

——. Clipping files: Richard J. Daley, Richard M. Daley, Carter Harrison I, Carter Harrison II, Newton N. Minnow, and Harold Washington.

——. "Haymarket Affair Digital Collection." Chicago Historical Society. http://www.chicagohs.org/hadc/index.html.

——. "History Files: Century of Progress." Chicago Historical Society. http://www.chicagohs.org/history/century.html.

——. "History Files: The Stockyards, Back of the Yards." Chicago Historical Society. http://www.chicagohs.org/history/stockyard/stock6.html.

Chicago Tribune. Online historic archive. http://www.chicagotribune.com.

Chudacoff, Howard P. *The Evolution of American Urban Society.* Englewood Cliffs, N.J.: Prentice-Hall, 1975.

City of Chicago, Commission on Chicago Landmarks. "Chess Records, Office and Studio, 2120 South Michigan Avenue: Preliminary Staff Summary of Information." 1989.

City of Chicago, 2006 Proposed Budget. http://egov.cityofchicago.org.

——. "Essanay Studios, 1333–45 West Argyle Street: Preliminary Staff Summary of Information." 1996.

City of Chicago, Film Office. "Famous Titles: Television." http://www.ci.chi.il.us/FilmOffice/famous.html.

Clapp, Elizabeth J. "The Chicago Juvenile Court Movement in the 1890s." Paper given at the Centre for Urban History, University of Leichester, 1995.

Clifton, James A. "September 14, 1883: The Last Great Indian Treaty in the Old Northwest." *Chicago History* (Summer 1980): 91–6.

Cohen, Adam and Elizabeth Taylor. *American Pharaoh, Mayor Richard J. Daley: His Battle for Chicago and the Nation.* Boston: Little, Brown and Company, 2000.

Cohen, Lizabeth. *Making a New Deal: Industrial Workers in Chicago, 1919–1939.* Cambridge: Cambridge University Press, 1990.

Cohn, Lawrence. *Nothing But the Blues: The Music and the Musicians.* New York: Abbeville Press, 1993.

Condit, Carl. *The Chicago School of Architecture: A History of Commercial and Public Building in the Chicago Area 1875–1925.* Chicago: University of Chicago Press, 1964.

Crabb, Richard. *Radio's Beautiful Day: An Account of the First Five Decades of Broadcasting in America Based on the Experience of Everett Mitchell.* Aberdeen, S.D.: North Plains Press, 1983.

Crate & Barrel. "About Us." www.crateandbarrel.com.

Cronon, William. *Nature's Metropolis: Chicago and the Great West.* New York: W. W. Norton & Company, 1991.

Darling, Sharon S. *Chicago Ceramics & Glass: An Illustrated History from 1871 to 1933.* Chicago: Chicago Historical Society and University of Chicago Press, 1979.

——. *Chicago Furniture: Art, Craft & Industry, 1833–1983.* Chicago: Chicago Historical Society in association with W. W. Norton & Company, 1984.

——. *Chicago Metalsmiths: An Illustrated History.* Chicago: Chicago Historical Society, 1977.

Derber, Milton. *Labor in Illinois: The Affluent Years, 1945–1980.* Urbana: University of Illinois Press, 1989.

Dewey, John. *The School and Society.* New York: McClure, Phillips & Co., 1985.

Doherty, Richard Paul. "The Origin and Development of Chicago-O'Hare Airport." Ph.D. diss., Ball State University, 1970.

Douglas, George H. *Rail City: Chicago U.S.A.* San Diego: Howell-North Books, 1981.

Drake, St. Clair and Horace R. Cayton. *Black Metropolis: A Study of Negro Life in a Northern City.* Chicago: University of Chicago Press, 1993.

Duis, Perry R. *Challenging Chicago: Coping with Everyday Life, 1837–1920.* Urbana and Chicago: University of Illinois Press, 1998.

——. *Chicago: Creating New Traditions.* Chicago: Chicago Historical Society, 1976.

——. "Whose City? Public and Private Places in Nineteenth Century Chicago." *Chicago History* 12:1 (1983): 23.

——. "Yesterday's City (The Elevator)." *Chicago History* 16:2 (Summer 1987): 64–72.

——. "Yesterday's City, The Lakefront: Chicago's Selling Point." *Chicago History* 17:1+2 (Spring/Summer 1988): 106–118.

Duis, Perry R. and Glen E. Holt. "Chicago As It Was: Bright Lights, Hard Times of White City II." *Chicago* magazine (August 1978).

——. "Derby Day at Washington Park." *Chicago* magazine (December 1978).

Duis, Perry R. and Scott La France. *We've Got a Job to Do: Chicagoans and World War II*. Chicago: Chicago Historical Society, 1992.

Eagen, Michael J. "Court Limits Disclosure Requirements: Privacy Rights and Safety Concerns Outweigh Union's Right of Disclosure to Home Addresses of Permanent Strike Replacements." Siegel, O'Connor, Schiff & Zangari, P.C. http://www.soszlaw.com/Pubs/LAW/limits.html.

Eastland Disaster Historical Society. "Learn About Saturday, July 24, 1915." http://www.eastlanddisaster.org.

"The Edgewater Beach Hotel." *Chicago History* 23:2 (Fall 1994): 20–43.

Emmet, Boris and John E. Jeuck. *Catalogers and Counters: A History of Sears, Roebuck & Co.* Chicago: University of Chicago Press, 1950.

Evans, Sara M. *Born for Liberty: A History of Women in America.* New York: Free Press, 1997.

Farber, David. *Chicago '68.* Chicago & London: University of Chicago Press, 1988.

Foner, Eric and John A. Garraty, eds. *The Reader's Companion to American History.* Boston: Houghton Mifflin Company, 1991.

Fowler, Bertram B. *Men, Meat and Miracles.* New York: Julian Messner, 1952.

Frazier, Arthur H. "The Military Frontier: Fort Dearborn." *Chicago History* (Summer 1980): 80–82.

Gelfand, Mark I. *A Nation of Cities: The Federal Government and Urban America 1933–65.* New York: Oxford University Press, 1975.

Gems, Gerald R. "Not Only a Game." *Chicago History* 18:2 (Summer 1989): 4–21.

Gilbert, Paul and Charles Lee Bryson. *Chicago and Its Makers: A Narrative of Events from the Day of the Frits White Man to the Inception of the Second World's Fair.* Chicago: Felix Mendelsohn, 1929.

Gill, Brendan. *Many Masks: A Life of Frank Lloyd Wright.* New York: Putnam, 1987.

Gillette, Howard F., Jr. "White City, Capital City." *Chicago History* 18:4 (Winter 1989–90): 26–45.

"The Golden Age of Cycling." *Chicago History* (Summer 1967): 97–108.

Gordon, Ann D. "Investigating the Eastland Disaster." *Chicago History* 10:2 (Summer 1981): 74–85.

Greising, David. *Brokers, Bagmen, and Moles: Fraud and Corruption in the Chicago Futures Market.* New York: Wiley, 1991.

Griffin, Al. "The Ups and Downs of Riverview Park." *Chicago History* 4:1 (Spring 1975): 14–22.

Grossman, James R., Ann Durkin Keating, and Janice L. Reiff, eds. *The Encyclopedia of Chicago.* Chicago and London: University of Chicago Press, 2004.

Grossman, James R. *Land of Hope: Chicago, Black Southerners, and the Great Migration.* Chicago: University of Chicago Press, 1989.

Halker, Clark. "Banding Together." *Chicago History* 18:2 (Summer 1989): 40–59.

Hall, Peter. *Cities in Civilization.* New York: Pantheon, 1998.

Harris, Neil, Wim de Wit, James Gilbert, and Robert W. Rydell. *Grand Illusions: Chicago's World's Fair of 1893.* Chicago: Chicago Historical Society, 1994.

Hirsch, Arnold R. *Making the Second Ghetto: Race & Housing in Chicago 1940–1960.* Cambridge and New York: Cambridge University Press, 1983.

Hirsch, Susan E., Robert I. Goler, and Sam Bass Warner, Jr. *A City Comes of Age: Chicago in the 1890s.* Chicago: Chicago Historical Society, 1990.

"Historical Background." Back of the Yards Neighborhood Council. http://www.bync.org/history_background/index.cfm.

"History: A.G. Spalding–Our Founder." Spalding Sports Worldwide. http://www.spalding.com/about/ag_Spalding.html.

"A History of Chicago's Northerly Island." Openlands Project. http://www.openlands.org/policy.asp?pgid=247.

"History of Edison Motion Pictures–the Kinetoscope." http://memory.loc.gove/ammem/edhtml/edmvhist.html.

"History of the World Famous Harlem Globetrotters." Mannie Jackson Presents the Original Harlem Globetrotters. http://harlemglobetrotters.com/history/index.php.

Hofstadter, Richard. *The Age of Reform: From Bryan to F.D.R.* New York: Alfred A. Knopf, 1955.

Hofstadter, Richard, ed. *The Progressive Movement 1900–1915.* Englewood Cliffs, N.J.: Prentice-Hall, 1963.

Holt, Glen E. and Dominic A. Pacyga. *Chicago: A Historical Guide to the Neighborhoods, The Loop and South Side.* Chicago: Chicago Historical Society, 1979.

Holt, Glen E. "Private Plans for Public Spaces: The Origins of Chicago's Park System, 1850–1875." *Chicago History* 8:3 (Fall 1979): 173–84.

"Indiana Dunes National Lakeshore." National Park Service. http://www.nps.gov/indu/index.htm.

Interview with Eldon Hatch, Chicago livestock trader. Conducted by Olivia Mahoney at the Chicago Historical Society, June 25, 2004.

Jackson, Kenneth T. *Crabgrass Frontier: The Suburbanization of the United States.* New York: Oxford University Press, 1985.

Jackson, Kenneth T. and Stanley K. Schultz. *Cities in American History.* New York: Alfred A. Knopf, 1972.

Jahant, Charles A. "Chicago: Center of the Silent Film Industry." *Chicago History* 3:1 (Spring/Summer 1974): 45–53.

"Jazz, A Film by Ken Burns." PBS. http://www.pbs.org/jazz.

Justin's Letter, October 14, 1871. Archives & Manuscript Collection, Chicago Historical Society.

Kaplan, Wendy, ed. *"The Art That is Life:" The Arts & Crafts Movement in America 1875–1920.* Boston: Museum of Fine Arts, 1987.

Keating, Ann D. *Building Chicago: Suburban Developers and the Creation of a Divided Metropolis.* Columbus: Ohio State University, 1988.

Kenney, William Howard. *Chicago Jazz: A Cultural History 1904–1930.* New York and Oxford: Oxford University Press, 1993.

Kogan, Bernard R. "Chicago's Pier." *Chicago History* 5:1 (Spring 1976): 28–38.

Lamb, John. "Early Days on the Illinois & Michigan Canal." *Chicago History* 3:3 (Winter 1974–1975): 168–76.

Laurie, Clayton D. "Antilabor Mercenaries or Defenders of Public Order." *Chicago History* 20:3+4 (Fall/Winter 1991–92): 4–32.

Leach, William. *Land of Desire: Merchants, Power, and the Rise of a New American Culture.* New York: Vintage Books, 1993.

Lester, Robin. *Stagg's University: The Rise, Decline & Fall of Big-Time Football at Chicago.* Urbana and Champaign: University of Illinois Press, 1999.

Leven, Charles L. *The Mature Metropolis.* Lexington, Mass.: Lexington Books, 1978.

Mason, Roswell B. *Proclamation.* Chicago: October 10, 1871.

Mahoney, Olivia. *Douglas/Grand Boulevard: A Chicago Neighborhood.* Images of America. Charleston, S.C.: Arcadia, 2001.

——. *Edward F. Worst: Craftsman and Educator.* Chicago: Chicago Historical Society, 1985.

——. *Go West: Chicago and American Expansion.* Chicago: Chicago Historical Society, 1999.

Mayer, Harold M. "The Launching of Chicago: The Situation and the Site." *Chicago History* 9:2 (Summer 1980): 68–79.

Mayer, Harold M. and Richard C. Wade. *Chicago: Growth of a Metropolis.* Chicago: University of Chicago Press, 1969.

McKelvey, Blake. *The Urbanization of America, 1860–1915.* New Brunswick, N.J.: Rutgers University Press, 1963.

Melville, Tom. "Yesterday's City, A League of His Own: William Hulbert and the Founding of the National League." *Chicago History* 29:2 (Fall 2000): 44–57.

Merriner, James L. "Chicago's Political Conventions: From the 'Smoke-Filled' Room to 'The Whole World is Watching.'" *Illinois Issues* (August 1996): 12–16. http://www.lib.niu.edu/ipo/ii960812.html.

Metcalfe, Ralph, Jr. "The Blues, Chicago Style." *Chicago History* 3:1 (Spring/Summer 1974): 4–13.

"Millennium Park, Chicago." www.millenniumpark.org.

Miller, Donald L. *City of the Century: The Epic of Chicago and the Making of America.* New York: Simon & Schuster, 1996.

Miller, Ross. "The Great Fire and the Myth of Chicago." *Chicago History* 19:1+2 (Spring/Summer 1990): 5–31.

"Motorola History." Motorola, Inc. http://www.motorola.com/content/0,,115–110,00.html.

Museum of Broadcast Communications. *Encyclopedia of Television,* assorted articles. http://www.museum.tv/archives/etv/index.html.

Nestor, Agnes. *A Brief History of the International Glove Workers Union of America.* Milwaukee: 1942.

Newman, Scott A. "Jazz Age Chicago: Urban Leisure from 1893 to 1945." Scott A. Newman. http://chicago.urban-history.org/mainmenu.htm.

O'Brien, Ellen and Lyle Benedict. "Chicago Historical Information, 1915, July 24: Eastland Disaster." Chicago Public Library. http://www.chipublib.org/004chicago/disasters/eastland.html.

Odell, John. "Curator's Corner: The All-Stars Are Not the Only Stars." 2003 http://www.baseballhalloffame.org/.

Official Catalog, International Live Stock Exposition. Chicago: P. F. Pettibone & Co., 1901.

"The Official Site of the Chicago Bears." Chicago Bears. http://www.chicagobears.com/.

"The Official Site of the Chicago Blackhawks." Chicago Blackhawks. http://www.chicagoblackhawks.com/.

"The Official Site of the Chicago Cubs." Major League Baseball Advance Media. http://chicago.cubs.mlb.com/NASApp/mlb/index.jsp?c_id=chc.

"The Official Site of the Chicago White Sox." Major League Baseball Advanced Media. http://chicago.whitesox.mlb.com/NASApp/mlb/index.jsp?c_id=cws.

"Our History." Chicago Board of Trade. http://www.cbot.com.

Pacyga, Dominic A. "Crisis and Community: The Back of the Yards 1921." *Chicago History* 6:3 (Fall 1977): 167–176.

Pacyga, Dominic A. and Ellen Skerrett. *Chicago: City of Neighborhoods, Histories and Tours.* Chicago: Loyola University Press, 1986.

Painter, Nell Irvin. *Standing at Armageddon: The United States 1877–1919.* New York: W. W. Norton & Company, 1989.

Palen, J. John. *The Urban World.* New York: McGraw-Hill, 1981.

Patikin, Sheldon and Robert Klein. *The Second City: Backstage at the World's Greatest Comedy Theater.* Naperville, Illinois: Sourcebooks, 2000.

Peretti, Burton W. "White Hot Jazz." *Chicago History* 17:3+4 (Fall/Winter 1988–1989): 26–41.

Peterson, Jacqueline. "Goodbye, Madore Beaubien: The Americanization of Early Chicago Society." *Chicago History* 9:2 (Summer 1980): 98–111.

Petrakis, Harry Mark. *The Founder's Touch: The Life of Paul Galvin of Motorola.* New York: McGraw-Hill, 1965.

Pierce, Bessie Louise. *A History of Chicago, 1848–1871.* New York: Alfred A. Knopf, 1940.

"Pro Football Firsts." 2006 http://www.profootballhof.com/history/.

"Pump Room History." The Pump Room, Omni Ambassador East. http://www.pumproom.com/history/html.

Quaife, Milo Hilton. *The Development of Chicago, 1674–1914*. Chicago: The Caxton Club, 1916.

Ralph, James R. Jr. *Northern Protest: Martin Luther King, Jr., Chicago, and the Civil Rights Movement*. Cambridge: Harvard University Press, 1993.

Randall, John D. *History of the Building Construction in Chicago*. 2nd Edition. Urbana: University of Illinois Press, 1999.

Read, Charlotte J. "The Battles for the Indiana Dunes: The 1966 Legislation." Save the Dunes Council. http://www.savedunes.org/html/66.30th.html.

Reed, Christopher Robert. "A Century of Progress, Issues of Race at the 1933 World's Fair: Old Plantation Show." http://www.xroads.virginia.edu/~UG00/30n1/worldfair/plantsho.htm.

Reiff, Janice L., James R. Grossman, and Ann Durkin Keating, eds. *The Electronic Encyclopedia of Chicago*. Chicago: Chicago Historical Society, The Newberry Library, and Northwestern University, 2005. http://www.encyclopedia.chicagohistory.org.

Rhodes, Richard. *The Making of the Atomic Bomb*. New York: Touchstone, 1986.

Rice, William. "In a Glaze of Glory: The Star-Dusted Pump Room Celebrates 65 Years." *Chicago Tribune* magazine.

"Riverview Park." *Amusement Park History, 2002*. http://history.amusementparks.com/riverviewmain.html.

Rose, Julie K. "The World's Columbian Exposition: Idea, Experience, Aftermath." Julie K. Rose. http://xroads.virginia.edu/~MA96/WCE/title.html.

Ross, Norman. "Looking Backward: Confession of an Opera Addict." *Chicago History* 8:3 (Fall 1979): 170–172.

Royko, Mike. *Boss: Richard J. Daley of Chicago*. New York: E. P. Dutton, 1971.

Ruth, David E. "Chicago's Public Enemy." *Chicago History* 26:2 (Summer 1997): 5–41.

Rybczynski, Witold. *City Life: Urban Expectations in a New World*. New York: Scribner, 1995.

Samuels, Rich. http://www.richsamuels.com.

Sandweiss, Eric. *St. Louis: The Evolution of an American Urban Landscape*. Philadelphia: Temple University Press, 2001.

Sawislak, Karen. "Smoldering City." *Chicago History* 17:3+4 (Fall/Winter 1988–89): 70–101.

Schlesinger, Arthur M. *The Rise of the City, 1878–1898*. New York: MacMillan, 1933.

Schneirov, Richard. "Chicago's Great Upheaval of 1877." *Chicago History* 9:1 (Spring 1980): 2–17.

Schreier, Barbara A. *Becoming American Women: Clothing and the Jewish Immigrant Experience, 1880–1920*. Chicago: Chicago Historical Society, 1994.

Schultz, Rima Lunin and Adele Hast, eds. *Women Building Chicago, 1790–1900: A Biographical Dictionary*. Bloomington and Indianapolis: Indiana University Press, 2001.

Segre, Emilio. *Enrico Fermi: Physicist*. Chicago: University of Chicago Press, 1987.

"SEIU Stronger Together." Service Employees Union International, AFL-CIO, CLC. http://www.seiu.org/.

Settle, Frank. "Nuclear Chemistry: Chain Reaction (December 2, 1942)." ChemCases.com. http://chemcases.com/2003version/nuclear/nc-05.htm.

Skinner, June. *Chicago Sketches: Urban Tales, Stories, and Legends from Chicago History*. Chicago: Wild Onion Books, 1995.

Smith, Carl. *The Dramas of Haymarket*. Chicago Historical Society and Northwestern University. http://www.chicagohs.org/dramas/overview/over.htm.

———. *The Great Chicago Fire and the Web of Memory*. Chicago Historical Society and Northwestern University. http://www.chicagohs.org/fire/index.html.

———. *Urban Disorder and the Shape of Belief: The Great Chicago Fire, the Haymarket Bomb, and the Model Town of Pullman*. Chicago: University of Chicago Press, 1995.

Smith, Page. *The Rise of Industrial America: A People's History of the Post-Reconstruction Era*. New York: McGraw-Hill, 1984.

Spear, Allan H. *Black Chicago: The Making of a Negro Ghetto, 1890–1920*. Chicago: University of Chicago Press, 1967.

"Stagg, Amos Alonzo." *Encyclopedia Britannica* 2006. Encyclopedia Britannica Premium Service. May 3, 2006 http://www.britannica.com/ed/article-9069361.

Steigerwald, David. *The Sixties and the End of Modern America*. New York: St. Martin's, 1995.

Steinberg, Joel. "Television Town." *Chicago History* 4:2 (Summer 1975): 108–117.

Stern, Leon, ed. *The Pullman Strike*. New York: Arno & the New York Times, 1969.

Straus, Terry, ed. *Indians of the Chicago Area*. Chicago: NAES College Press, 1990.

Straus, Terry and Grant P. Arndt, eds. *Native Chicago*. Chicago: McNaughton & Gunn, 1998.

Strauss, Anselm L. *Images of the American City*. New Brunswick, N.J.: Transaction Books, 1976.

Swenson, John F. "Jean Baptiste Point de Sable: The Founder of Modern Chicago." In *A Compendium of the Early History of Chicago in the Year 1835 When the Indians Left*, edited by Ulrich Danckers and Jane Meredith. River Forest, Ill.: Early Chicago, Inc., 2000.

Talbot-Stanway, Susan. "The Giant Jewel." *Chicago History* 22:2 (July 1993): 4–23.

Tanner, Helen Hornbeck, ed. *Atlas of Great Lakes Indian History*. Norman and London: University of Oklahoma Press, 1987.

Teaford, Jon C. *Cities of the Heartland: The Rise and Fall of the Industrial Midwest*. Bloomington: Indiana University Press, 1993.

———. *The Twentieth-Century American City*. Baltimore: Johns Hopkins University Press, 1993.

Thorn, John and Pete Palmer, with David Reuther. *Total Baseball*. New York: Warner Books, 1989.

Tone, Andrea. *Devices and Desires: A History of Contraceptives in America*. New York: Hill and Wang, 2001.

Tuttle, William M., Jr. *Race Riot: Chicago in the Red Summer of 1919*. Urbana and Chicago: University of Illinois Press, 1996.

Wade, Louise Carroll. *Chicago's Pride: The Stockyards, Packingtown, and Environs in the Nineteenth Century*. Urbana: University of Illinois Press, 1987.

Warner, Sam Bass, Jr. *The Urban Wilderness: A History of the American City*. New York: Harper & Row, 1972.

Weiler, N. Sue. "Walkout: The Chicago Men's Garment Worker's Strike, 1910–1911." *Chicago History* 8:4 (Winter 1979–80): 238–249.

Weiman, Jeanne Madeline. *The Fair Women*. Chicago: Academy Chicago, 1981.

Weinrott, Lester A. "Chicago Radio: The Glory Days." *Chicago History* 3:1 (Spring/Summer 1974): 14–22.

"Welcome to McCormick Place." McCormick Place Chicago, Metropolitan Pier and Exposition Authority. http://www.mccormickplace.com/.

"Welcome to Navy Pier." Navy Pier Chicago, Metropolitan Pier and Exposition Authority. http://www.navypier.com/.

Welding, Pete. "Gone To Mainstreet." Bluesland, E.P. Dutton, 1992. www.muddywaters.com.

Wendt, Lloyd and Herman Kogan. *Give the Lady What She Wants!* Chicago: Rand McNally & Company, 1952.

Wendt, Lloyd. *"Swift Walker": An Informal Biography of Gurdon Saltonstall Hubbard*. Lake Bluff, Ill.: Regnery Books, 1995.

WGBH. *American Experience: America 1900*. "People & Events: Scott Joplin & Ragtime." Public Broadcasting Service. http://www.pbs.org/wgbh/amex/1900/peopleevents/pande22.html.

———. *American Experience: Chicago: City of the Century*. "People & Events: World's Columbian Exposition of 1893: The Midway." Public Broadcasting Service. http://www.pbs.org/wgbh/amex/chicago/peopleevents/e_midway/html.

———. *American Experience: Chicago: City of the Century*. "People & Events: Cyrus McCormick (1809–1884)." Public Broadcasting Service. http://www.pbs.org/wgbh/amex/chicago/peopleevents/p_mccormick.html.

———. *American Experience: The Pill*. "People & Events." Public Broadcasting Service. http://www.pbs.org/wgbh/amex/pill/peopleevents/index.html.

White, Morton and Lucia. *The Intellectual Versus the City, From Thomas Jefferson to Frank Lloyd Wright*. Cambridge: Harvard University Press, 1962.

"Who is Louis Armstrong?" *Louis Armstrong House & Archives*. Queens College, New York, 2002-03. www.satchmo.net/bio.

Wikipedia, the Free Encyclopedia. http://en.wikipedia.org.

Wilson, William J. *When Work Disappears: The World of the New Urban Poor*. New York: Vintage Books, 1996.

de Wit, Wim. *Louis Sullivan: The Function of Ornament*. New York: W. W. Norton, 1986.

Young, David M. *Chicago Maritime: An Illustrated History*. DeKalb: Northern Illinois University Press, 2001.

Zukowsky, John. *Chicago Architecture 1872–1922, Birth of a Metropolis*. Munich: Prestel-Verlag, in association with The Art Institute of Chicago, 1987.

INDEX

Page references in *italics* indicate illustrations. Illustrations with identifiable subjects are separately indexed unless the subject is discussed on the same page.